GETTING OUT OF HOPE

First Edition

Printed by Gauvin in Gatineau, Quebec, Canada

Library and Archives Canada Cataloguing in Publication

Cadelli, James, author, illustrator
    Getting out of hope / James Cadelli.

ISBN 978-1-77262-014-6 (softcover)
    1. Graphic novels. I. Title.

PN6733.C33G48 2017   741.5'971   C2017-900278-3

Conundrum Press
Wolfville, Nova Scotia, Canada
www.conundrumpress.com

Distribution in Canada: Litdistco
Distribution in UK: Turnaround
Distribution in US: Consortium

Conundrum Press acknowledges the financial support of the Canada Council
for the Arts, the government of Canada through the Canada Book Fund, and
the Province of Nova Scotia's Creative Industries Fund toward its publishing
activities.

Canada Council
for the Arts

NOVA SCOTIA

Canada

To all the cherry pickers in BC
(and the locals who hate them)

CHAPTER 1

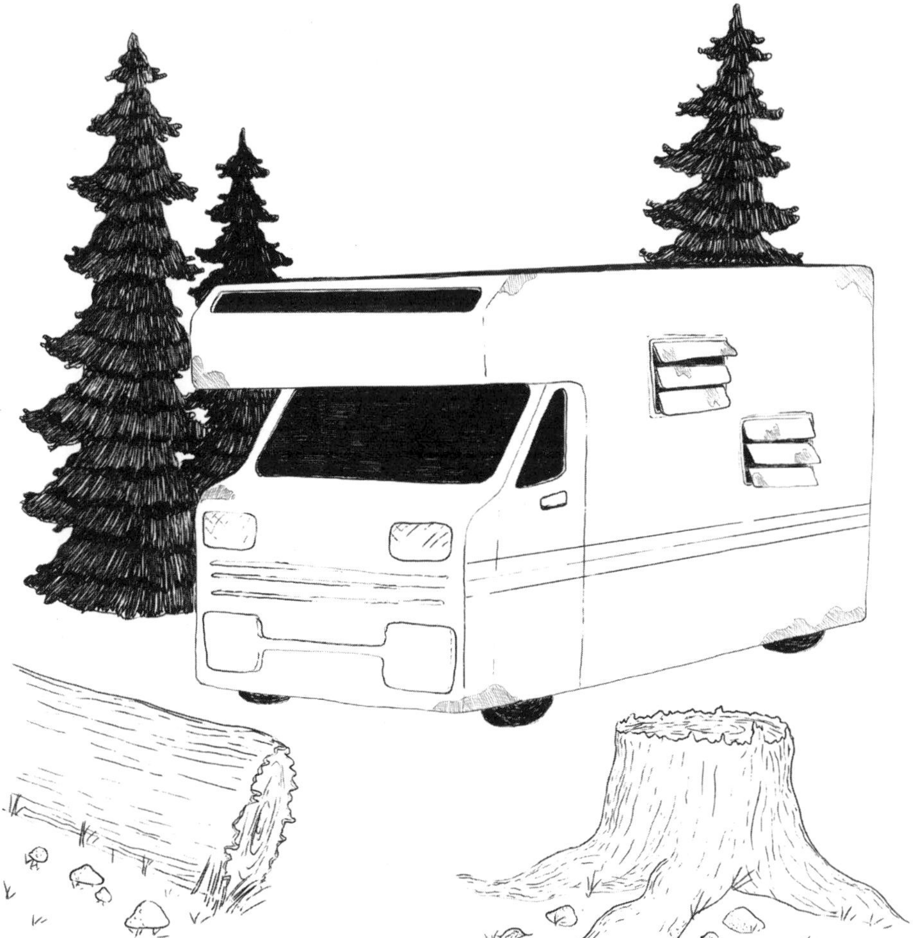

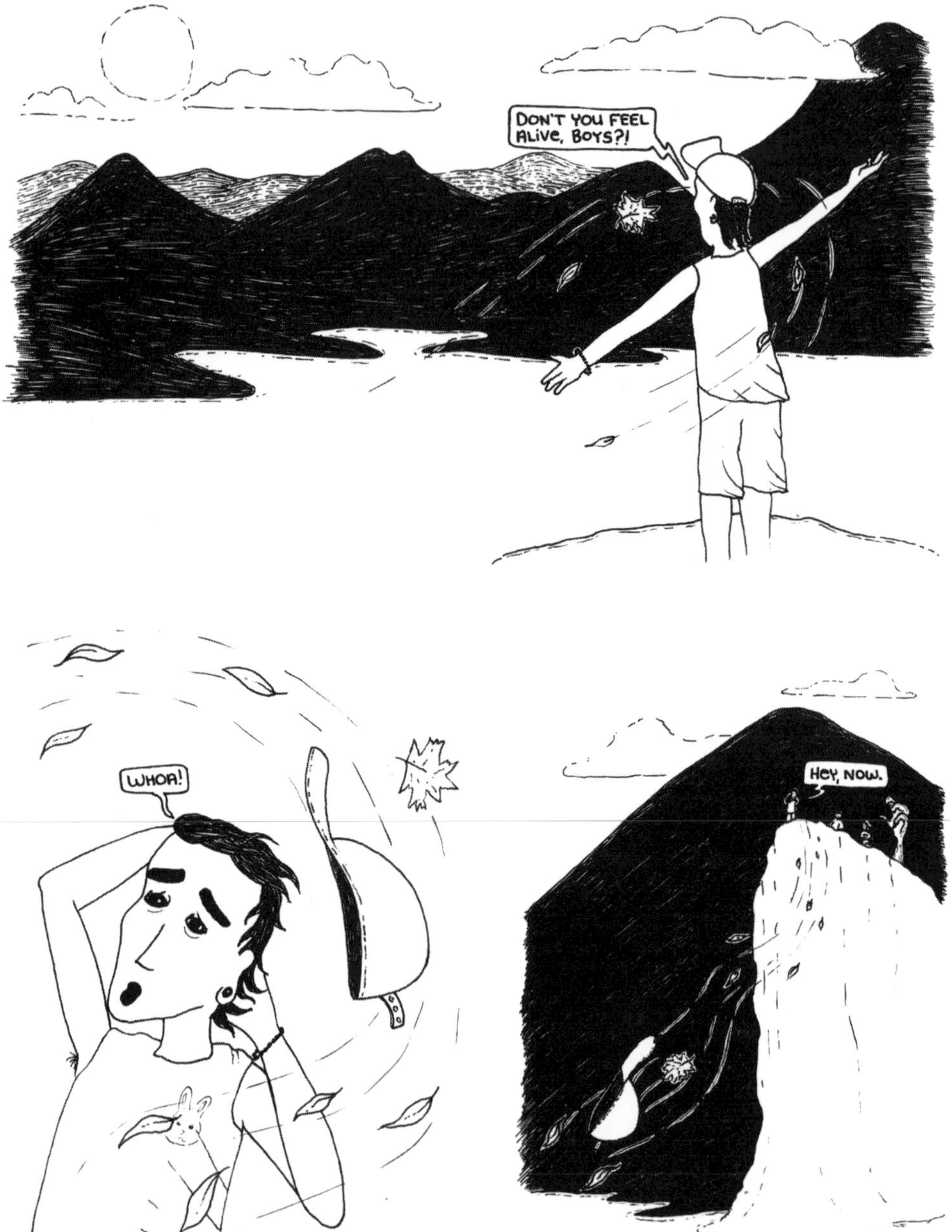
DON'T YOU FEEL ALIVE, BOYS?!
WHOA!
HEY, NOW.

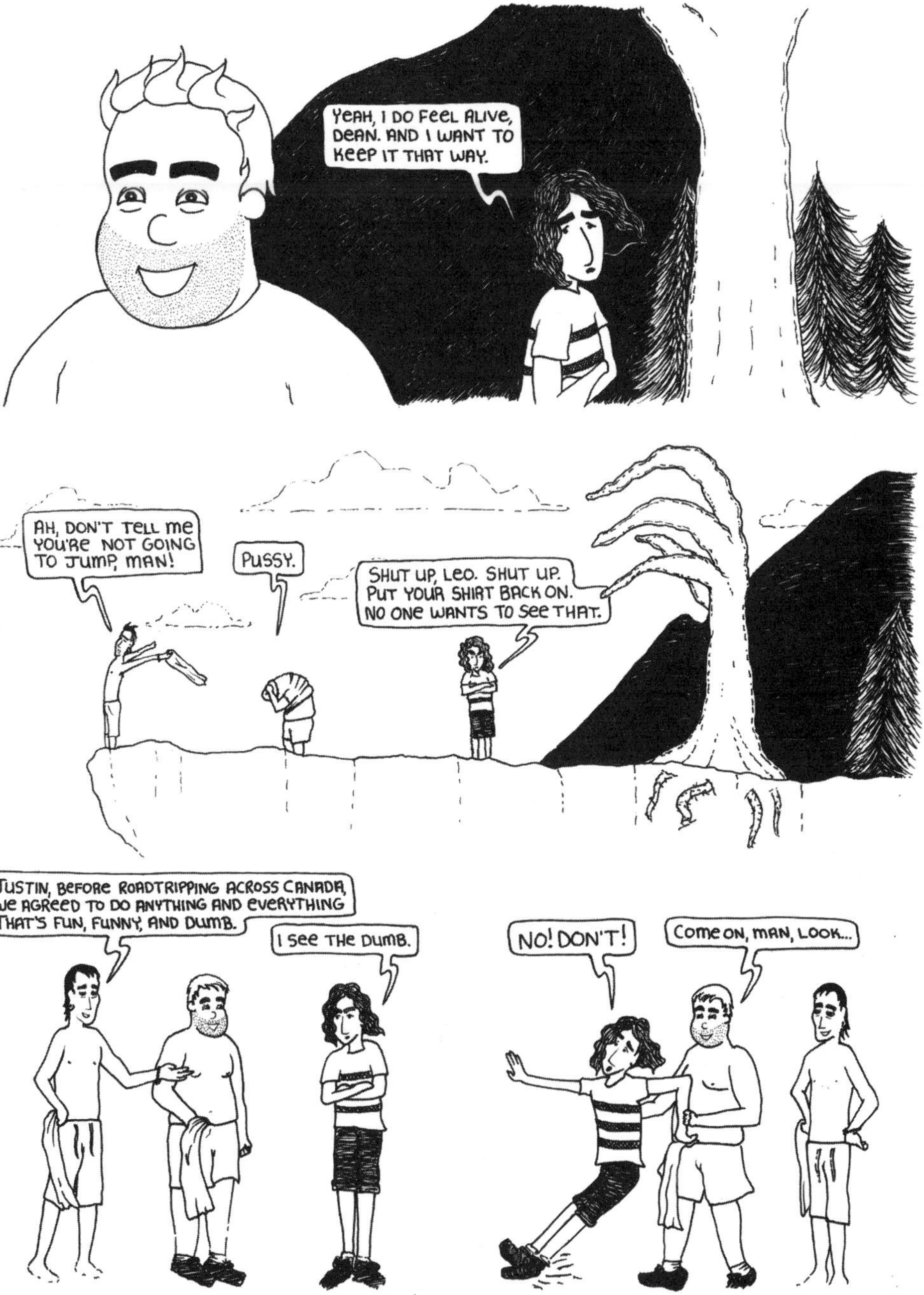
YEAH, I DO FEEL ALIVE, DEAN. AND I WANT TO KEEP IT THAT WAY.
AH, DON'T TELL ME YOU'RE NOT GOING TO JUMP, MAN!
PUSSY.
SHUT UP, LEO. SHUT UP. PUT YOUR SHIRT BACK ON. NO ONE WANTS TO SEE THAT.
JUSTIN, BEFORE ROADTRIPPING ACROSS CANADA, WE AGREED TO DO ANYTHING AND EVERYTHING THAT'S FUN, FUNNY, AND DUMB.
I SEE THE DUMB.
NO! DON'T!
COME ON, MAN, LOOK...

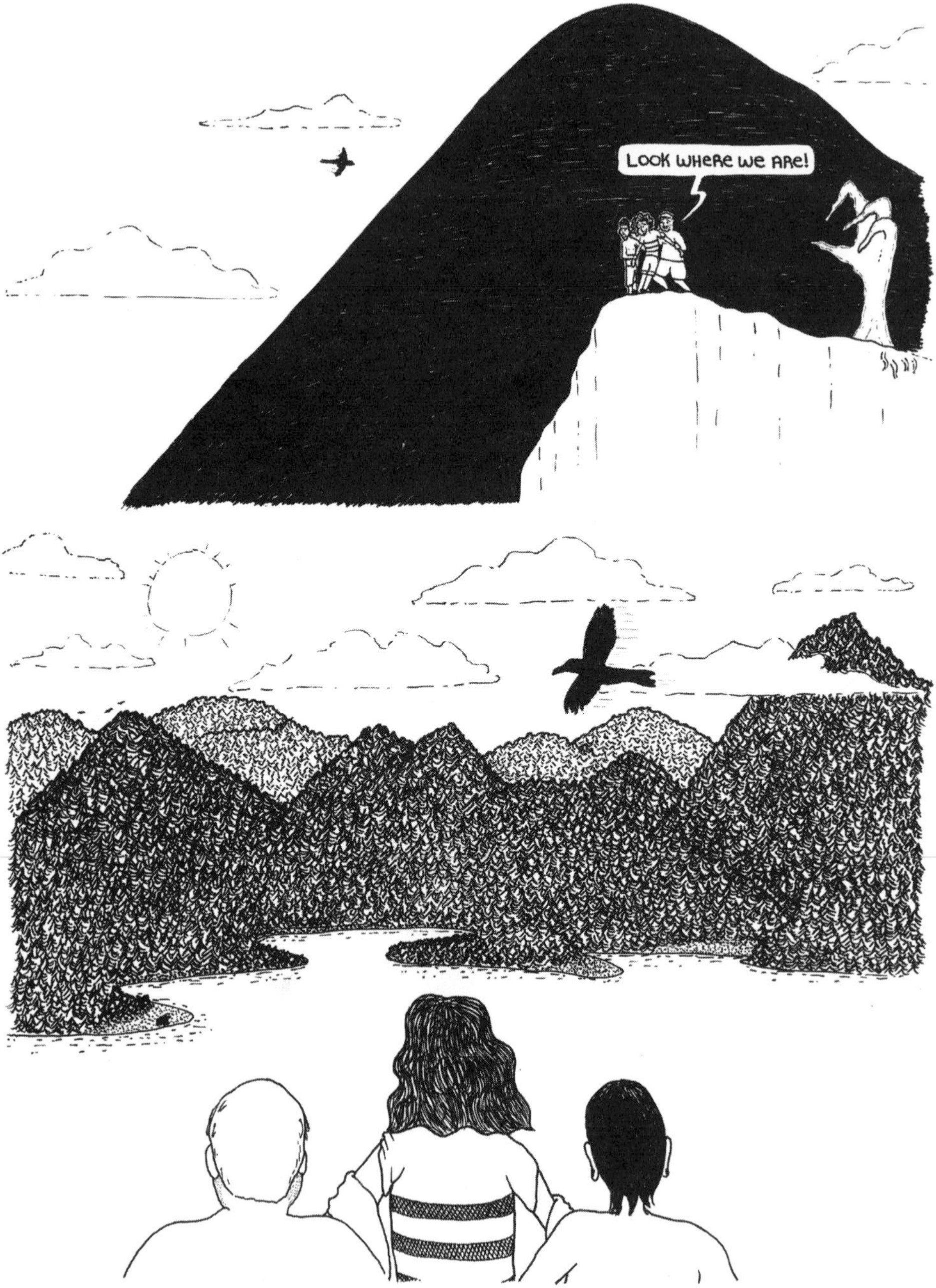
LOOK WHERE WE ARE!

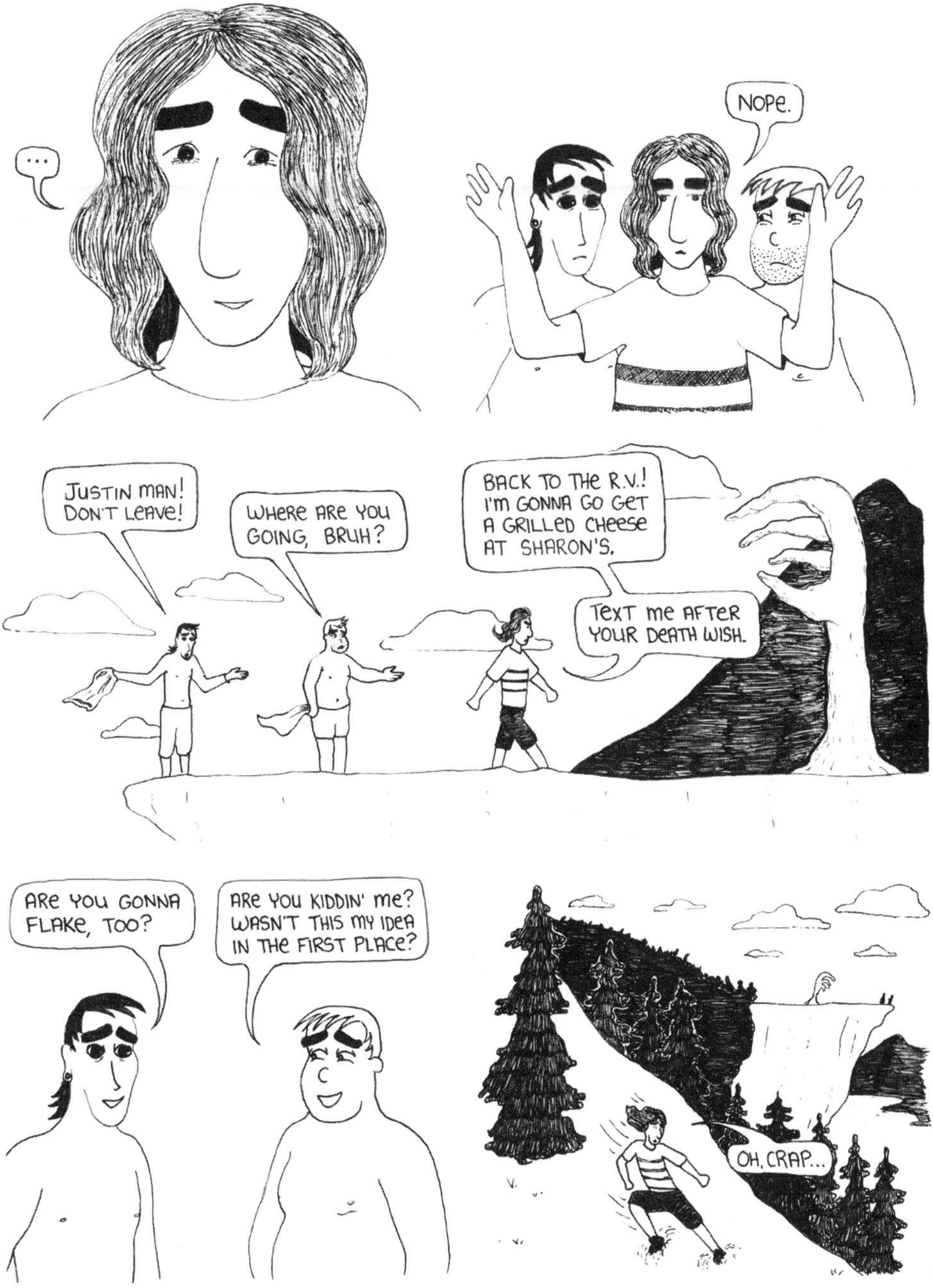
...
NOPE.
JUSTIN MAN! DON'T LEAVE!
WHERE ARE YOU GOING, BRUH?
BACK TO THE R.V.! I'M GONNA GO GET A GRILLED CHEESE AT SHARON'S.
TEXT ME AFTER YOUR DEATH WISH.
ARE YOU GONNA FLAKE, TOO?
ARE YOU KIDDIN' ME? WASN'T THIS MY IDEA IN THE FIRST PLACE?
OH, CRAP...

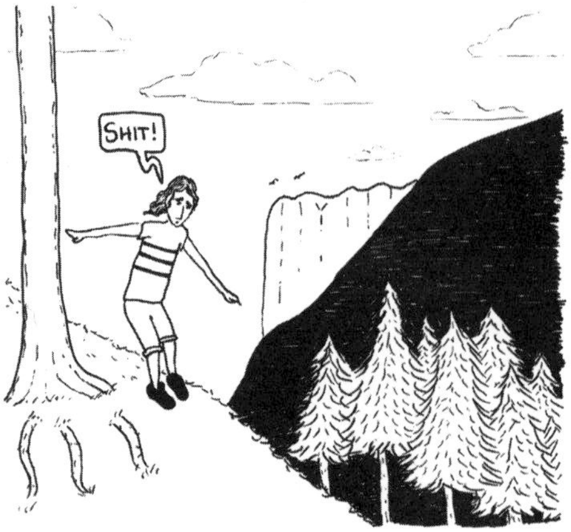
SHIT!
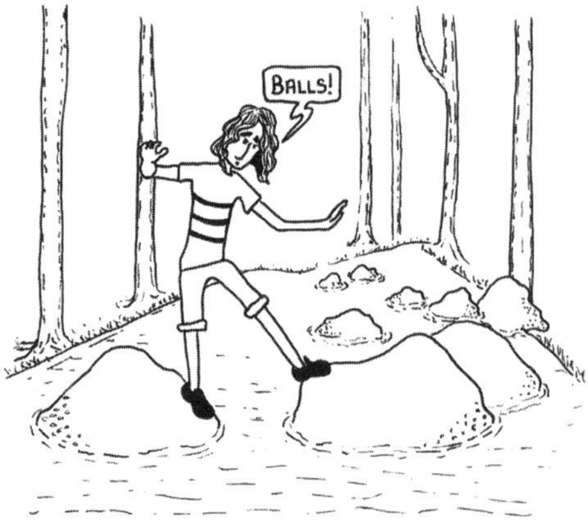
BALLS!
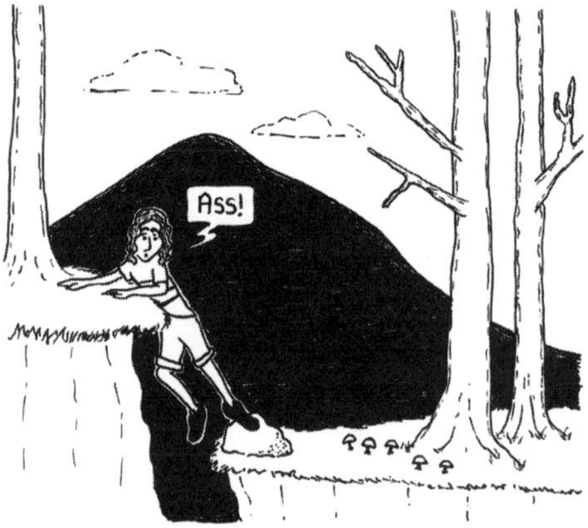
ASS!
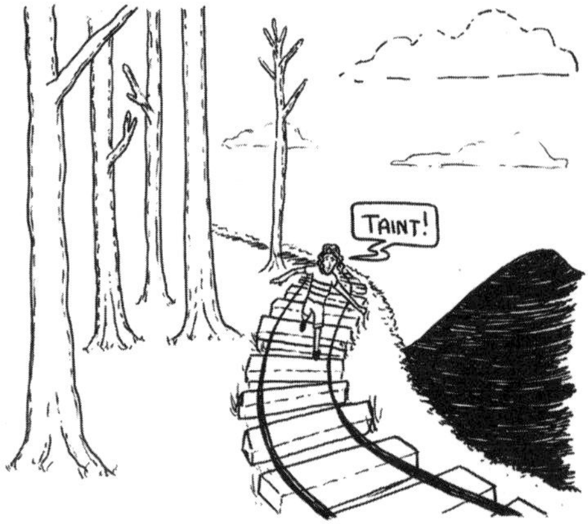
TAINT!
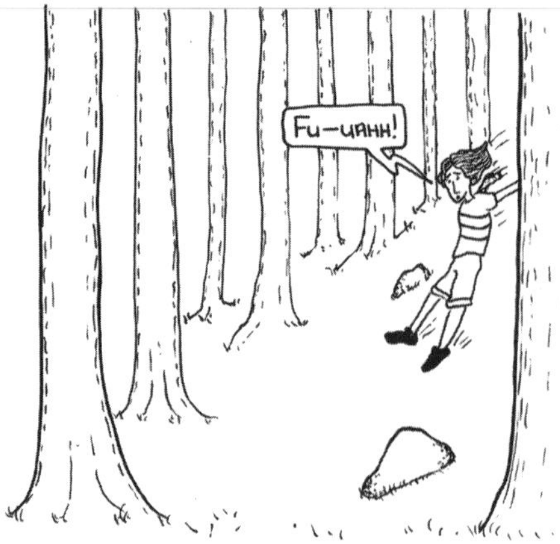
FU-UAHH!
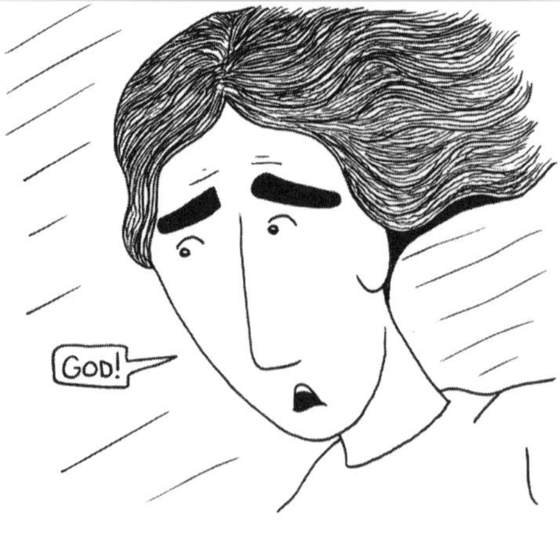
GOD!

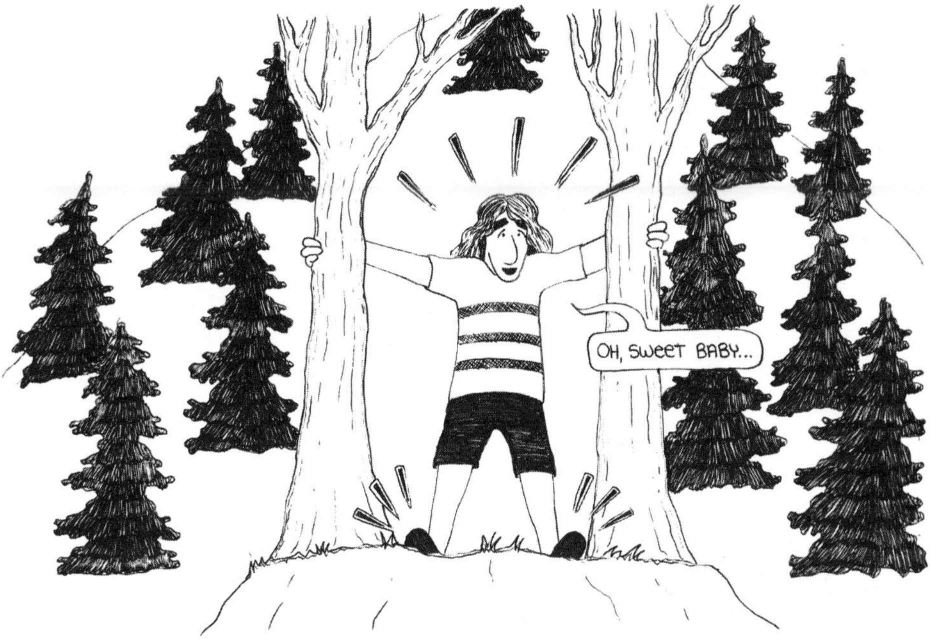
OH, SWEET BABY...

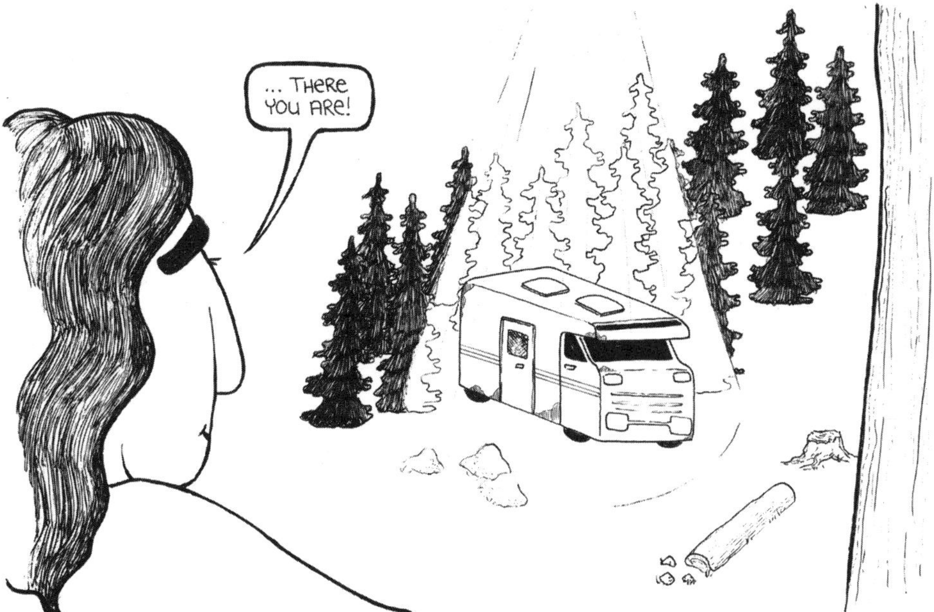
... THERE YOU ARE!

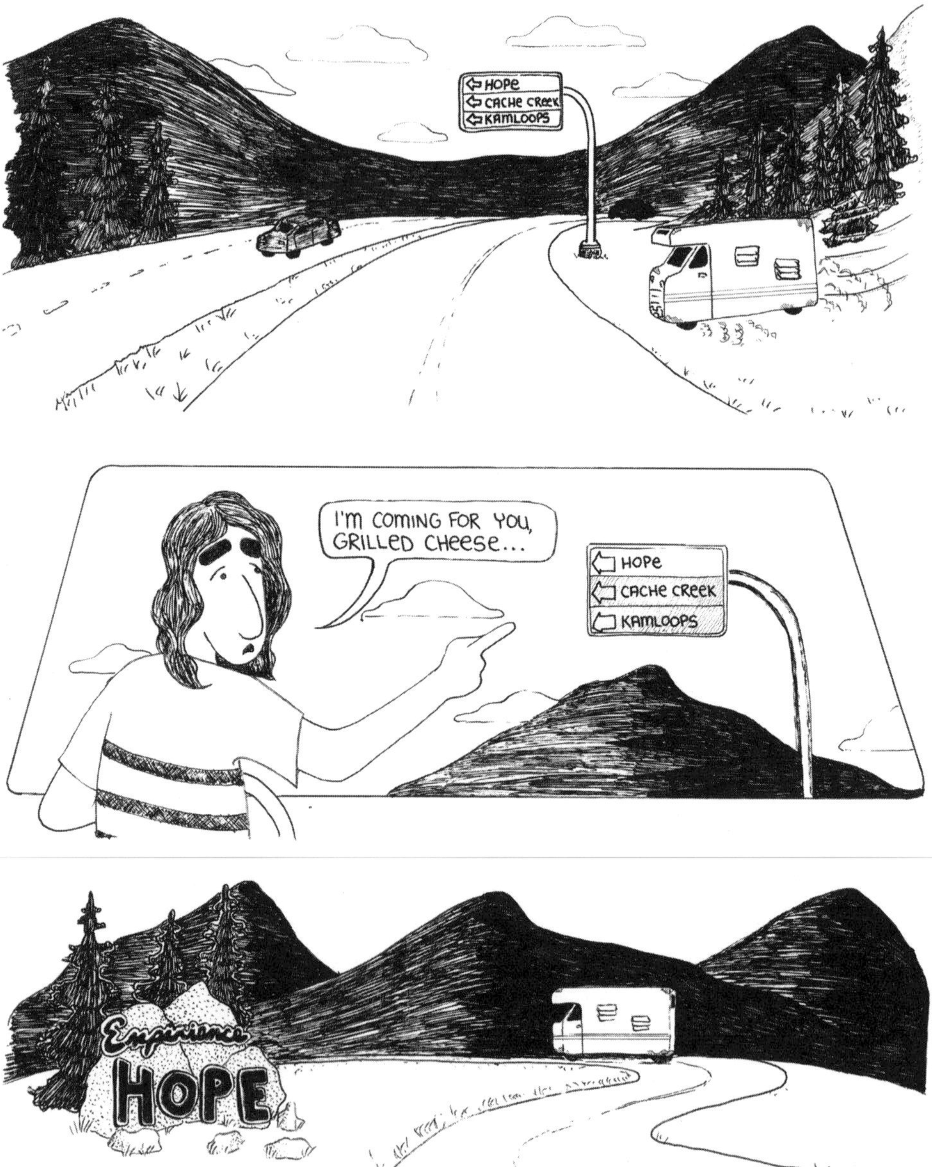
HOPE
CACHE CREEK
KAMLOOPS
I'M COMING FOR YOU, GRILLED CHEESE...
HOPE
CACHE CREEK
KAMLOOPS
Experience
HOPE

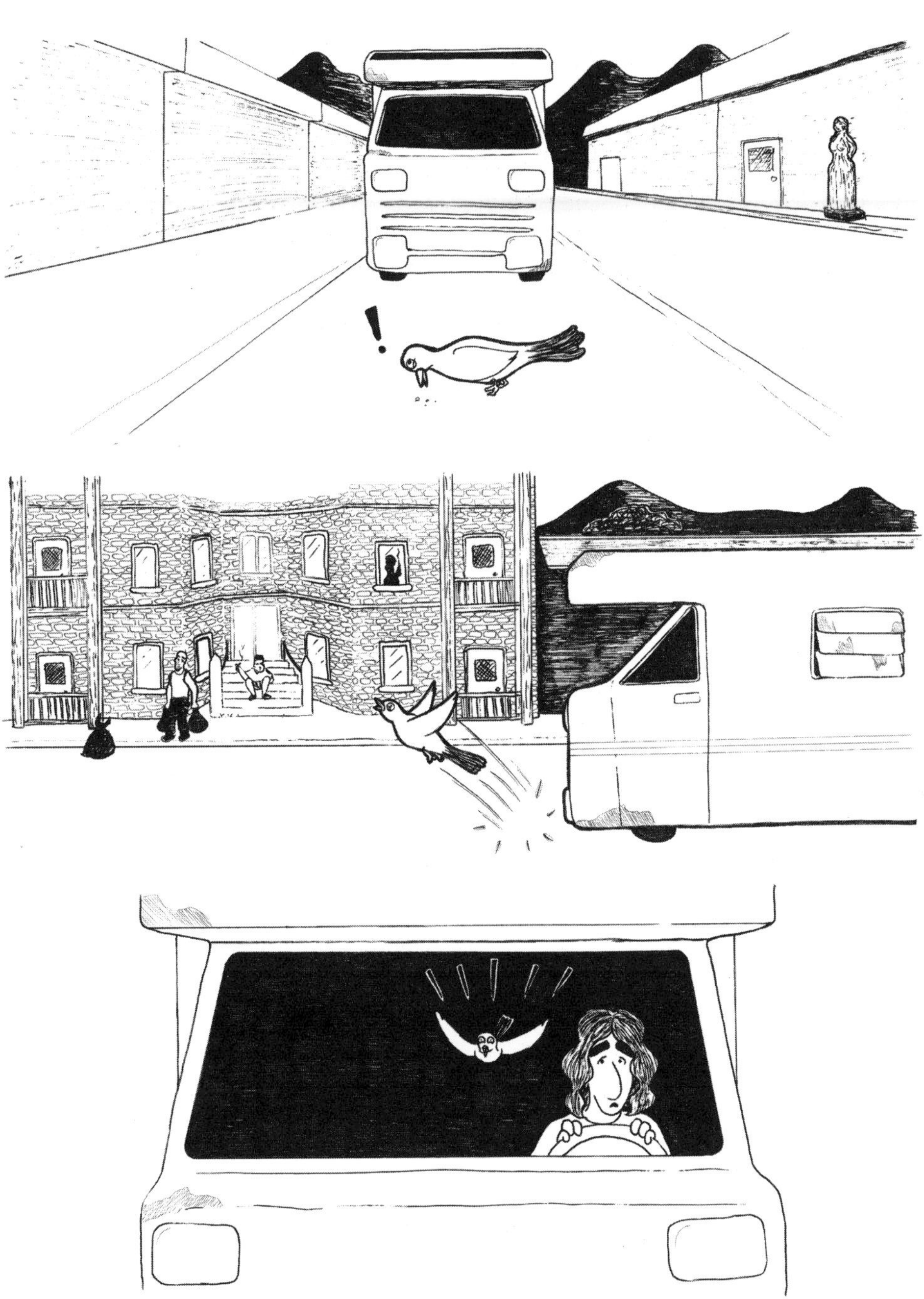

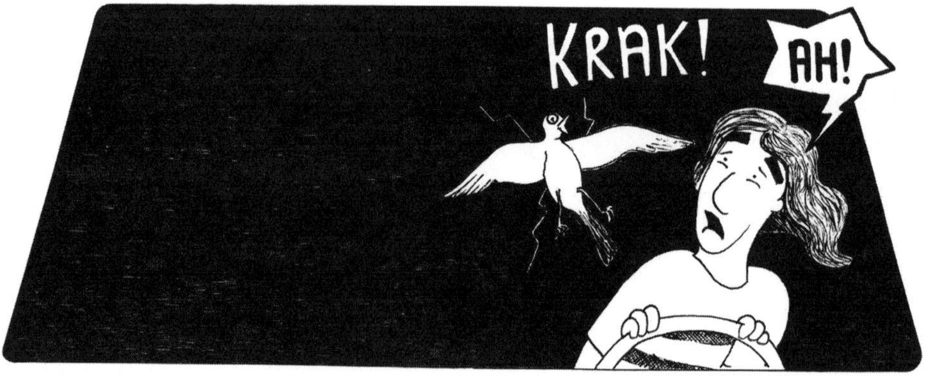
KRAK!
AH!

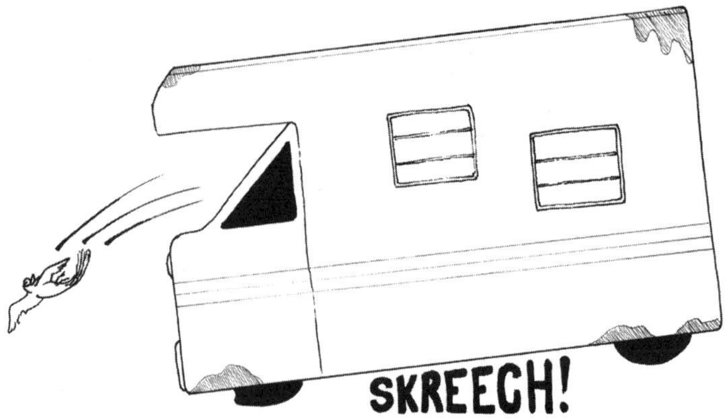
SKREECH!

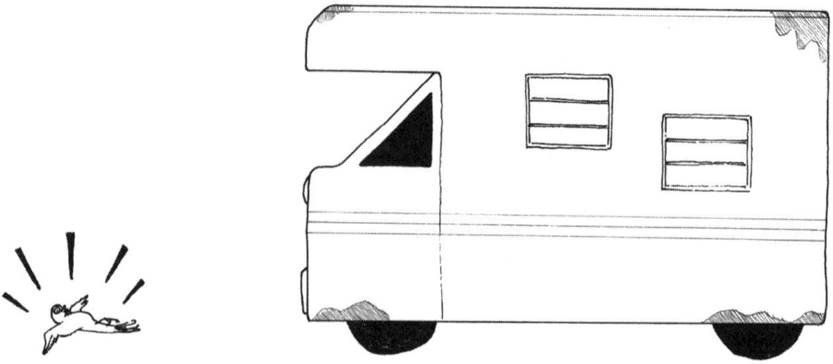

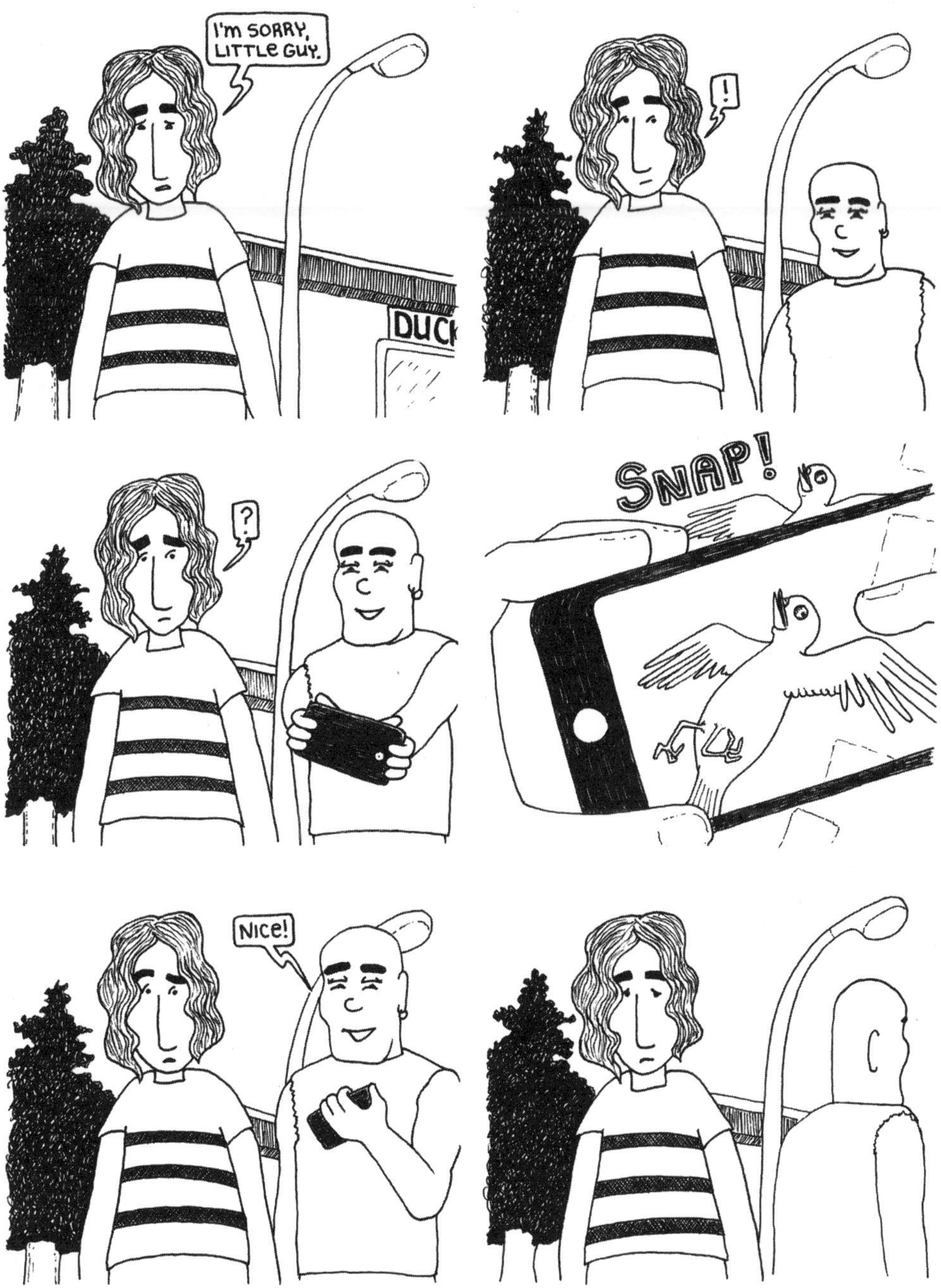
I'm SORRY, LITTLE GUY.
DUCK
!
?
SNAP!
Nice!

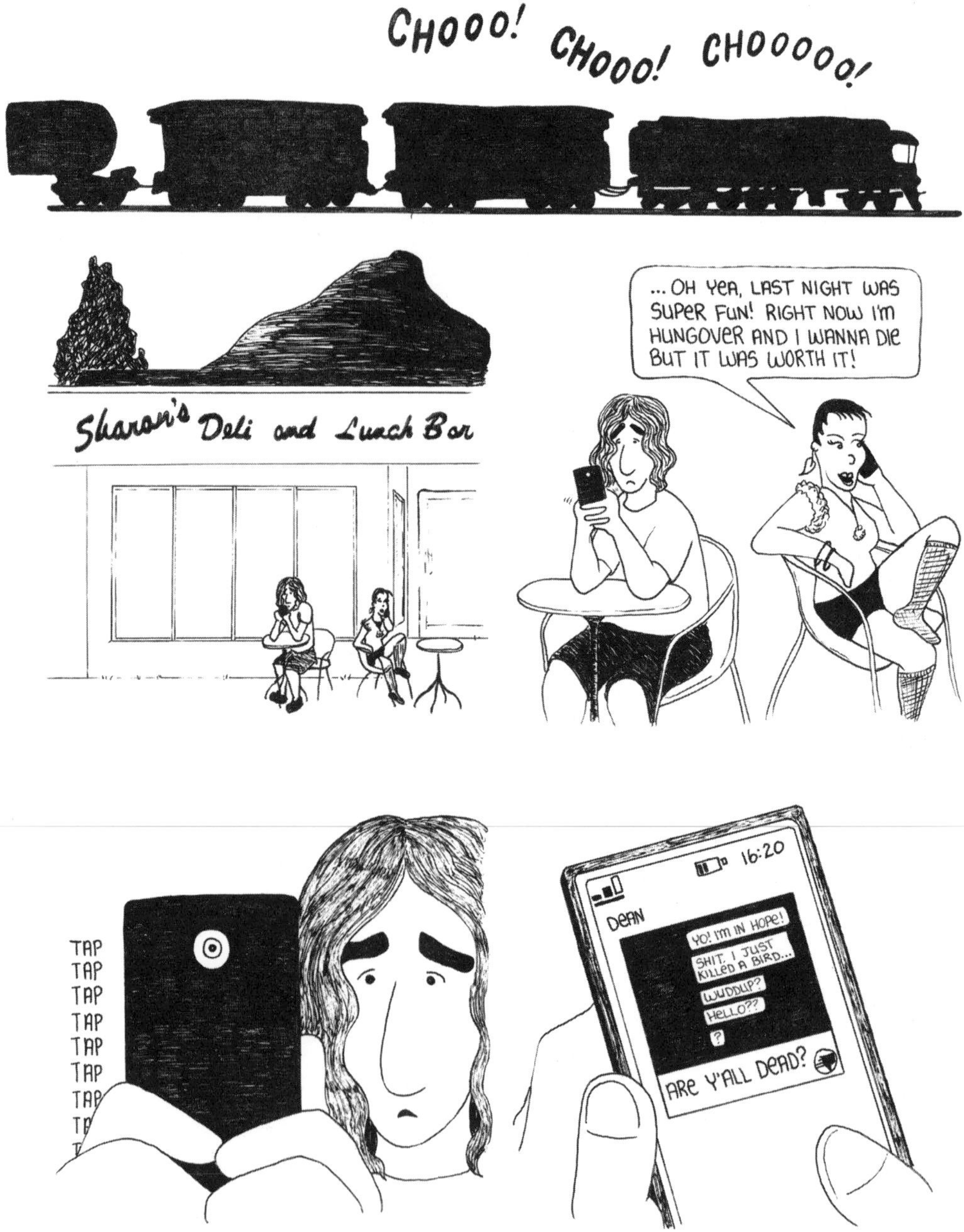
CHOOO! CHOOO! CHOOOOO!
Sharon's Deli and Lunch Bar
... OH YEA, LAST NIGHT WAS SUPER FUN! RIGHT NOW I'M HUNGOVER AND I WANNA DIE BUT IT WAS WORTH IT!
TAP
TAP
TAP
TAP
TAP
TAP
TAP
16:20
DEAN
YO! I'M IN HOPE!
SHIT. I JUST KILLED A BIRD...
WUDDUP?
HELLO??
?
ARE Y'ALL DEAD?

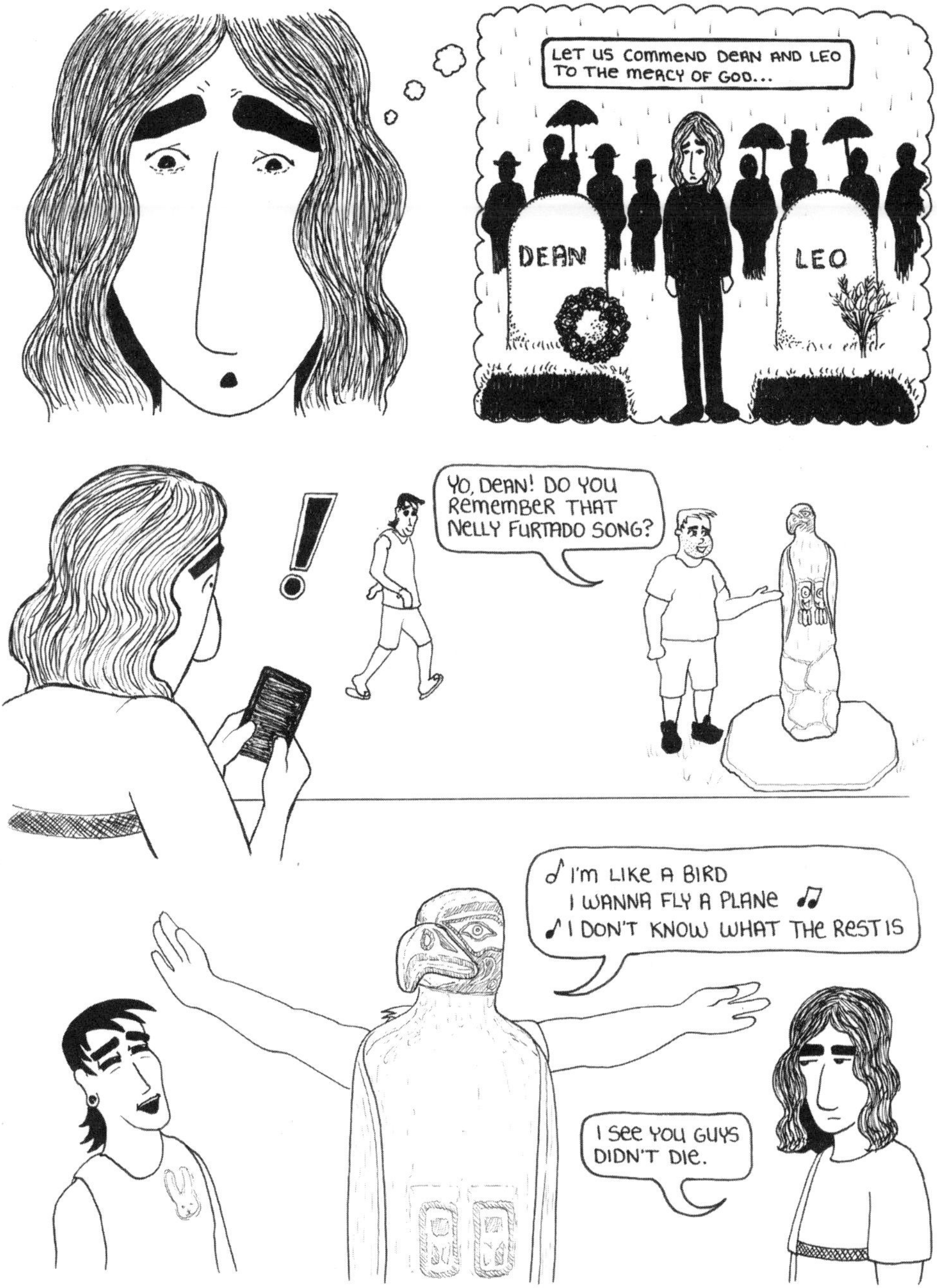
LET US COMMEND DEAN AND LEO TO THE MERCY OF GOD...
DEAN
LEO
YO, DEAN! DO YOU REMEMBER THAT NELLY FURTADO SONG?
I'M LIKE A BIRD
I WANNA FLY A PLANE
I DON'T KNOW WHAT THE REST IS
I SEE YOU GUYS DIDN'T DIE.

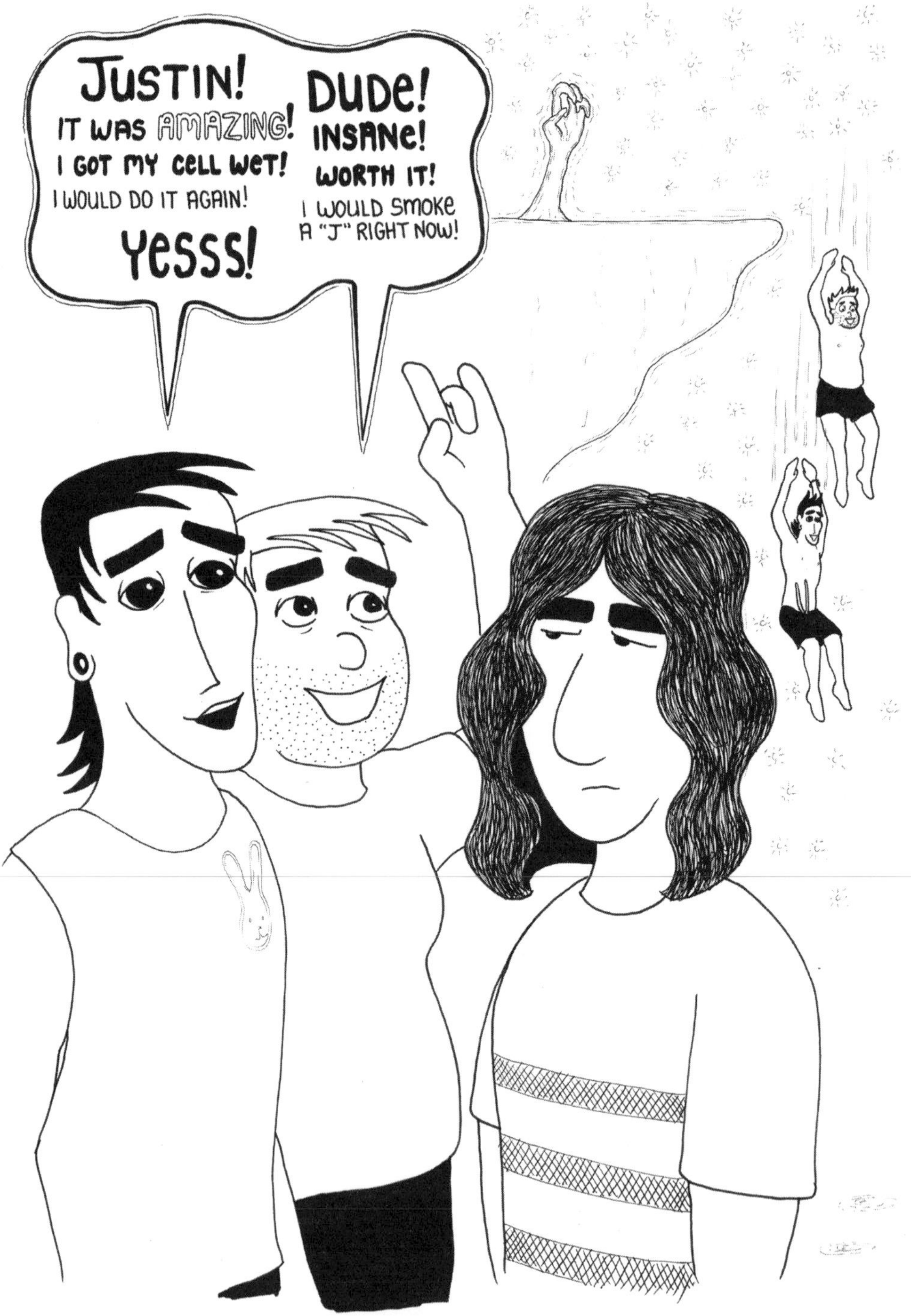
JUSTIN! IT WAS AMAZING! I GOT MY CELL WET! I WOULD DO IT AGAIN! YESSS!
DUDE! INSANE! WORTH IT! I WOULD SMOKE A "J" RIGHT NOW!

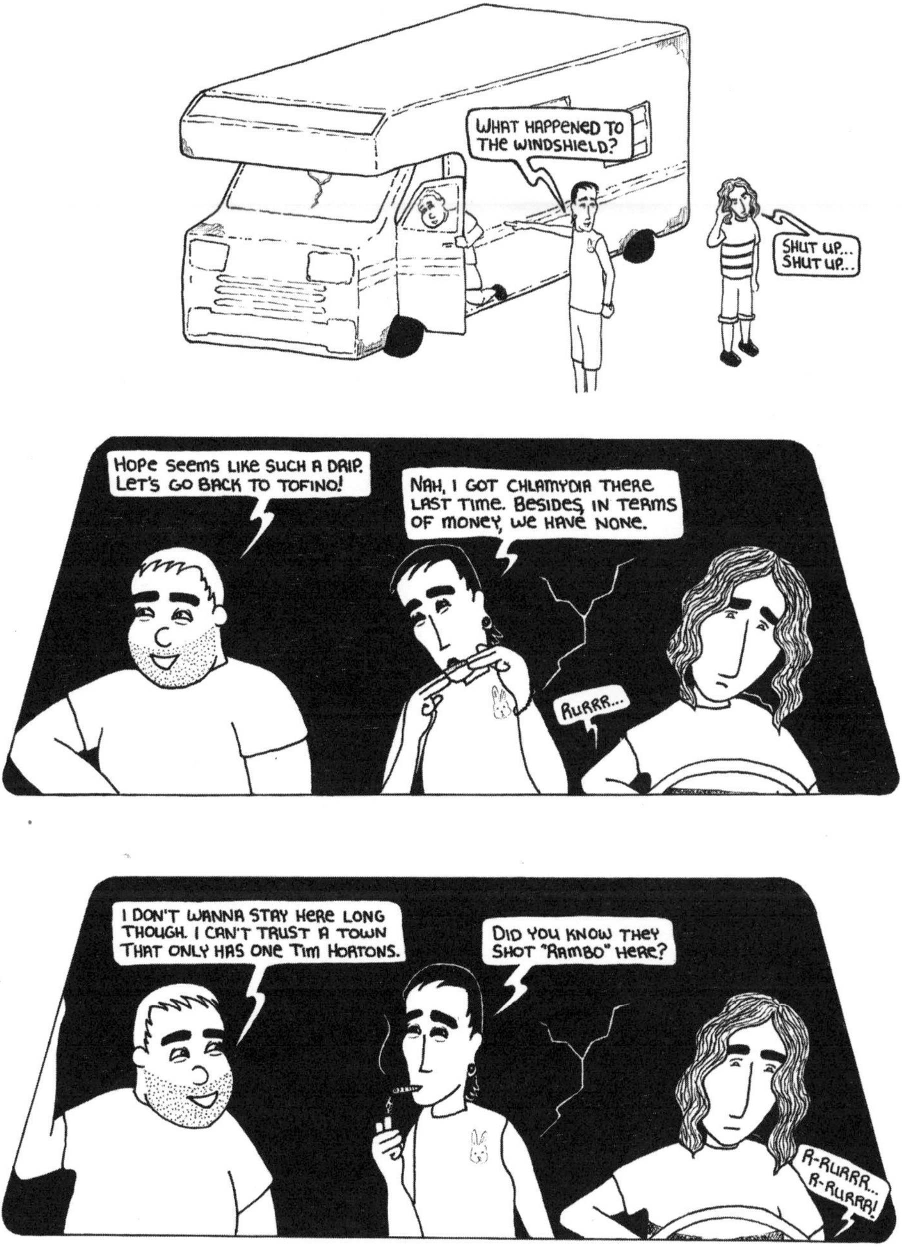
WHAT HAPPENED TO THE WINDSHIELD?
SHUT UP... SHUT UP...
HOPE SEEMS LIKE SUCH A DRIP. LET'S GO BACK TO TOFINO!
NAH, I GOT CHLAMYDIA THERE LAST TIME. BESIDES, IN TERMS OF MONEY, WE HAVE NONE.
RURRR...
I DON'T WANNA STAY HERE LONG THOUGH. I CAN'T TRUST A TOWN THAT ONLY HAS ONE TIM HORTONS.
DID YOU KNOW THEY SHOT "RAMBO" HERE?
R-RURRR... R-RURRR!

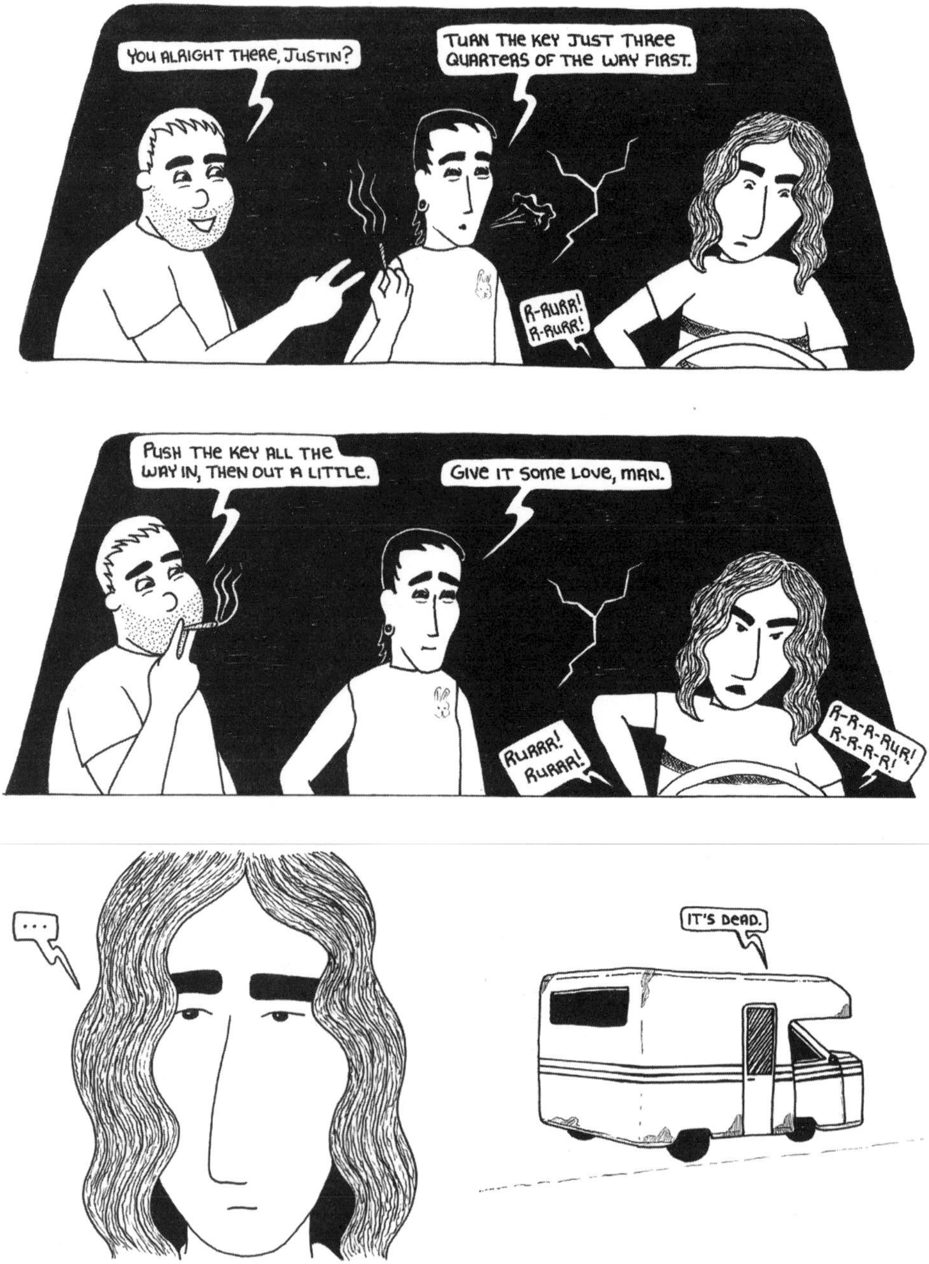
YOU ALRIGHT THERE, JUSTIN?
TURN THE KEY JUST THREE QUARTERS OF THE WAY FIRST.
R-RURR! R-RURR!
PUSH THE KEY ALL THE WAY IN, THEN OUT A LITTLE.
GIVE IT SOME LOVE, MAN.
RURRR! RURRR!
R-R-R-RUR! R-R-R-R!
...
IT'S DEAD.

CHAPTER 2

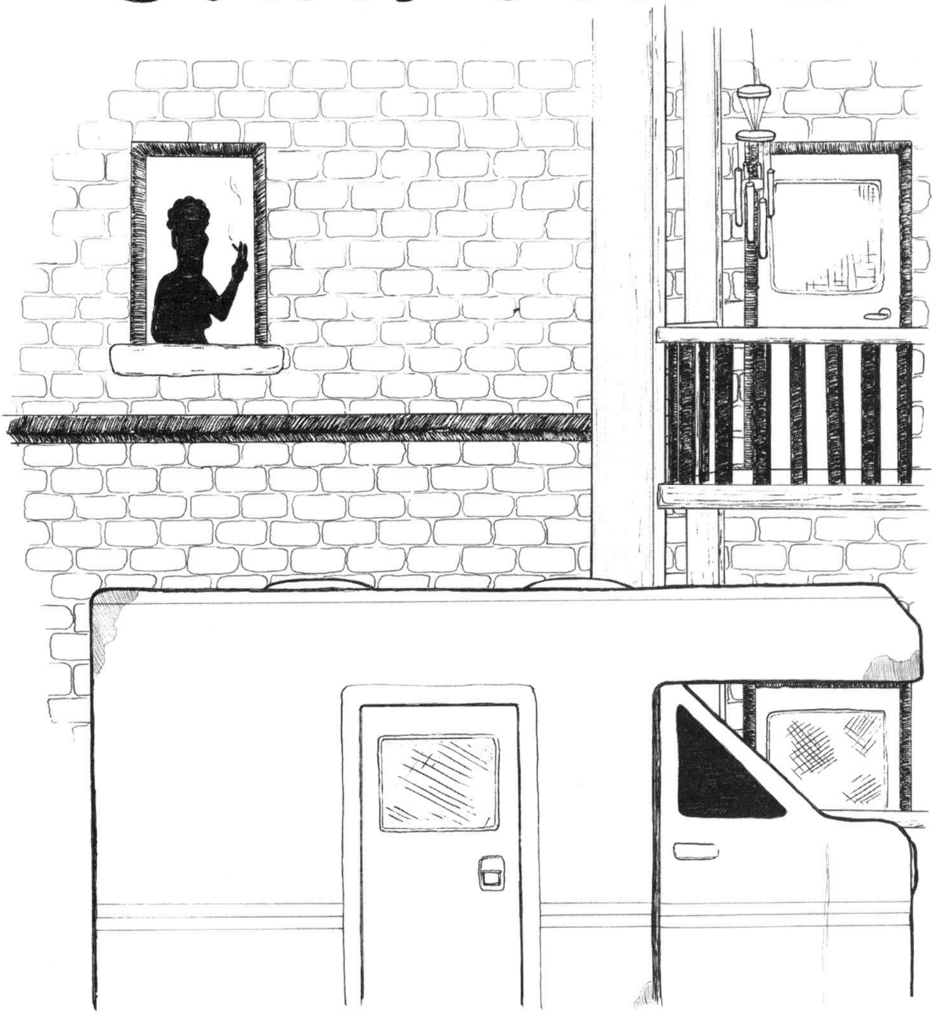

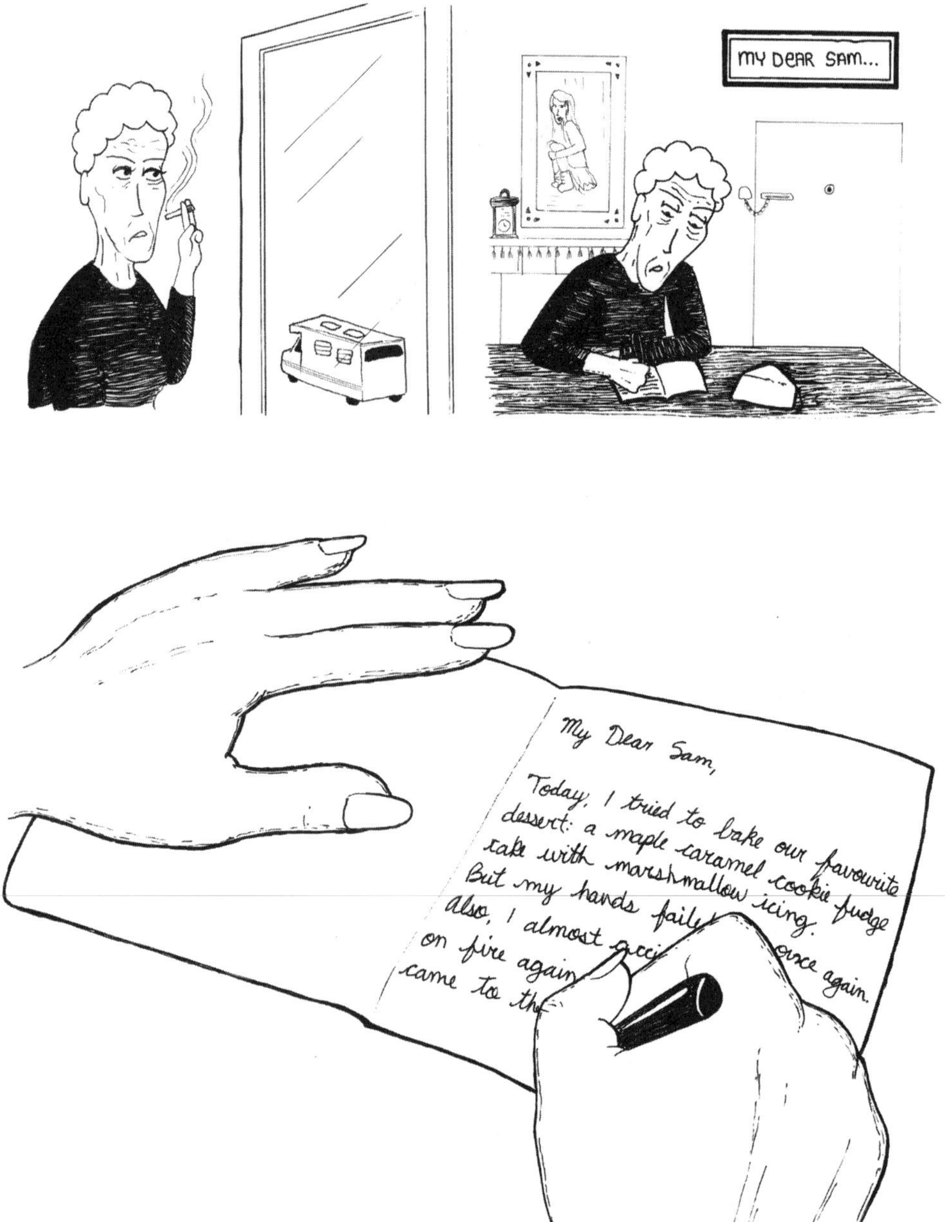

MY DEAR SAM...
My Dear Sam,
Today, I tried to bake our favourite
dessert: a maple caramel cookie fudge
cake with marshmallow icing.
But my hands fail
Also, I almost
once again.
on fire again
came to the

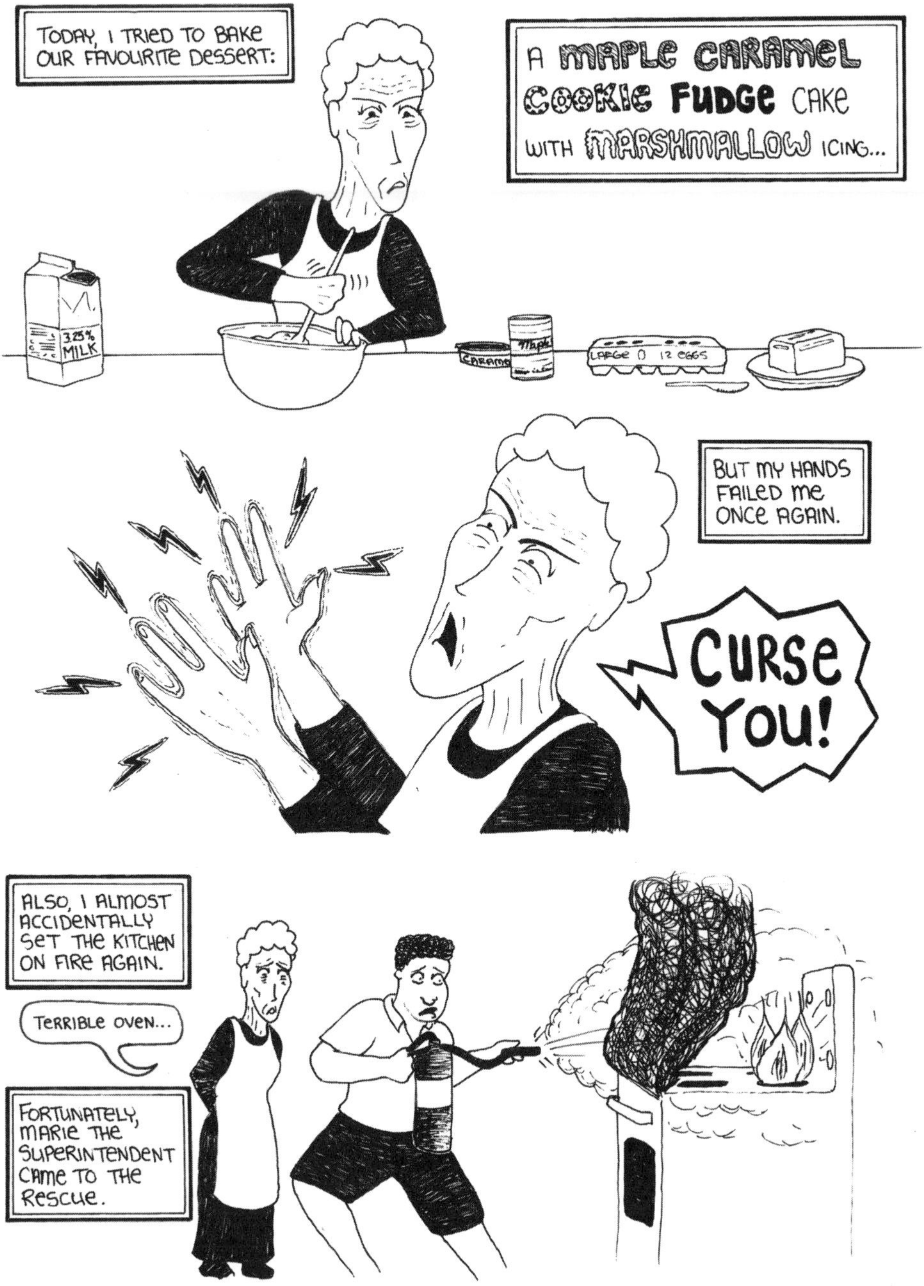
TODAY, I TRIED TO BAKE OUR FAVOURITE DESSERT:
A MAPLE CARAMEL COOKIE FUDGE CAKE WITH MARSHMALLOW ICING...
3.25% MILK
CARAMEL
Maple
LARGE 12 EGGS
BUT MY HANDS FAILED ME ONCE AGAIN.
CURSE YOU!
ALSO, I ALMOST ACCIDENTALLY SET THE KITCHEN ON FIRE AGAIN.
TERRIBLE OVEN...
FORTUNATELY, MARIE THE SUPERINTENDENT CAME TO THE RESCUE.

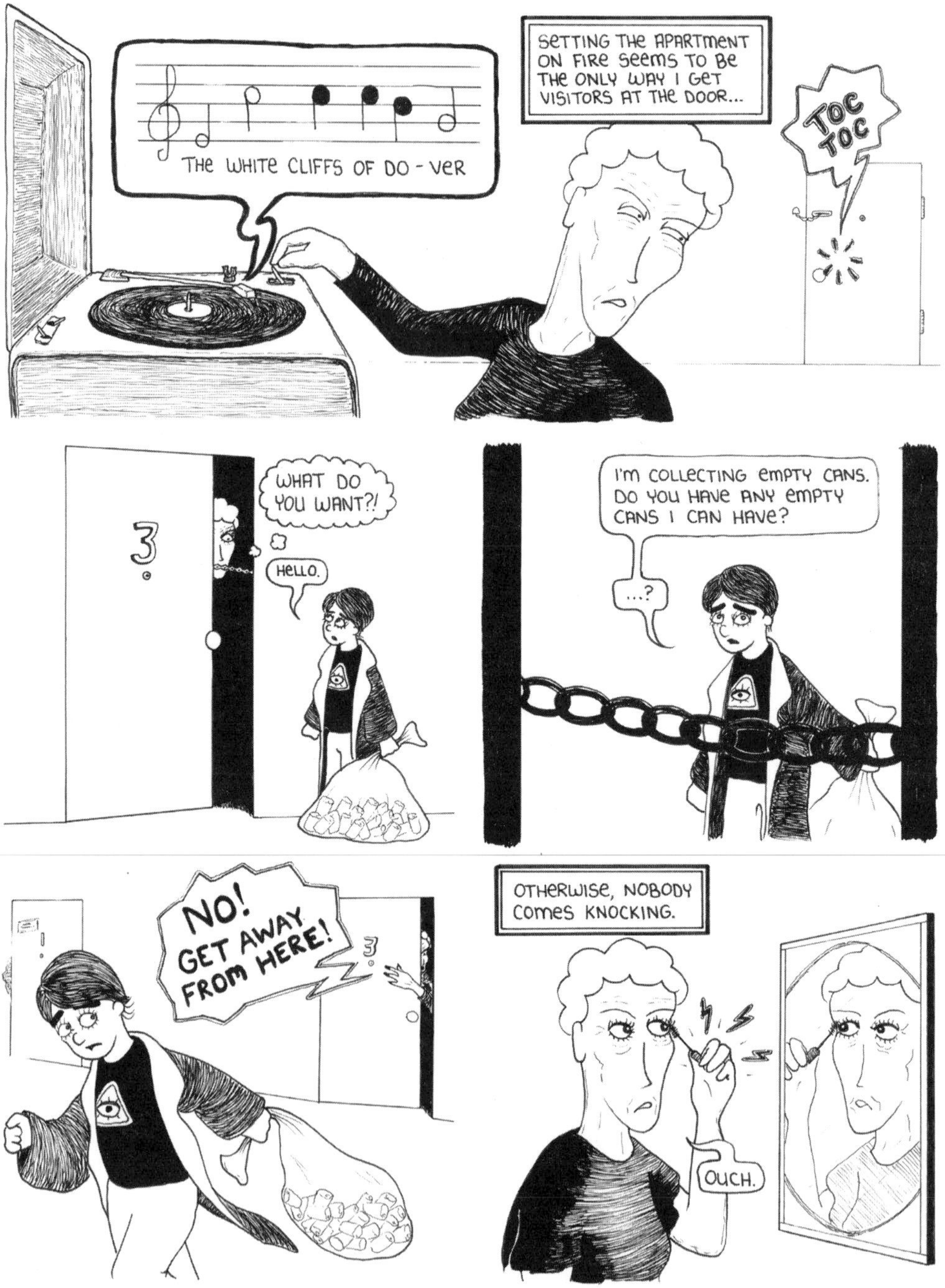
THE WHITE CLIFFS OF DO - VER
SETTING THE APARTMENT ON FIRE SEEMS TO BE THE ONLY WAY I GET VISITORS AT THE DOOR...
TOC TOC
3
WHAT DO YOU WANT?!
HELLO.
I'M COLLECTING EMPTY CANS. DO YOU HAVE ANY EMPTY CANS I CAN HAVE?
...?
NO! GET AWAY FROM HERE!
3
OTHERWISE, NOBODY COMES KNOCKING.
OUCH.

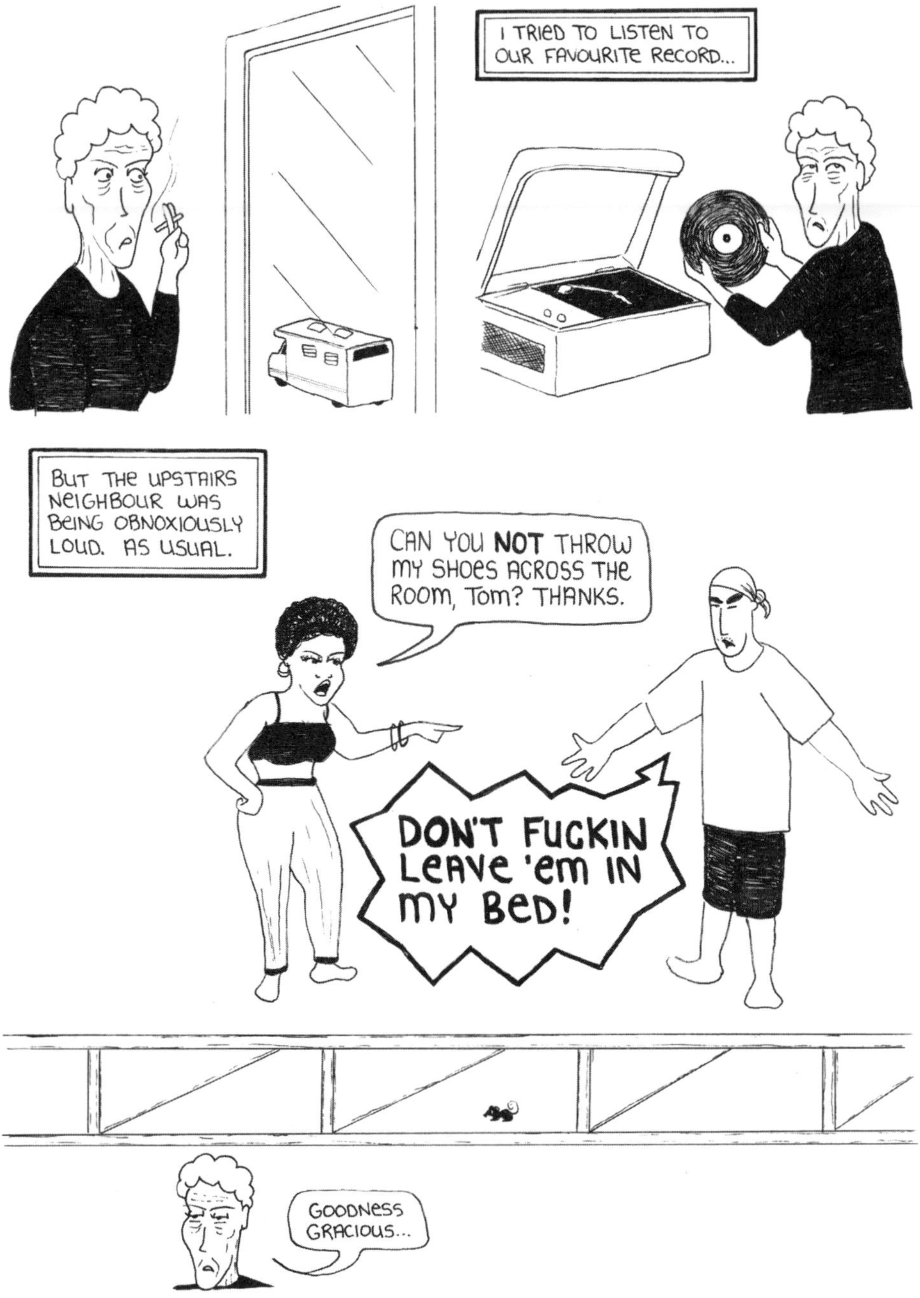
I TRIED TO LISTEN TO OUR FAVOURITE RECORD...
BUT THE UPSTAIRS NEIGHBOUR WAS BEING OBNOXIOUSLY LOUD. AS USUAL.
CAN YOU **NOT** THROW MY SHOES ACROSS THE ROOM, Tom? THANKS.
DON'T FUCKIN LEAVE 'em IN MY BED!
GOODNESS GRACIOUS...

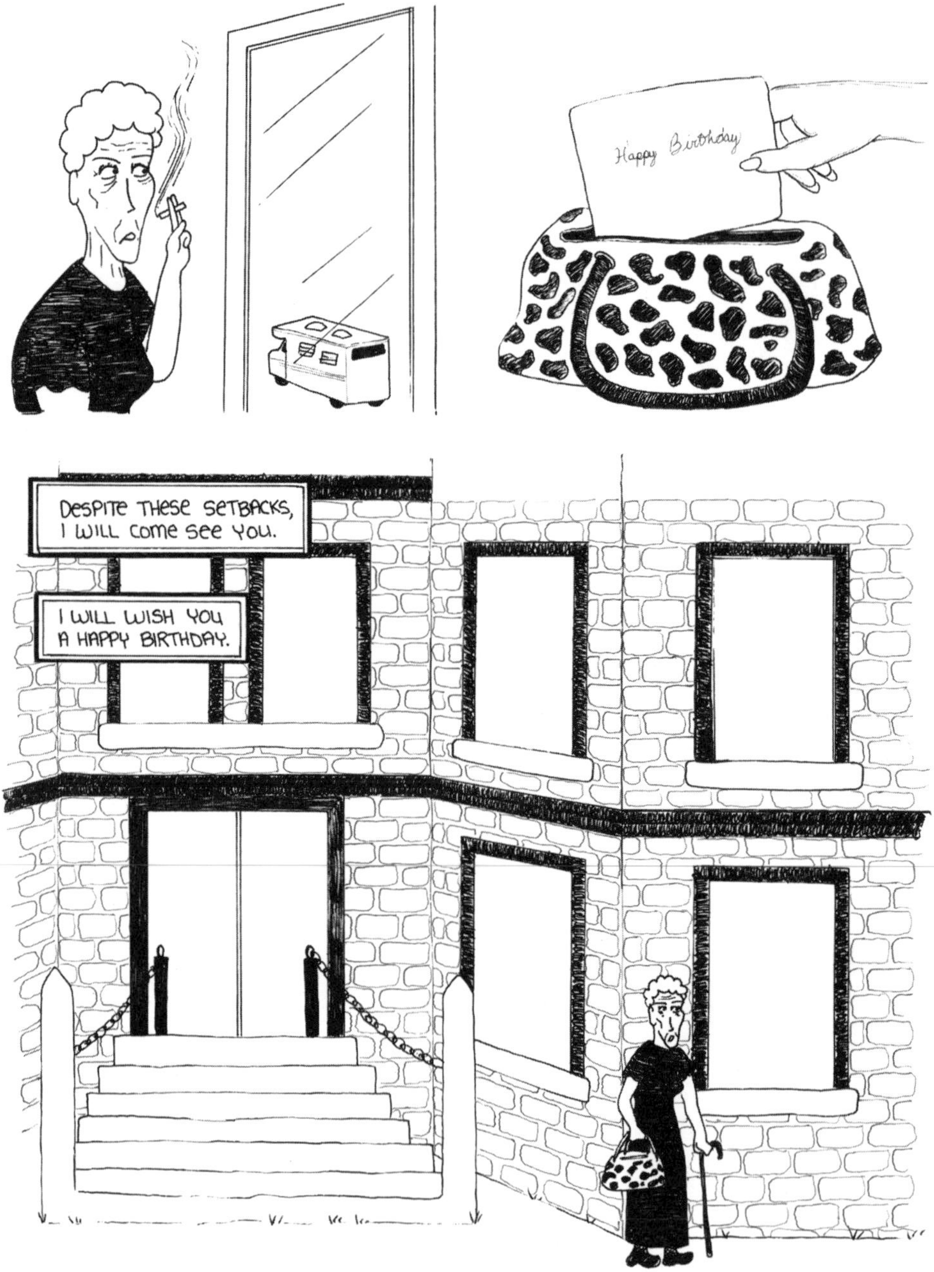
Happy Birthday
DESPITE THESE SETBACKS, I WILL COME SEE YOU.
I WILL WISH YOU A HAPPY BIRTHDAY.

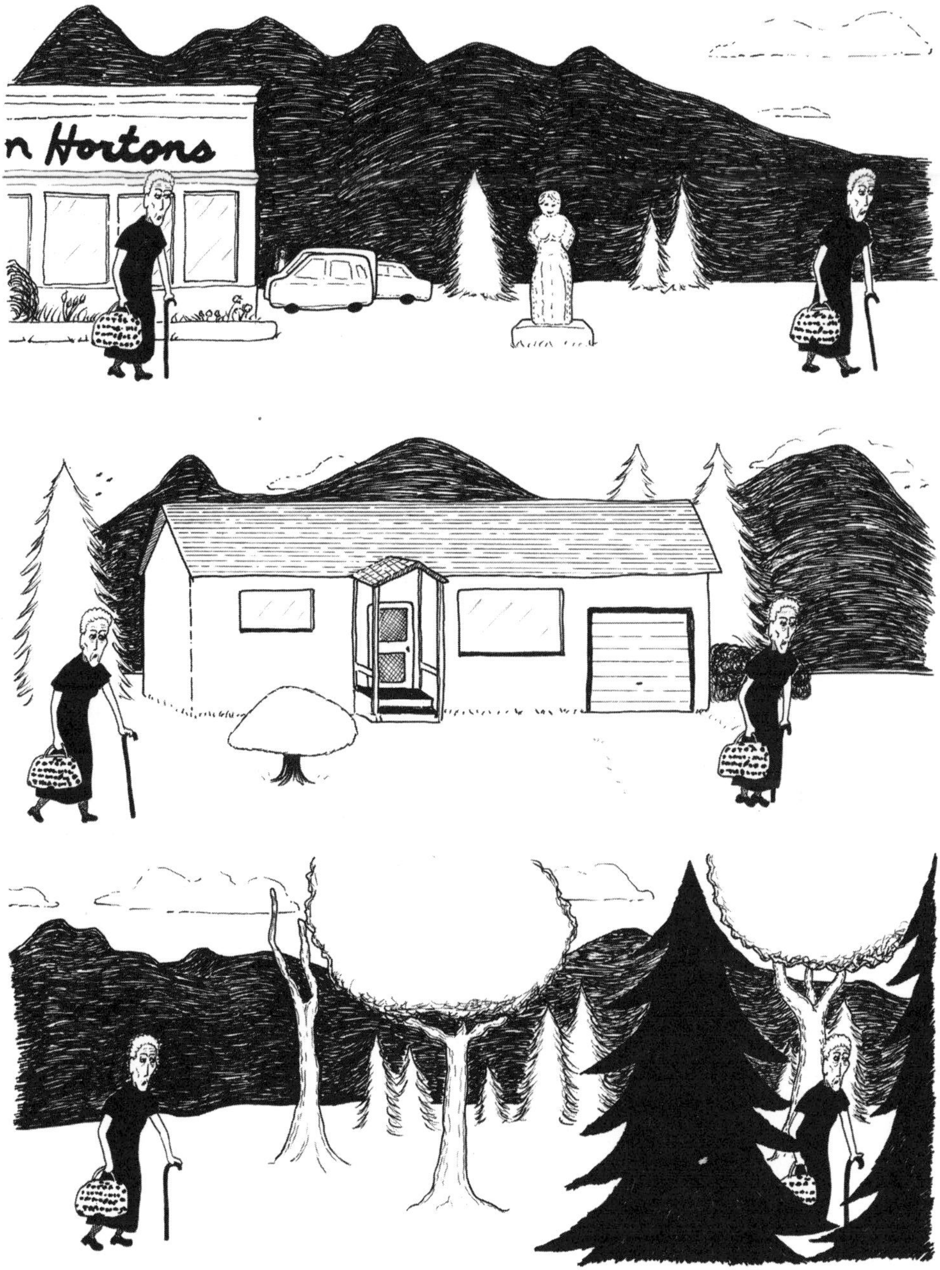
n Hortons

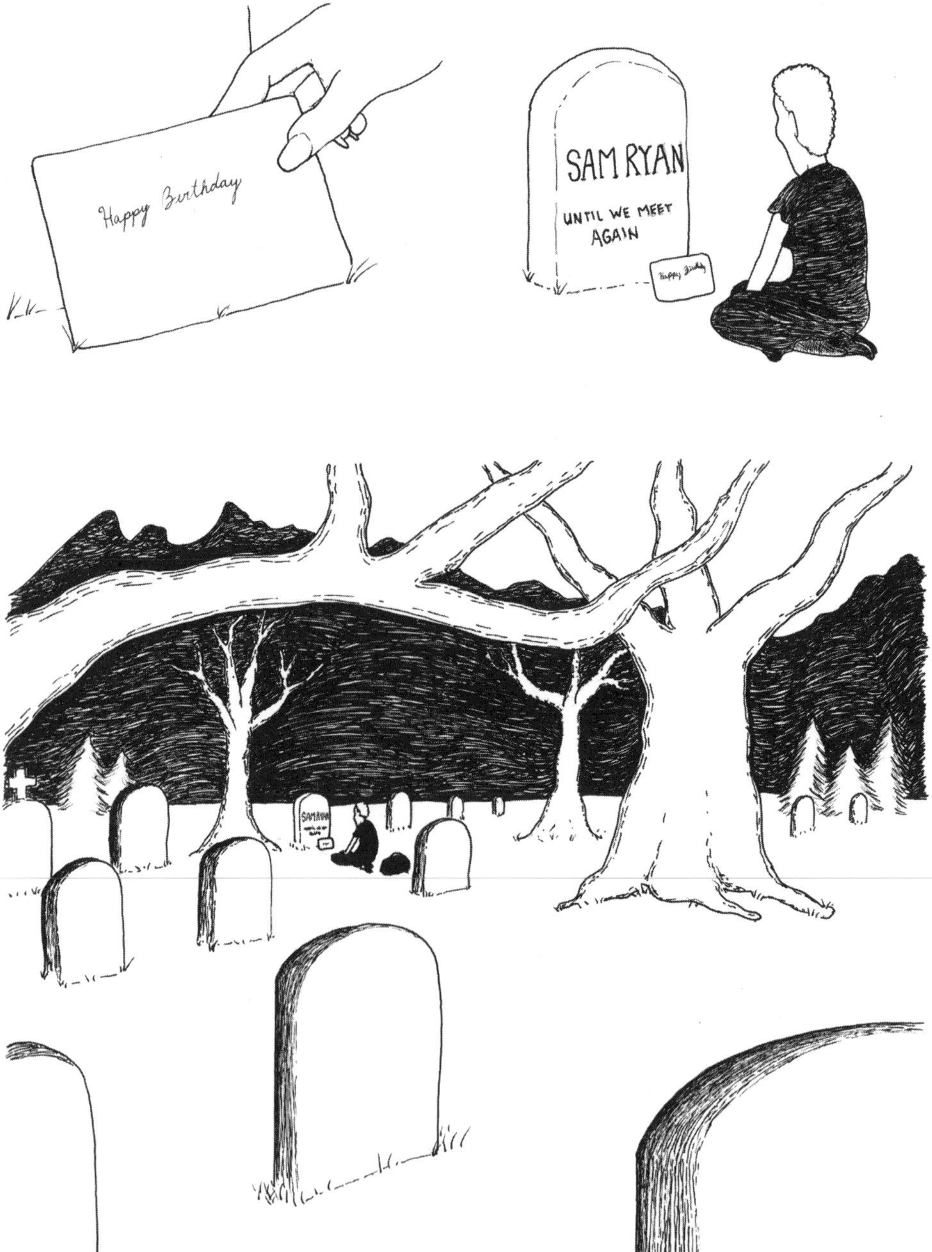
Happy Birthday
SAM RYAN
UNTIL WE MEET AGAIN
Happy Birthday

CHAPTER 3

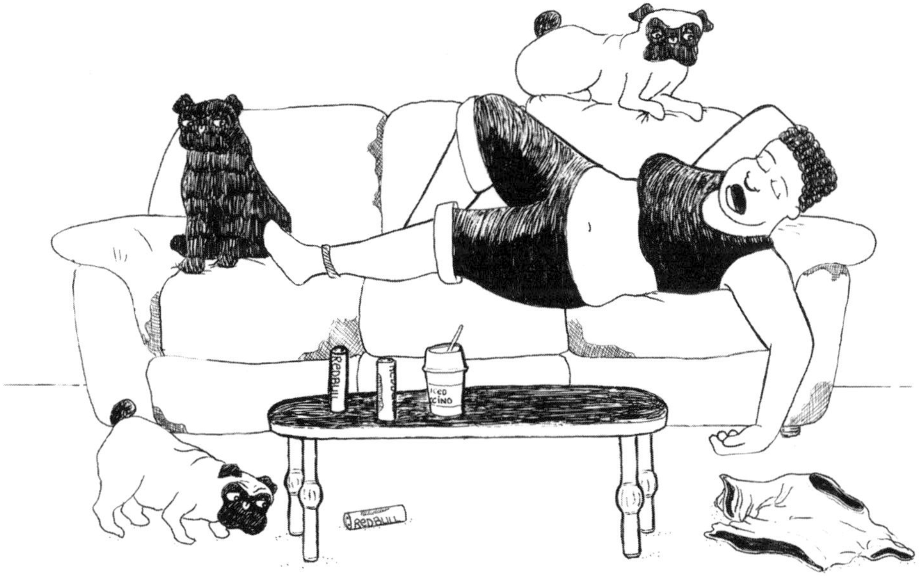

REDBULL
REDBULL
ICED
CINO
REDBULL

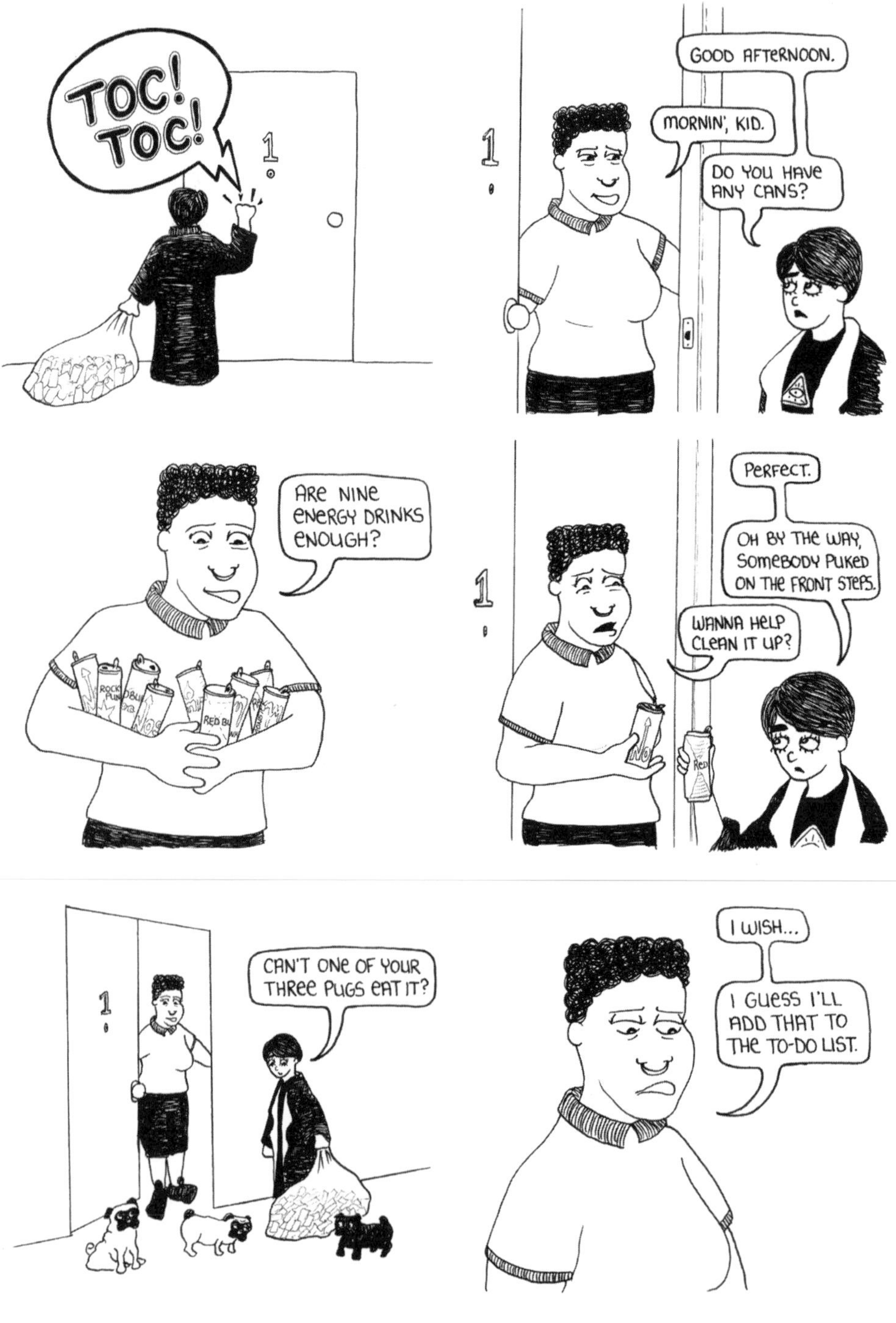
TOC! TOC!
1
GOOD AFTERNOON.
MORNIN', KID.
DO YOU HAVE ANY CANS?
ARE NINE ENERGY DRINKS ENOUGH?
ROCK
RED BU
NOS
PERFECT.
OH BY THE WAY, SOMEBODY PUKED ON THE FRONT STEPS.
WANNA HELP CLEAN IT UP?
CAN'T ONE OF YOUR THREE PUGS EAT IT?
I WISH...
I GUESS I'LL ADD THAT TO THE TO-DO LIST.

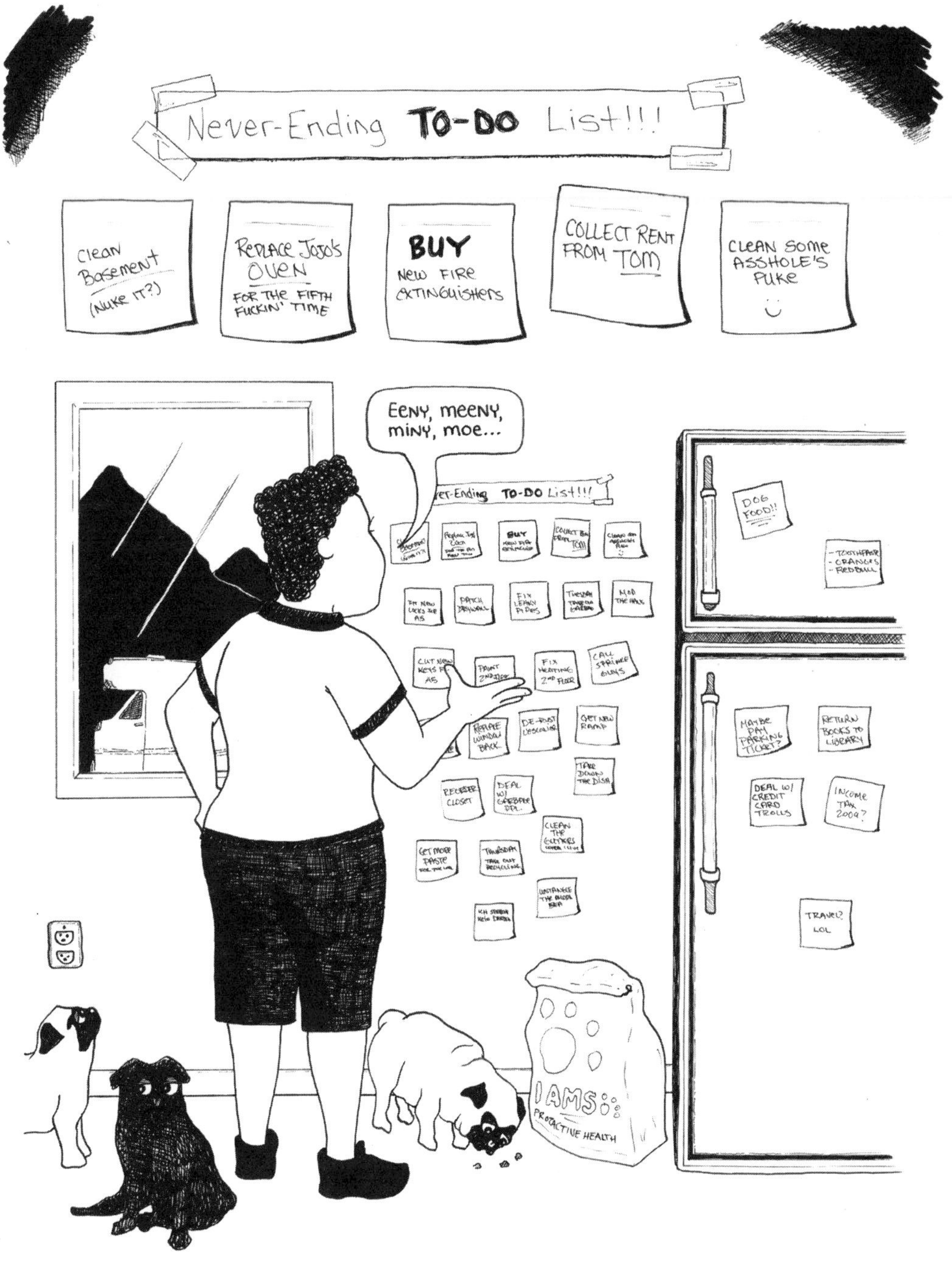
Never-Ending TO-DO List!!!
Clean Basement (Nuke it?)
Replace Jojo's OVEN FOR THE FIFTH FUCKIN' TIME
BUY New Fire extinguishers
COLLECT RENT FROM TOM
CLEAN SOME ASSHOLE'S PUKE
Eeny, meeny, miny, moe...
PATCH DRYWALL
GET NEW RAMP
TAKE DOWN THE DISH
CLEAN THE GUTTERS
DOG FOOD!!
- TOOTHPASTE - ORANGES - REDBULL
MAYBE PAY PARKING TICKET?
RETURN BOOKS TO LIBRARY
DEAL W/ CREDIT CARD TROLLS
INCOME TAX 2009?
TRAVEL? LOL
IAMS
PROACTIVE HEALTH

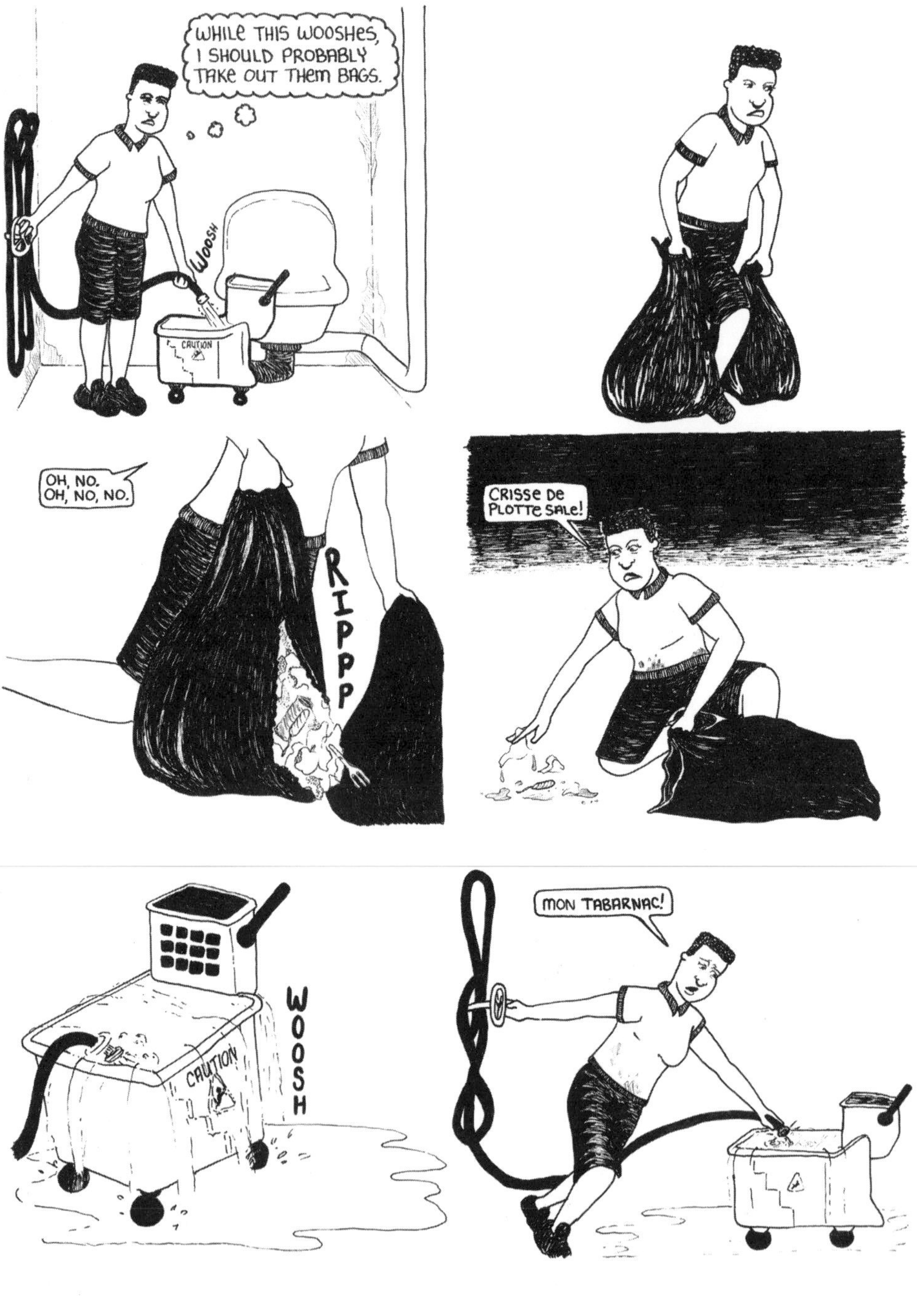
WHILE THIS WOOSHES, I SHOULD PROBABLY TAKE OUT THEM BAGS.
WOOSH
CAUTION
OH, NO. OH, NO, NO.
RIPPP
CRISSE DE PLOTTE SALE!
CAUTION
WOOSH
MON TABARNAC!

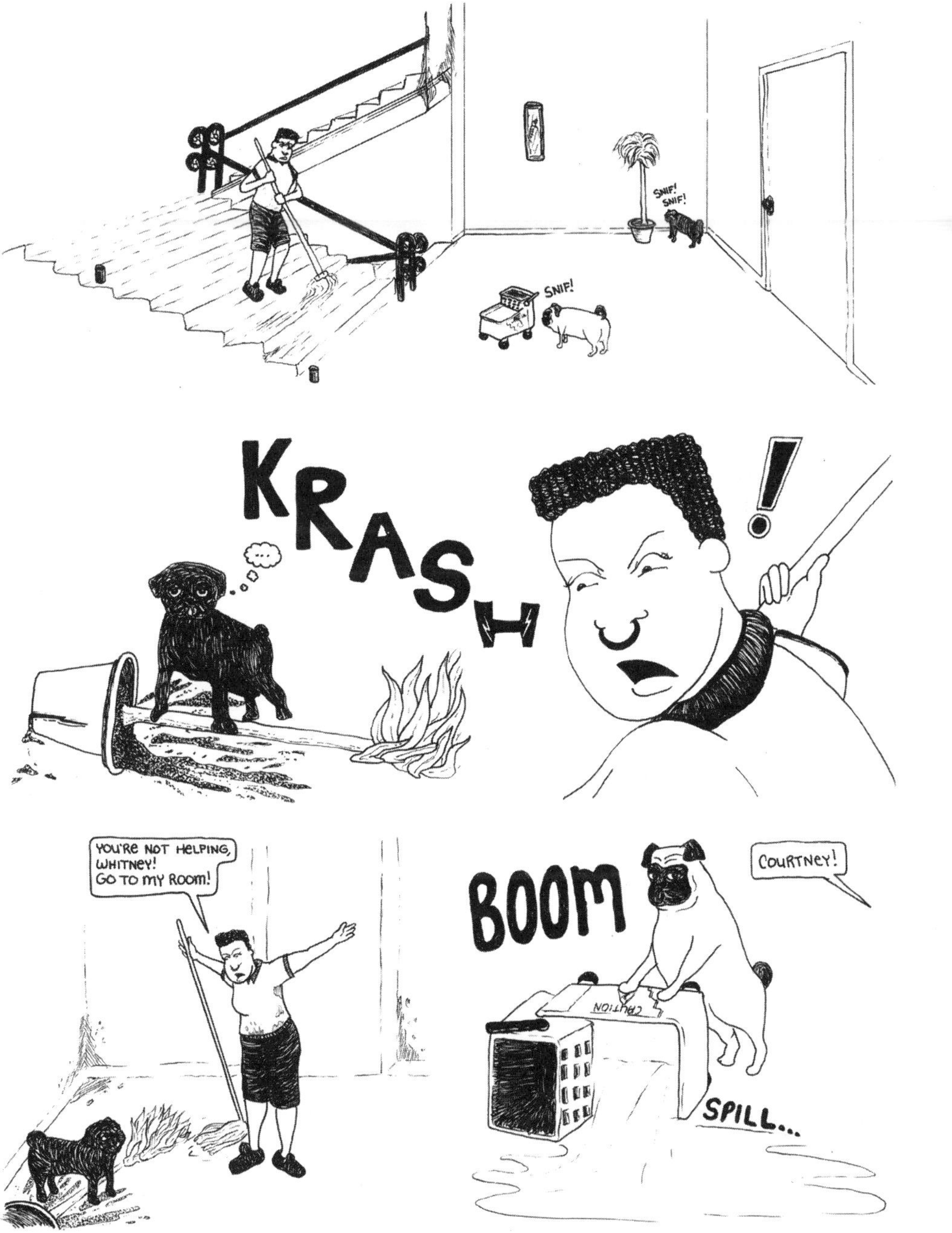
SNIF!
SNIF!
SNIF!
KRASH
...
!
YOU'RE NOT HELPING, WHITNEY! GO TO MY ROOM!
BOOM
COURTNEY!
CAUTION
SPILL...

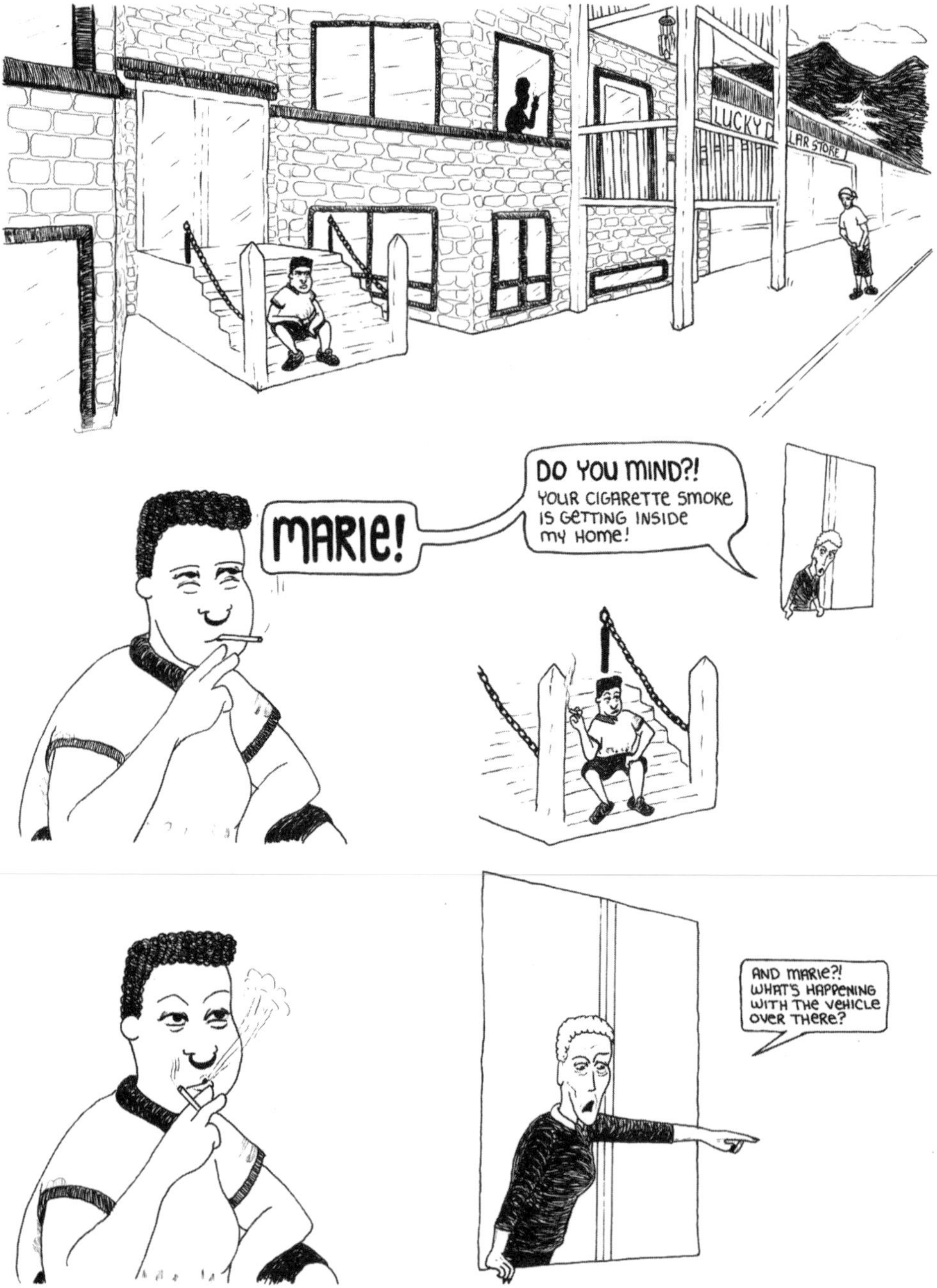
MARIE!
DO YOU MIND?! YOUR CIGARETTE SMOKE IS GETTING INSIDE MY HOME!
AND MARIE?! WHAT'S HAPPENING WITH THE VEHICLE OVER THERE?

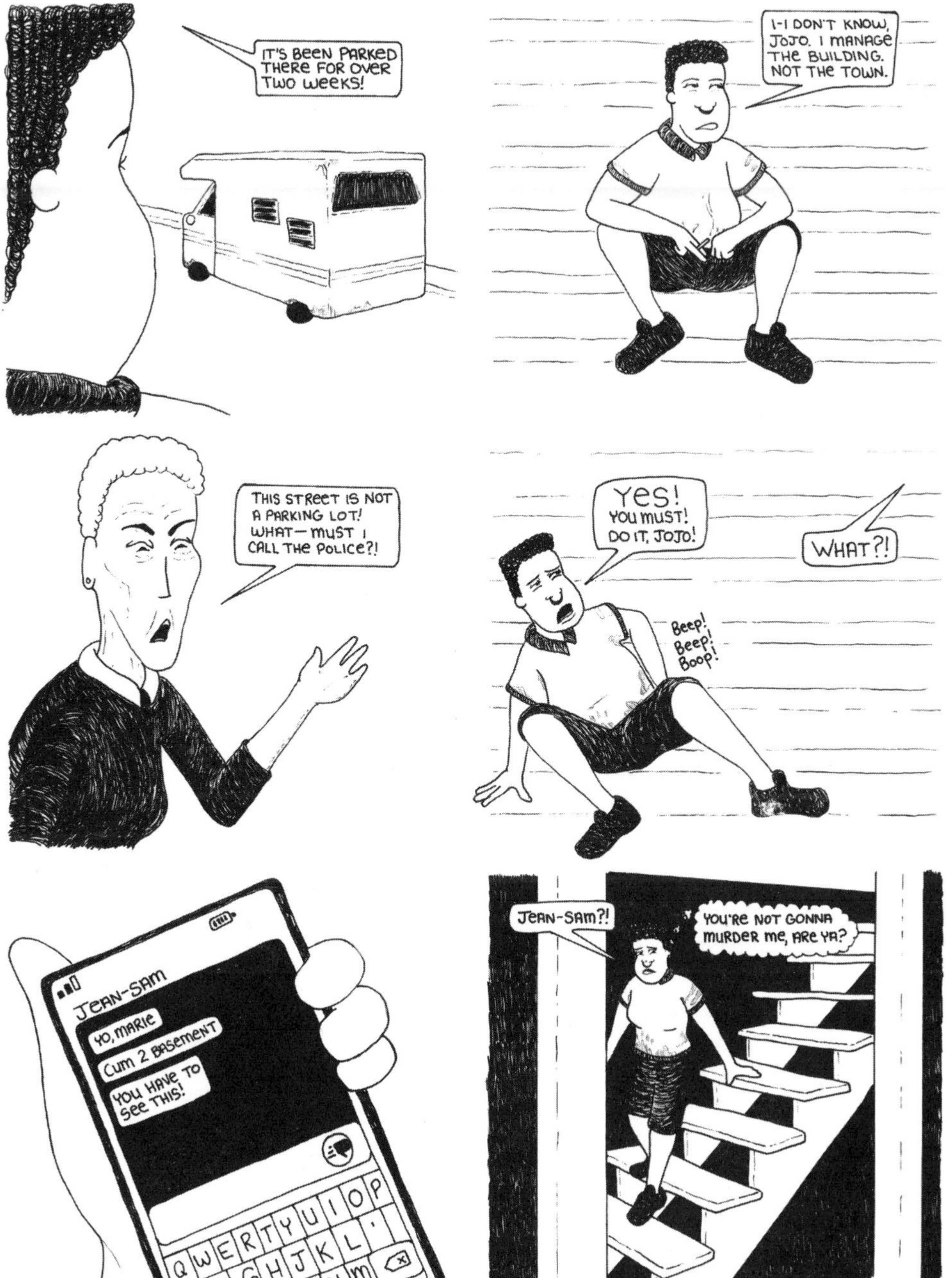
IT'S BEEN PARKED THERE FOR OVER TWO WEEKS!
I-I DON'T KNOW, JOJO. I MANAGE THE BUILDING. NOT THE TOWN.
THIS STREET IS NOT A PARKING LOT! WHAT—MUST I CALL THE POLICE?!
YES! YOU MUST! DO IT, JOJO!
WHAT?!
Beep! Beep! Boop!
JEAN-SAM
YO, MARIE
Cum 2 BASEMENT
YOU HAVE TO SEE THIS!
JEAN-SAM?!
YOU'RE NOT GONNA MURDER ME, ARE YA?

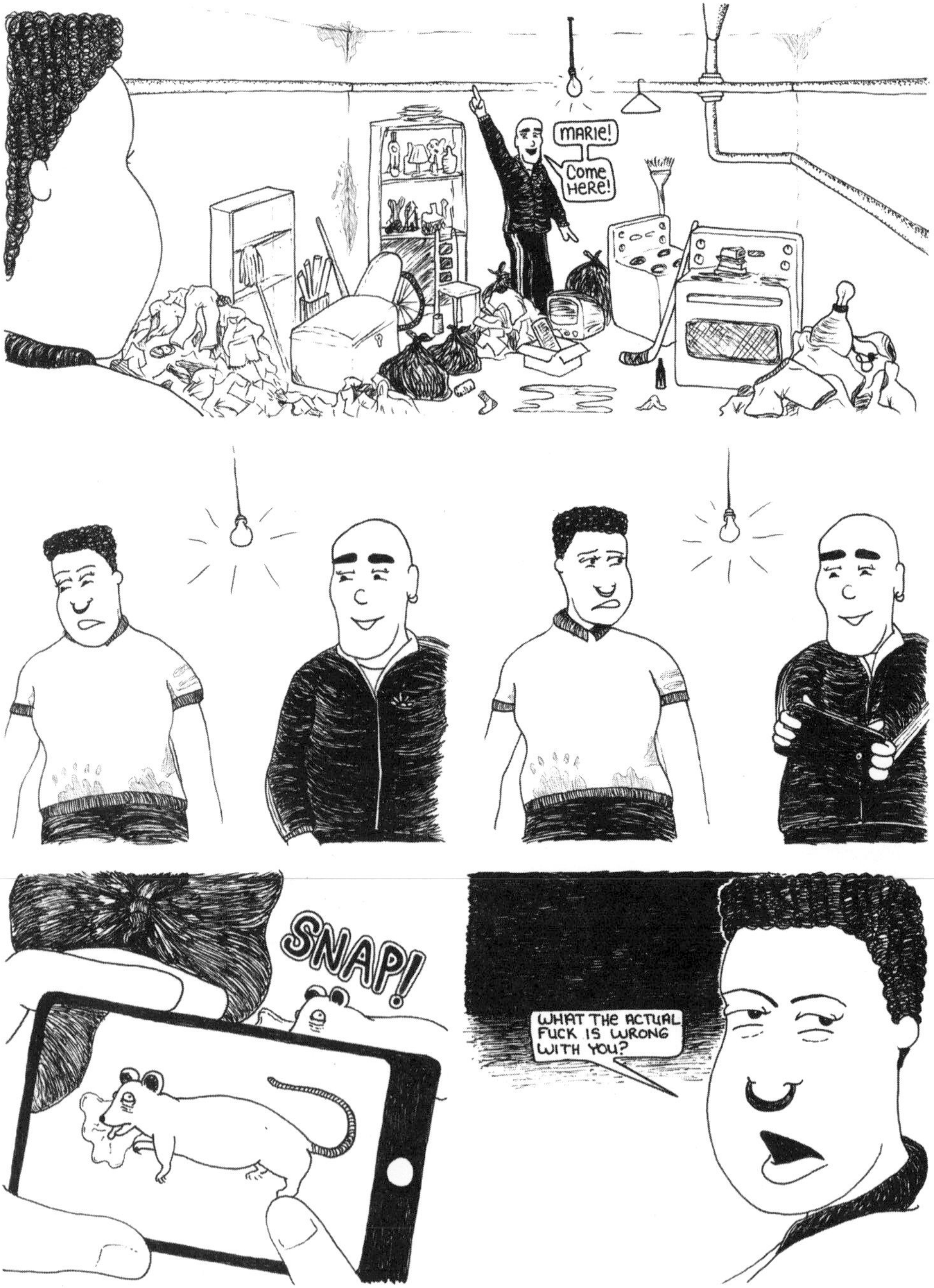
MARIE!
Come HERE!
SNAP!
WHAT THE ACTUAL FUCK IS WRONG WITH YOU?

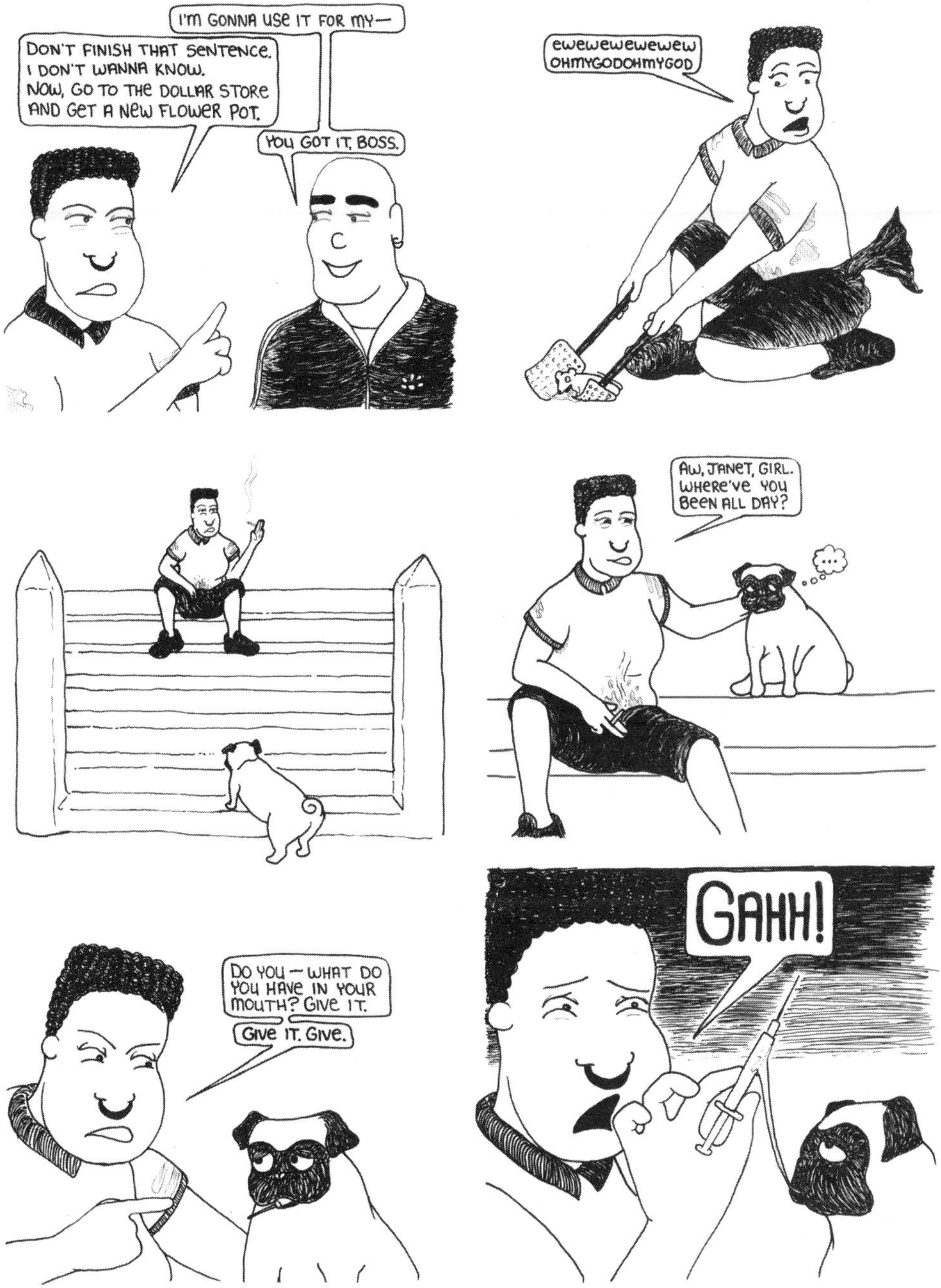
I'M GONNA USE IT FOR MY—
DON'T FINISH THAT SENTENCE. I DON'T WANNA KNOW. NOW, GO TO THE DOLLAR STORE AND GET A NEW FLOWER POT.
YOU GOT IT, BOSS.
EWEWEWEWEWEWEW OHMYGODOHMYGOD
AW, JANET, GIRL. WHERE'VE YOU BEEN ALL DAY?
...
DO YOU — WHAT DO YOU HAVE IN YOUR MOUTH? GIVE IT.
GIVE IT. GIVE.
GAHH!

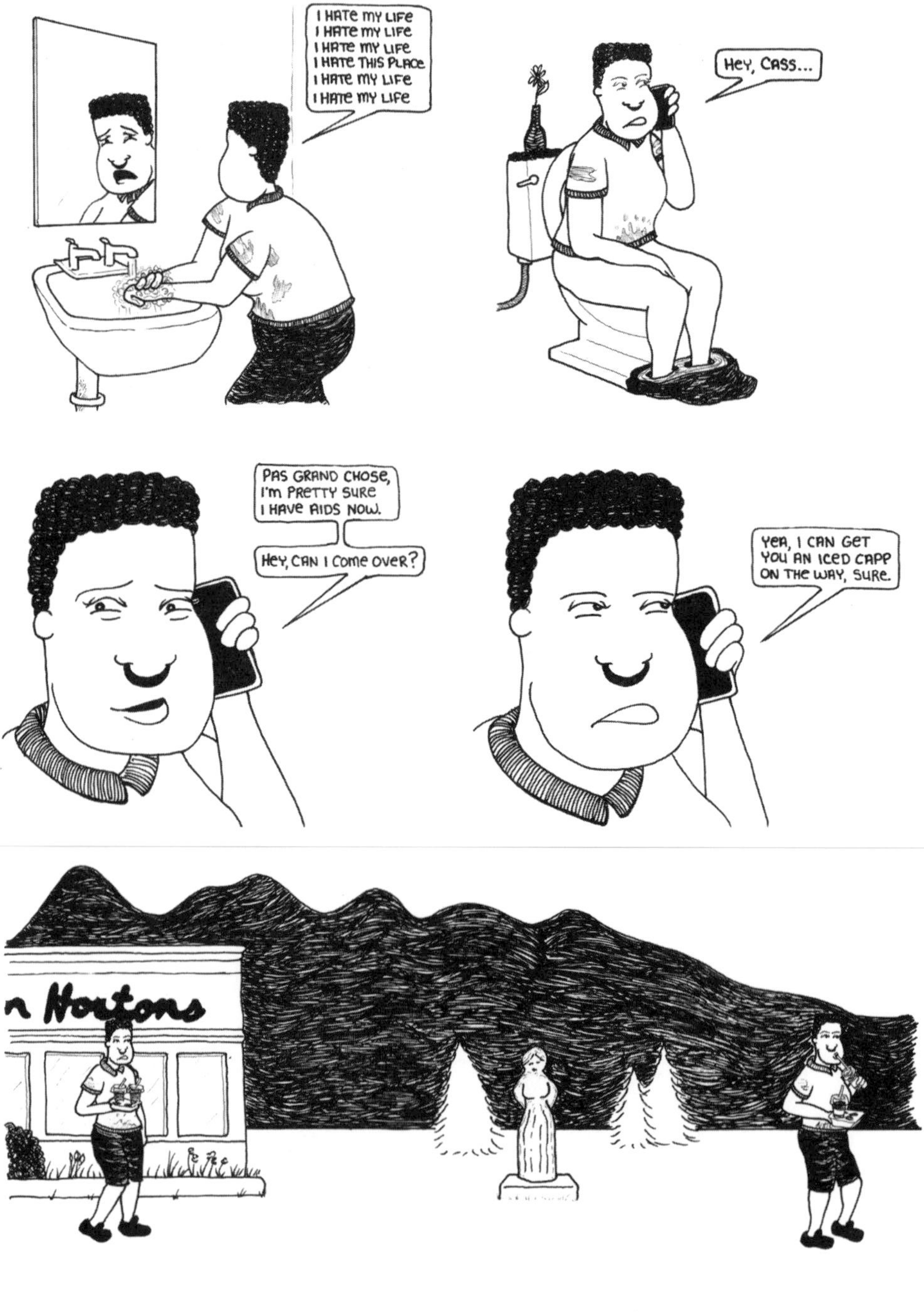
I HATE MY LIFE
I HATE MY LIFE
I HATE MY LIFE
I HATE THIS PLACE
I HATE MY LIFE
I HATE MY LIFE
HEY, CASS...
PAS GRAND CHOSE, I'M PRETTY SURE I HAVE AIDS NOW.
HEY, CAN I COME OVER?
YEA, I CAN GET YOU AN ICED CAPP ON THE WAY, SURE.
n Hortons

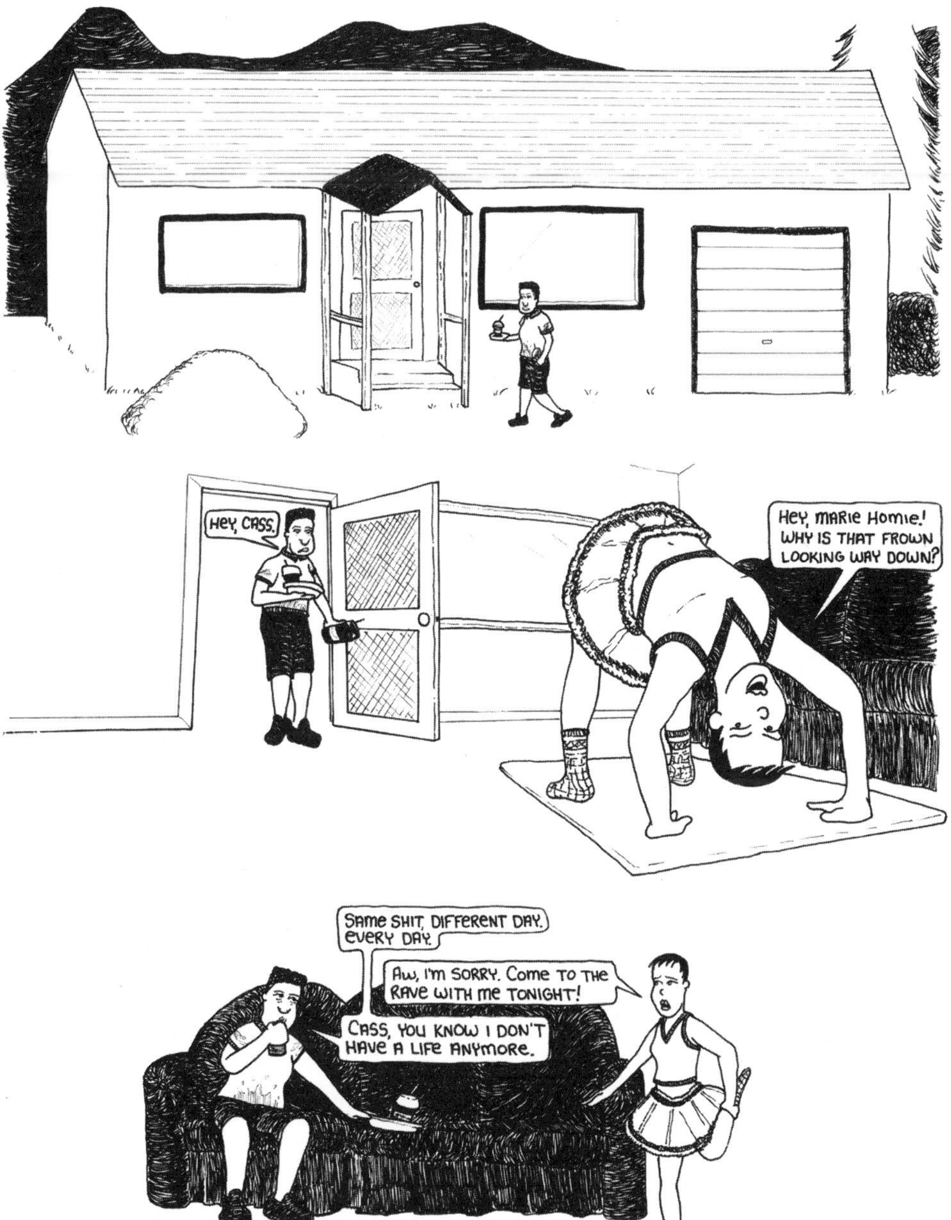
HEY, CASS.
Hey, marie Homie! WHY IS THAT FROWN LOOKING WAY DOWN?
Same SHIT, DIFFERENT DAY. every DAY.
Aw, I'm SORRY. Come TO THE RAVE WITH me TONIGHT!
CASS, YOU KNOW I DON'T HAVE A LIFE ANYMORE.

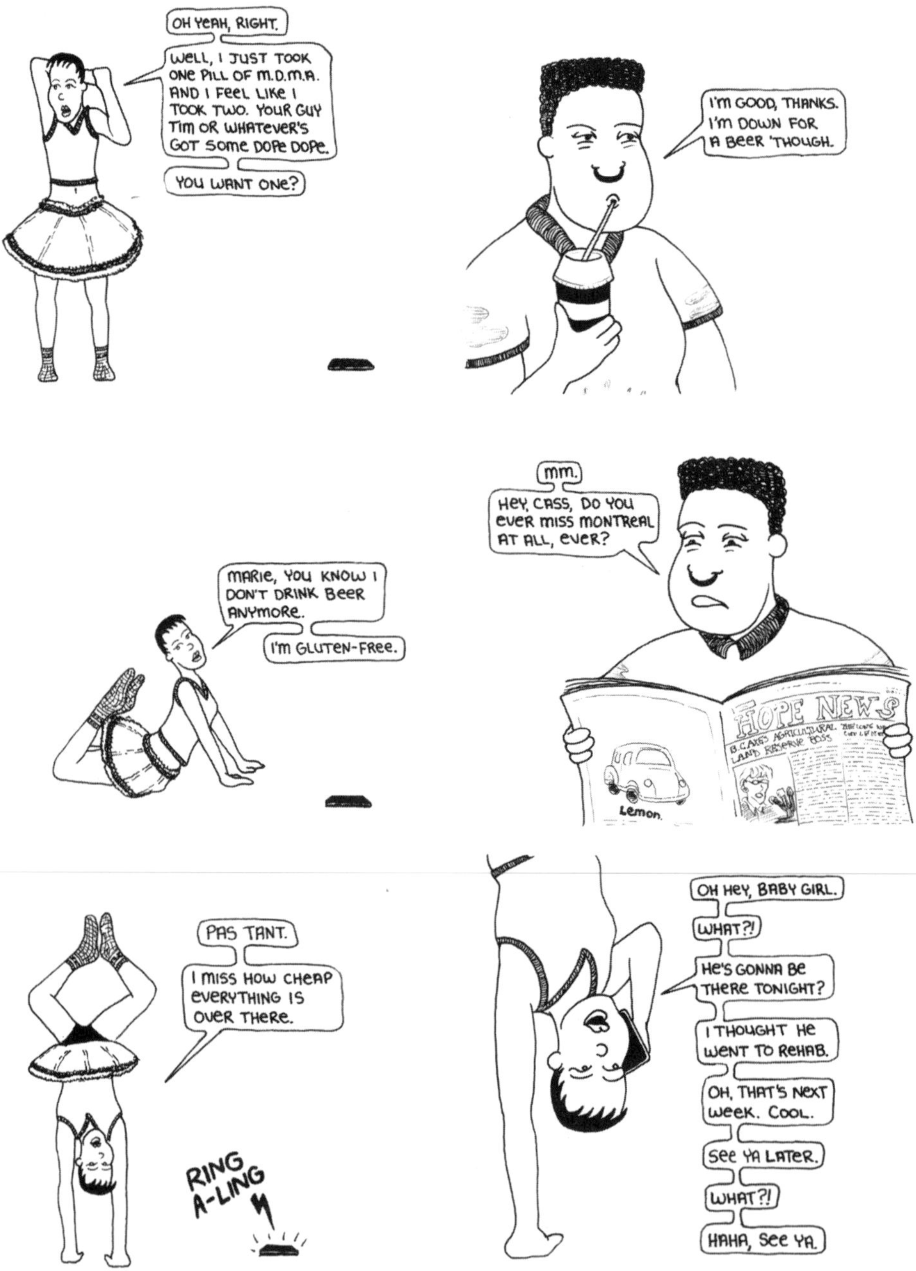
OH YEAH, RIGHT.
WELL, I JUST TOOK ONE PILL OF M.D.M.A. AND I FEEL LIKE I TOOK TWO. YOUR GUY TIM OR WHATEVER'S GOT SOME DOPE DOPE.
YOU WANT ONE?
I'M GOOD, THANKS. I'M DOWN FOR A BEER 'THOUGH.
MARIE, YOU KNOW I DON'T DRINK BEER ANYMORE.
I'M GLUTEN-FREE.
MM.
HEY, CASS, DO YOU EVER MISS MONTREAL AT ALL, EVER?
HOPE NEWS
B.C. AXES AGRICULTURAL LAND RESERVE BOSS
LEMON.
PAS TANT.
I MISS HOW CHEAP EVERYTHING IS OVER THERE.
RING A-LING
OH HEY, BABY GIRL.
WHAT?!
HE'S GONNA BE THERE TONIGHT?
I THOUGHT HE WENT TO REHAB.
OH, THAT'S NEXT WEEK. COOL.
SEE YA LATER.
WHAT?!
HAHA, SEE YA.

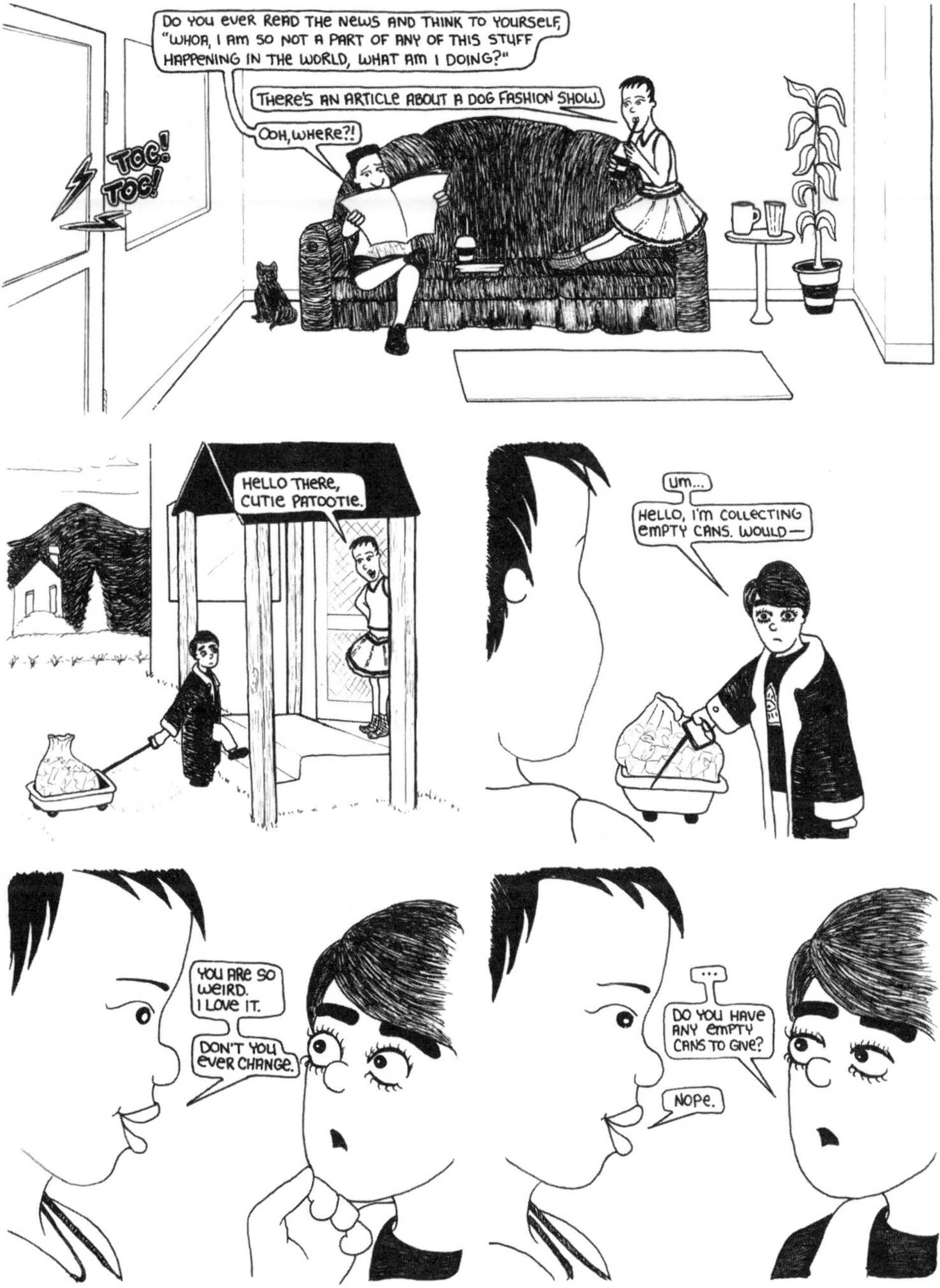
TOC! TOC!
DO YOU EVER READ THE NEWS AND THINK TO YOURSELF, "WHOA, I AM SO NOT A PART OF ANY OF THIS STUFF HAPPENING IN THE WORLD, WHAT AM I DOING?"
THERE'S AN ARTICLE ABOUT A DOG FASHION SHOW.
OOH, WHERE?!
HELLO THERE, CUTIE PATOOTIE.
UM...
HELLO, I'M COLLECTING EMPTY CANS. WOULD—
YOU ARE SO WEIRD. I LOVE IT.
DON'T YOU EVER CHANGE.
...
DO YOU HAVE ANY EMPTY CANS TO GIVE?
NOPE.

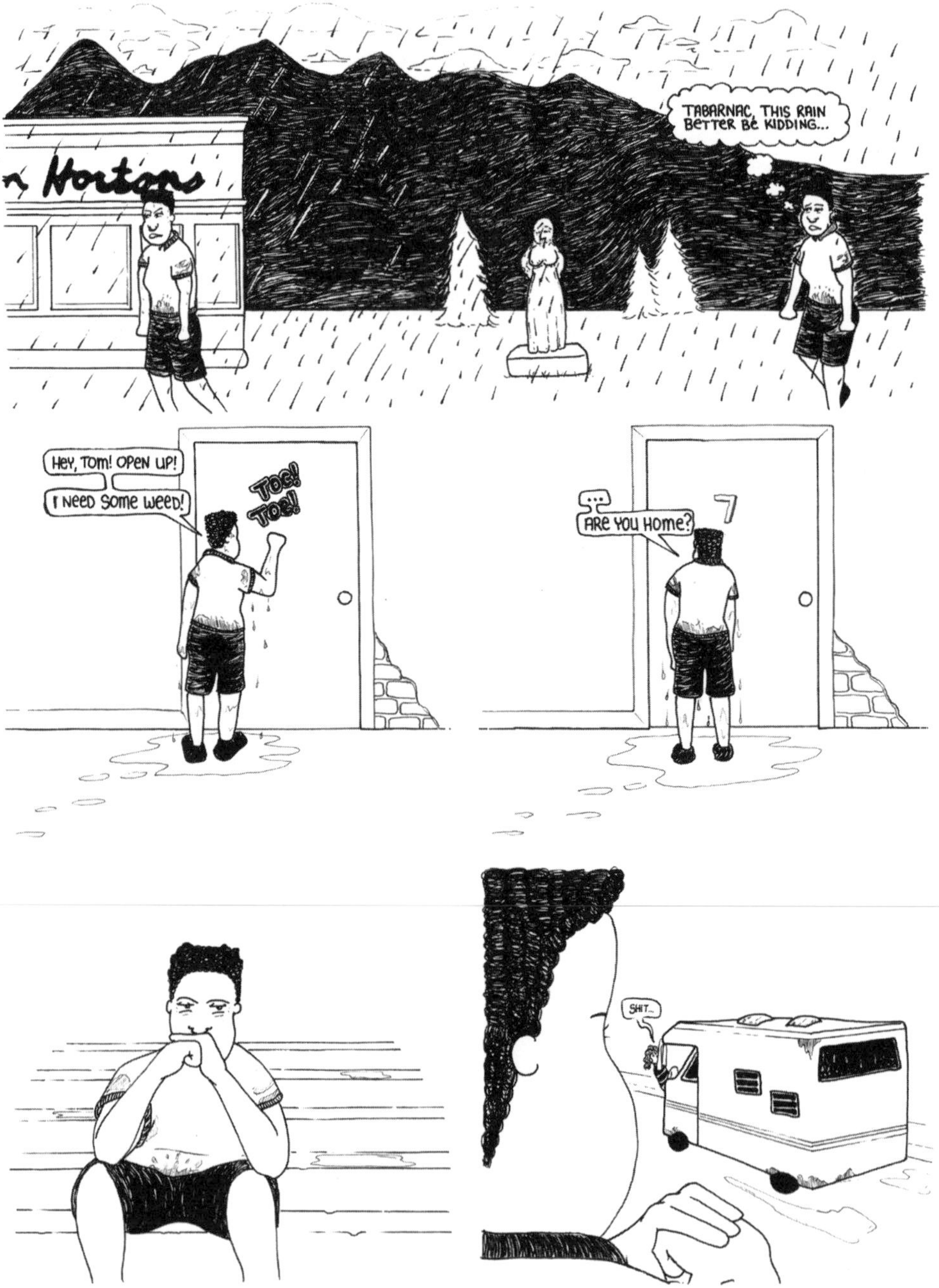
Hortons
TABARNAC, THIS RAIN BETTER BE KIDDING...
HEY, TOM! OPEN UP!
I NEED SOME WEED!
TOC! TOC!
...
ARE YOU HOME?
SHIT...

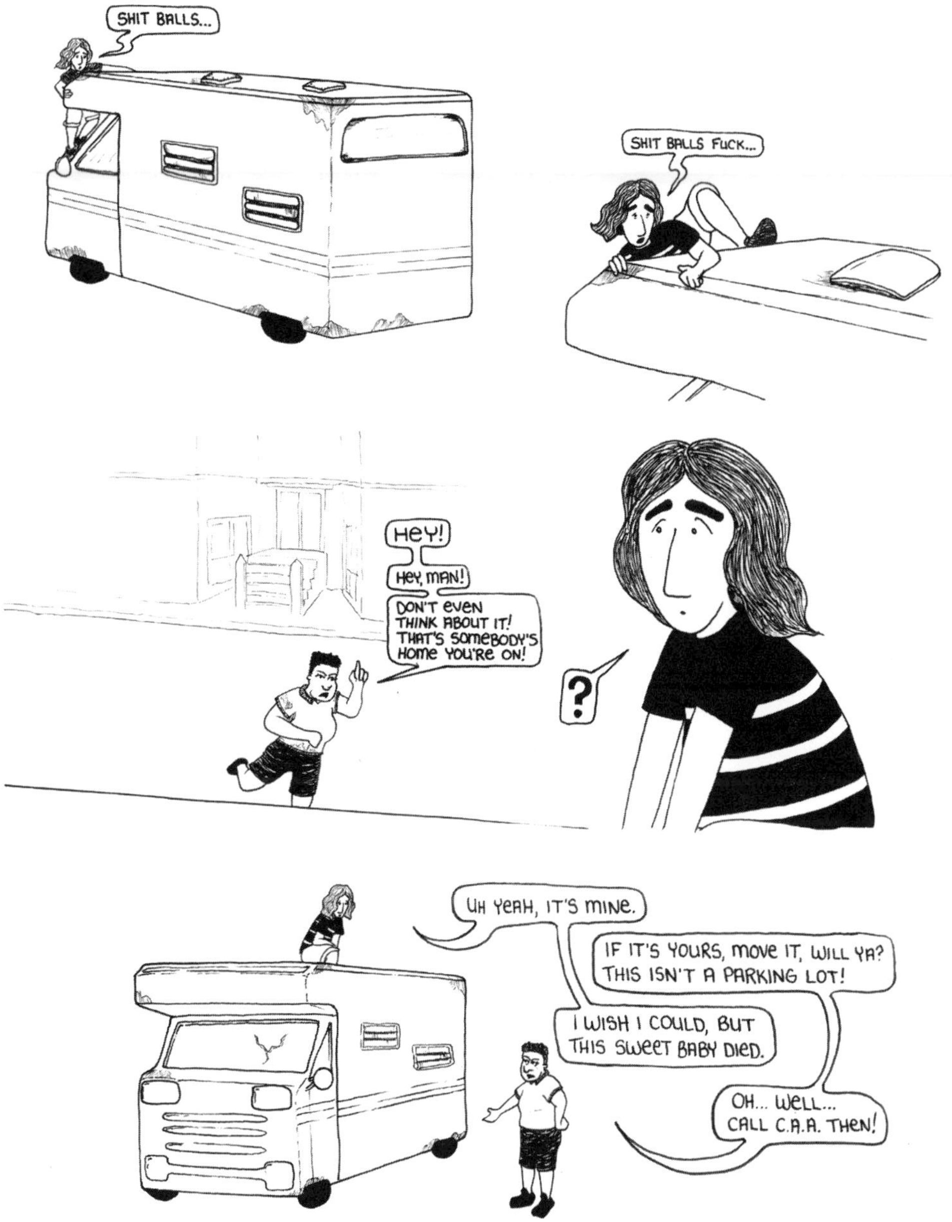
SHIT BALLS...
SHIT BALLS FUCK...
HEY!
HEY, MAN!
DON'T EVEN THINK ABOUT IT! THAT'S SOMEBODY'S HOME YOU'RE ON!
?
UH YEAH, IT'S MINE.
IF IT'S YOURS, MOVE IT, WILL YA? THIS ISN'T A PARKING LOT!
I WISH I COULD, BUT THIS SWEET BABY DIED.
OH... WELL... CALL C.A.A. THEN!

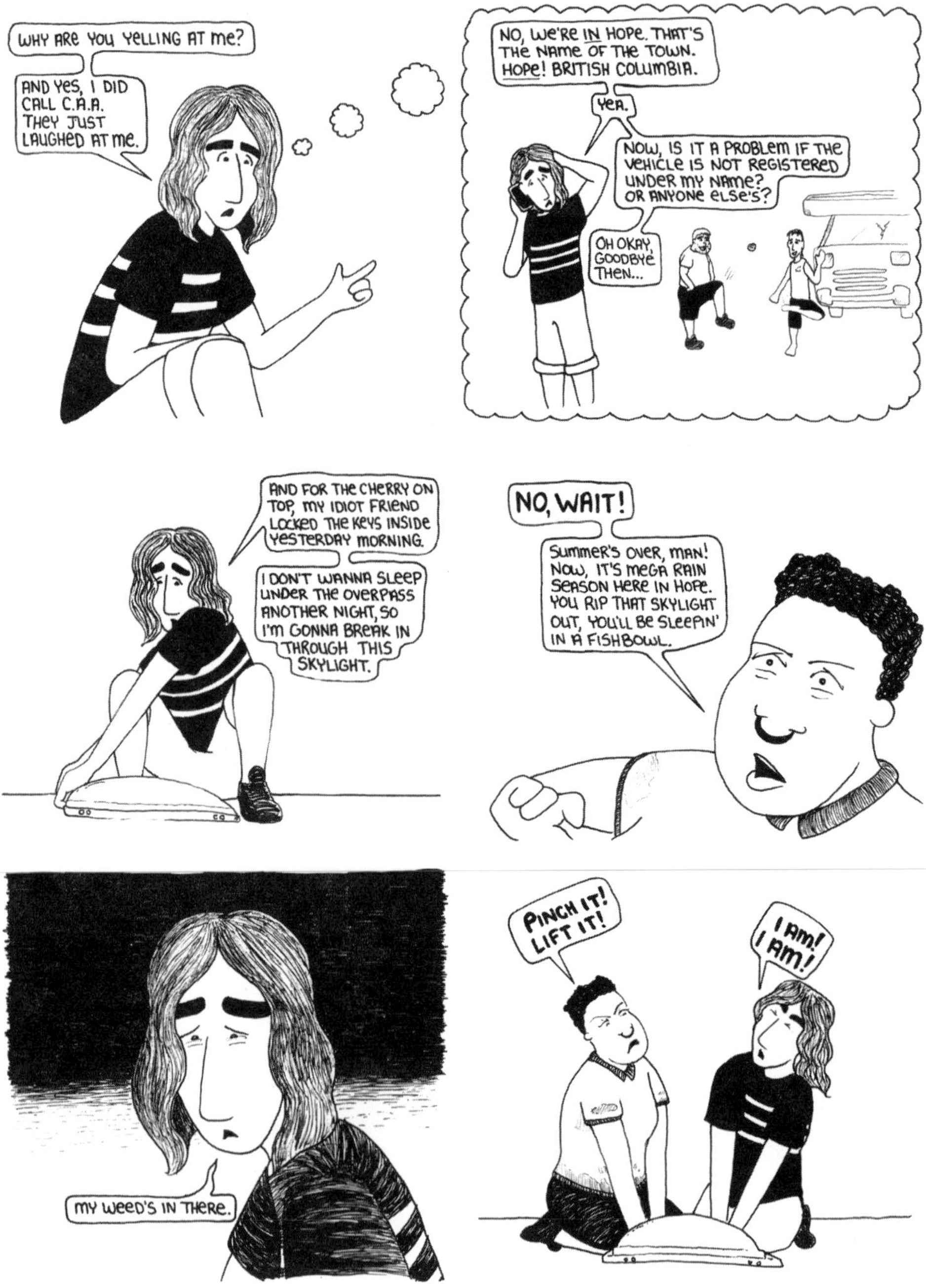
WHY ARE YOU YELLING AT ME?
AND YES, I DID CALL C.A.A. THEY JUST LAUGHED AT ME.
NO, WE'RE IN HOPE. THAT'S THE NAME OF THE TOWN. HOPE! BRITISH COLUMBIA.
YEA.
NOW, IS IT A PROBLEM IF THE VEHICLE IS NOT REGISTERED UNDER MY NAME? OR ANYONE ELSE'S?
OH OKAY, GOODBYE THEN...
AND FOR THE CHERRY ON TOP, MY IDIOT FRIEND LOCKED THE KEYS INSIDE YESTERDAY MORNING.
I DON'T WANNA SLEEP UNDER THE OVERPASS ANOTHER NIGHT, SO I'M GONNA BREAK IN THROUGH THIS SKYLIGHT.
NO, WAIT!
SUMMER'S OVER, MAN! NOW, IT'S MEGA RAIN SEASON HERE IN HOPE. YOU RIP THAT SKYLIGHT OUT, YOU'LL BE SLEEPIN' IN A FISHBOWL.
MY WEED'S IN THERE.
PINCH IT! LIFT IT!
I AM! I AM!

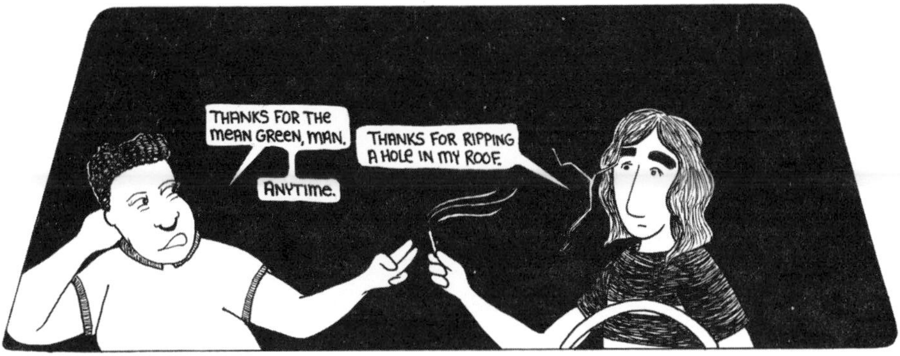
THANKS FOR THE MEAN GREEN, MAN.
ANYTIME.
THANKS FOR RIPPING A HOLE IN MY ROOF.

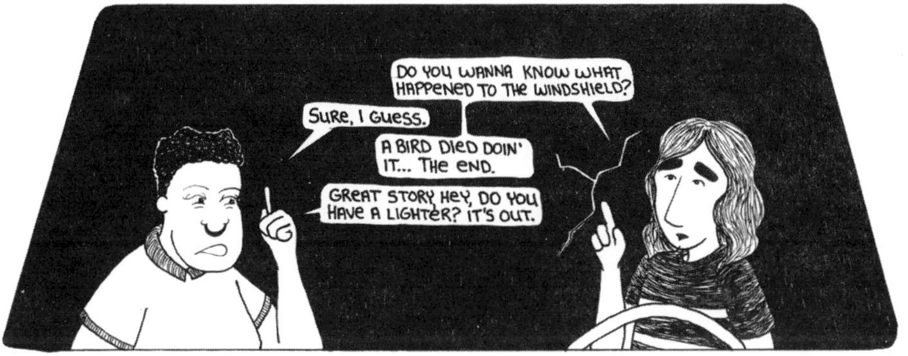
DO YOU WANNA KNOW WHAT HAPPENED TO THE WINDSHIELD?
SURE, I GUESS.
A BIRD DIED DOIN' IT... THE END.
GREAT STORY HEY, DO YOU HAVE A LIGHTER? IT'S OUT.

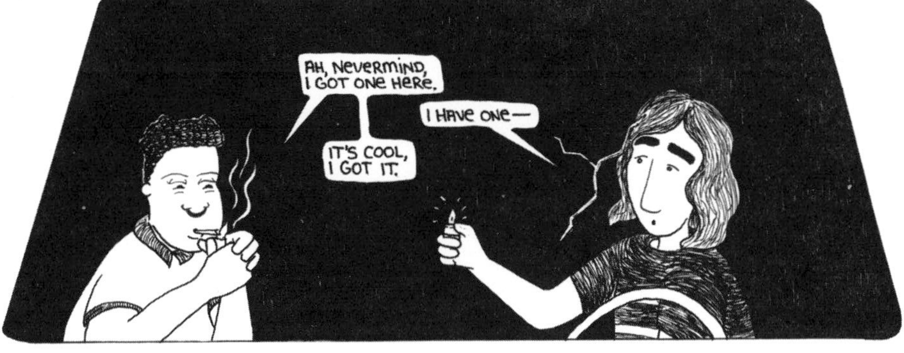
AH, NEVERMIND, I GOT ONE HERE.
I HAVE ONE—
IT'S COOL, I GOT IT.

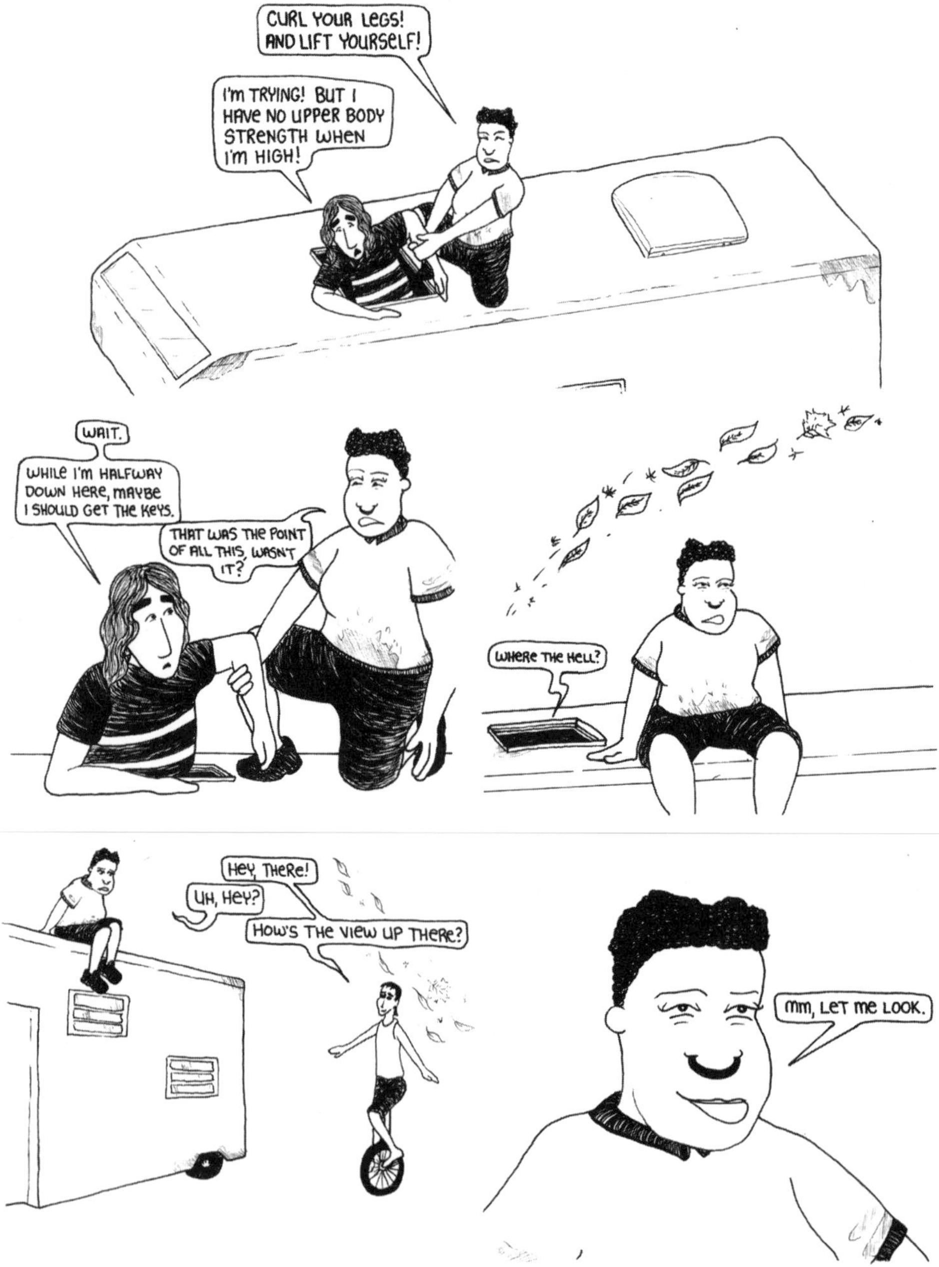
CURL YOUR LEGS! AND LIFT YOURSELF!
I'M TRYING! BUT I HAVE NO UPPER BODY STRENGTH WHEN I'M HIGH!
WAIT.
WHILE I'M HALFWAY DOWN HERE, MAYBE I SHOULD GET THE KEYS.
THAT WAS THE POINT OF ALL THIS, WASN'T IT?
WHERE THE HELL?
HEY, THERE!
UH, HEY?
HOW'S THE VIEW UP THERE?
MM, LET ME LOOK.

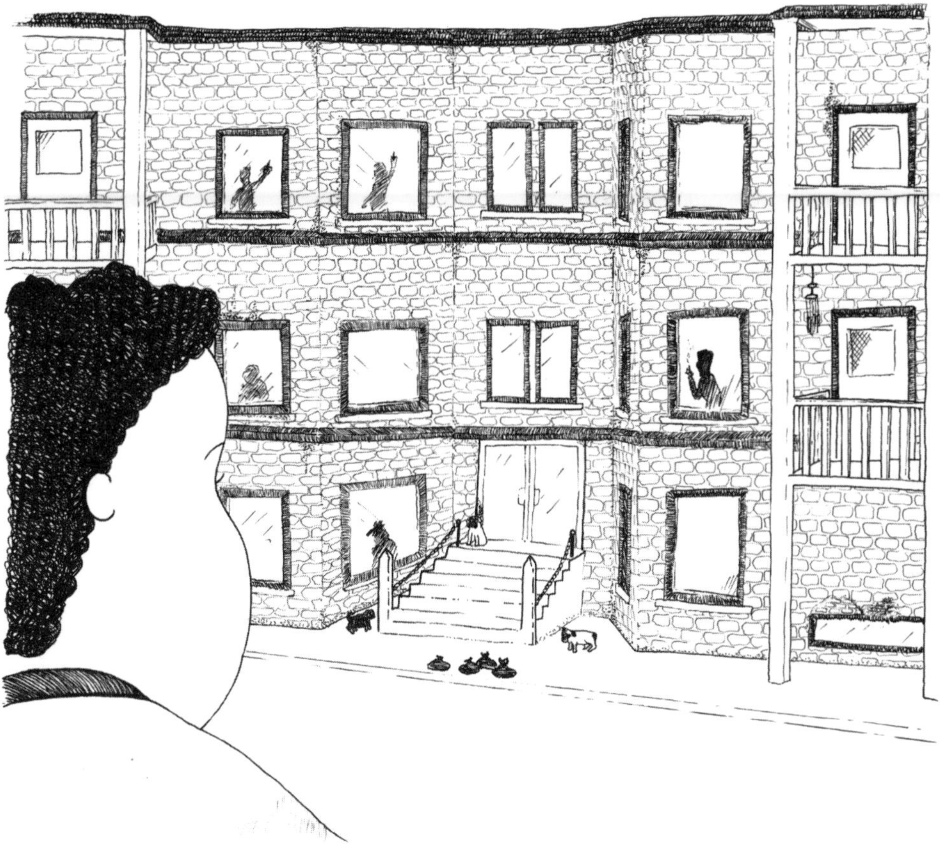

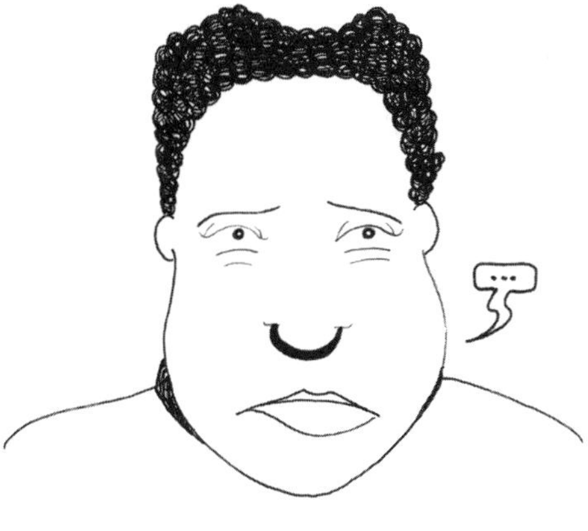
...

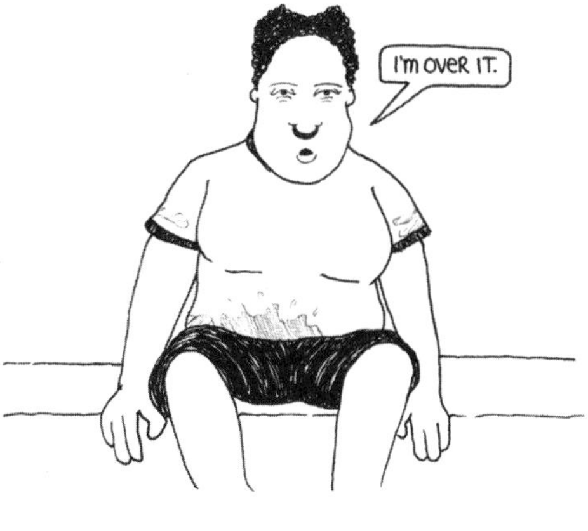
I'm OVER IT.

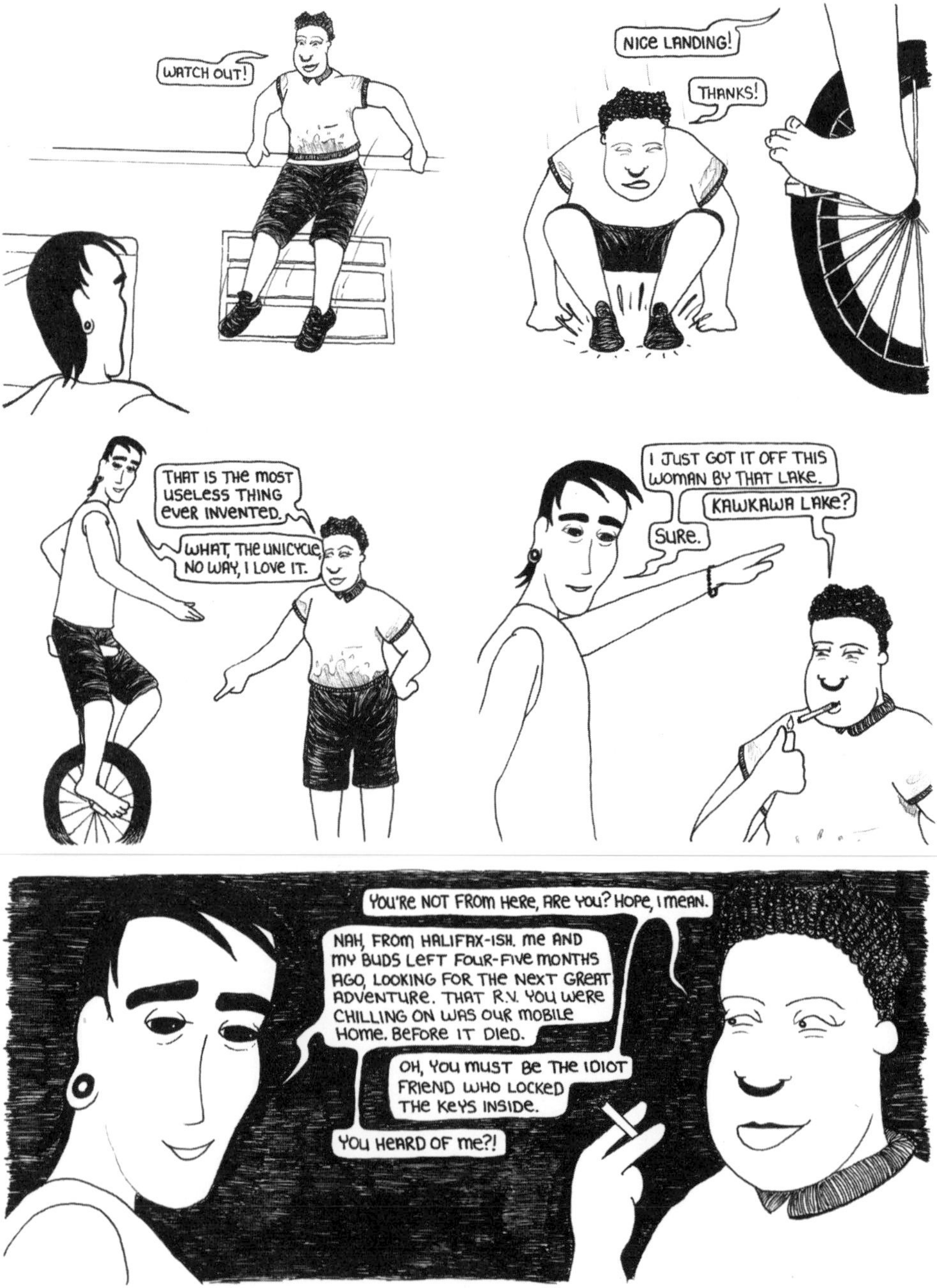
WATCH OUT!
NICE LANDING!
THANKS!
THAT IS THE MOST USELESS THING EVER INVENTED.
WHAT, THE UNICYCLE, NO WAY, I LOVE IT.
I JUST GOT IT OFF THIS WOMAN BY THAT LAKE.
KAWKAWA LAKE?
SURE.
YOU'RE NOT FROM HERE, ARE YOU? HOPE, I MEAN.
NAH, FROM HALIFAX-ISH. ME AND MY BUDS LEFT FOUR-FIVE MONTHS AGO, LOOKING FOR THE NEXT GREAT ADVENTURE. THAT R.V. YOU WERE CHILLING ON WAS OUR MOBILE HOME. BEFORE IT DIED.
OH, YOU MUST BE THE IDIOT FRIEND WHO LOCKED THE KEYS INSIDE.
YOU HEARD OF ME?!

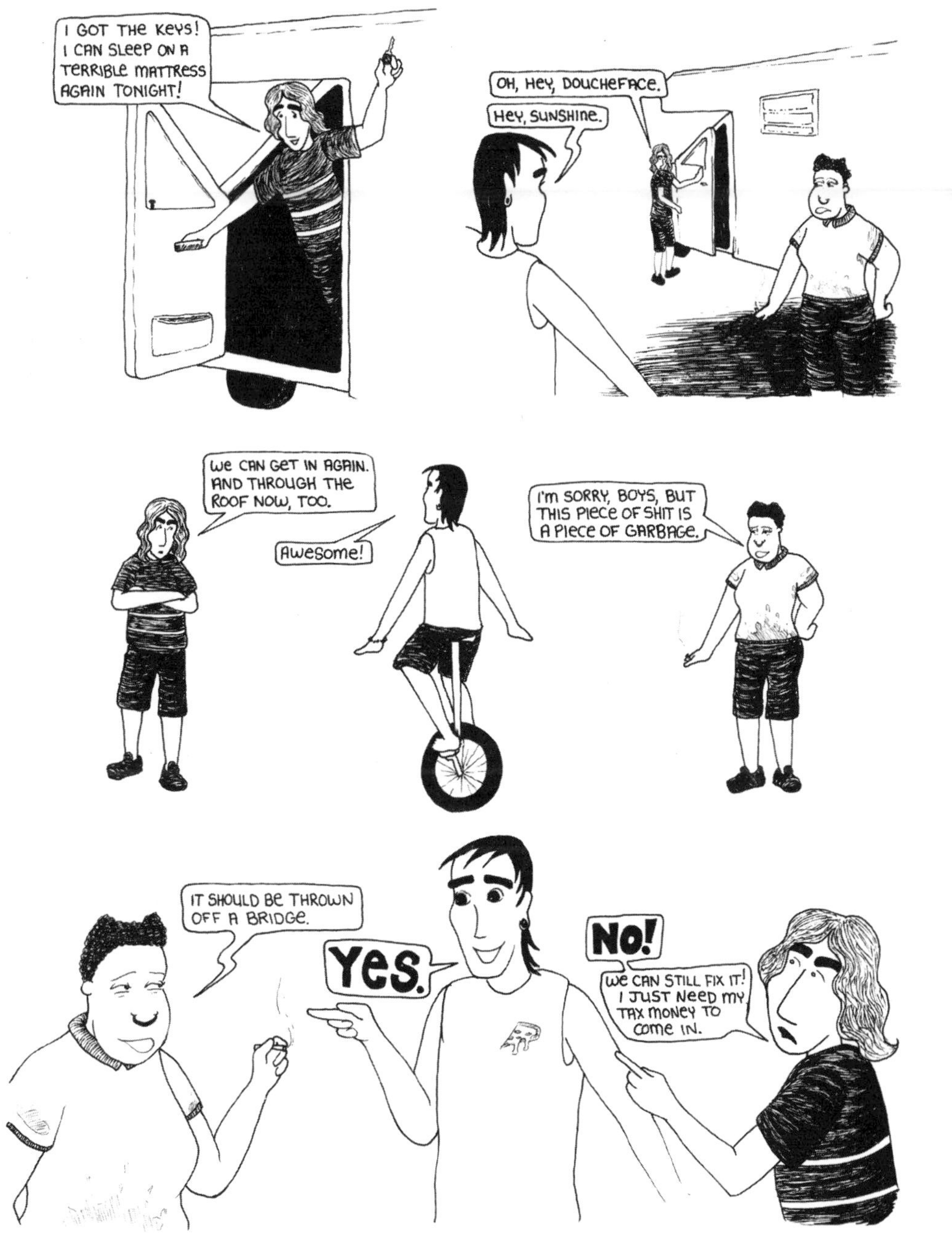
I GOT THE KEYS! I CAN SLEEP ON A TERRIBLE MATTRESS AGAIN TONIGHT!
OH, HEY, DOUCHEFACE.
HEY, SUNSHINE.
WE CAN GET IN AGAIN. AND THROUGH THE ROOF NOW, TOO.
AWESOME!
I'M SORRY, BOYS, BUT THIS PIECE OF SHIT IS A PIECE OF GARBAGE.
IT SHOULD BE THROWN OFF A BRIDGE.
YES.
NO!
WE CAN STILL FIX IT! I JUST NEED MY TAX MONEY TO COME IN.

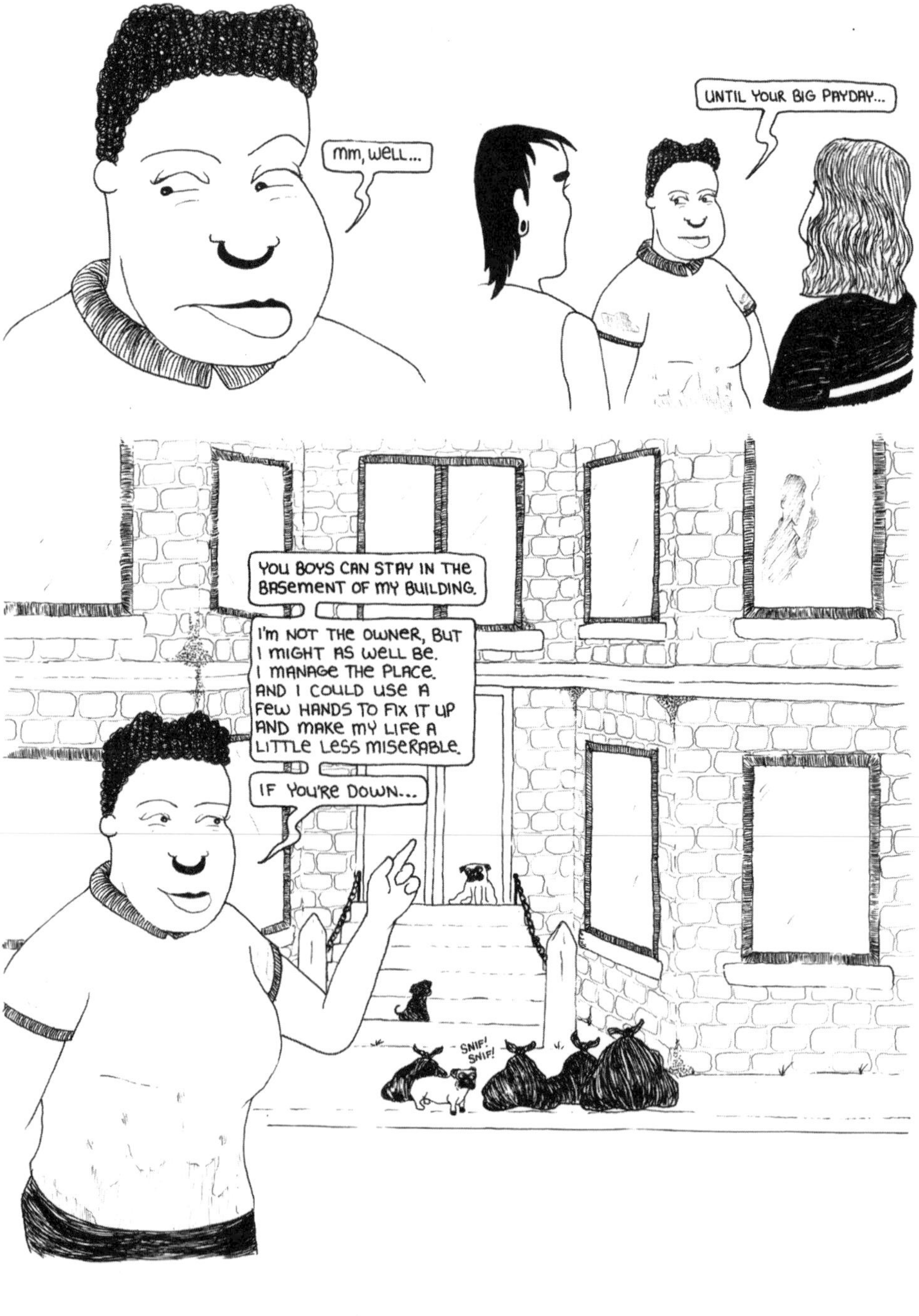
mm, WELL...
UNTIL YOUR BIG PAYDAY...
YOU BOYS CAN STAY IN THE BASEMENT OF MY BUILDING.
I'M NOT THE OWNER, BUT I MIGHT AS WELL BE. I MANAGE THE PLACE. AND I COULD USE A FEW HANDS TO FIX IT UP AND MAKE MY LIFE A LITTLE LESS MISERABLE.
IF YOU'RE DOWN...
SNIF! SNIF!

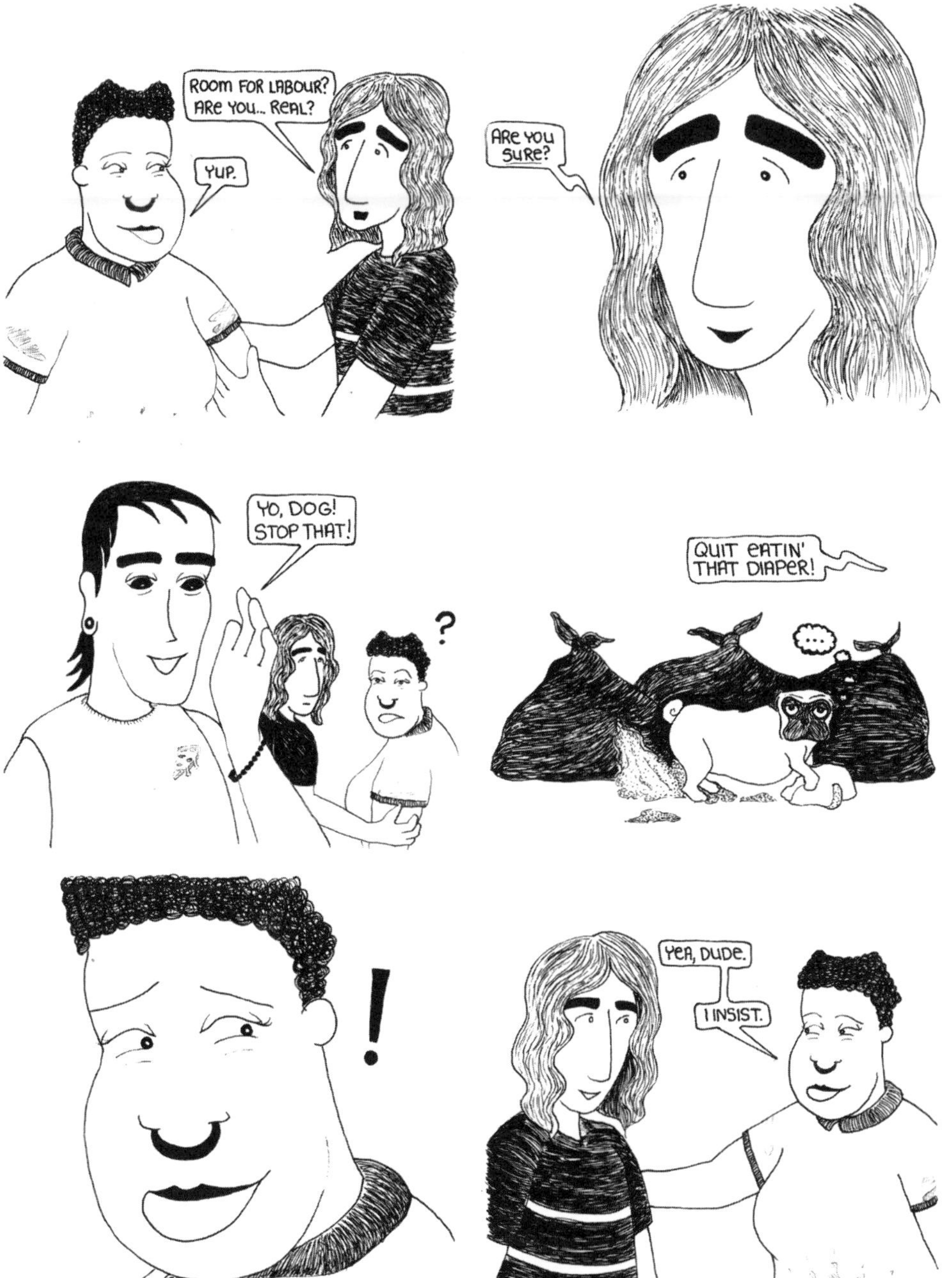
ROOM FOR LABOUR? ARE YOU... REAL?
YUP.
ARE YOU SURE?
YO, DOG! STOP THAT!
?
QUIT EATIN' THAT DIAPER!
...
!
YEA, DUDE.
I INSIST.

CHAPTER 4

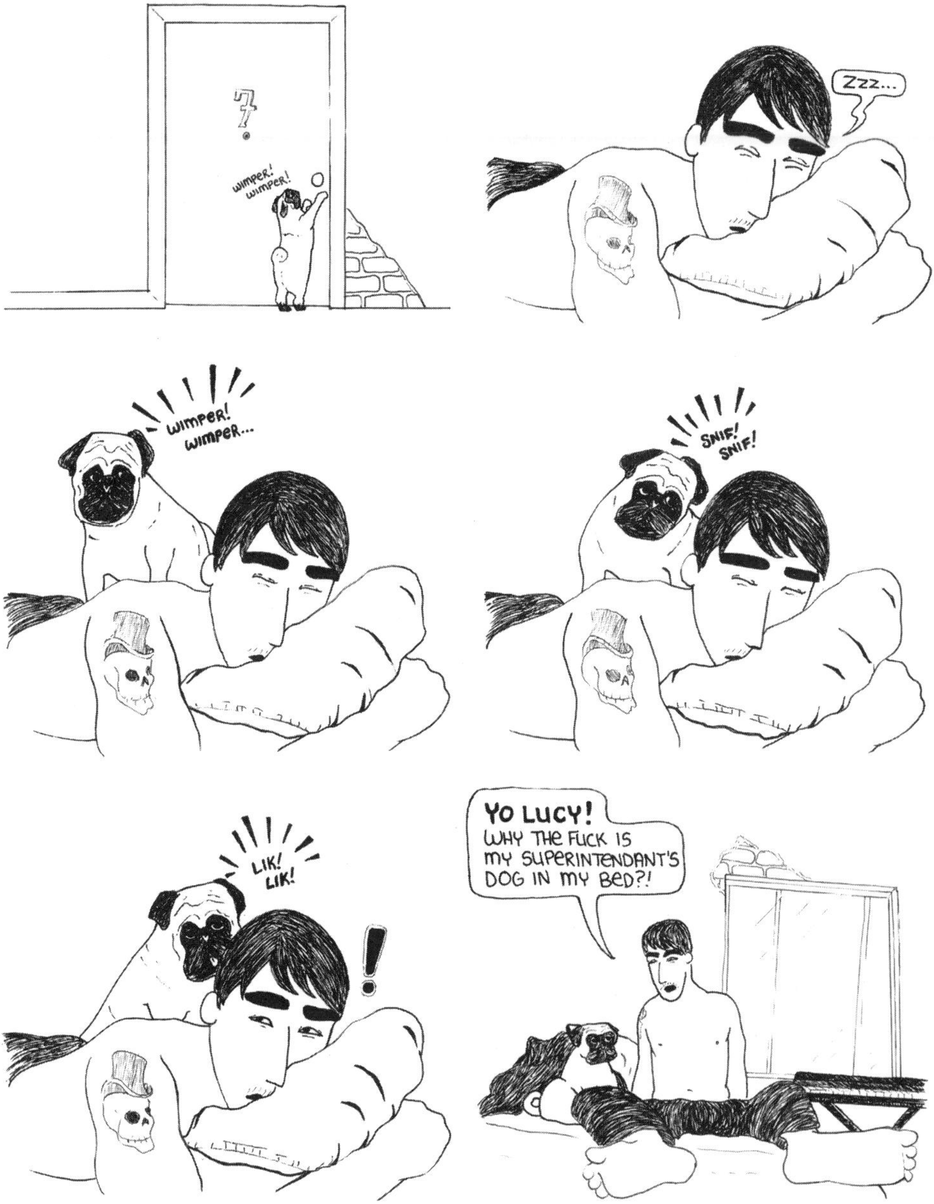

wimper! wimper!
Zzz...
WIMPER! WIMPER...
SNIF! SNIF!
LIK! LIK!
!
YO LUCY!
WHY THE FUCK IS MY SUPERINTENDANT'S DOG IN MY BED?!

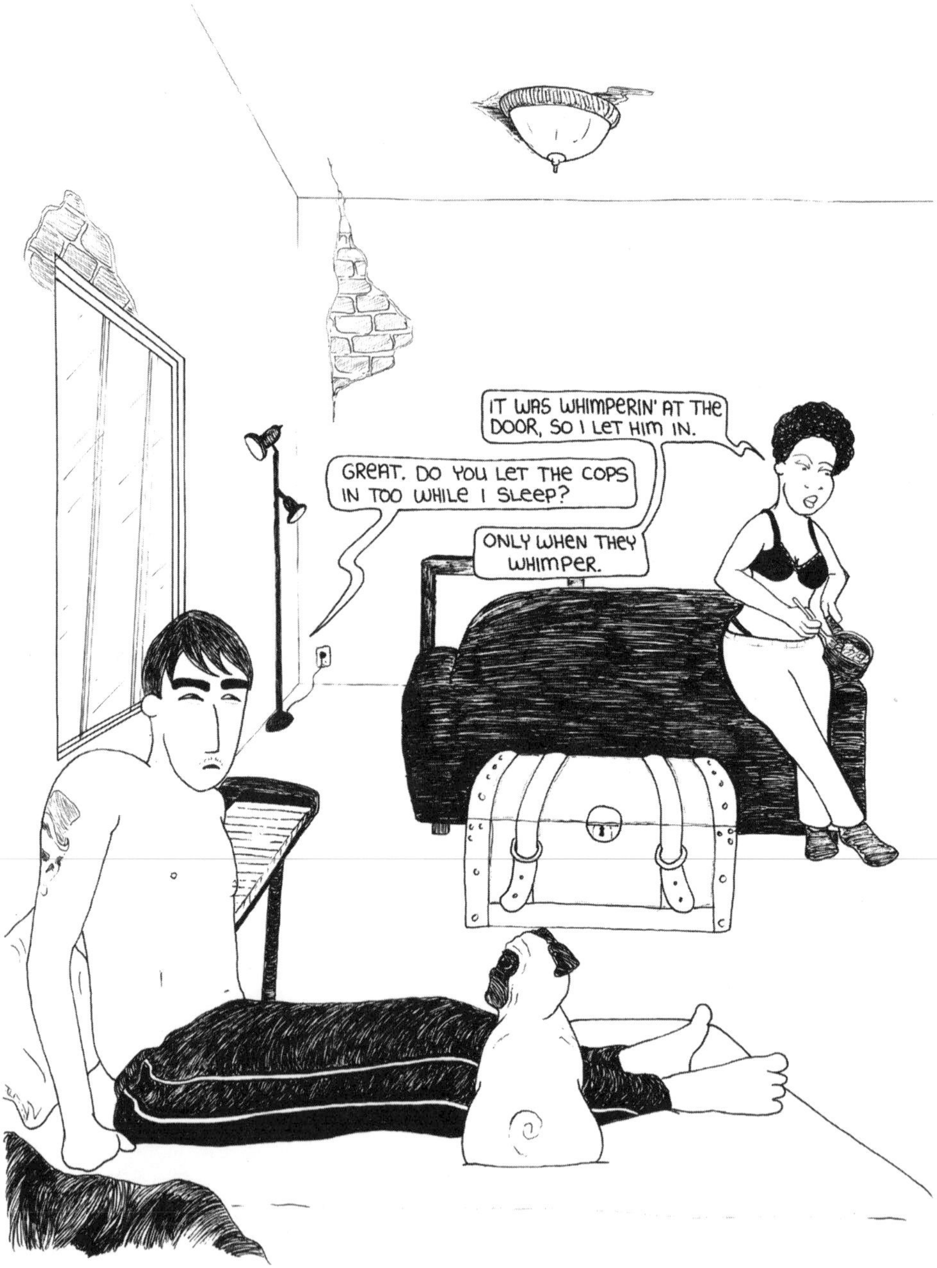
GREAT. DO YOU LET THE COPS IN TOO WHILE I SLEEP?
IT WAS WHIMPERIN' AT THE DOOR, SO I LET HIM IN.
ONLY WHEN THEY WHIMPER.

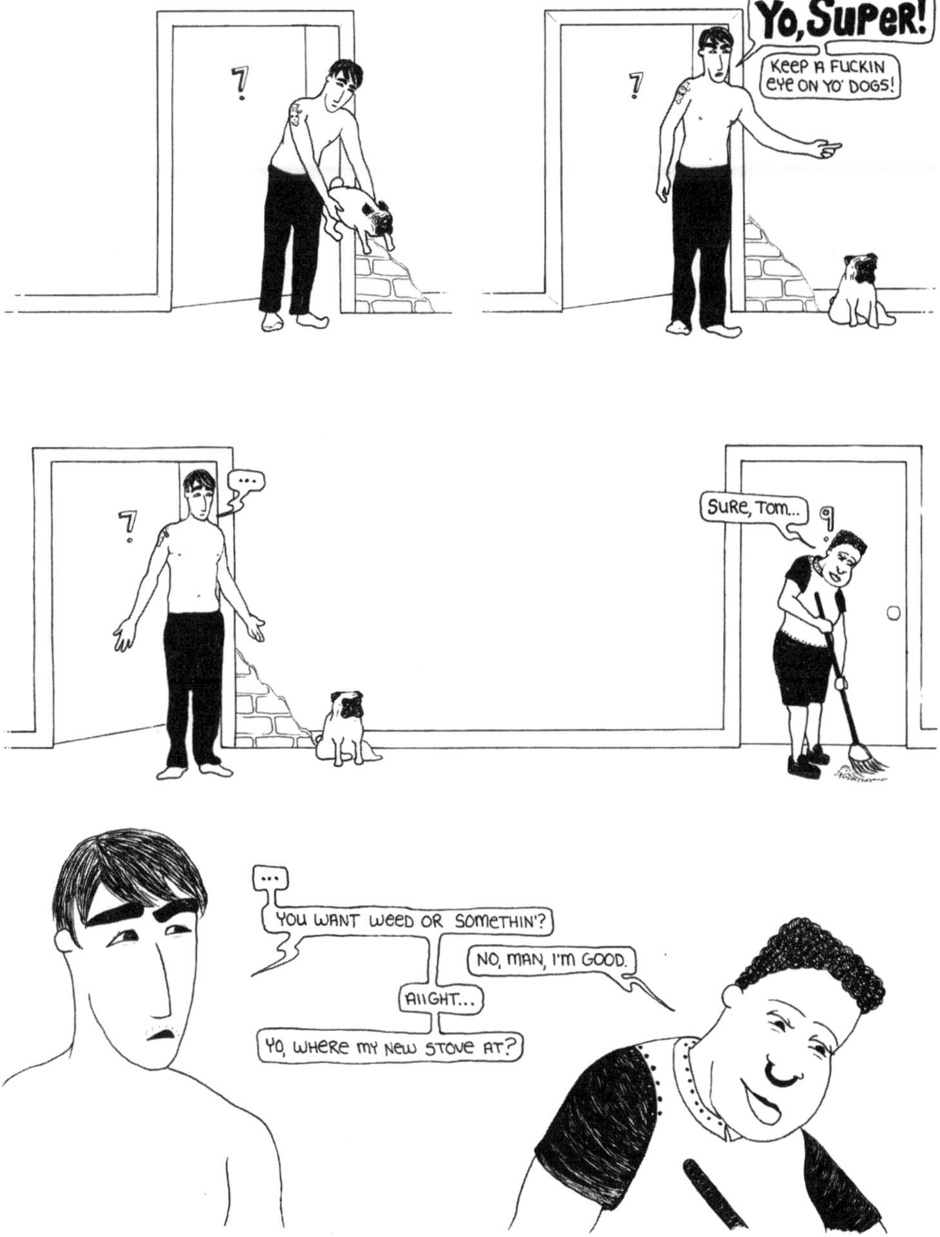
Yo, Super!
Keep a fuckin eye on yo' dogs!
...
Sure, Tom...
...
You want weed or somethin'?
No, man, I'm good.
Aiight...
Yo, where my new stove at?

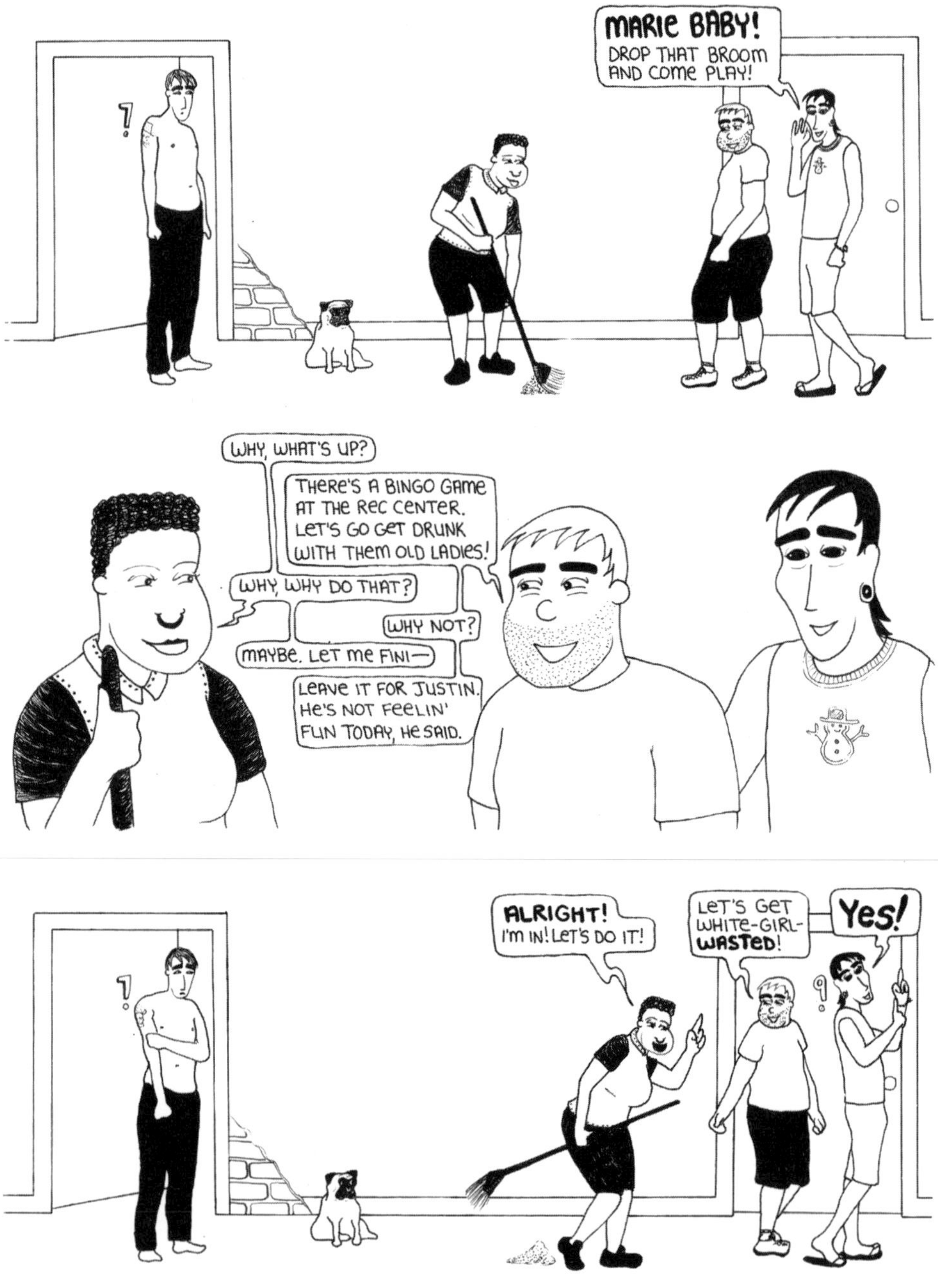
MARIE BABY! DROP THAT BROOM AND COME PLAY!
WHY, WHAT'S UP?
THERE'S A BINGO GAME AT THE REC CENTER. LET'S GO GET DRUNK WITH THEM OLD LADIES!
WHY, WHY DO THAT?
WHY NOT?
MAYBE. LET ME FINI—
LEAVE IT FOR JUSTIN. HE'S NOT FEELIN' FUN TODAY, HE SAID.
ALRIGHT! I'M IN! LET'S DO IT!
LET'S GET WHITE-GIRL-WASTED!
Yes!

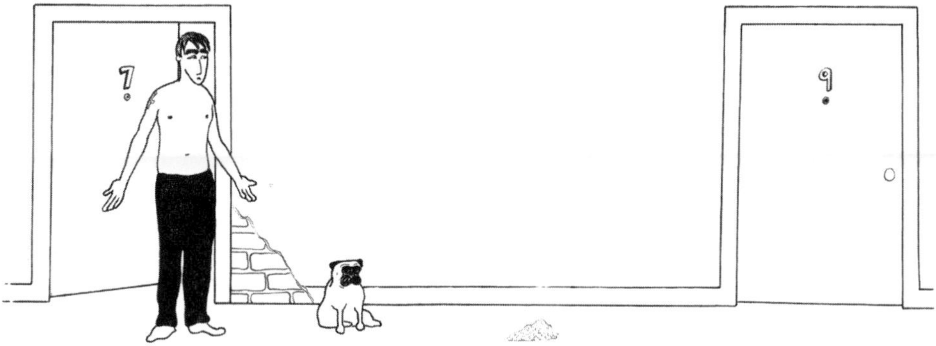

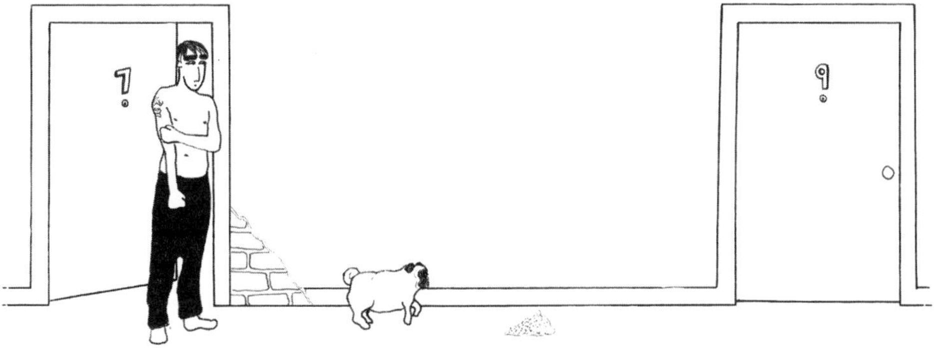

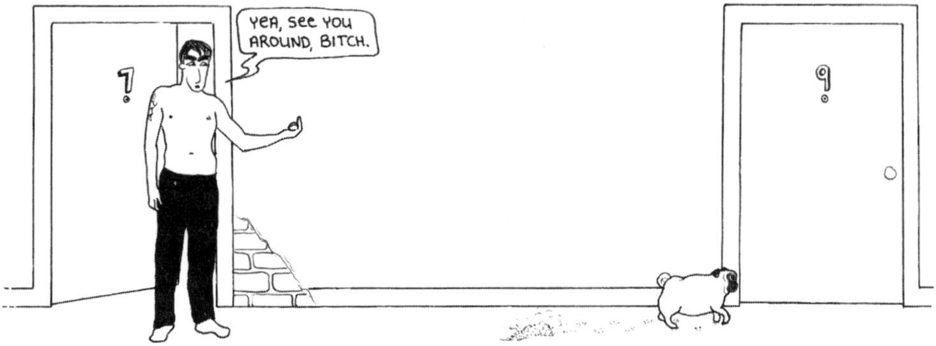
YEA, SEE YOU AROUND, BITCH.

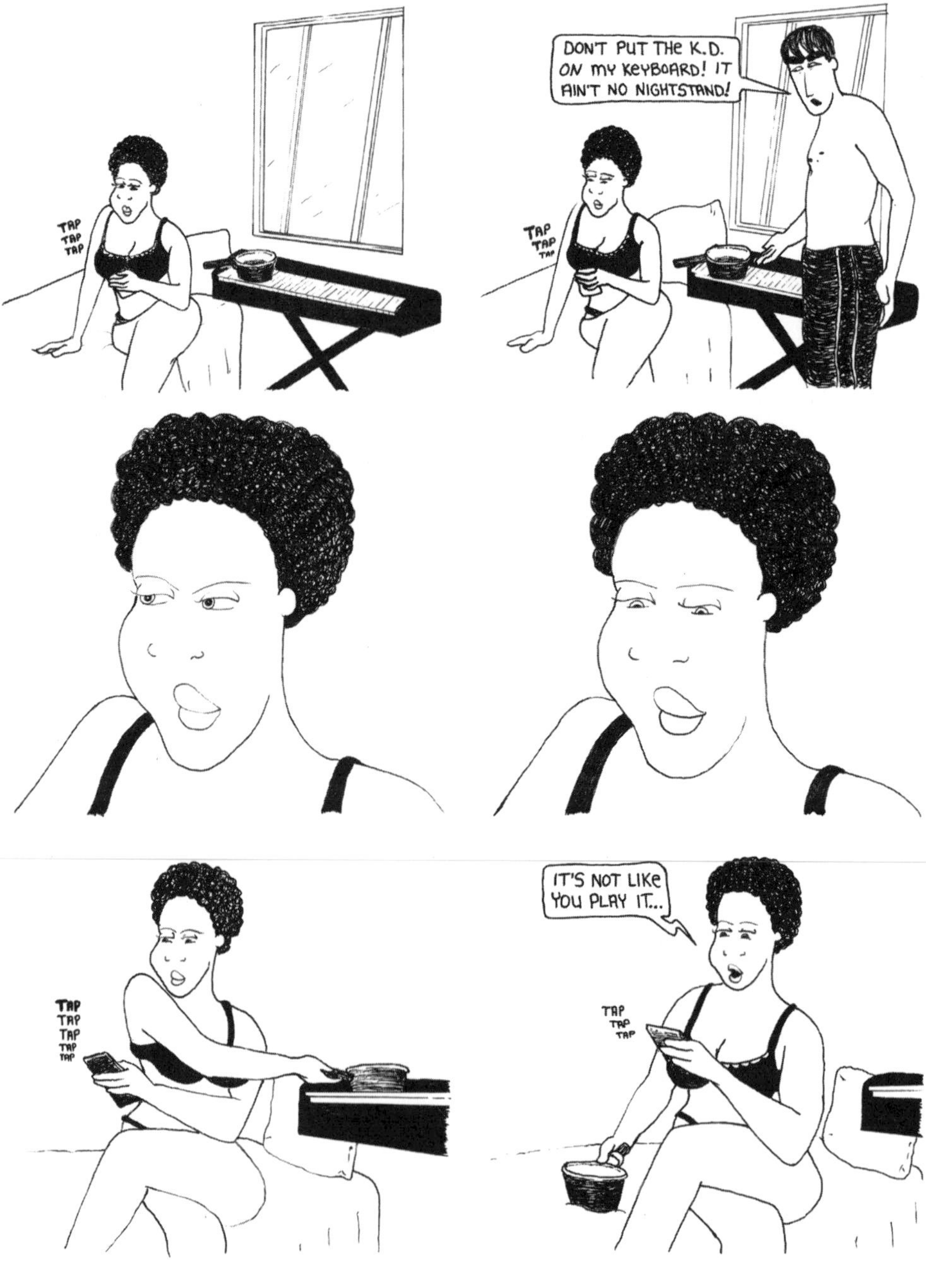
TAP
TAP
TAP
DON'T PUT THE K.D. ON MY KEYBOARD! IT AIN'T NO NIGHTSTAND!
TAP
TAP
TAP
TAP
TAP
TAP
TAP
TAP
IT'S NOT LIKE YOU PLAY IT...
TAP
TAP
TAP

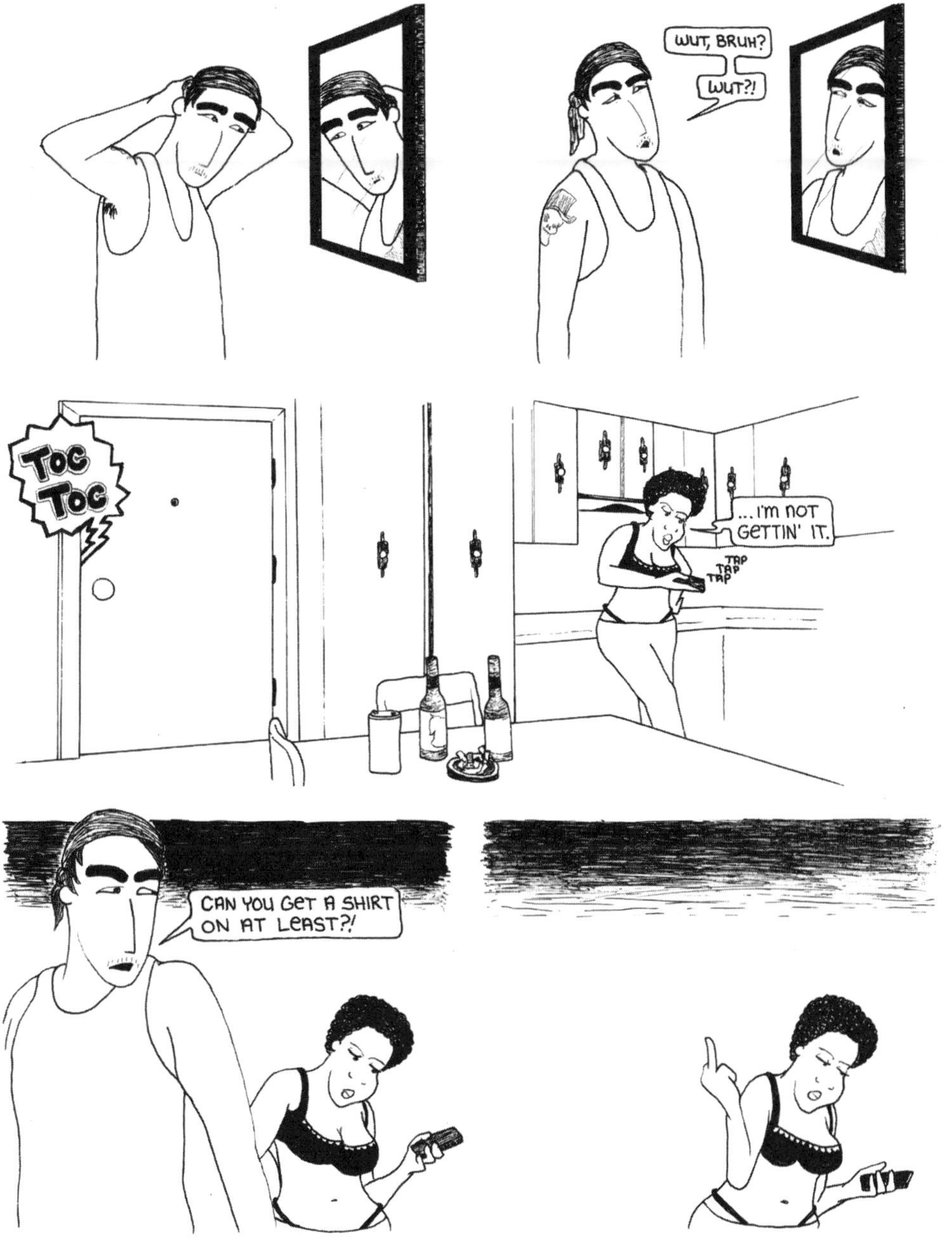
WUT, BRUH?
WUT?!
TOC
TOC
...I'M NOT GETTIN' IT.
TAP
TAP
TAP
CAN YOU GET A SHIRT ON AT LEAST?!

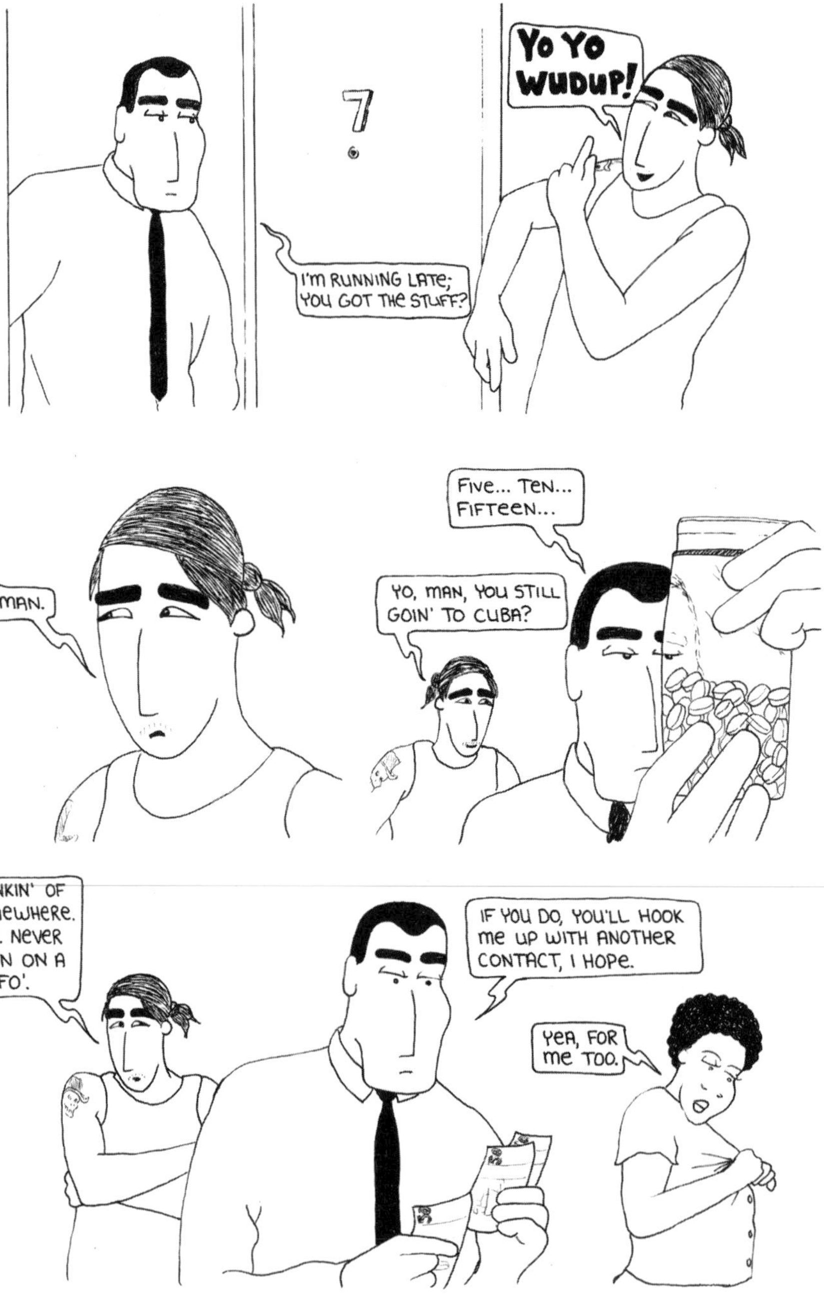
I'M RUNNING LATE; YOU GOT THE STUFF?
YO YO WUDUP!
...
YEA, MAN.
FIVE... TEN... FIFTEEN...
YO, MAN, YOU STILL GOIN' TO CUBA?
I WAS THINKIN' OF GOIN' SOMEWHERE. ANYWHERE. NEVER EVEN BEEN ON A PLANE BEFO'.
IF YOU DO, YOU'LL HOOK ME UP WITH ANOTHER CONTACT, I HOPE.
YEA, FOR ME TOO.

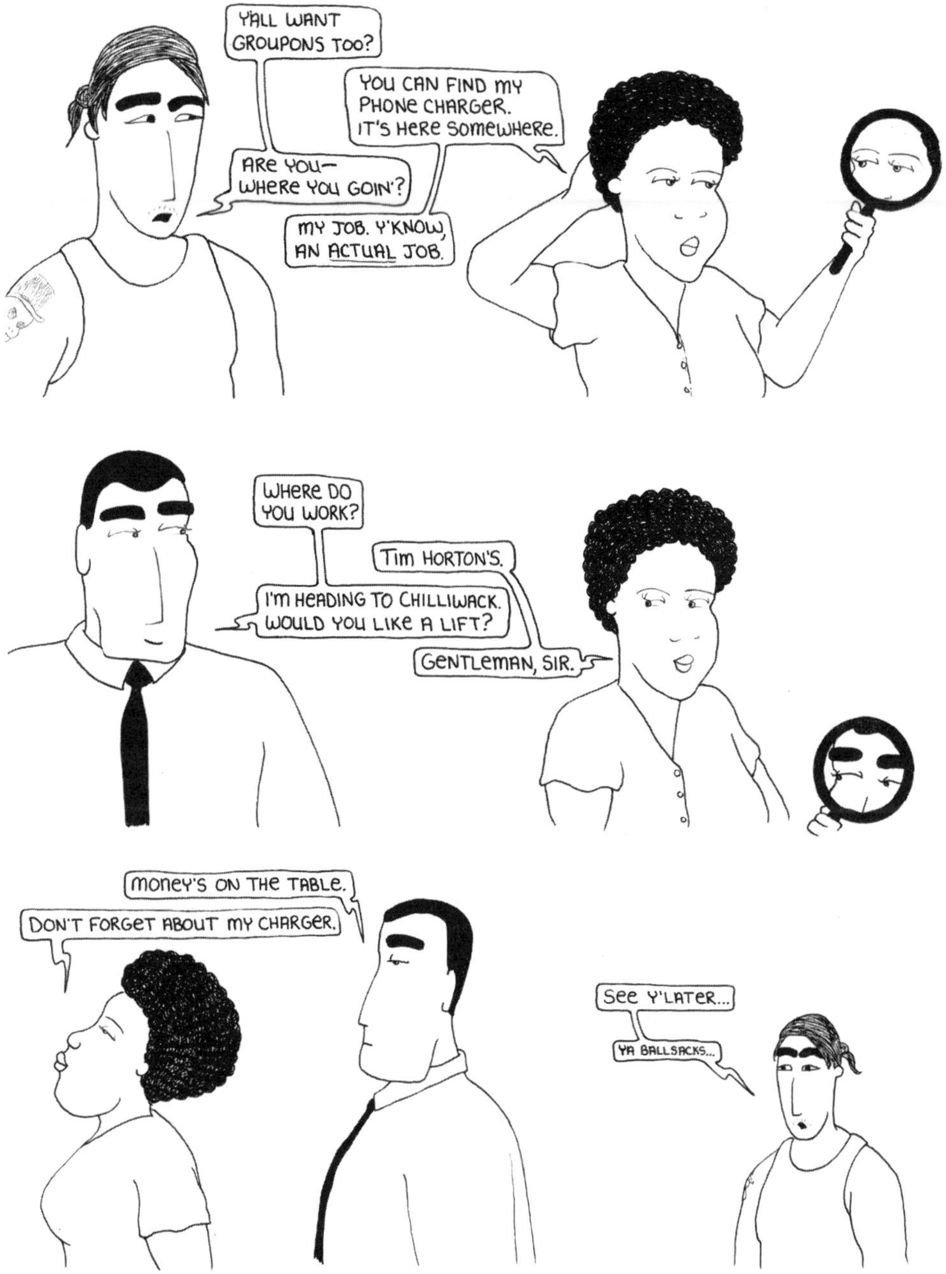
Y'ALL WANT GROUPONS TOO?
YOU CAN FIND MY PHONE CHARGER. IT'S HERE SOMEWHERE.
ARE YOU— WHERE YOU GOIN'?
MY JOB. Y'KNOW, AN ACTUAL JOB.
WHERE DO YOU WORK?
TIM HORTON'S.
I'M HEADING TO CHILLIWACK. WOULD YOU LIKE A LIFT?
GENTLEMAN, SIR.
MONEY'S ON THE TABLE.
DON'T FORGET ABOUT MY CHARGER.
SEE Y'LATER...
YA BALLSACKS...

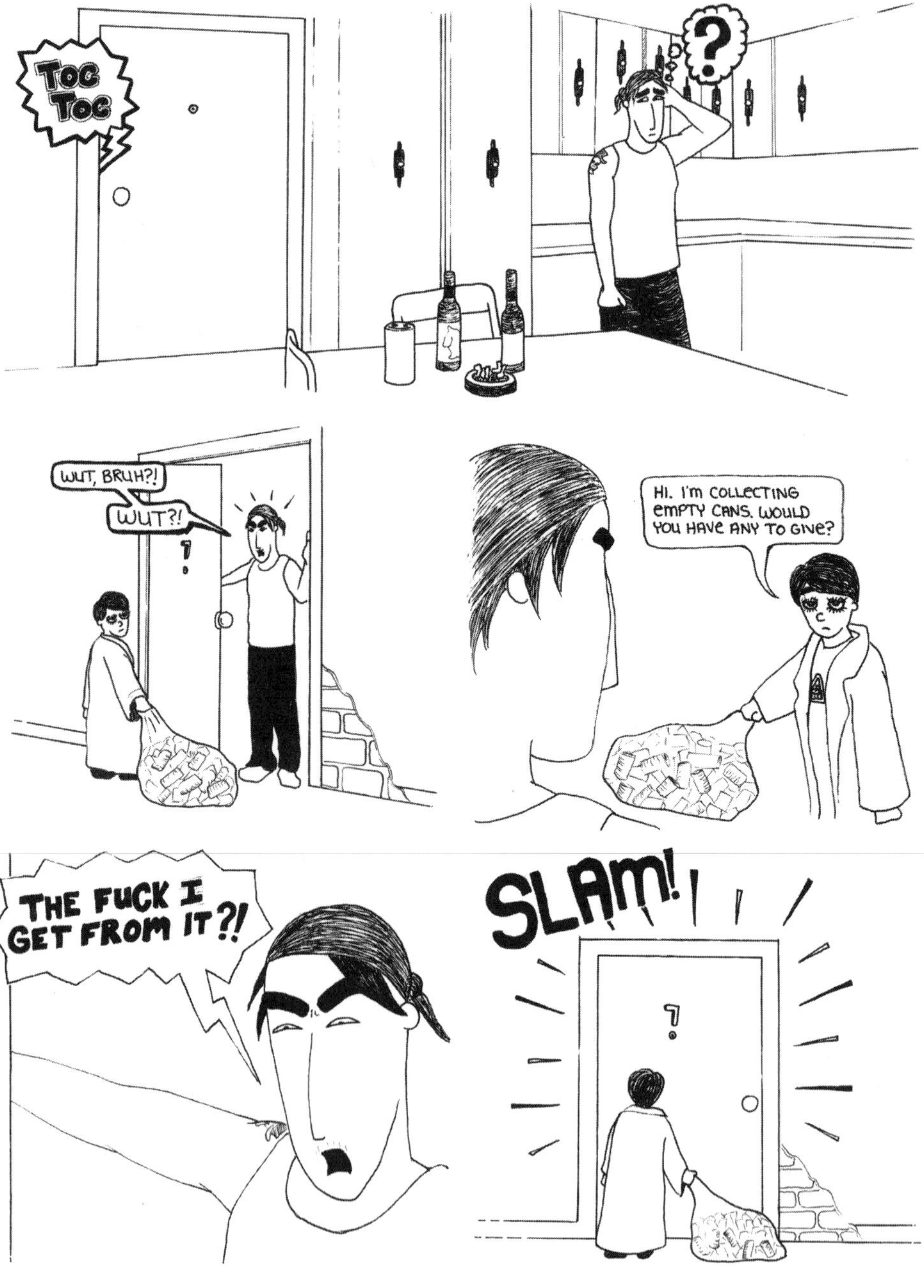
TOC TOC
?
WUT, BRUH?!
WUT?!
HI. I'm COLLECTING EMPTY CANS. WOULD YOU HAVE ANY TO GIVE?
THE FUCK I GET FROM IT?!
SLAM!

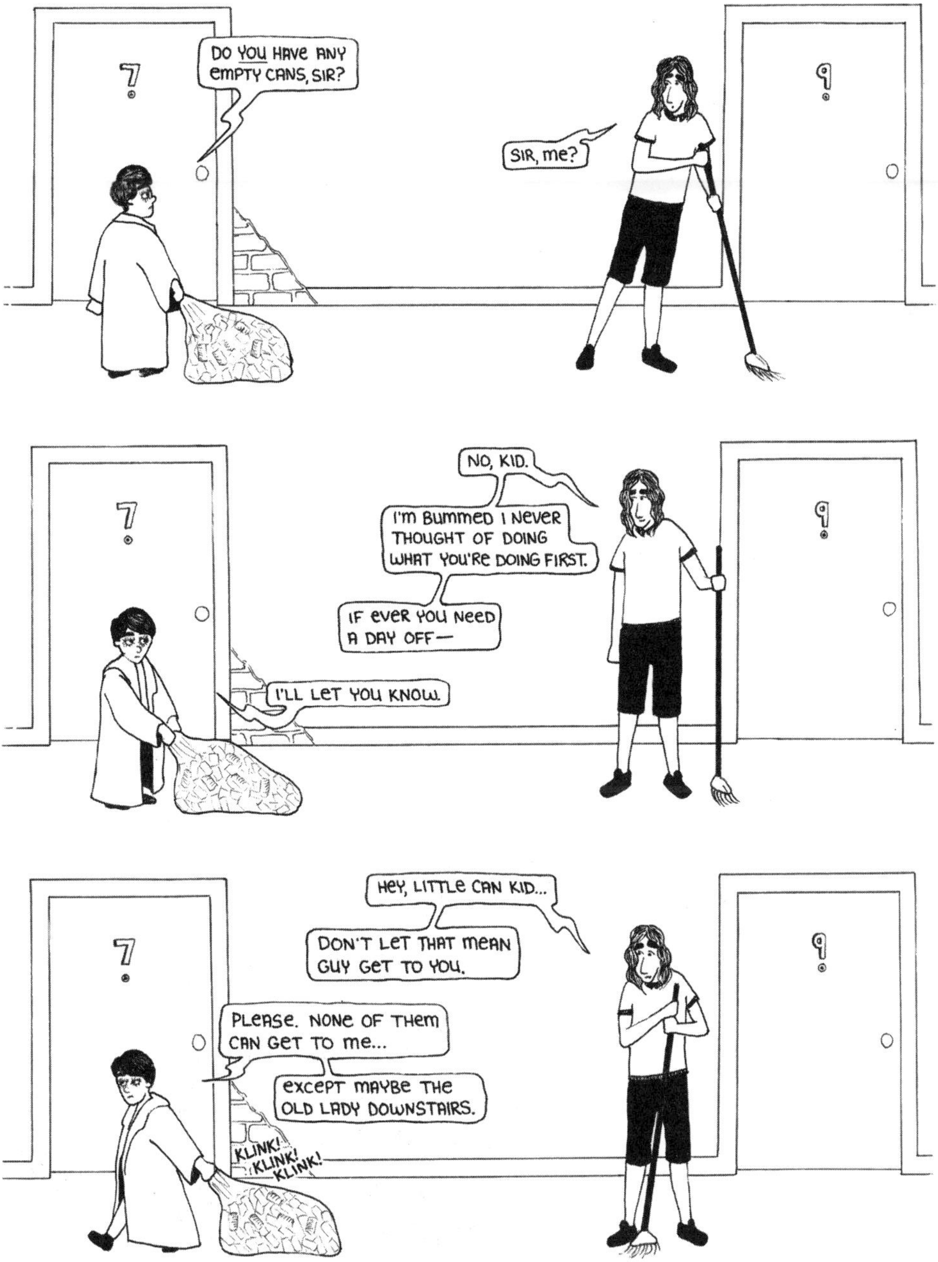
DO YOU HAVE ANY EMPTY CANS, SIR?
SIR, ME?
NO, KID.
I'M BUMMED I NEVER THOUGHT OF DOING WHAT YOU'RE DOING FIRST.
IF EVER YOU NEED A DAY OFF—
I'LL LET YOU KNOW.
HEY, LITTLE CAN KID...
DON'T LET THAT MEAN GUY GET TO YOU.
PLEASE. NONE OF THEM CAN GET TO ME...
EXCEPT MAYBE THE OLD LADY DOWNSTAIRS.
KLINK! KLINK! KLINK!

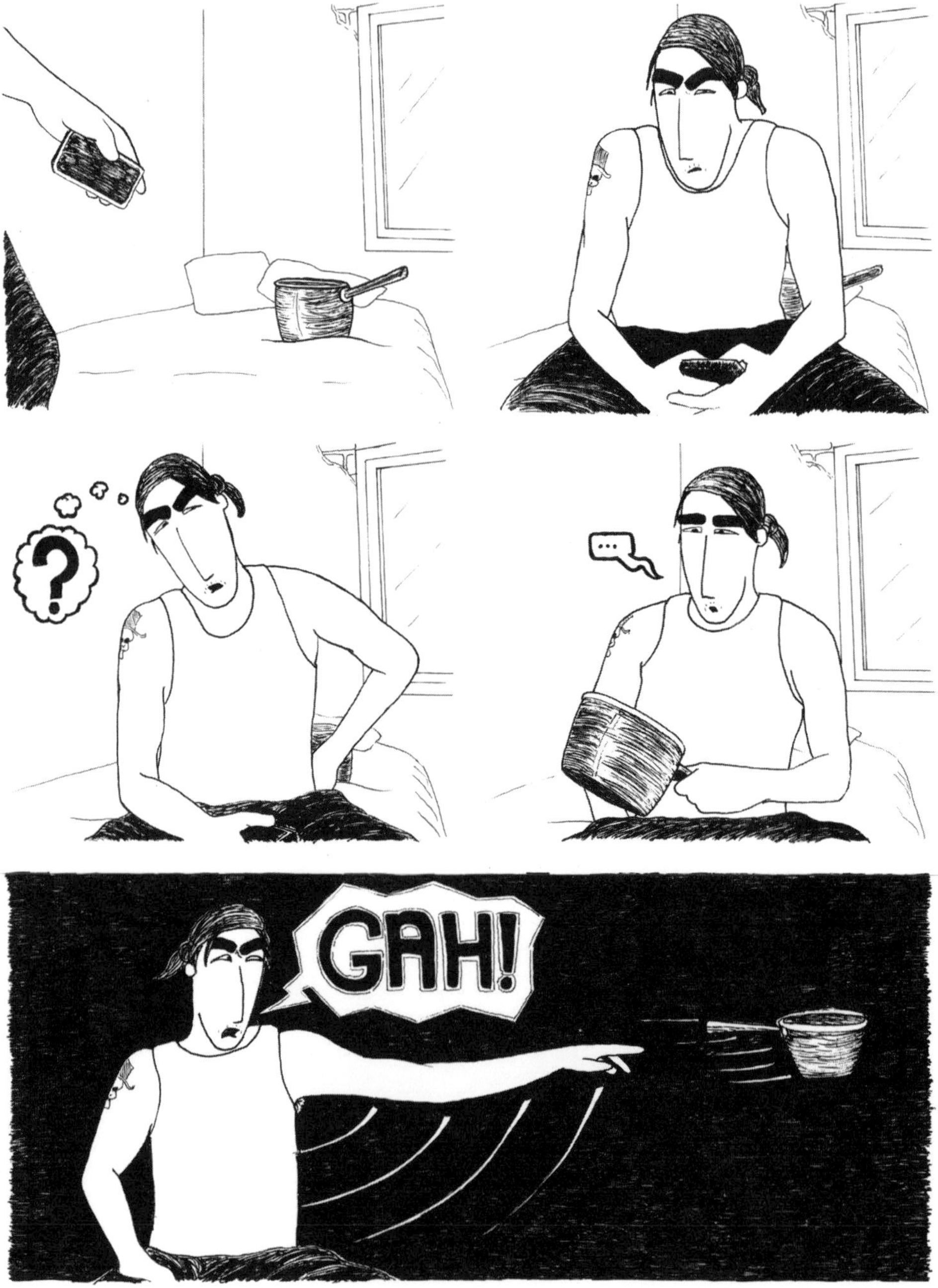
?
...
GAH!

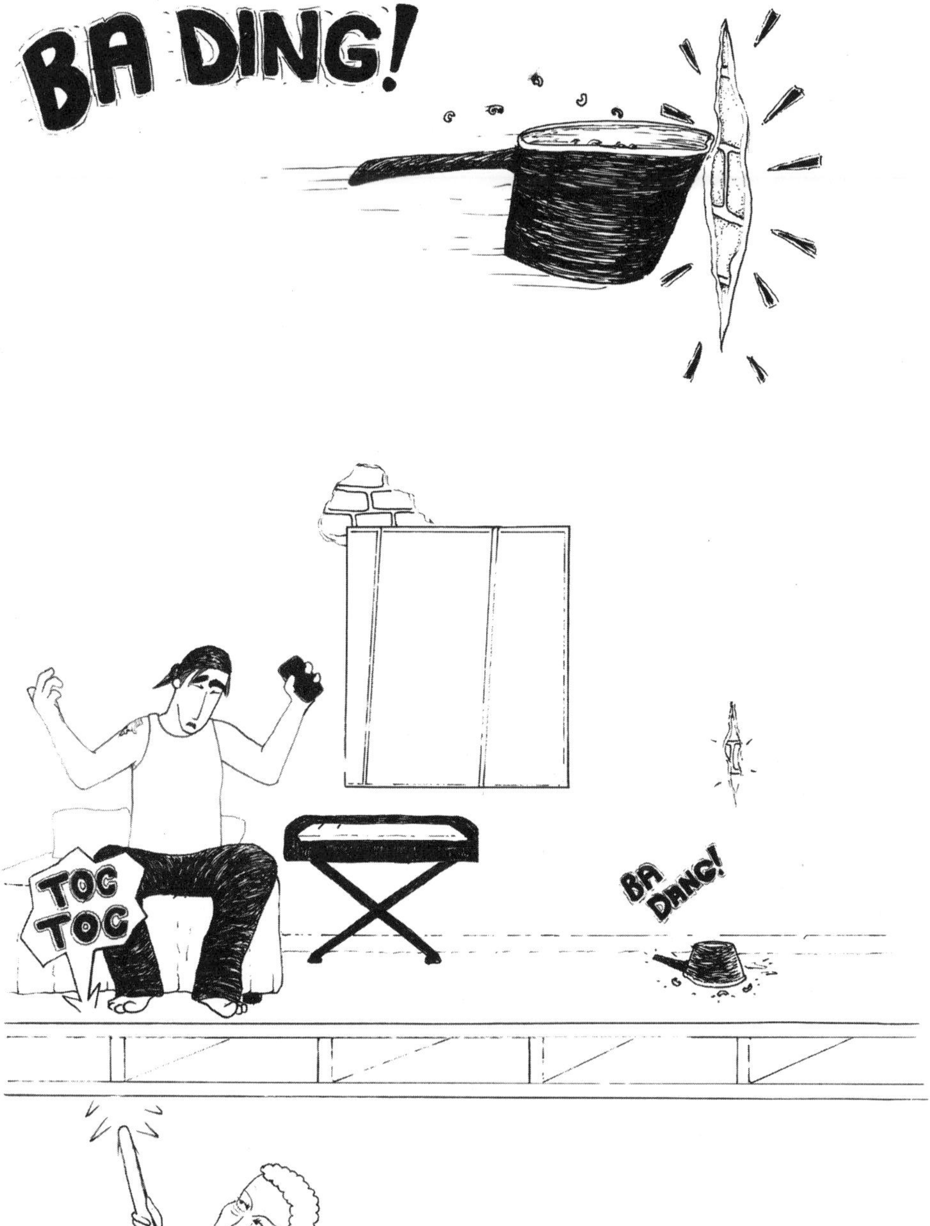
BA DING!
TOC TOC
BA DANG!

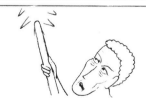

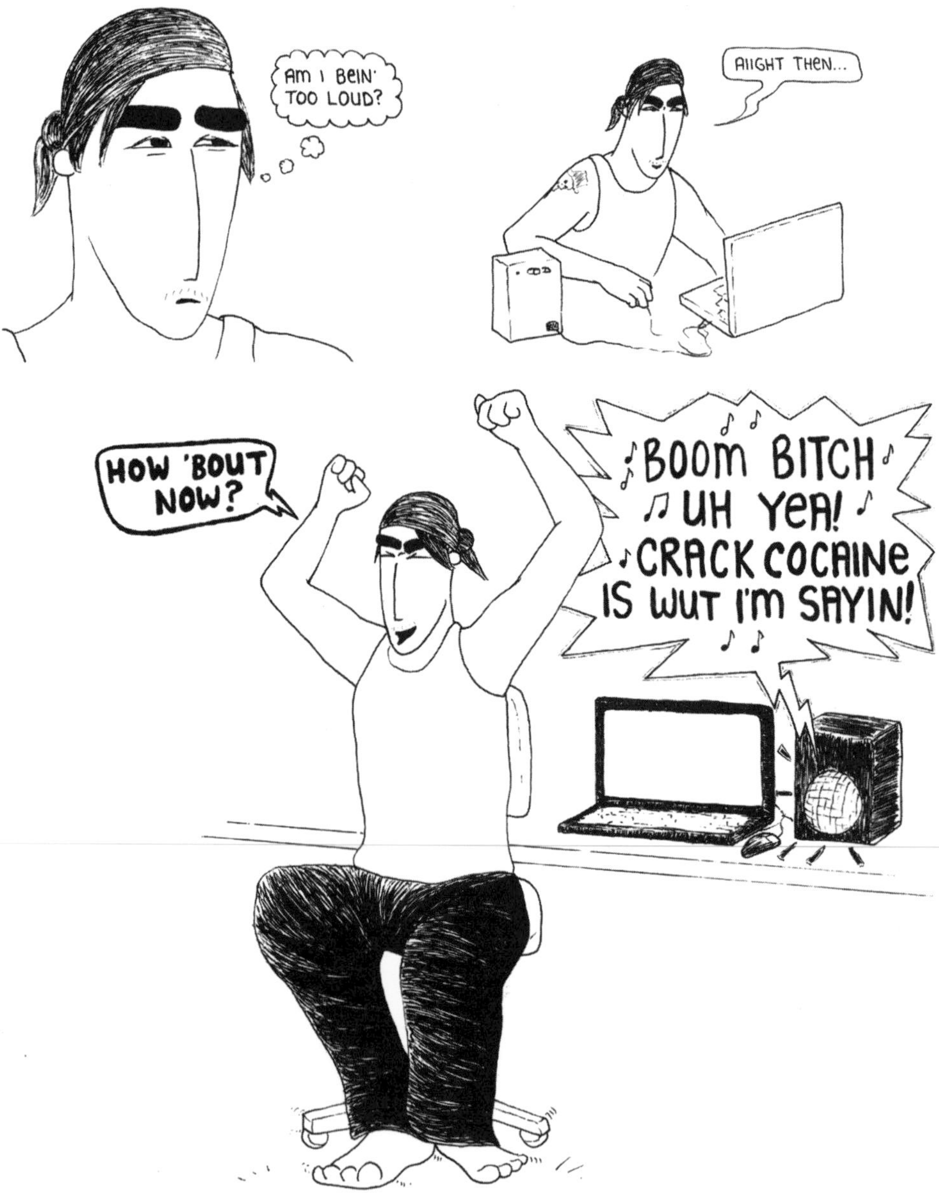
Am I BeIN' TOO LOUD?
AIIGHT THeN...
HOW 'BOUT NOW?
BOOm BITCH UH YeA! CRACK COCAINe IS WUT I'm SAYIN!

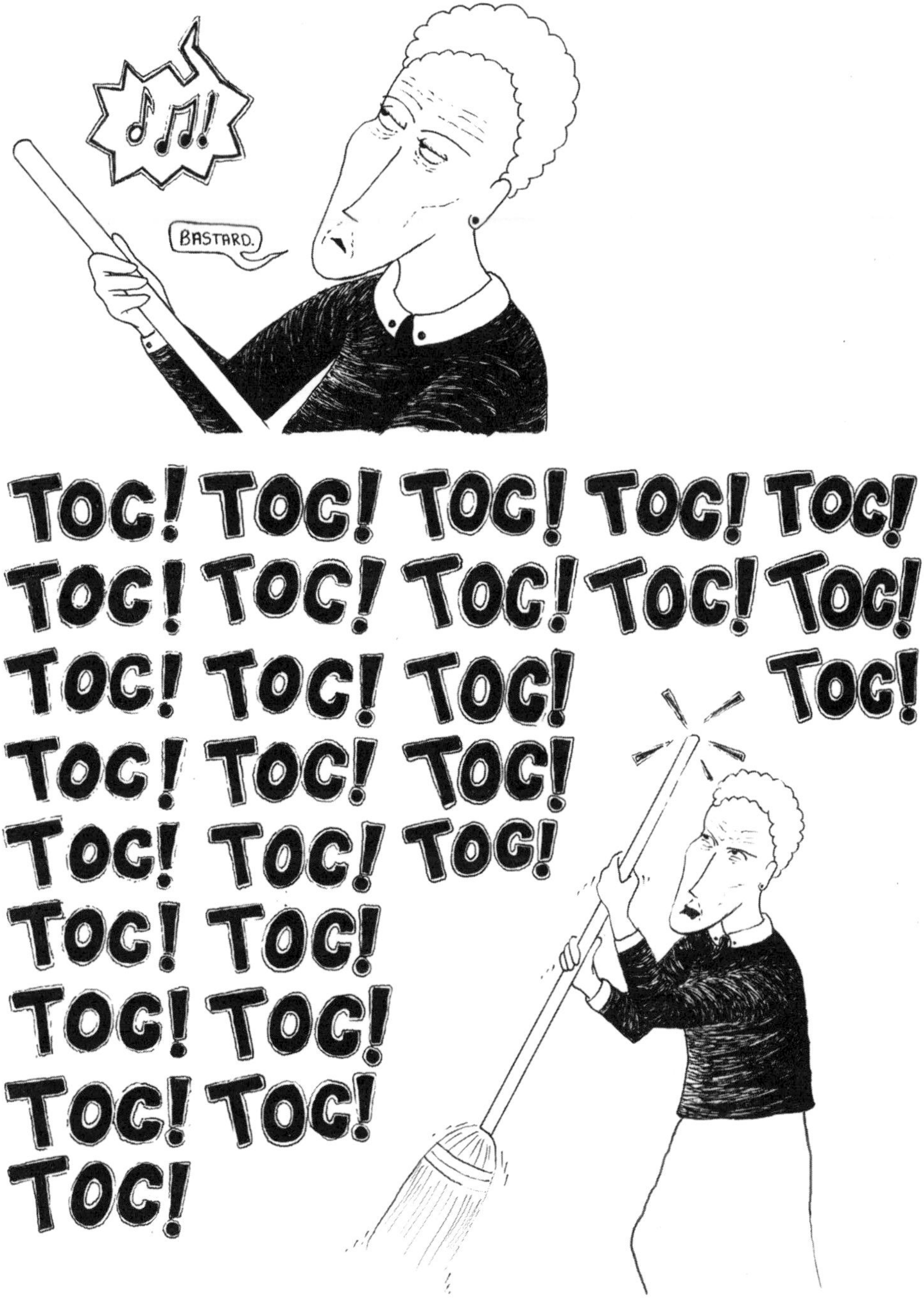
BASTARD.
TOC! TOC! TOC! TOC! TOC!
TOC! TOC! TOC! TOC! TOC!
TOC! TOC! TOC! TOC!
TOC! TOC! TOC!
TOC! TOC! TOC!
TOC! TOC!
TOC! TOC!
TOC! TOC!
TOC!

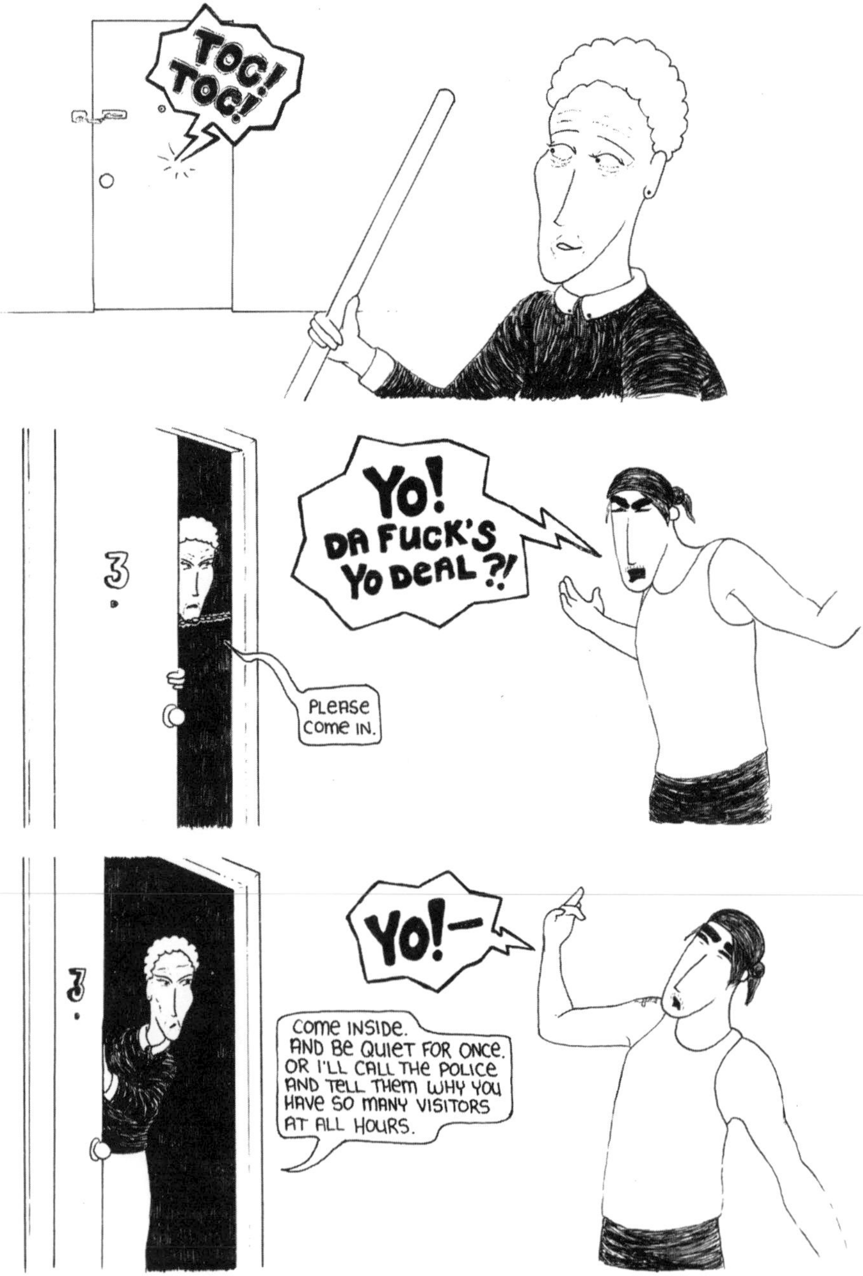
TOC! TOC!
YO! DA FUCK'S YO DEAL ?!
PLEASE COME IN.
YO!—
COME INSIDE. AND BE QUIET FOR ONCE. OR I'LL CALL THE POLICE AND TELL THEM WHY YOU HAVE SO MANY VISITORS AT ALL HOURS.

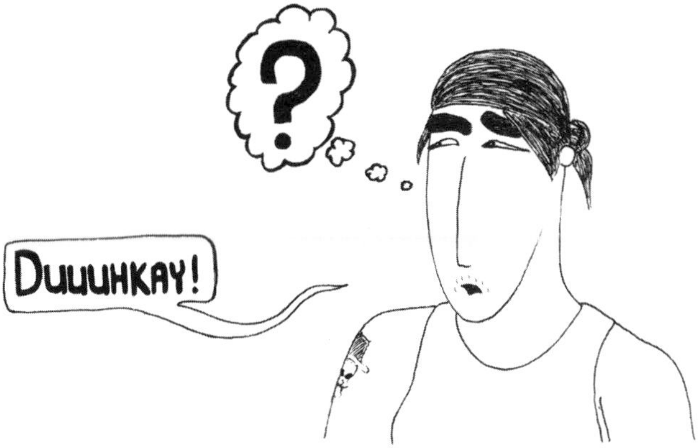
?
DUUUHKAY!

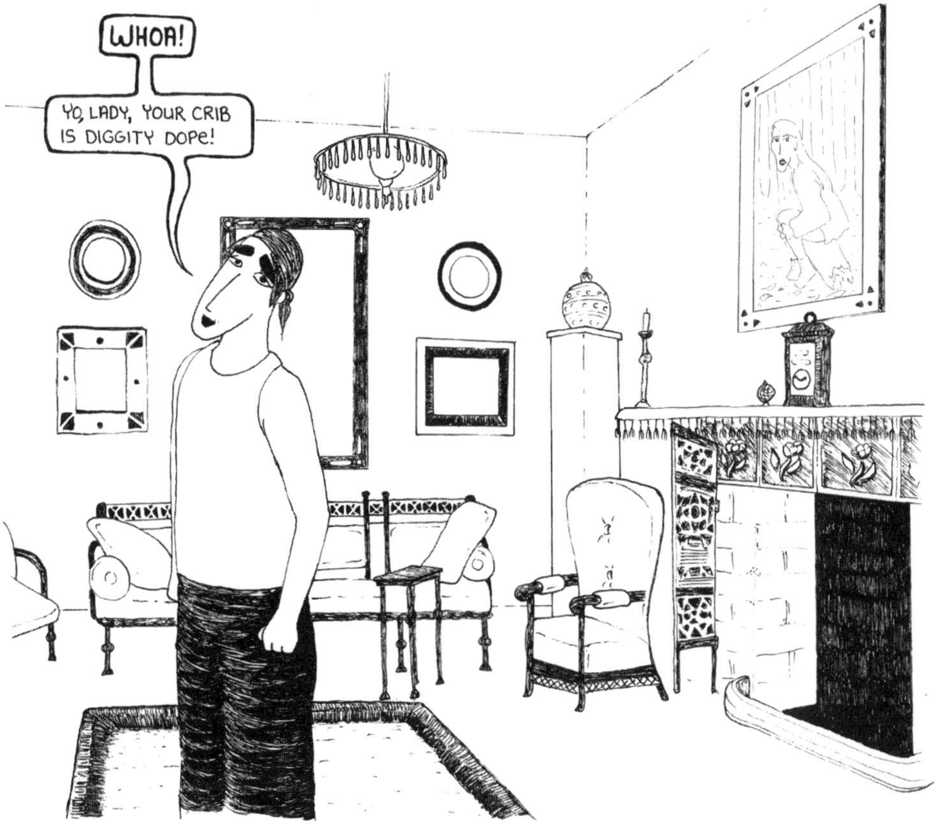
WHOA!
YO, LADY, YOUR CRIB IS DIGGITY DOPE!

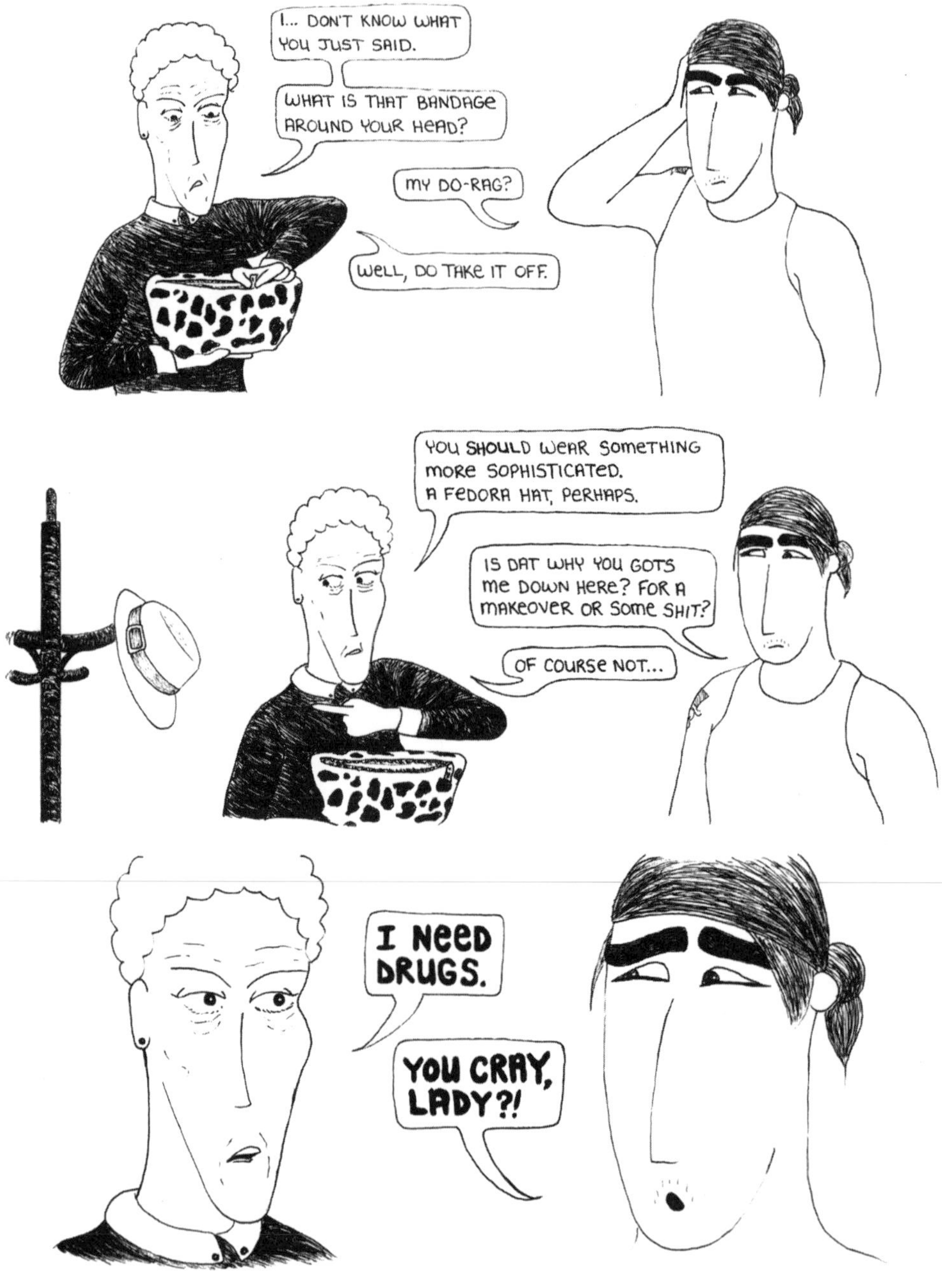
I... DON'T KNOW WHAT YOU JUST SAID.
WHAT IS THAT BANDAGE AROUND YOUR HEAD?
MY DO-RAG?
WELL, DO TAKE IT OFF.
YOU SHOULD WEAR SOMETHING MORE SOPHISTICATED. A FEDORA HAT, PERHAPS.
IS DAT WHY YOU GOTS ME DOWN HERE? FOR A MAKEOVER OR SOME SHIT?
OF COURSE NOT...
I NEED DRUGS.
YOU CRAY, LADY?!

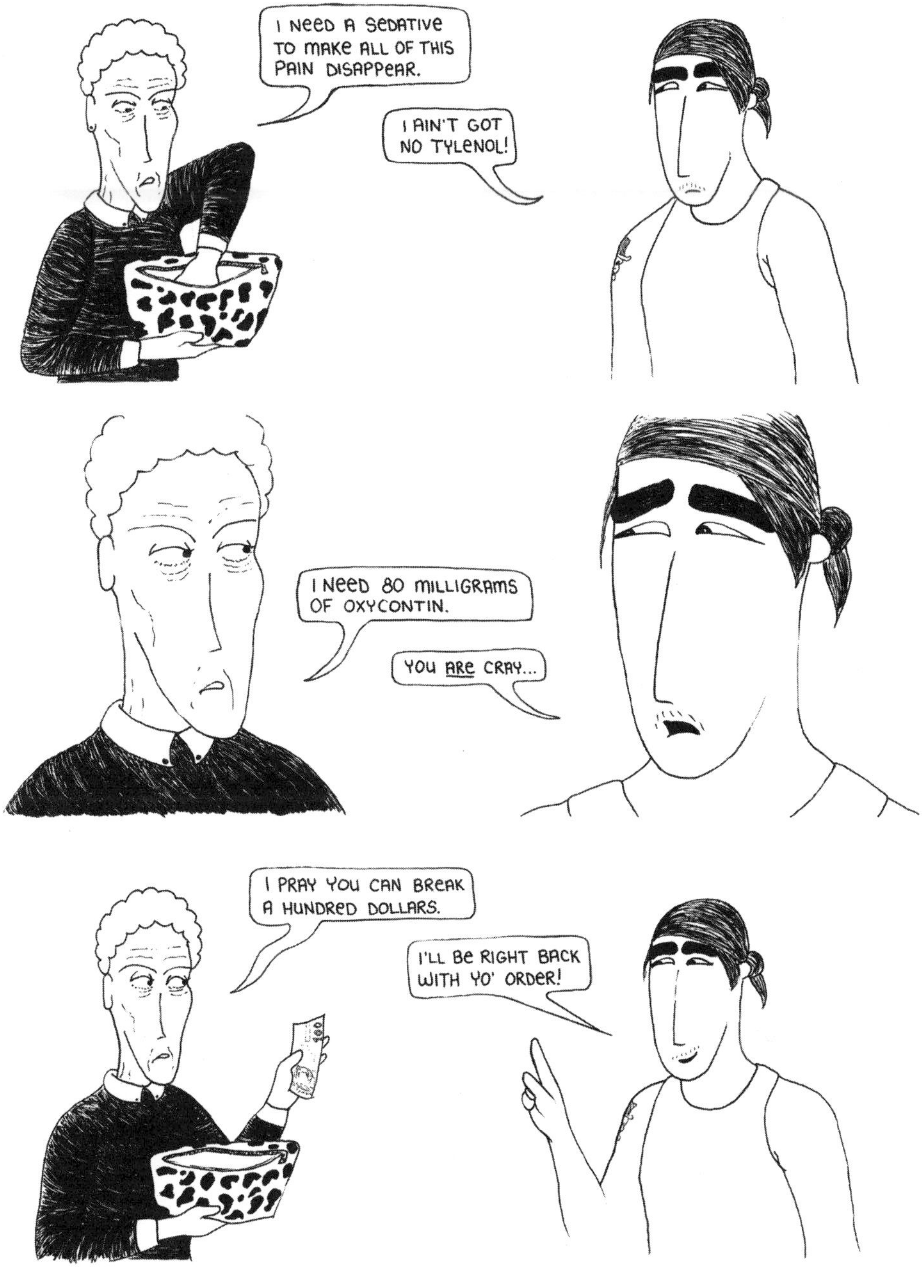
I NEED A SEDATIVE TO MAKE ALL OF THIS PAIN DISAPPEAR.
I AIN'T GOT NO TYLENOL!
I NEED 80 MILLIGRAMS OF OXYCONTIN.
YOU ARE CRAY...
I PRAY YOU CAN BREAK A HUNDRED DOLLARS.
I'LL BE RIGHT BACK WITH YO' ORDER!

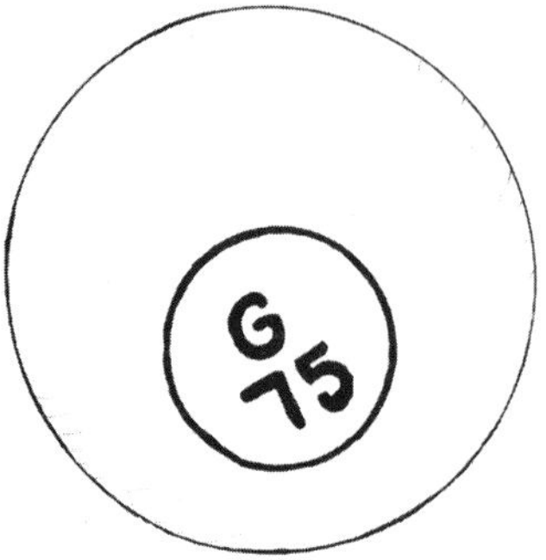
G
75

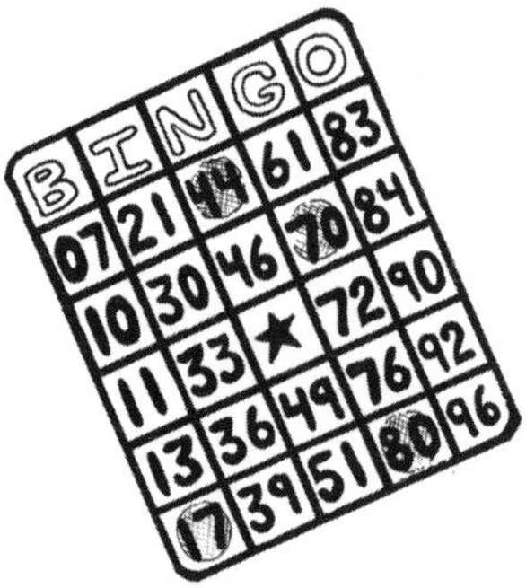
B I N G O
07 21 44 61 83
10 30 46 70 84
11 33 ★ 72 90
13 36 49 76 92
17 39 51 80 96

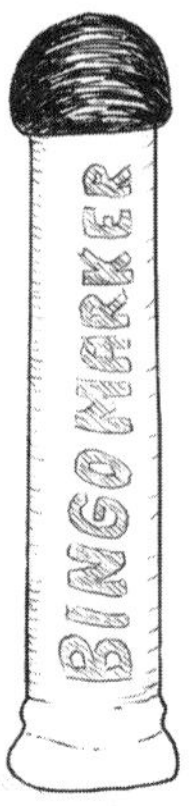
BINGO MARKER

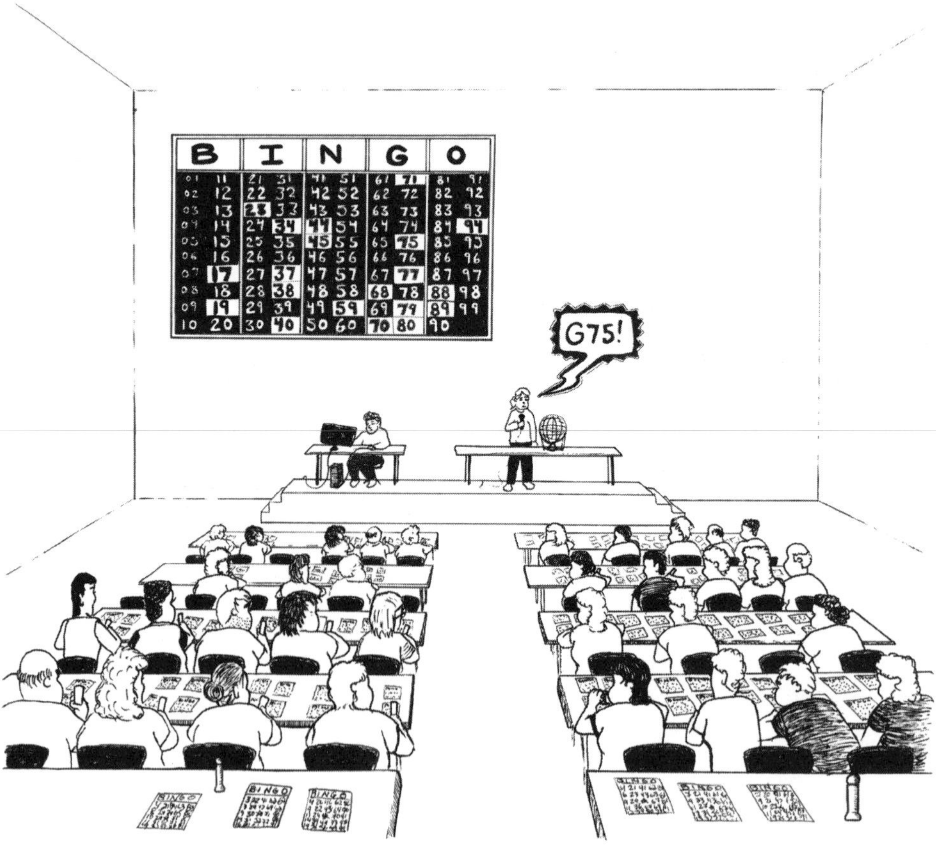
B I N G O
G75!

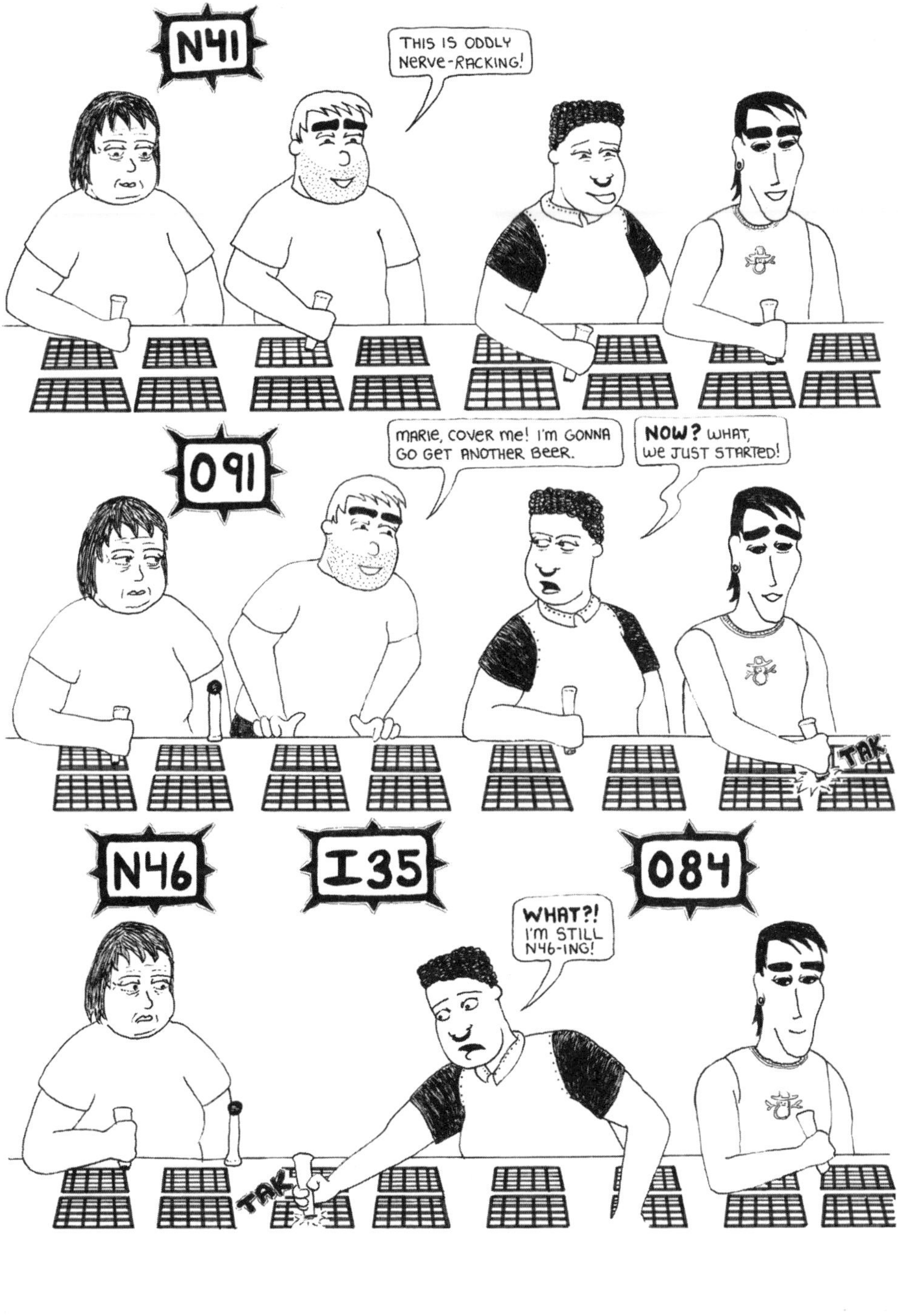
N41
THIS IS ODDLY NERVE-RACKING!
O91
MARIE, COVER ME! I'M GONNA GO GET ANOTHER BEER.
NOW? WHAT, WE JUST STARTED!
TAK
N46
I35
O84
WHAT?! I'M STILL N46-ING!
TAK

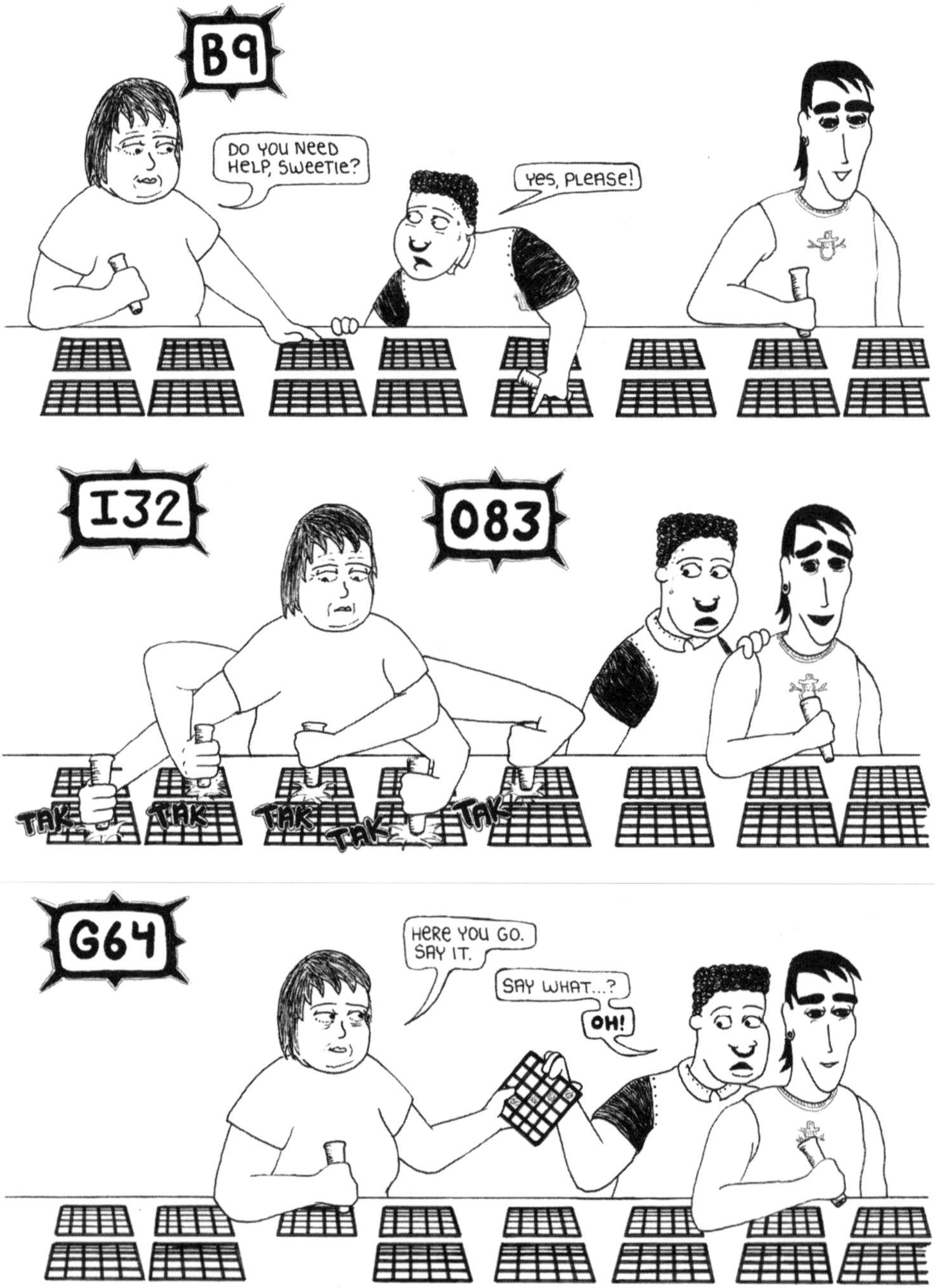
B9
DO YOU NEED HELP, SWEETIE?
YES, PLEASE!
I32
O83
TAK
TAK
TAK
TAK
TAK
G64
HERE YOU GO. SAY IT.
SAY WHAT...?
OH!

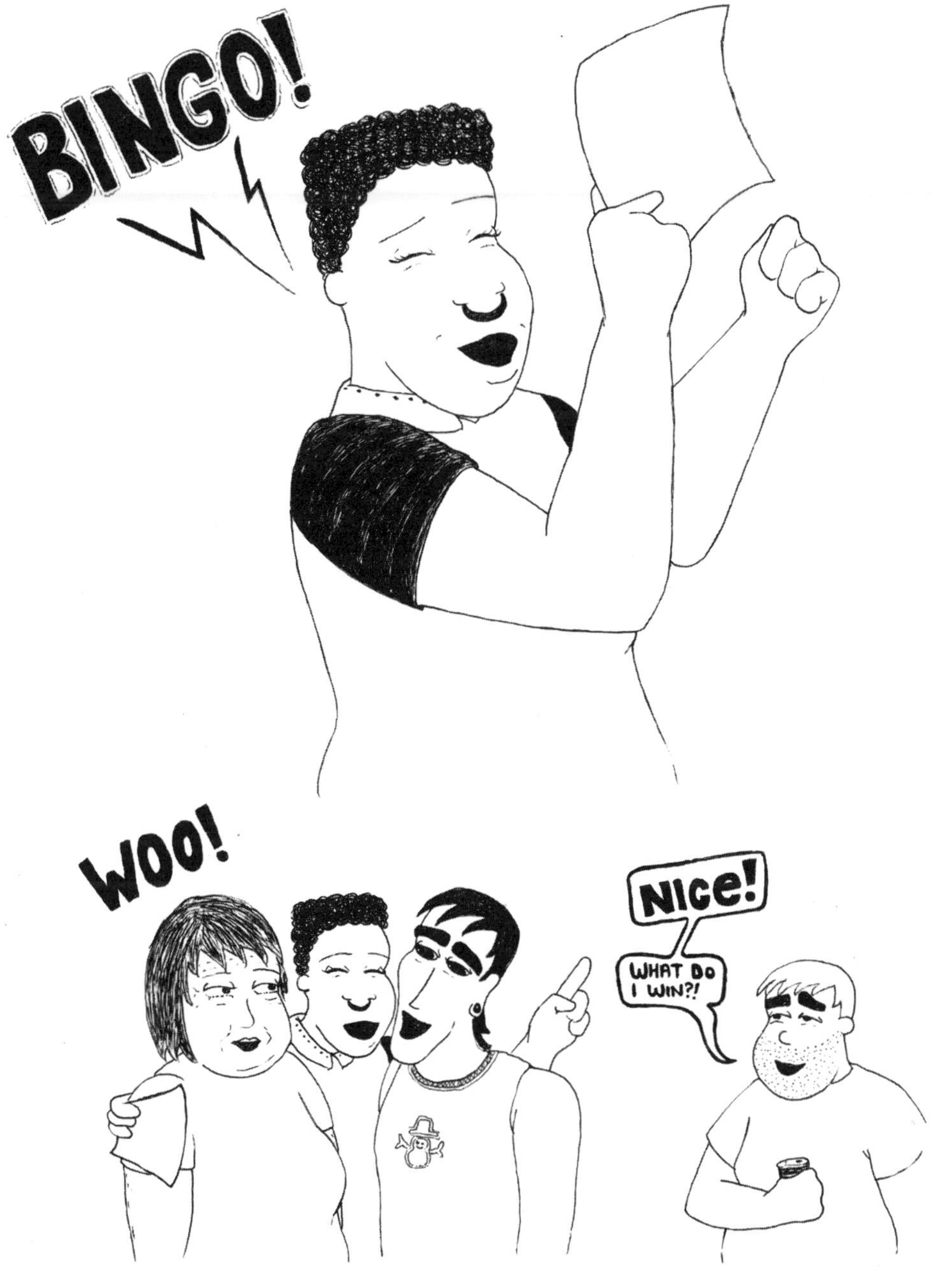
BINGO!
WOO!
NICE!
WHAT DO I WIN?!

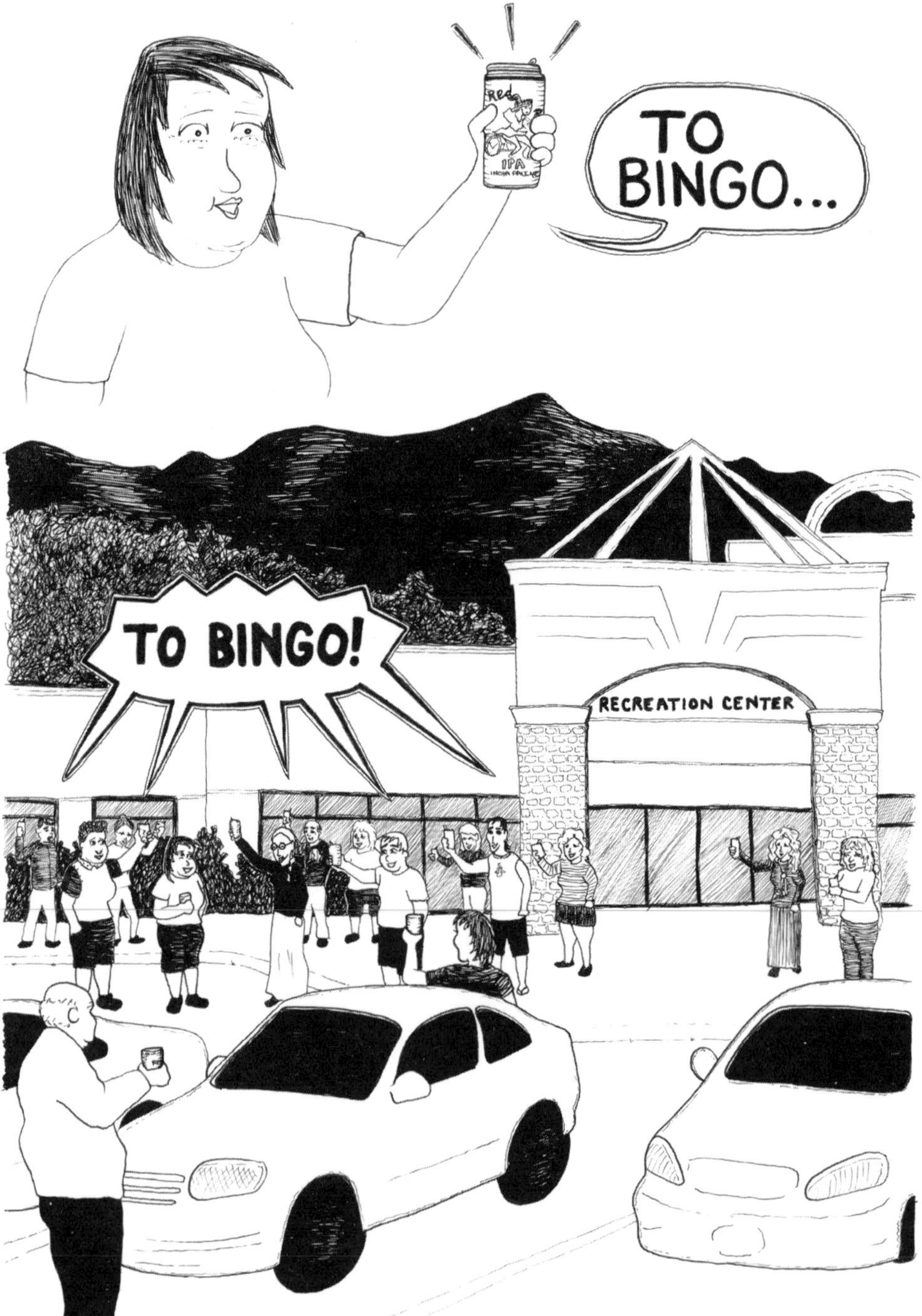
Red
IPA
TO BINGO...
TO BINGO!
RECREATION CENTER

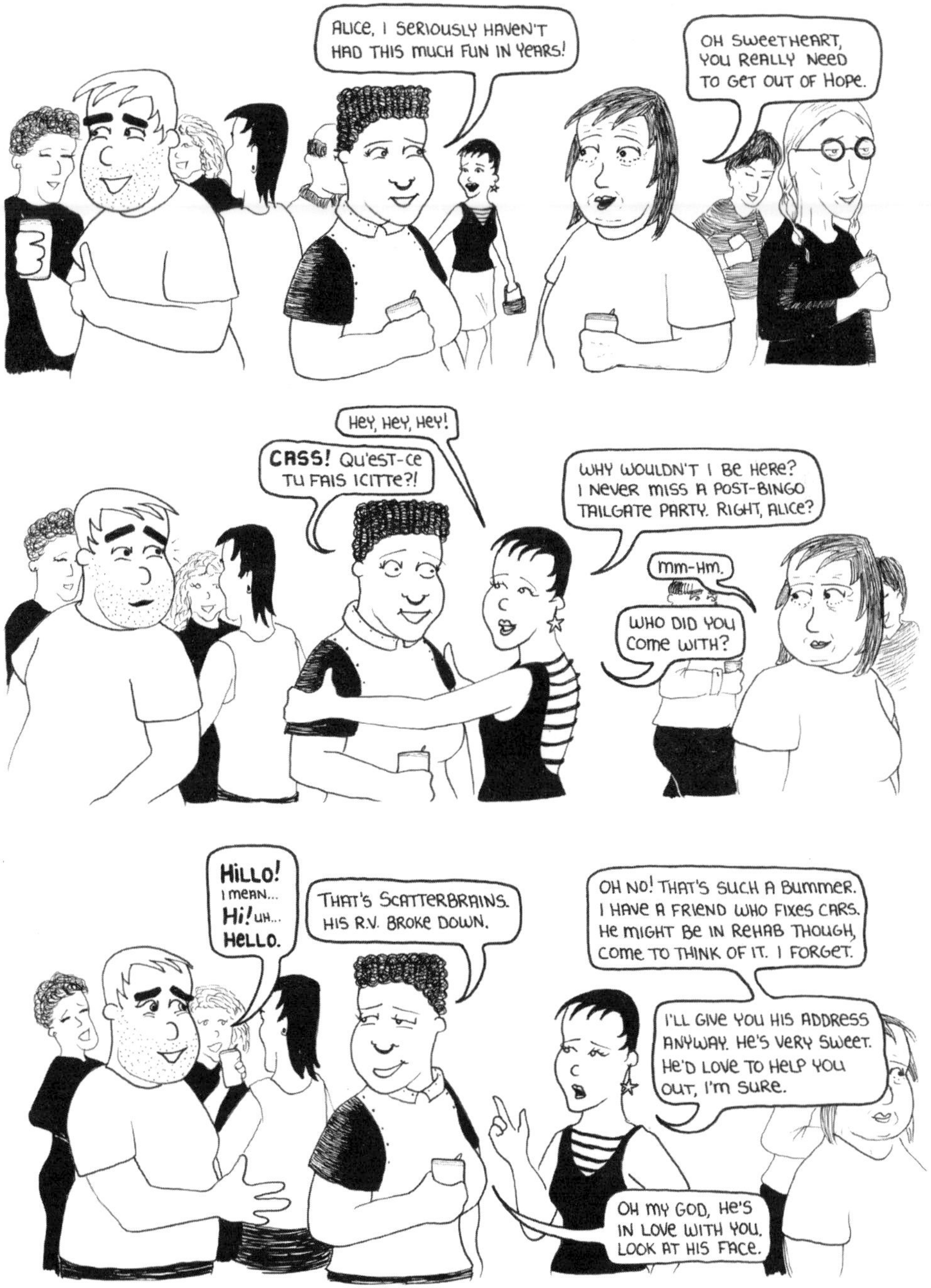
ALICE, I SERIOUSLY HAVEN'T HAD THIS MUCH FUN IN YEARS!
OH SWEETHEART, YOU REALLY NEED TO GET OUT OF HOPE.
HEY, HEY, HEY!
CASS! QU'EST-CE TU FAIS ICITTE?!
WHY WOULDN'T I BE HERE? I NEVER MISS A POST-BINGO TAILGATE PARTY. RIGHT, ALICE?
MM-HM.
WHO DID YOU COME WITH?
HILLO! I MEAN... HI! UH... HELLO.
THAT'S SCATTERBRAINS. HIS R.V. BROKE DOWN.
OH NO! THAT'S SUCH A BUMMER. I HAVE A FRIEND WHO FIXES CARS. HE MIGHT BE IN REHAB THOUGH, COME TO THINK OF IT. I FORGET.
I'LL GIVE YOU HIS ADDRESS ANYWAY. HE'S VERY SWEET. HE'D LOVE TO HELP YOU OUT, I'M SURE.
OH MY GOD, HE'S IN LOVE WITH YOU. LOOK AT HIS FACE.

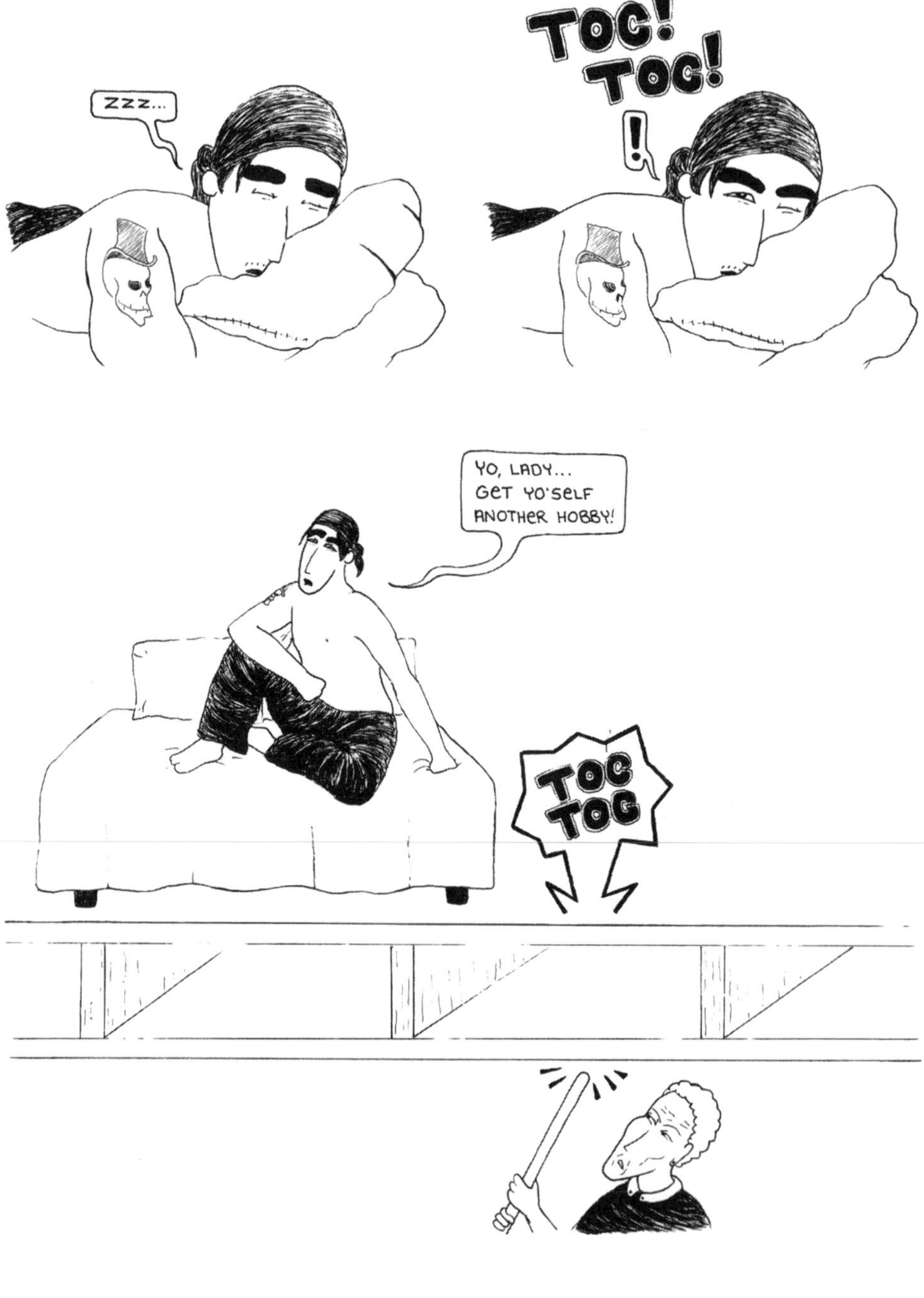
ZZZ...
TOC! TOC!
!
YO, LADY...
GET YO'SELF
ANOTHER HOBBY!
TOC
TOC

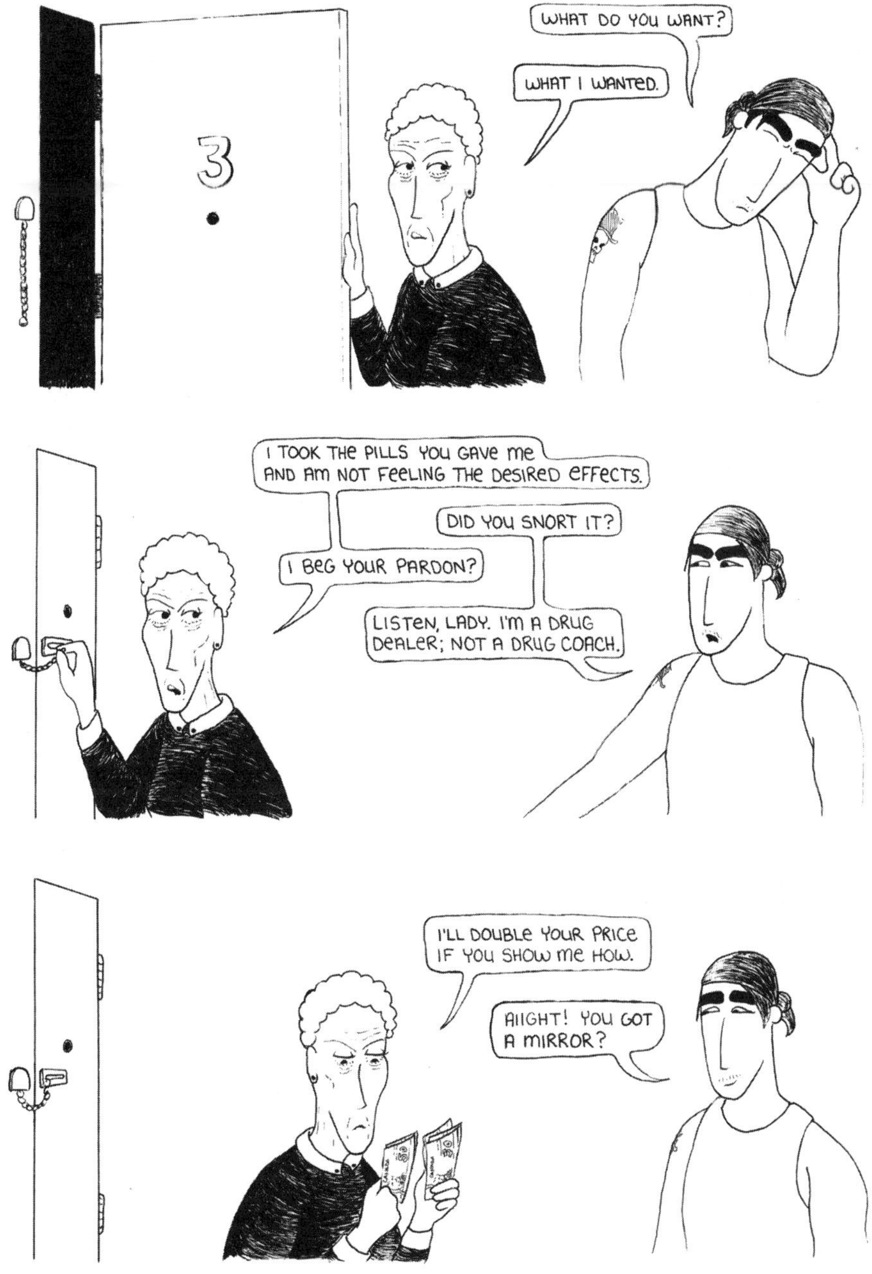
WHAT DO YOU WANT?
WHAT I WANTED.
I TOOK THE PILLS YOU GAVE ME AND AM NOT FEELING THE DESIRED EFFECTS.
DID YOU SNORT IT?
I BEG YOUR PARDON?
LISTEN, LADY. I'M A DRUG DEALER; NOT A DRUG COACH.
I'LL DOUBLE YOUR PRICE IF YOU SHOW ME HOW.
AIIGHT! YOU GOT A MIRROR?

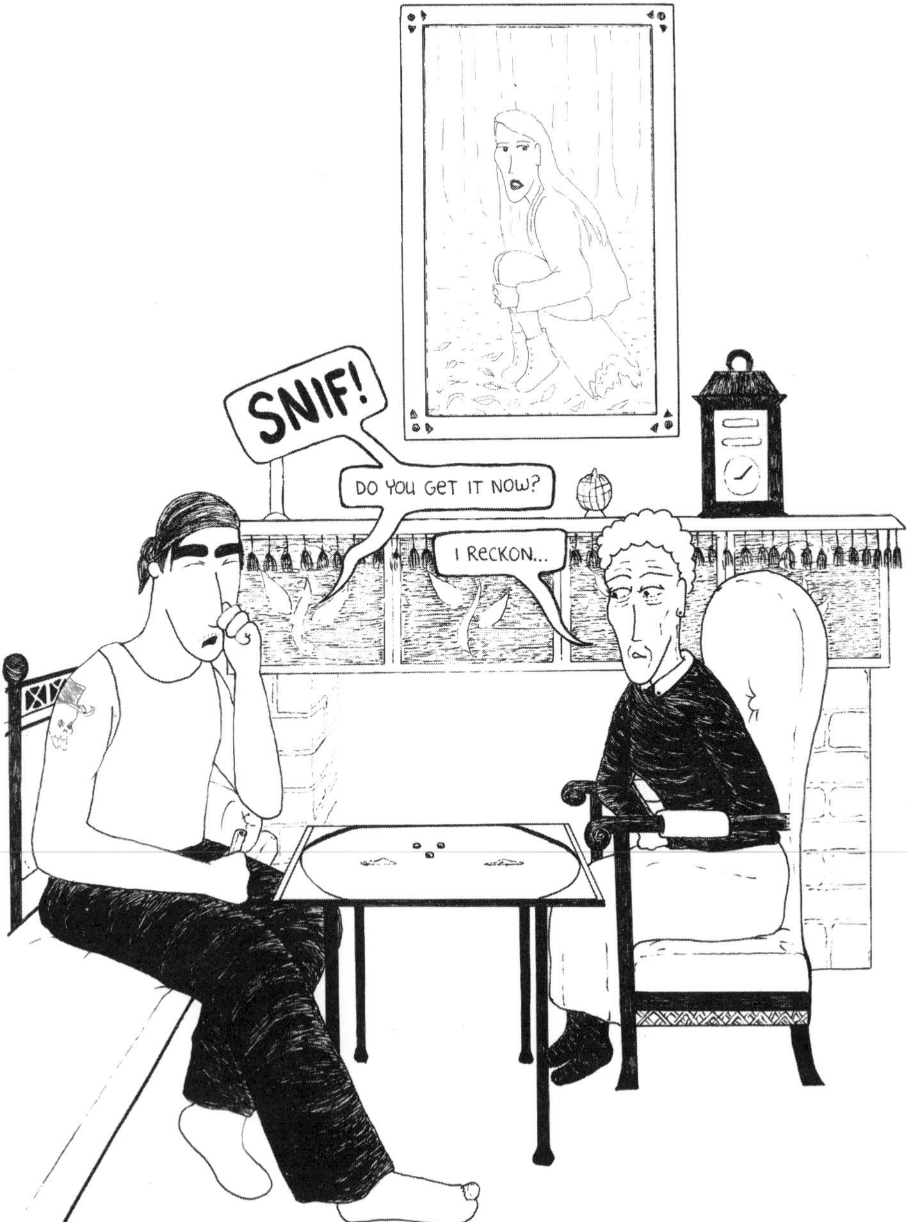
SNIF!
DO YOU GET IT NOW?
I RECKON...

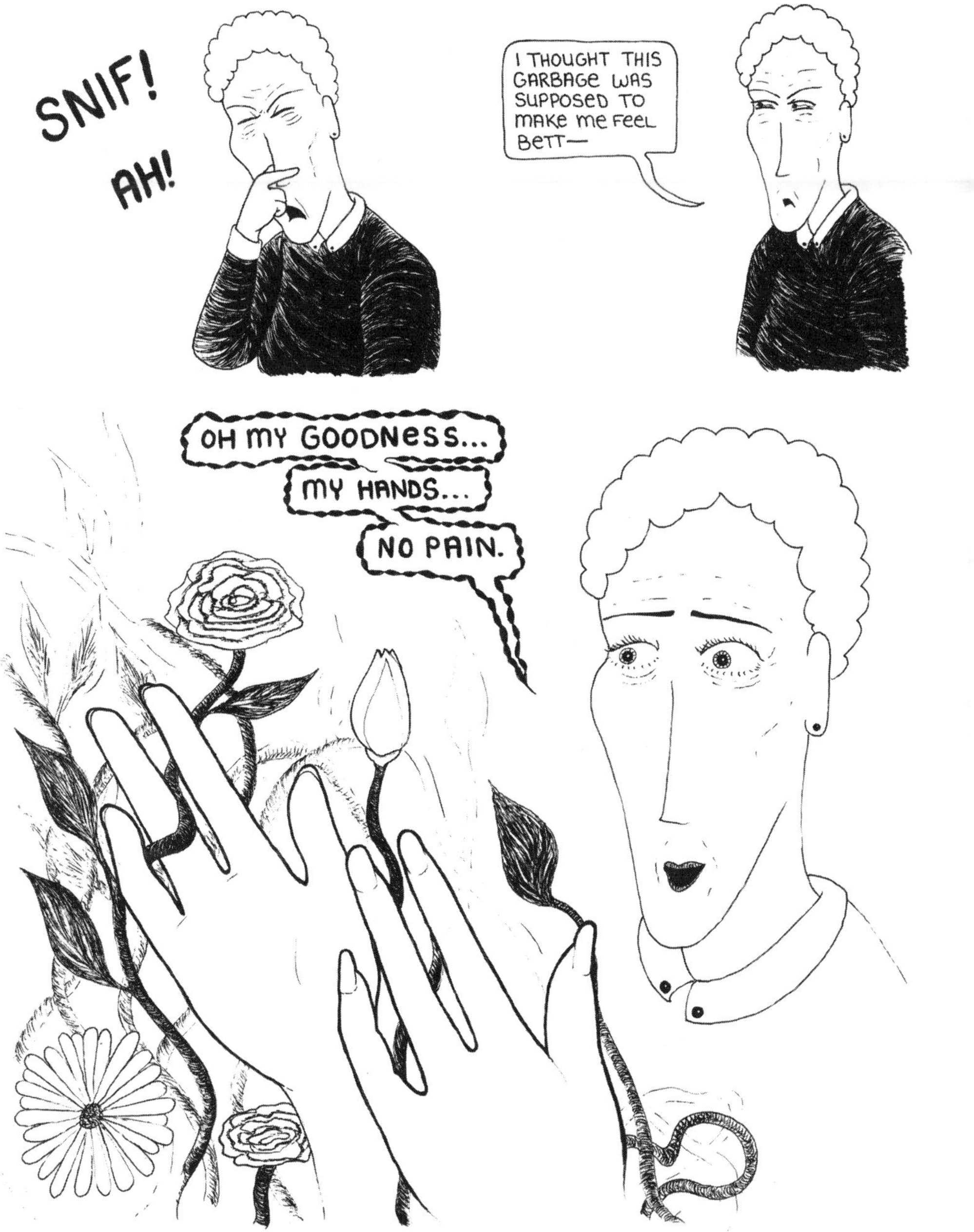
SNIF!
AH!
I THOUGHT THIS GARBAGE WAS SUPPOSED TO MAKE ME FEEL BETT—
OH MY GOODNESS...
MY HANDS...
NO PAIN.

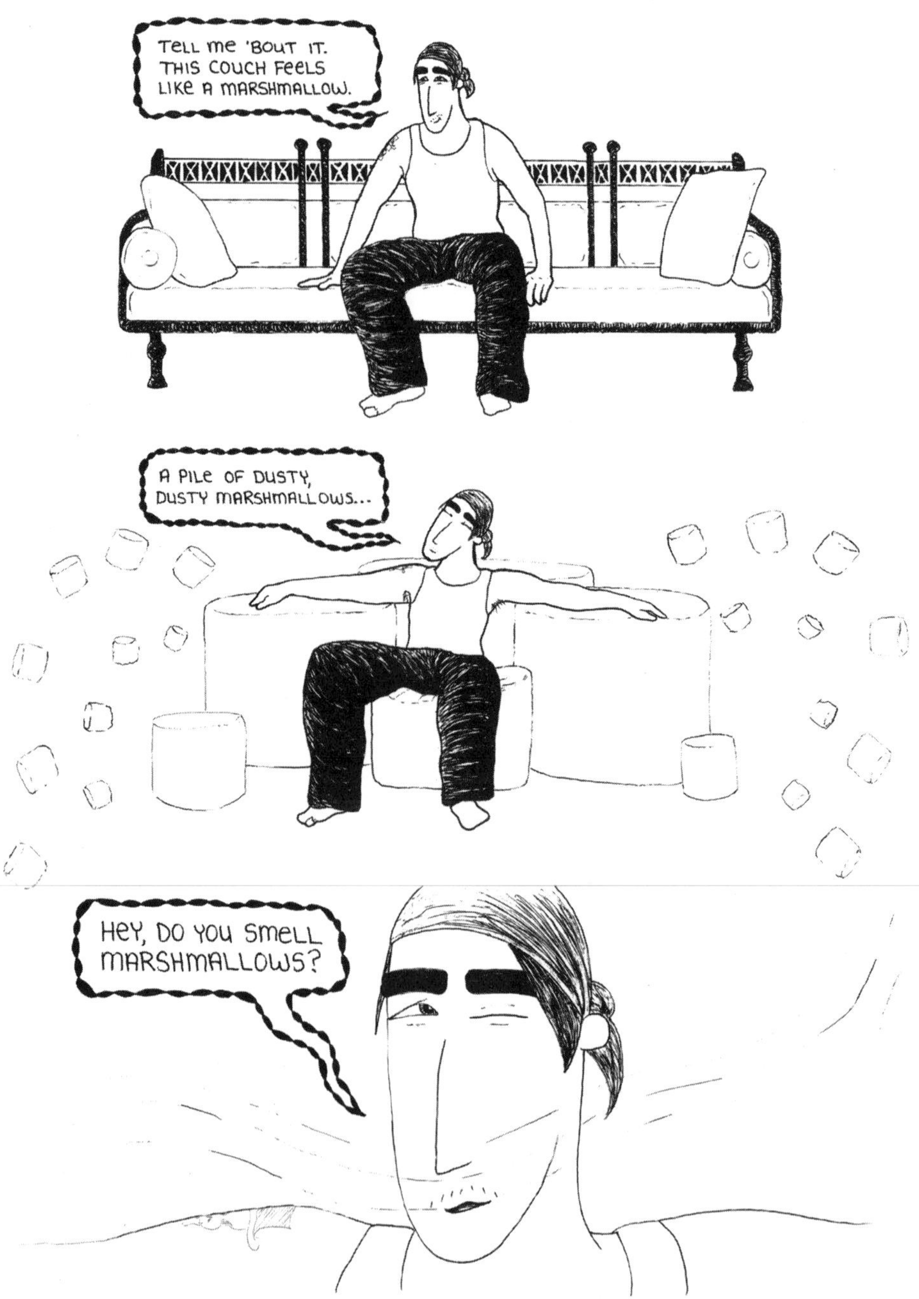
TELL ME 'BOUT IT. THIS COUCH FEELS LIKE A MARSHMALLOW.
A PILE OF DUSTY, DUSTY MARSHMALLOWS...
HEY, DO YOU SMELL MARSHMALLOWS?

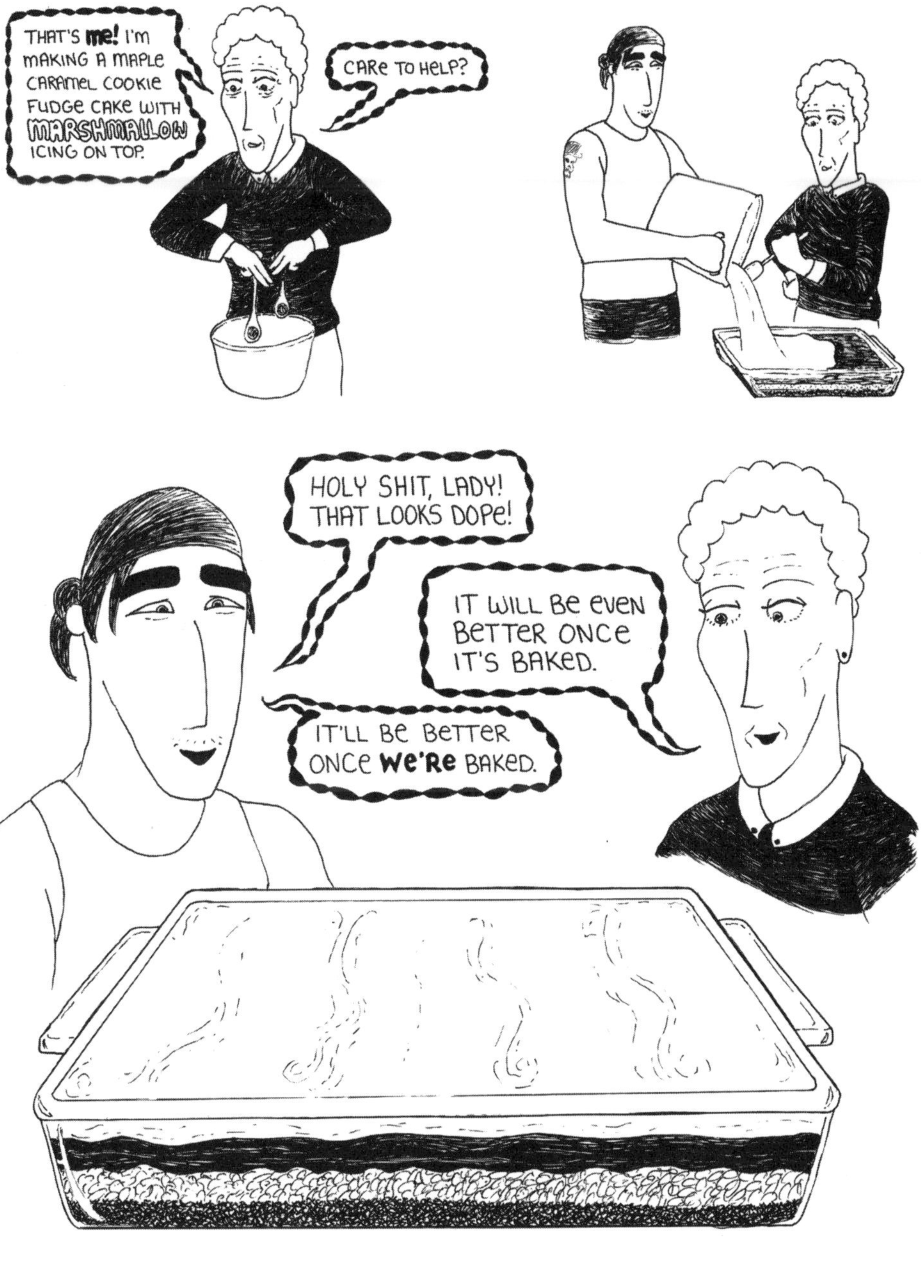
THAT'S me! I'M MAKING A MAPLE CARAMEL COOKIE FUDGE CAKE WITH MARSHMALLOW ICING ON TOP.
CARE TO HELP?
HOLY SHIT, LADY! THAT LOOKS DOPE!
IT WILL BE EVEN BETTER ONCE IT'S BAKED.
IT'LL BE BETTER ONCE WE'RE BAKED.

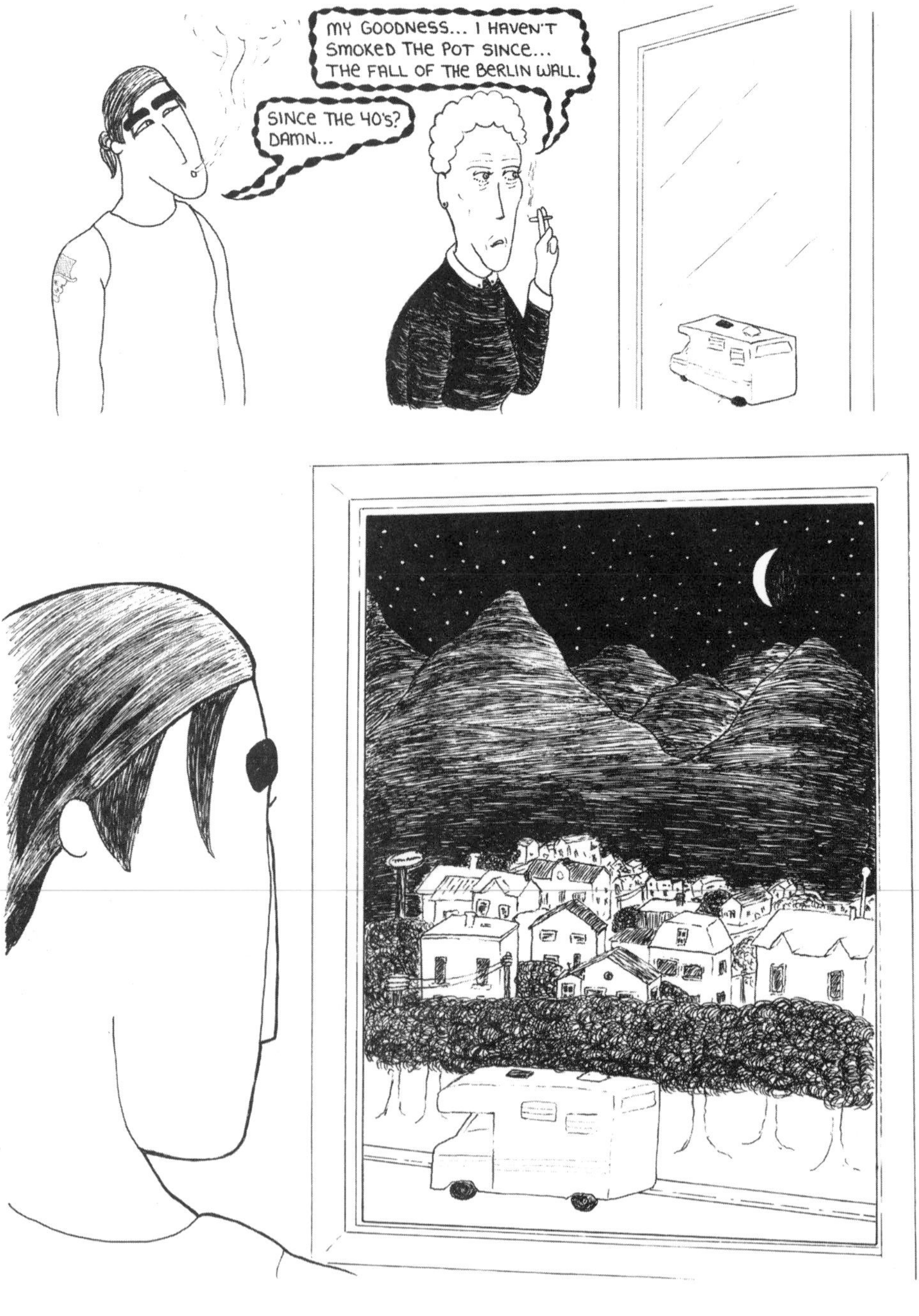
MY GOODNESS... I HAVEN'T SMOKED THE POT SINCE... THE FALL OF THE BERLIN WALL.
SINCE THE 40'S? DAMN...

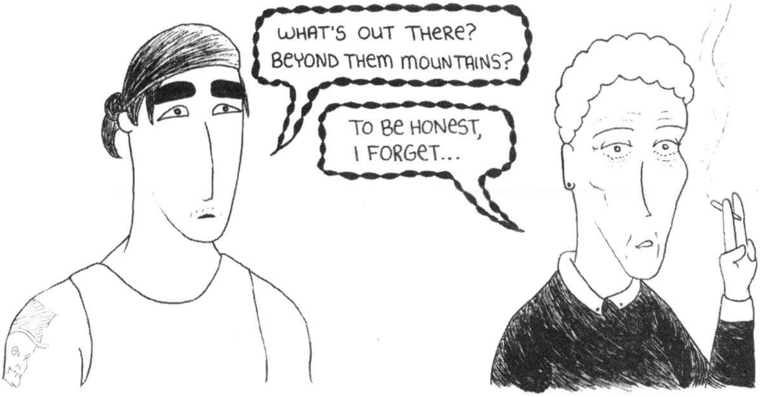
WHAT'S OUT THERE? BEYOND THEM MOUNTAINS?
TO BE HONEST, I FORGET...

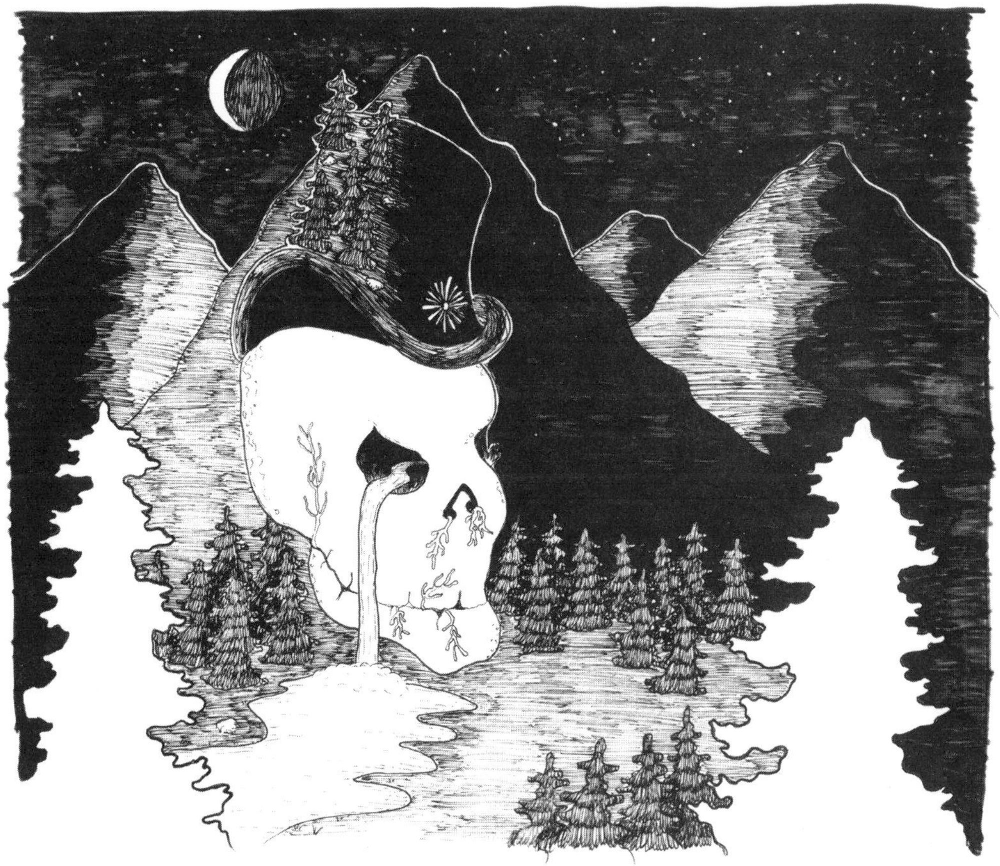

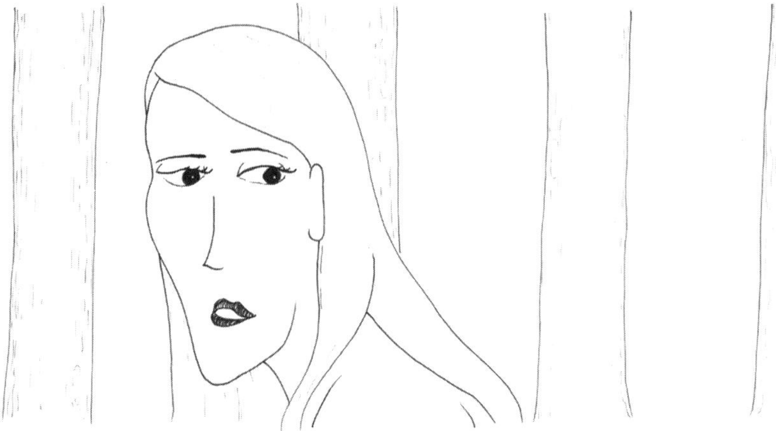

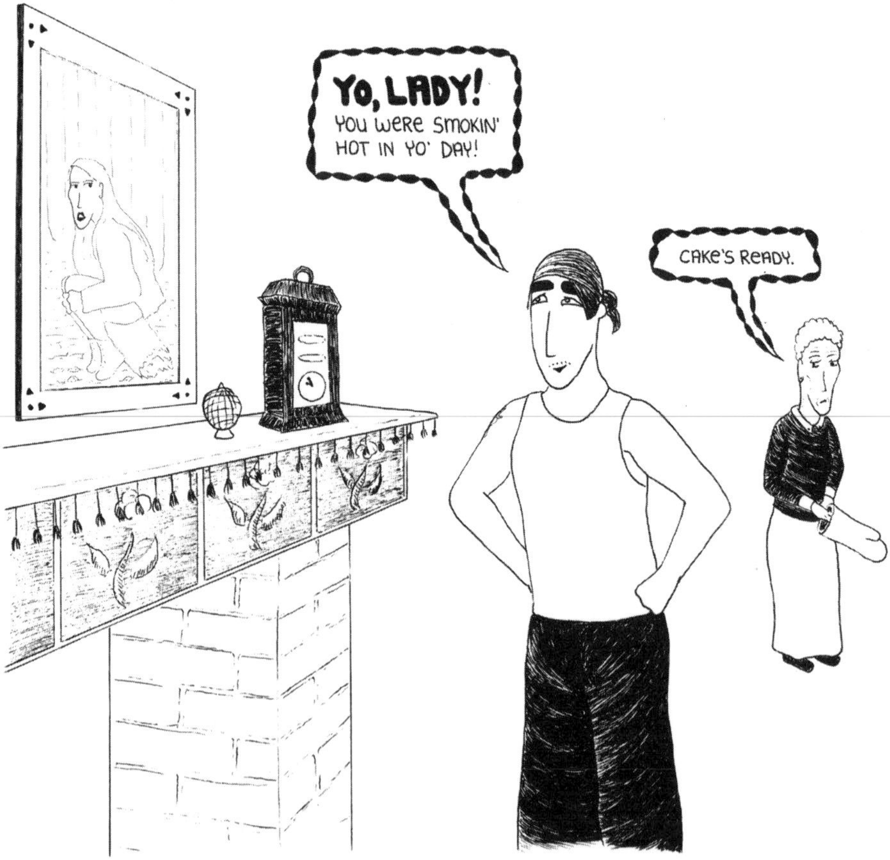
YO, LADY! YOU WERE SMOKIN' HOT IN YO' DAY!
CAKE'S READY.

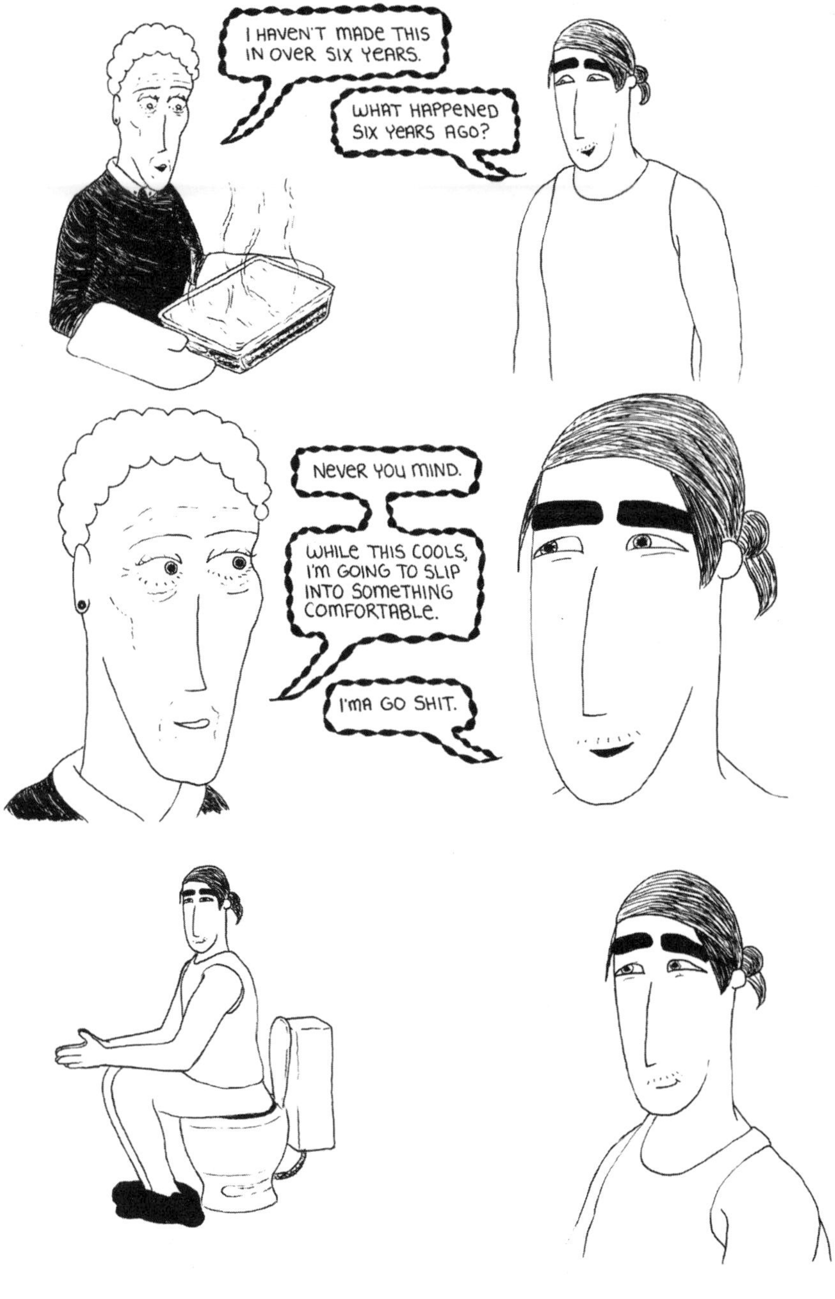

I HAVEN'T MADE THIS IN OVER SIX YEARS.
WHAT HAPPENED SIX YEARS AGO?
NEVER YOU MIND.
WHILE THIS COOLS, I'M GOING TO SLIP INTO SOMETHING COMFORTABLE.
I'MA GO SHIT.

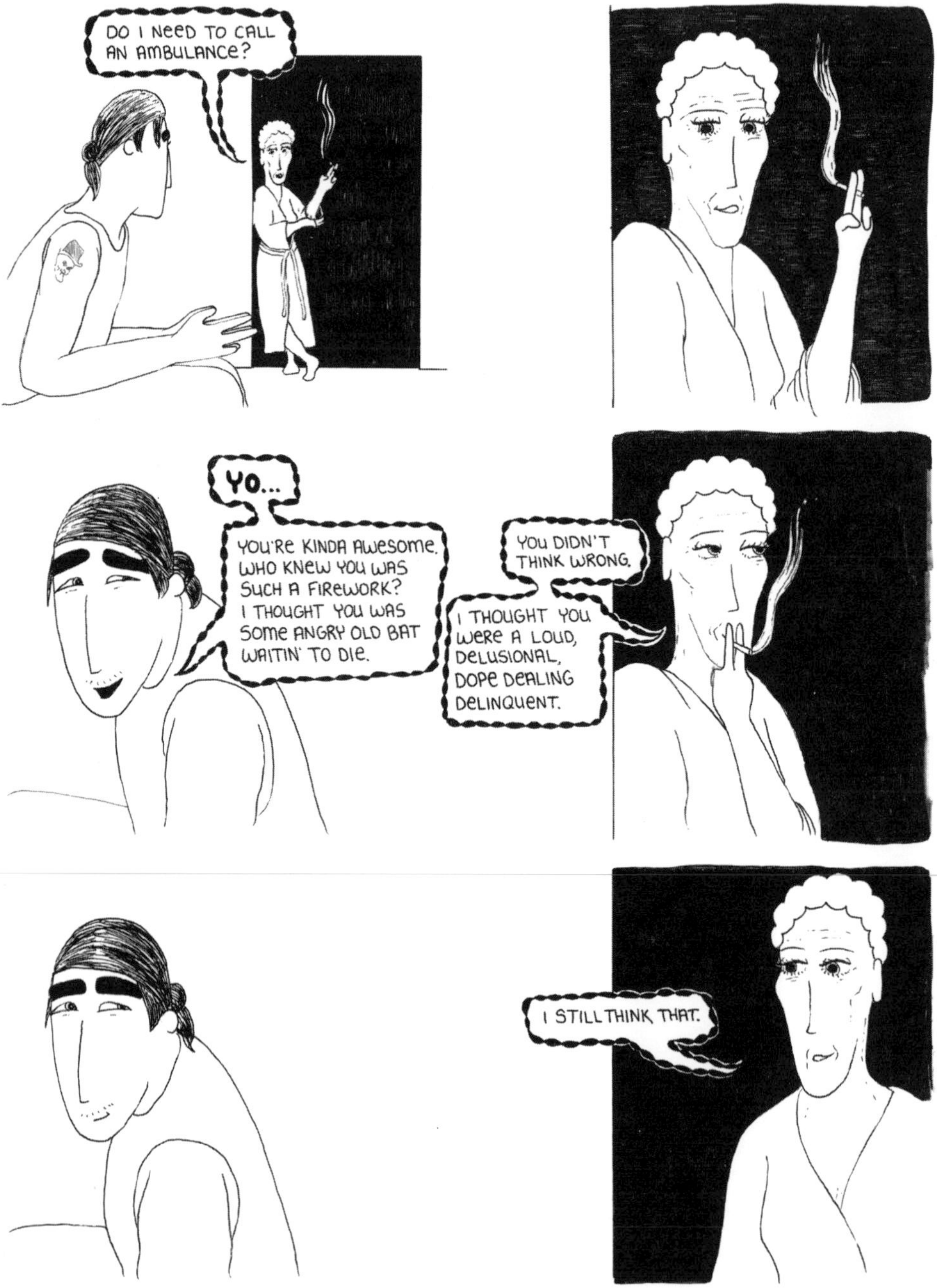
DO I NEED TO CALL AN AMBULANCE?
YO...
YOU'RE KINDA AWESOME. WHO KNEW YOU WAS SUCH A FIREWORK? I THOUGHT YOU WAS SOME ANGRY OLD BAT WAITIN' TO DIE.
YOU DIDN'T THINK WRONG.
I THOUGHT YOU WERE A LOUD, DELUSIONAL, DOPE DEALING DELINQUENT.
I STILL THINK THAT.

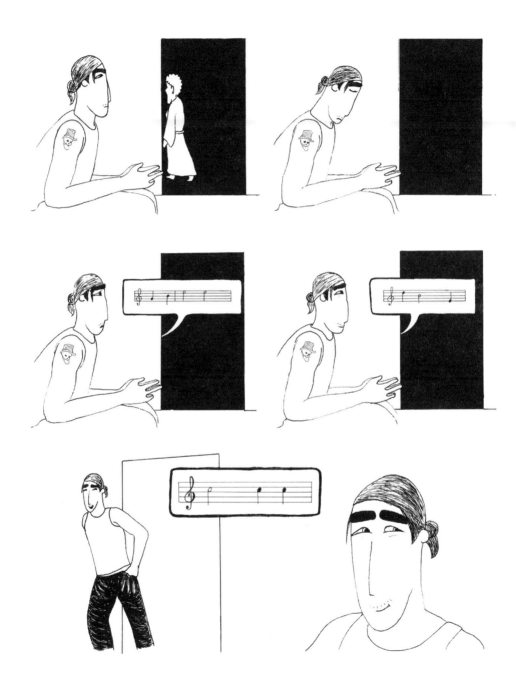

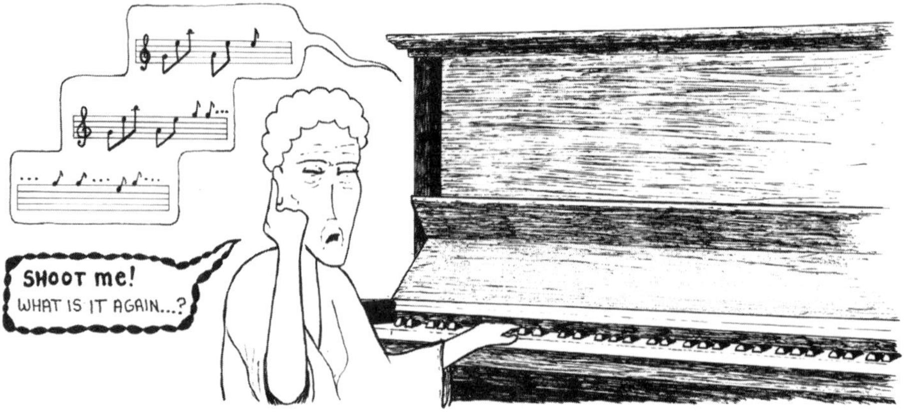
SHOOT me!
WHAT IS IT AGAIN...?

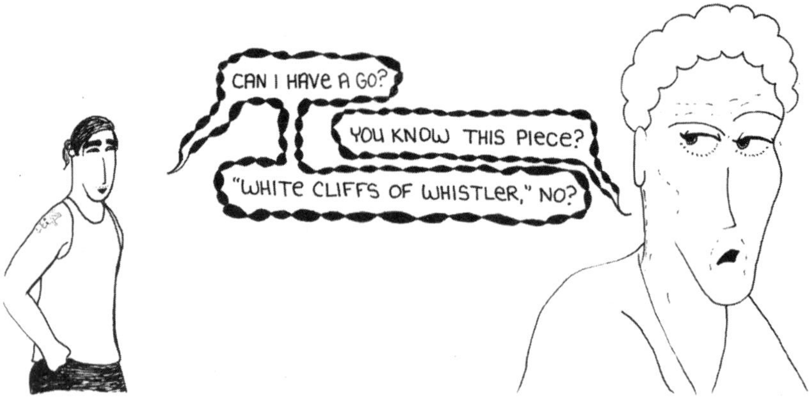
CAN I HAVE A GO?
YOU KNOW THIS PIECE?
"WHITE CLIFFS OF WHISTLER," NO?

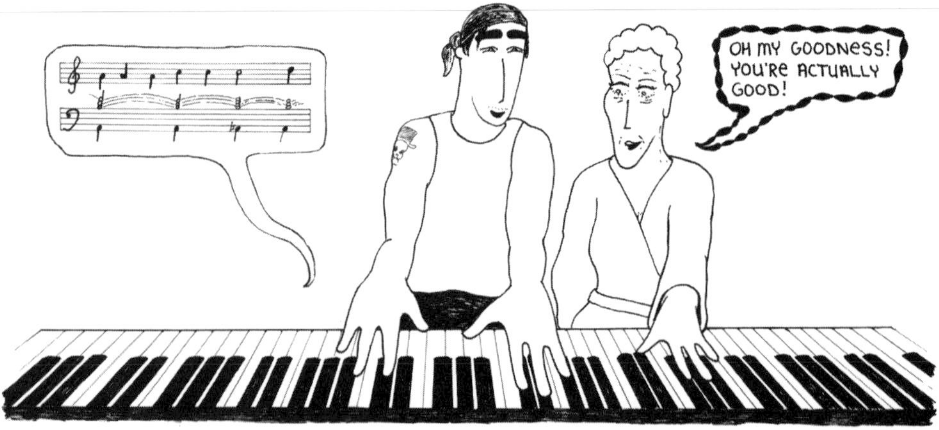
OH MY GOODNESS! YOU'RE ACTUALLY GOOD!

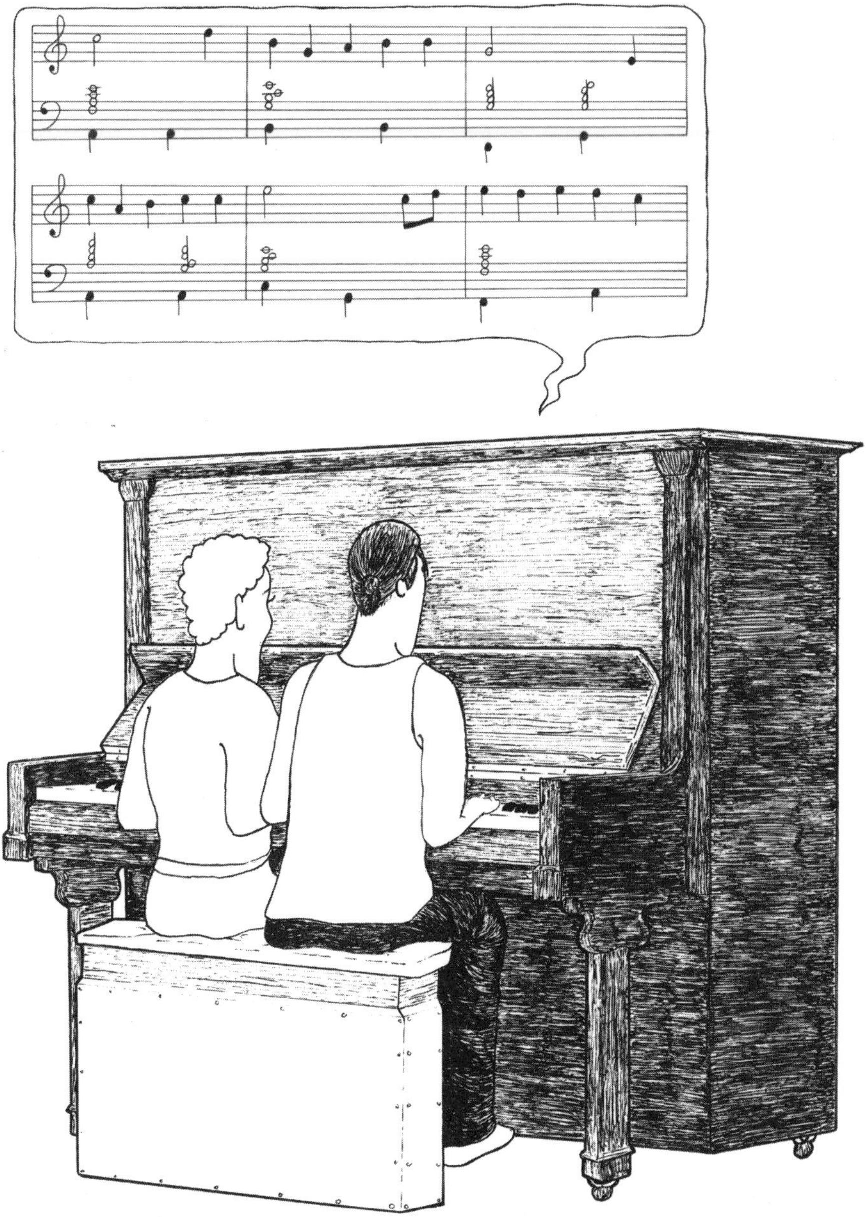

CHAPTER 5

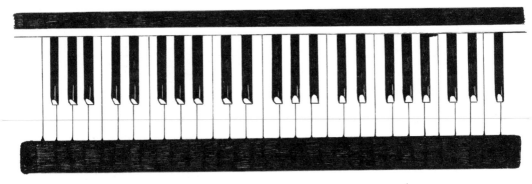

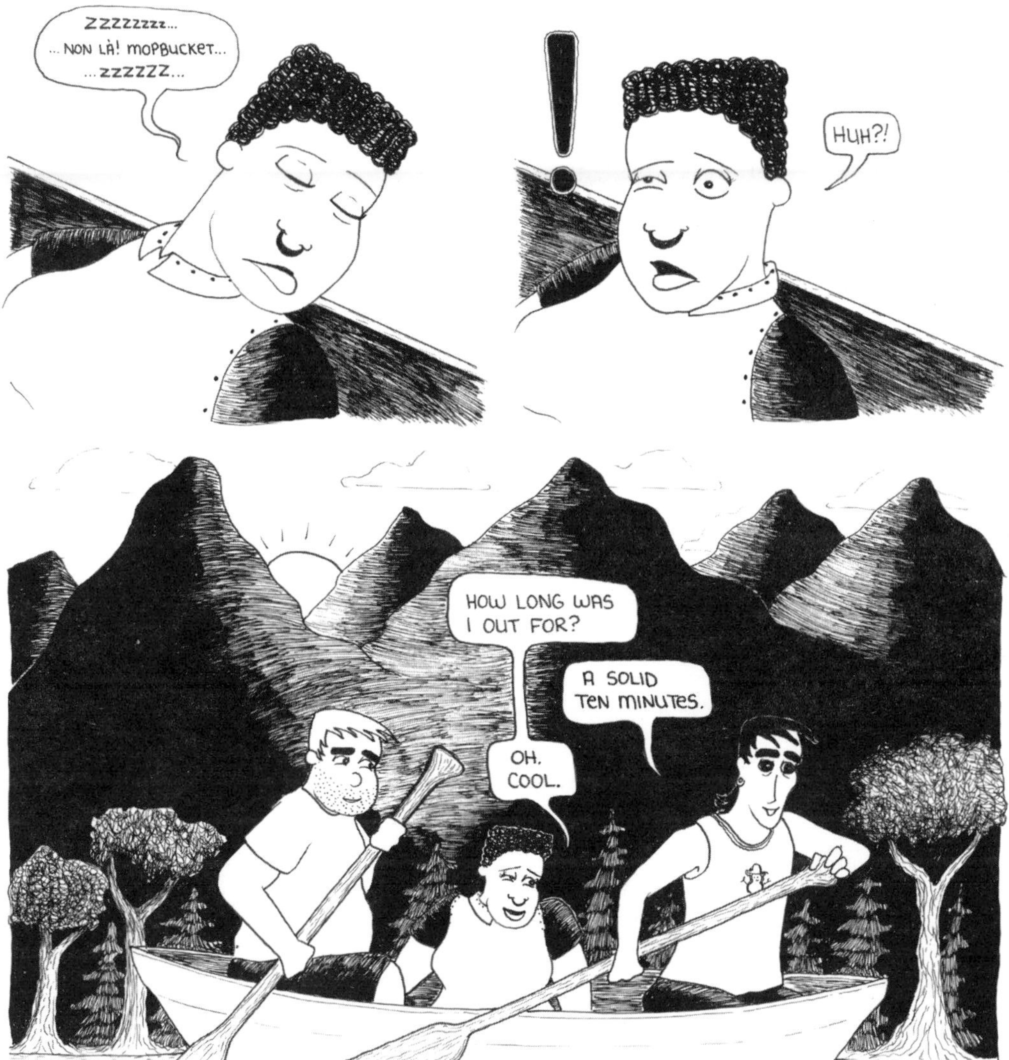
ZZZZZZZZ...
... NON LÀ! MOPBUCKET...
... ZZZZZZ...
HUH?!
HOW LONG WAS I OUT FOR?
A SOLID TEN MINUTES.
OH. COOL.

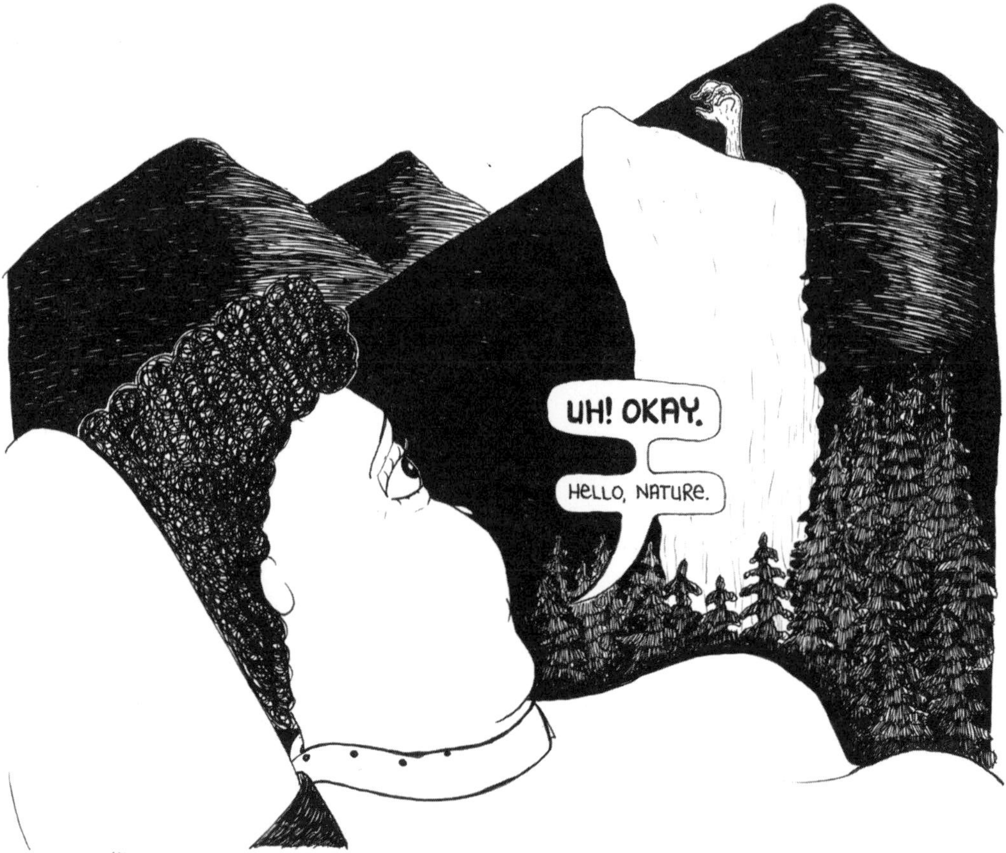
UH! OKAY.
HELLO, NATURE.

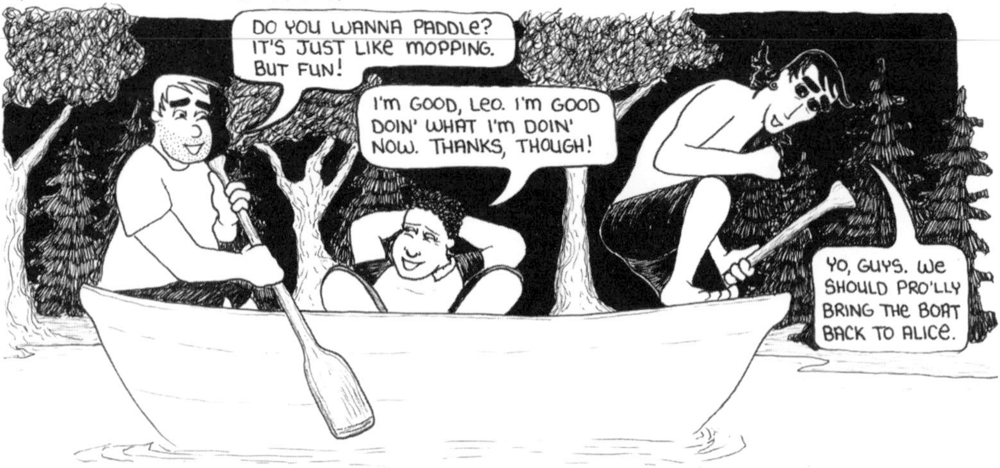
DO YOU WANNA PADDLE? IT'S JUST LIKE MOPPING. BUT FUN!
I'M GOOD, LEO. I'M GOOD DOIN' WHAT I'M DOIN' NOW. THANKS, THOUGH!
YO, GUYS. WE SHOULD PRO'LLY BRING THE BOAT BACK TO ALICE.

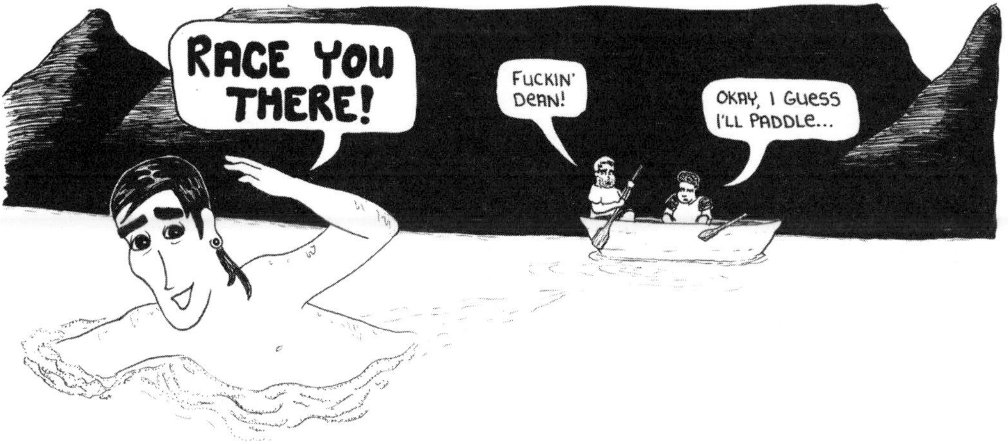
RACE YOU THERE!
FUCKIN' DEAN!
OKAY, I GUESS I'LL PADDLE...

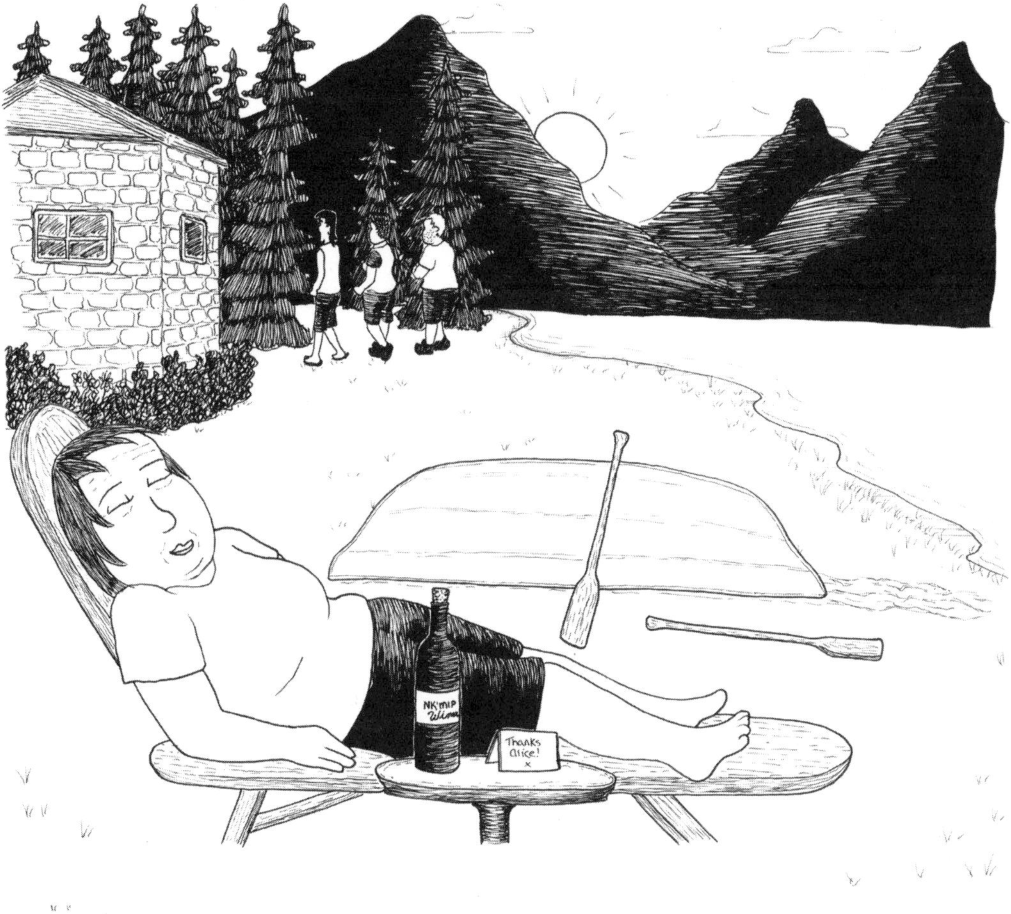
NK'MIP
Thanks Alice! x

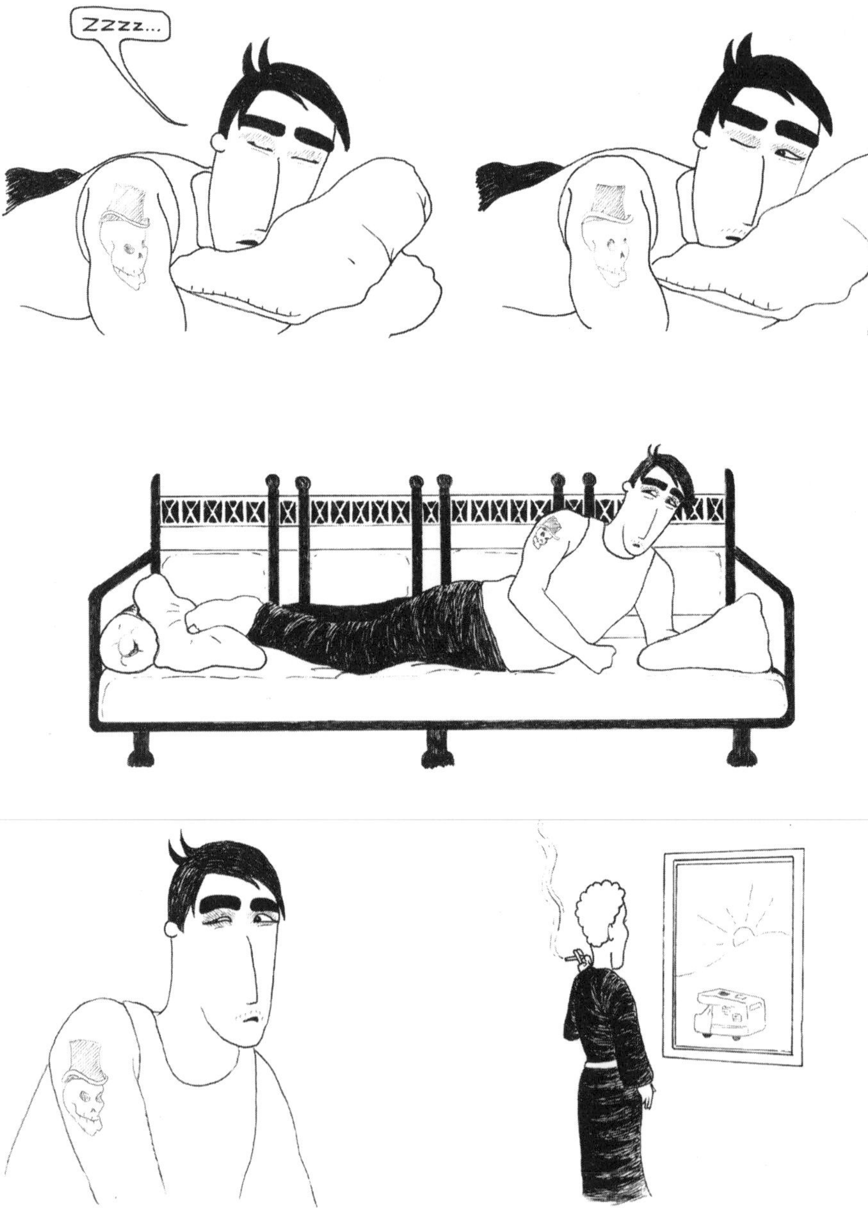
ZZZZ...

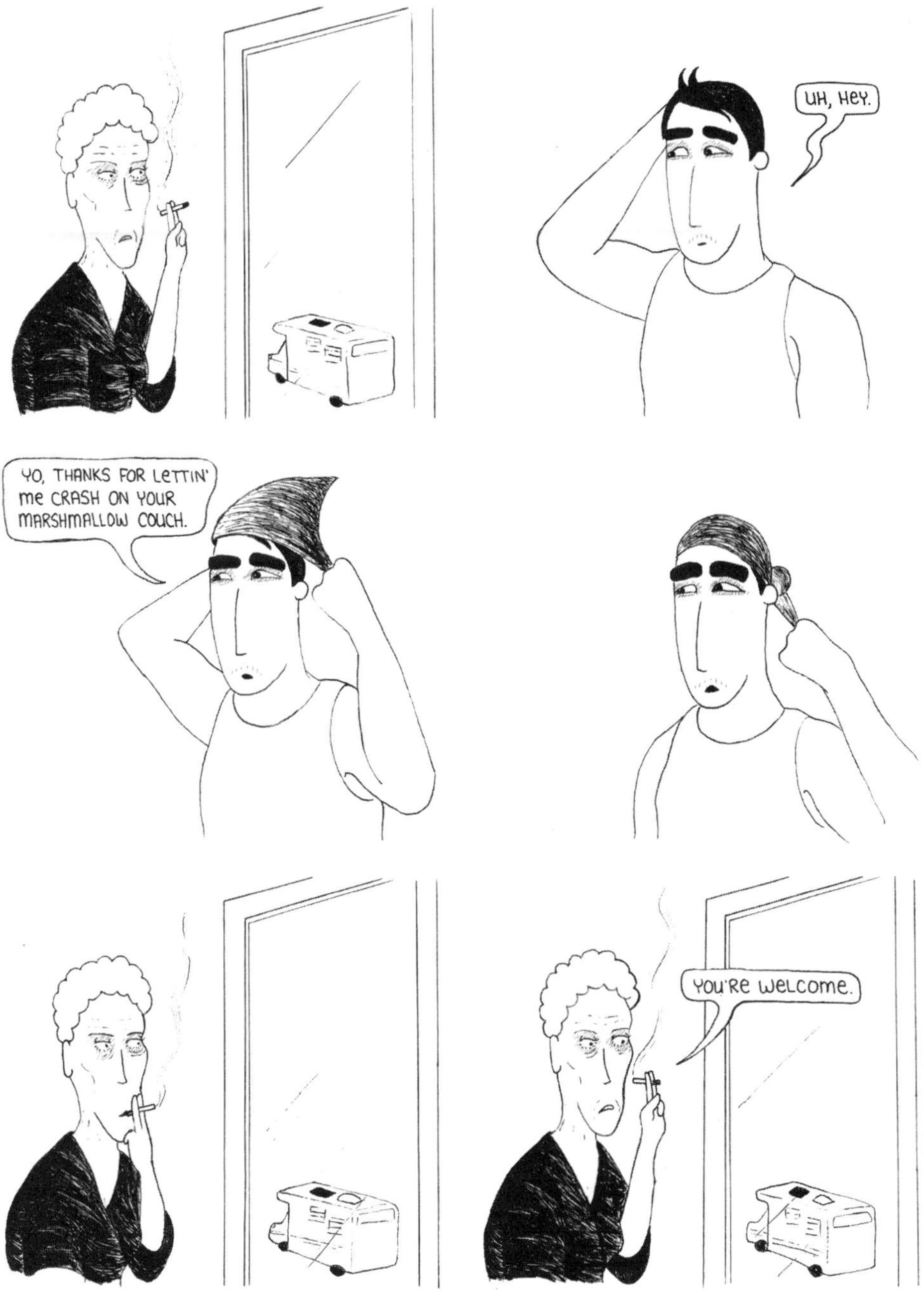
UH, HEY.
YO, THANKS FOR LETTIN' ME CRASH ON YOUR MARSHMALLOW COUCH.
YOU'RE WELCOME.

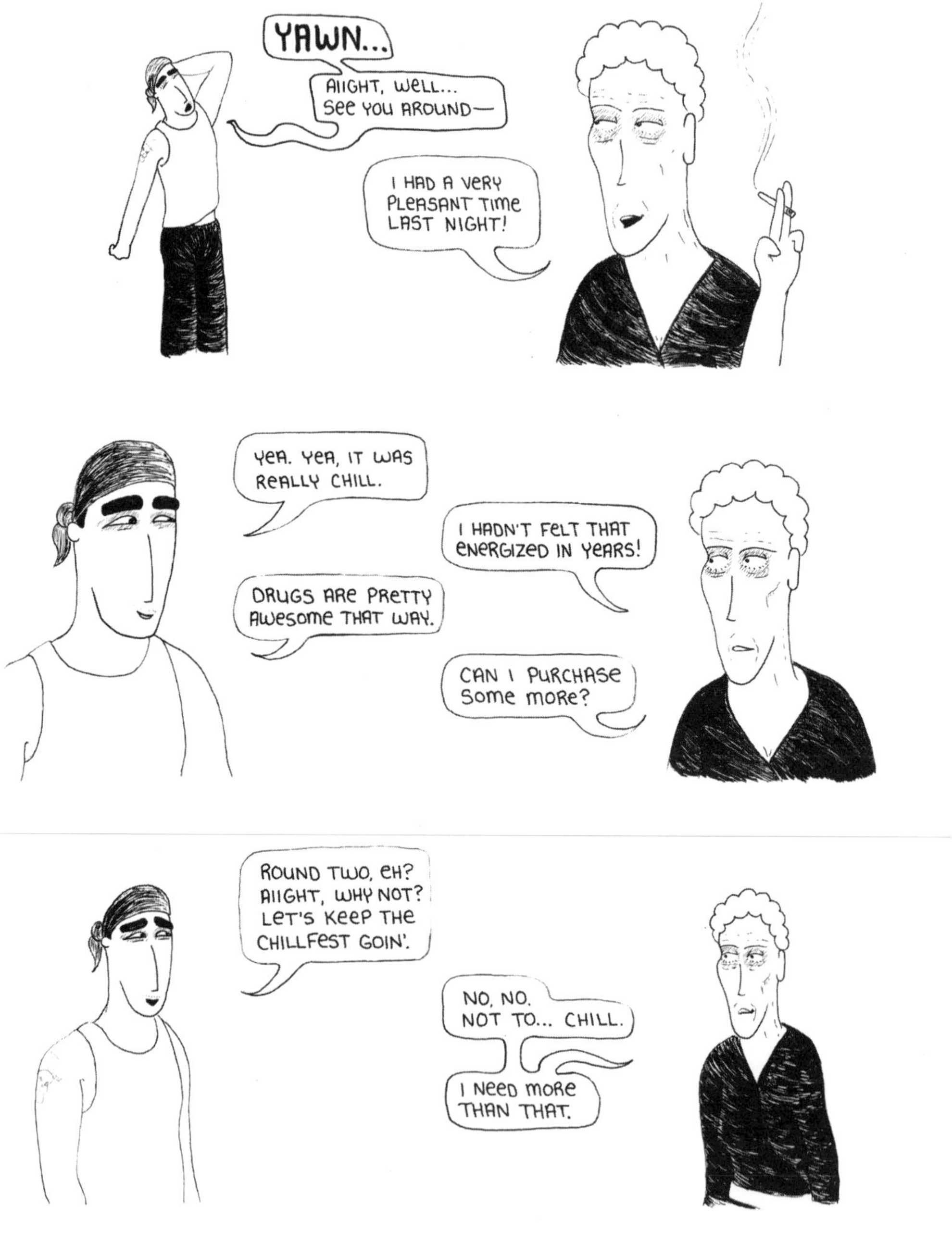
YAWN...
AIIGHT, WELL... SEE YOU AROUND—
I HAD A VERY PLEASANT TIME LAST NIGHT!
YEA. YEA, IT WAS REALLY CHILL.
I HADN'T FELT THAT ENERGIZED IN YEARS!
DRUGS ARE PRETTY AWESOME THAT WAY.
CAN I PURCHASE SOME MORE?
ROUND TWO, EH? AIIGHT, WHY NOT? LET'S KEEP THE CHILLFEST GOIN'.
NO, NO. NOT TO... CHILL.
I NEED MORE THAN THAT.

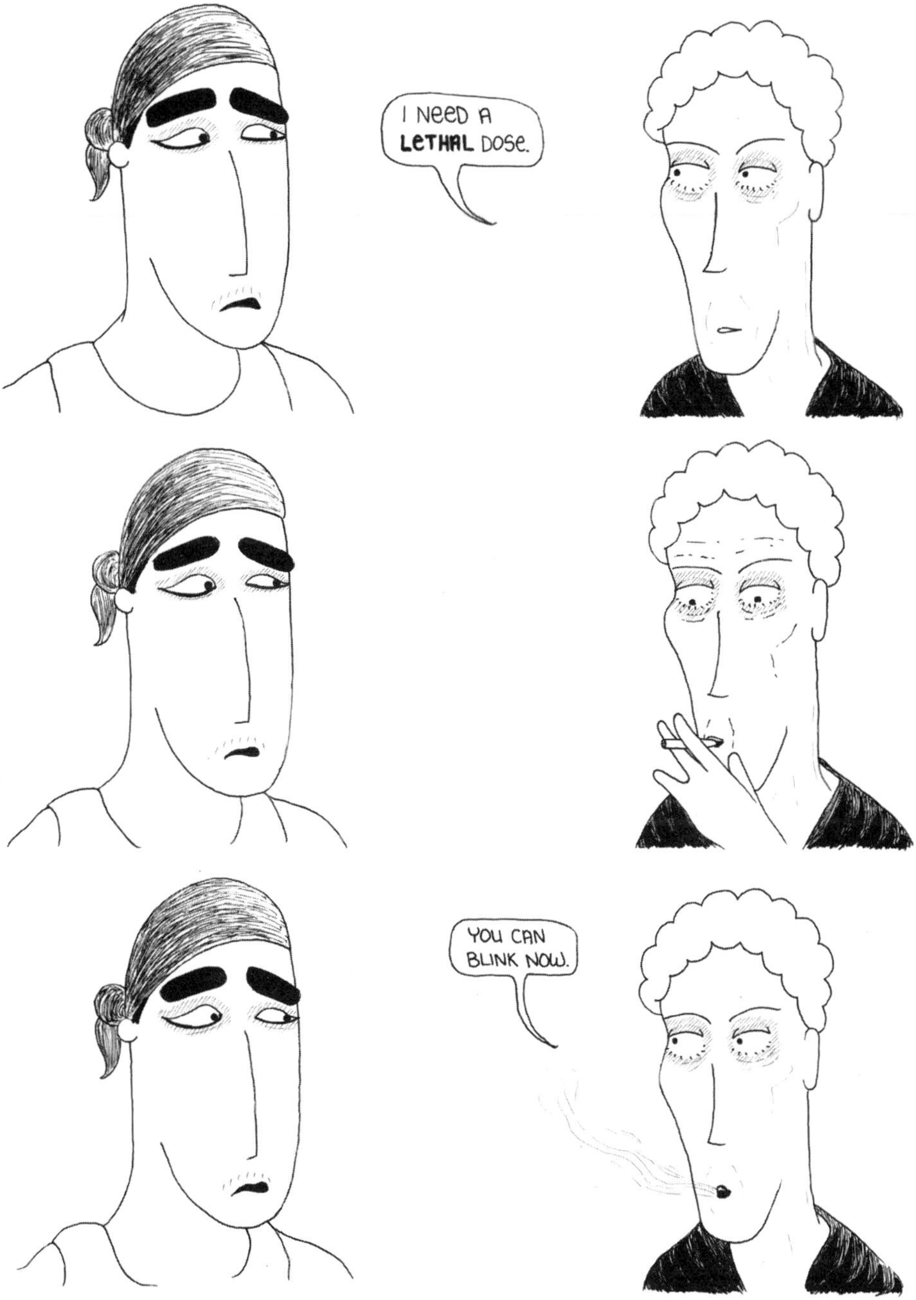
I NEED A LETHAL DOSE.
YOU CAN BLINK NOW.

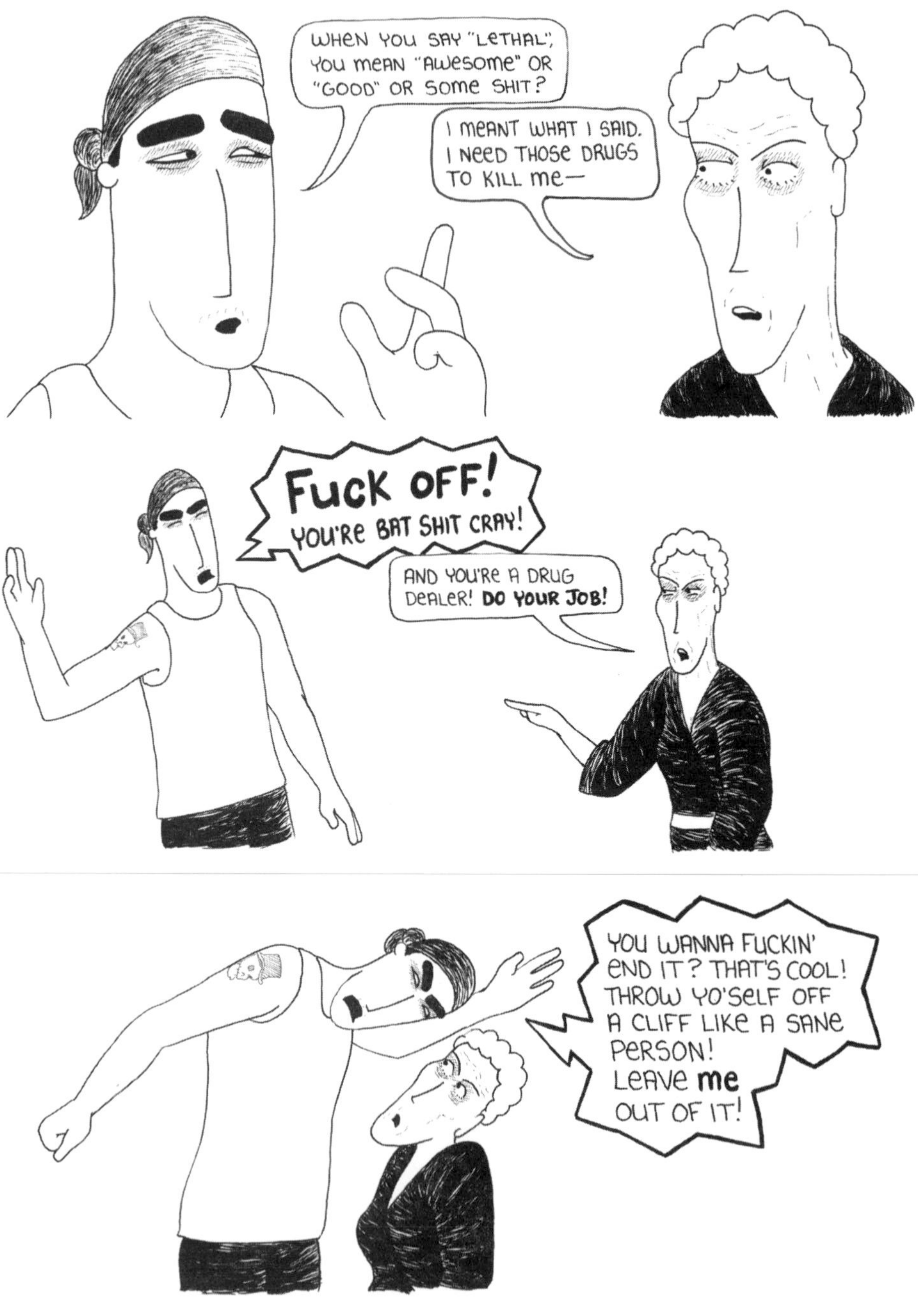
WHEN YOU SAY "LETHAL", YOU MEAN "AWESOME" OR "GOOD" OR SOME SHIT?
I MEANT WHAT I SAID. I NEED THOSE DRUGS TO KILL ME—
FUCK OFF! YOU'RE BAT SHIT CRAY!
AND YOU'RE A DRUG DEALER! **DO YOUR JOB!**
YOU WANNA FUCKIN' END IT? THAT'S COOL! THROW YO'SELF OFF A CLIFF LIKE A SANE PERSON! LEAVE **ME** OUT OF IT!

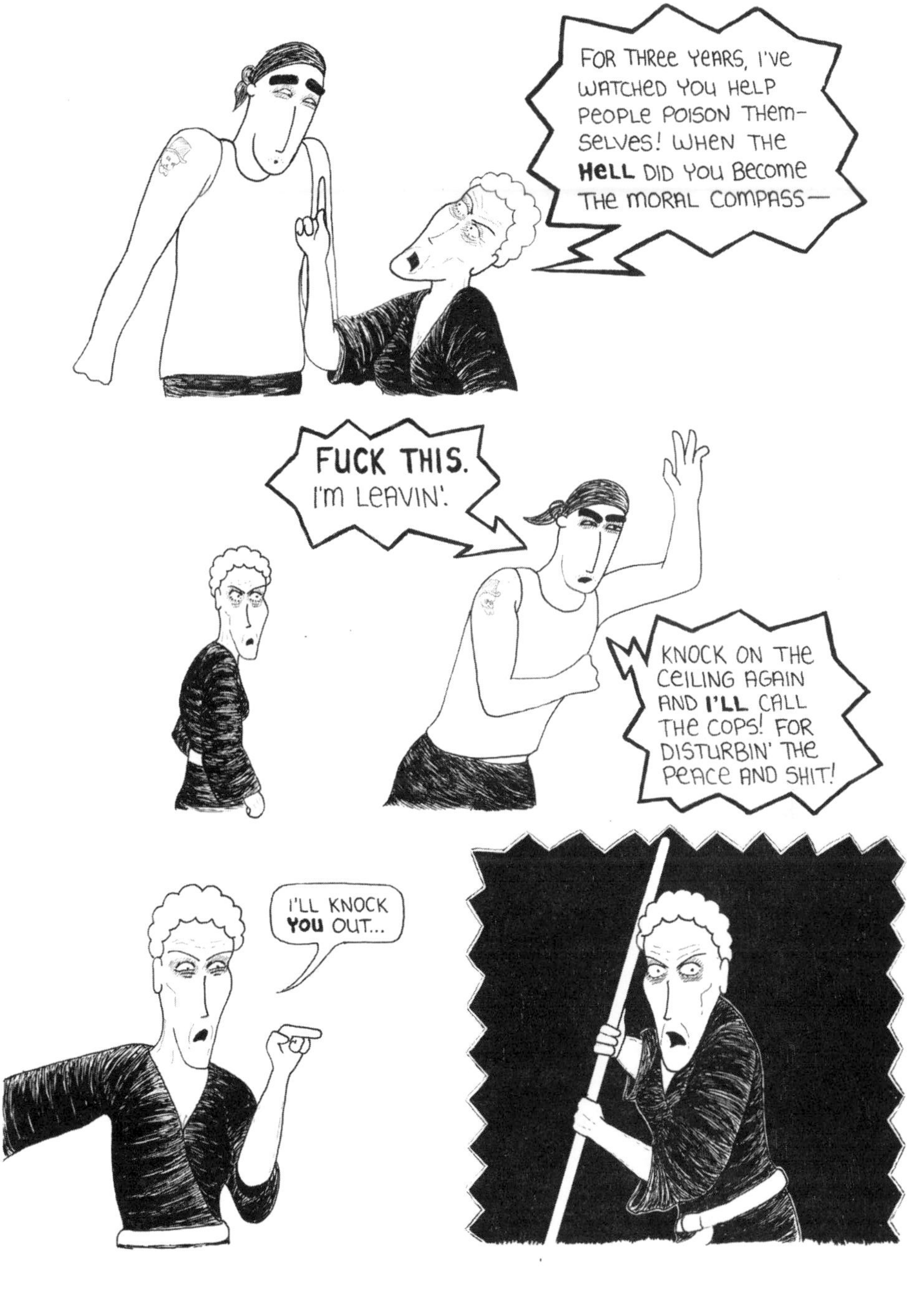
FOR THREE YEARS, I'VE WATCHED YOU HELP PEOPLE POISON THEM-SELVES! WHEN THE HELL DID YOU BECOME THE MORAL COMPASS—
FUCK THIS. I'M LEAVIN'.
KNOCK ON THE CEILING AGAIN AND I'LL CALL THE COPS! FOR DISTURBIN' THE PEACE AND SHIT!
I'LL KNOCK YOU OUT...

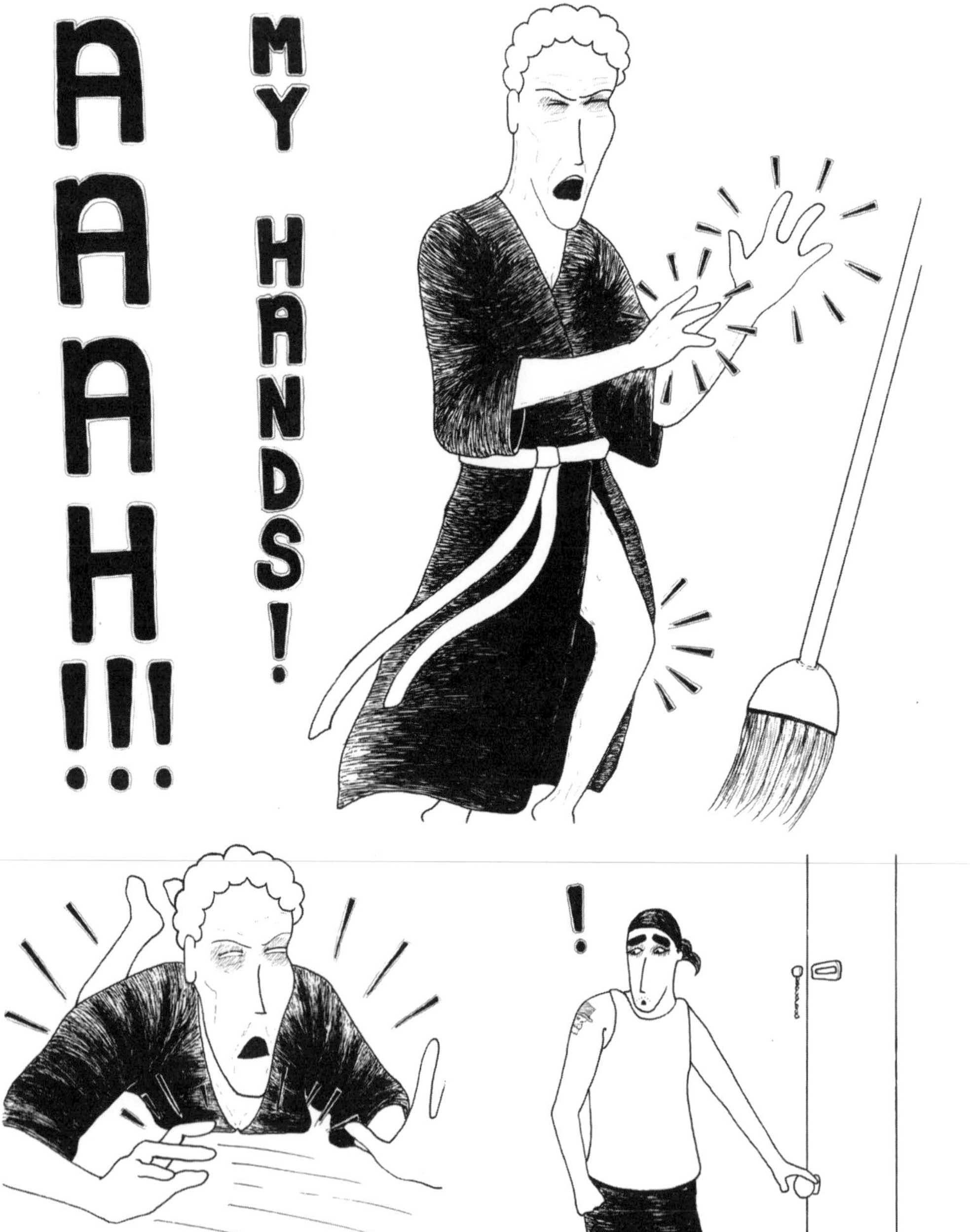
AAAH!!!
MY HANDS!
!

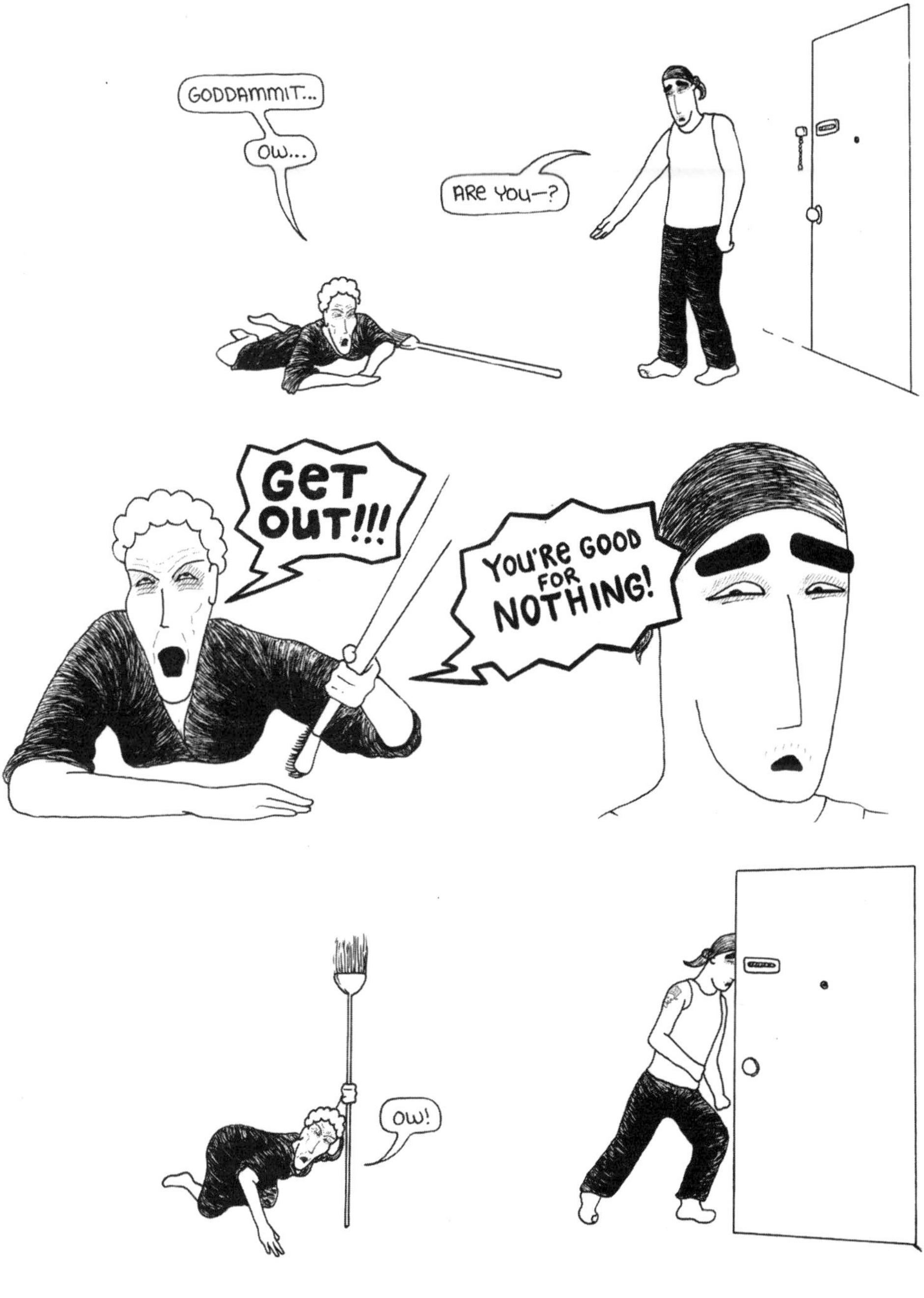
GODDAMMIT...
OW...
ARE YOU—?
GET OUT!!!
YOU'RE GOOD FOR NOTHING!
OW!

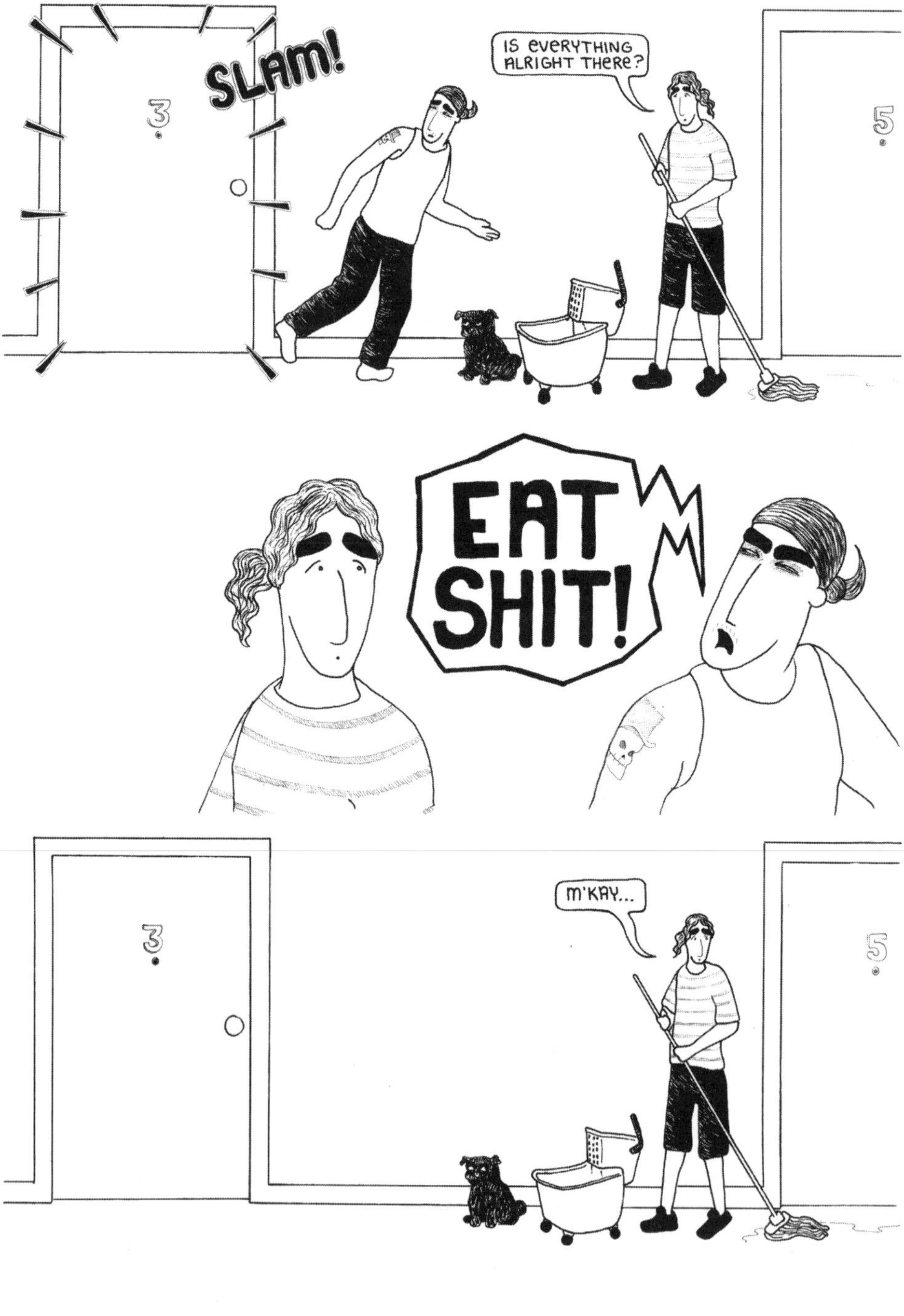
SLAM!
IS EVERYTHING ALRIGHT THERE?
3
5
EAT SHIT!
3
M'KAY...
5

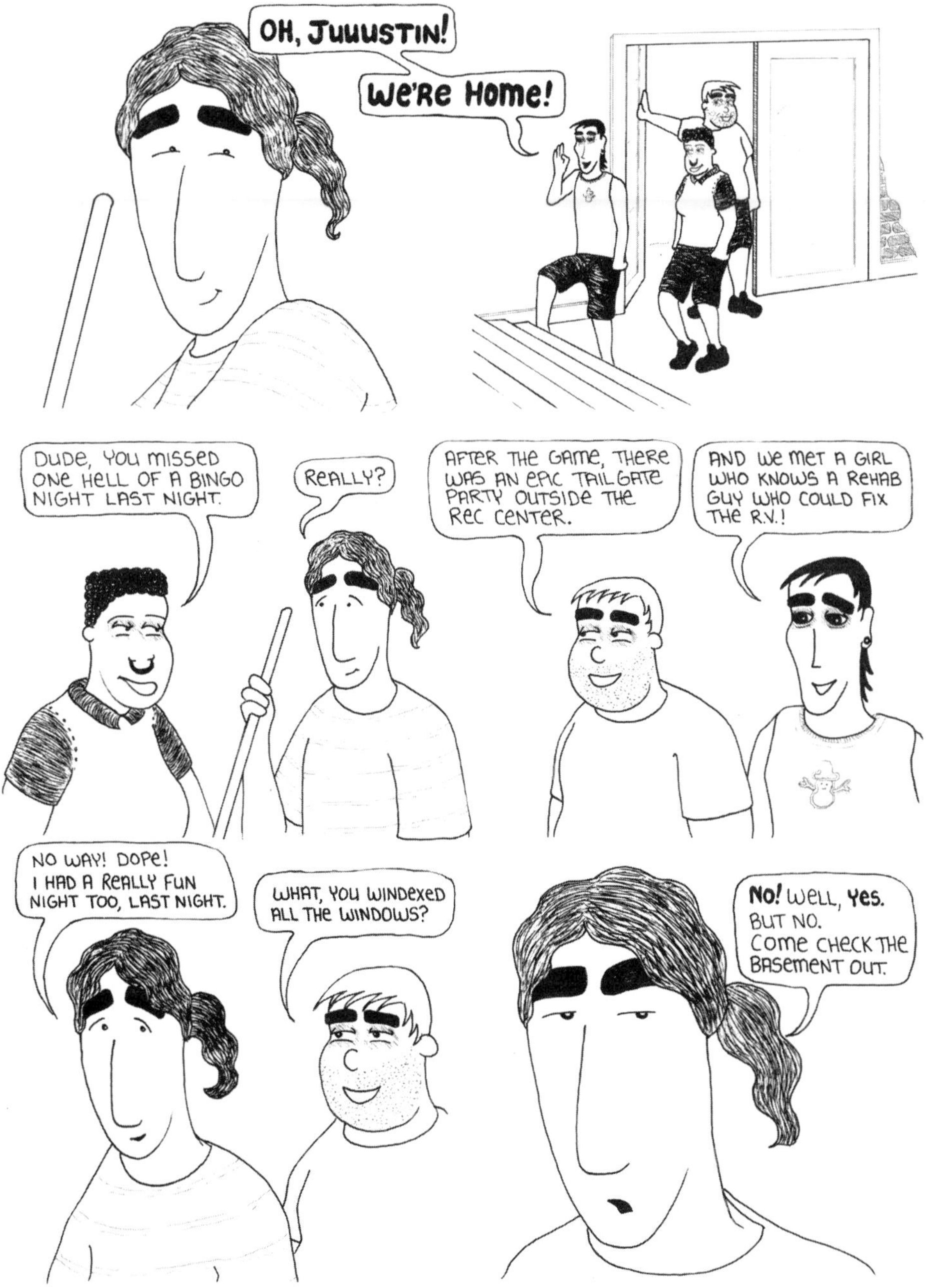
OH, JUUUSTIN!
WE'RE HOME!
DUDE, YOU MISSED ONE HELL OF A BINGO NIGHT LAST NIGHT.
REALLY?
AFTER THE GAME, THERE WAS AN EPIC TAILGATE PARTY OUTSIDE THE REC CENTER.
AND WE MET A GIRL WHO KNOWS A REHAB GUY WHO COULD FIX THE R.V.!
NO WAY! DOPE! I HAD A REALLY FUN NIGHT TOO, LAST NIGHT.
WHAT, YOU WINDEXED ALL THE WINDOWS?
NO! WELL, YES. BUT NO. COME CHECK THE BASEMENT OUT.

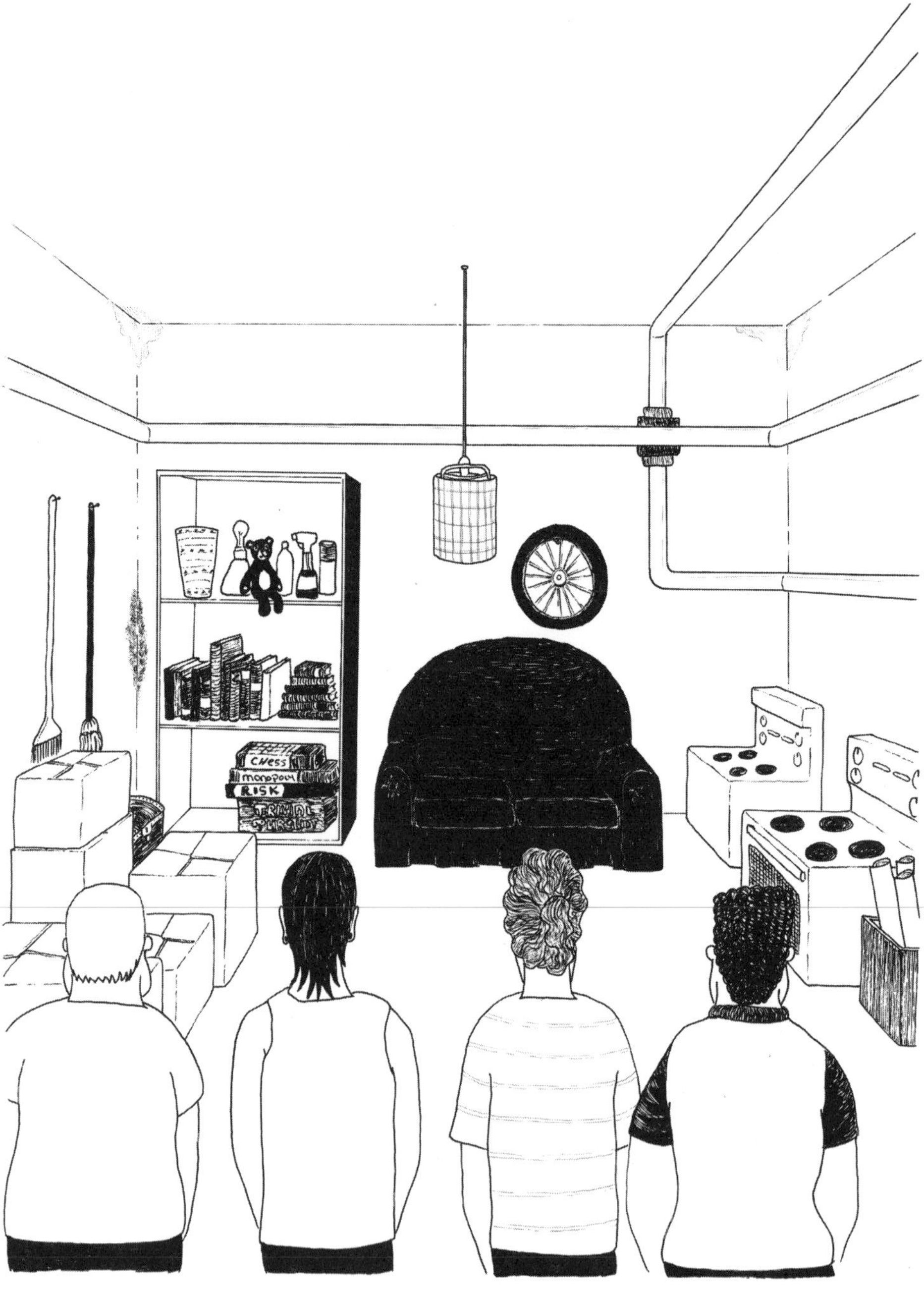
CHESS
monopoly
RISK
TRIVIAL

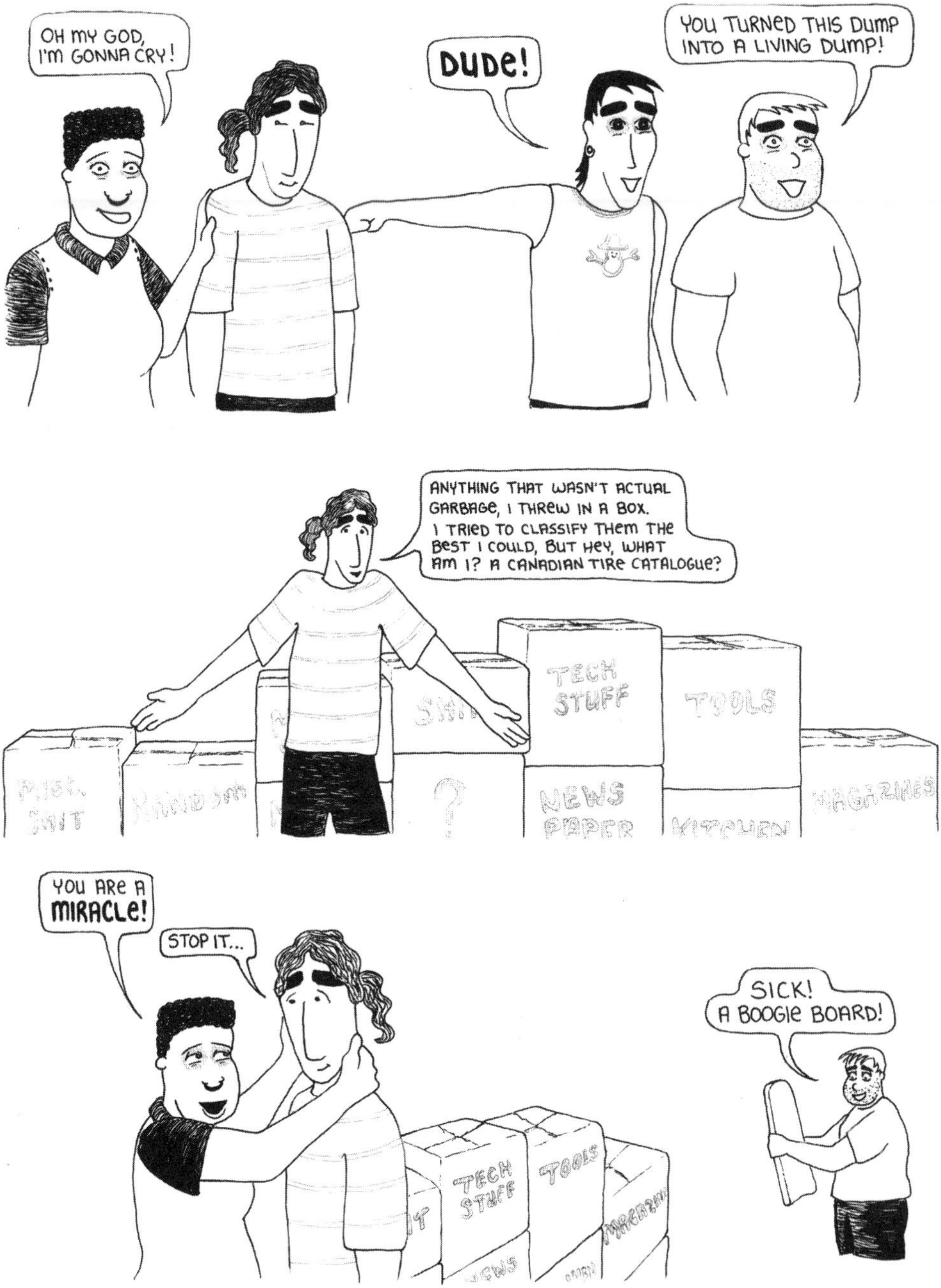
OH MY GOD, I'M GONNA CRY!
DUDE!
YOU TURNED THIS DUMP INTO A LIVING DUMP!
ANYTHING THAT WASN'T ACTUAL GARBAGE, I THREW IN A BOX. I TRIED TO CLASSIFY THEM THE BEST I COULD, BUT HEY, WHAT AM I? A CANADIAN TIRE CATALOGUE?
TECH STUFF
TOOLS
NEWS PAPER
KITCHEN
YOU ARE A MIRACLE!
STOP IT...
TECH STUFF
TOOLS
SICK! A BOOGIE BOARD!

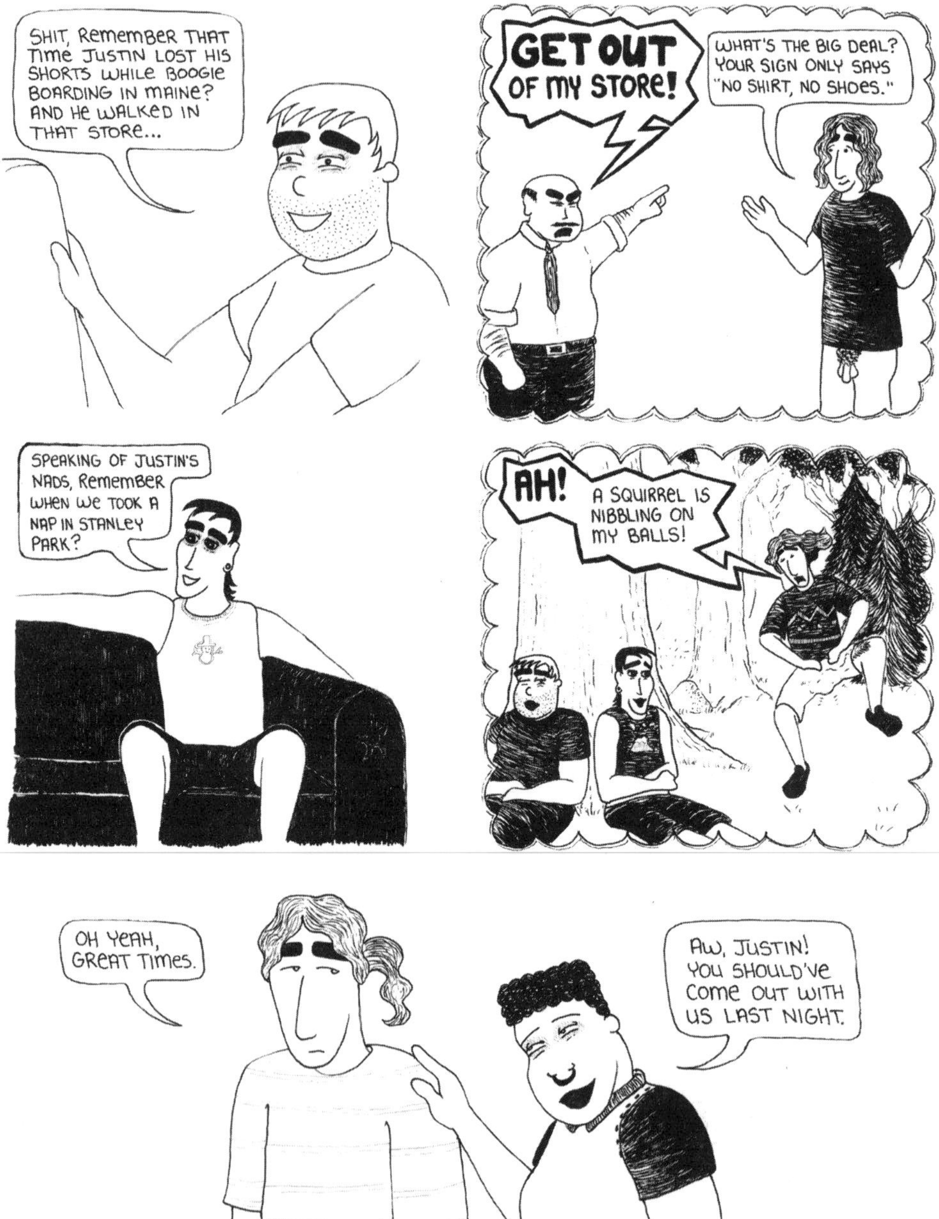
SHIT, REMEMBER THAT TIME JUSTIN LOST HIS SHORTS WHILE BOOGIE BOARDING IN MAINE? AND HE WALKED IN THAT STORE...
GET OUT OF MY STORE!
WHAT'S THE BIG DEAL? YOUR SIGN ONLY SAYS "NO SHIRT, NO SHOES."
SPEAKING OF JUSTIN'S NADS, REMEMBER WHEN WE TOOK A NAP IN STANLEY PARK?
AH!
A SQUIRREL IS NIBBLING ON MY BALLS!
OH YEAH, GREAT TIMES.
AW, JUSTIN! YOU SHOULD'VE COME OUT WITH US LAST NIGHT.

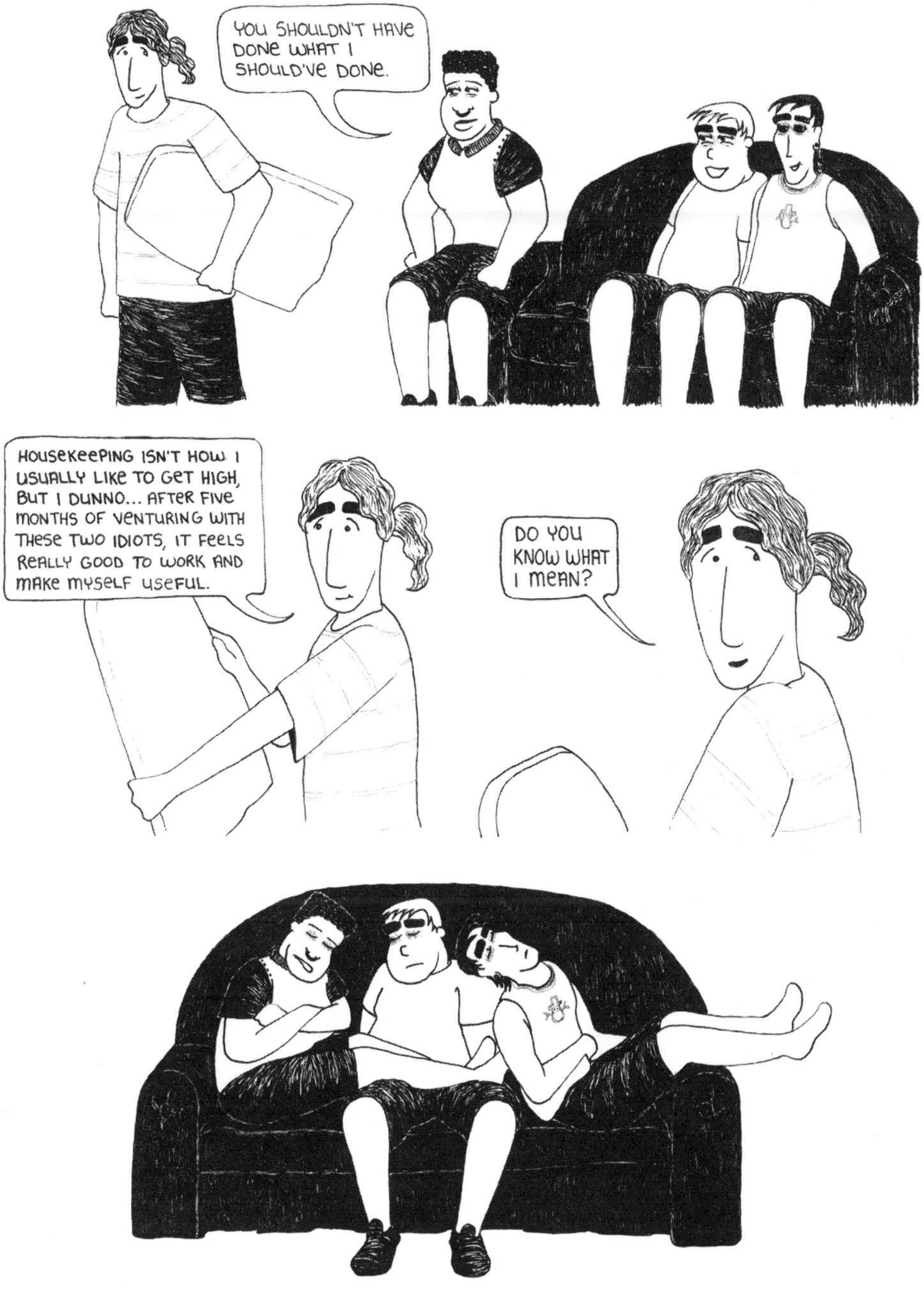
YOU SHOULDN'T HAVE DONE WHAT I SHOULD'VE DONE.
HOUSEKEEPING ISN'T HOW I USUALLY LIKE TO GET HIGH, BUT I DUNNO... AFTER FIVE MONTHS OF VENTURING WITH THESE TWO IDIOTS, IT FEELS REALLY GOOD TO WORK AND MAKE MYSELF USEFUL.
DO YOU KNOW WHAT I MEAN?

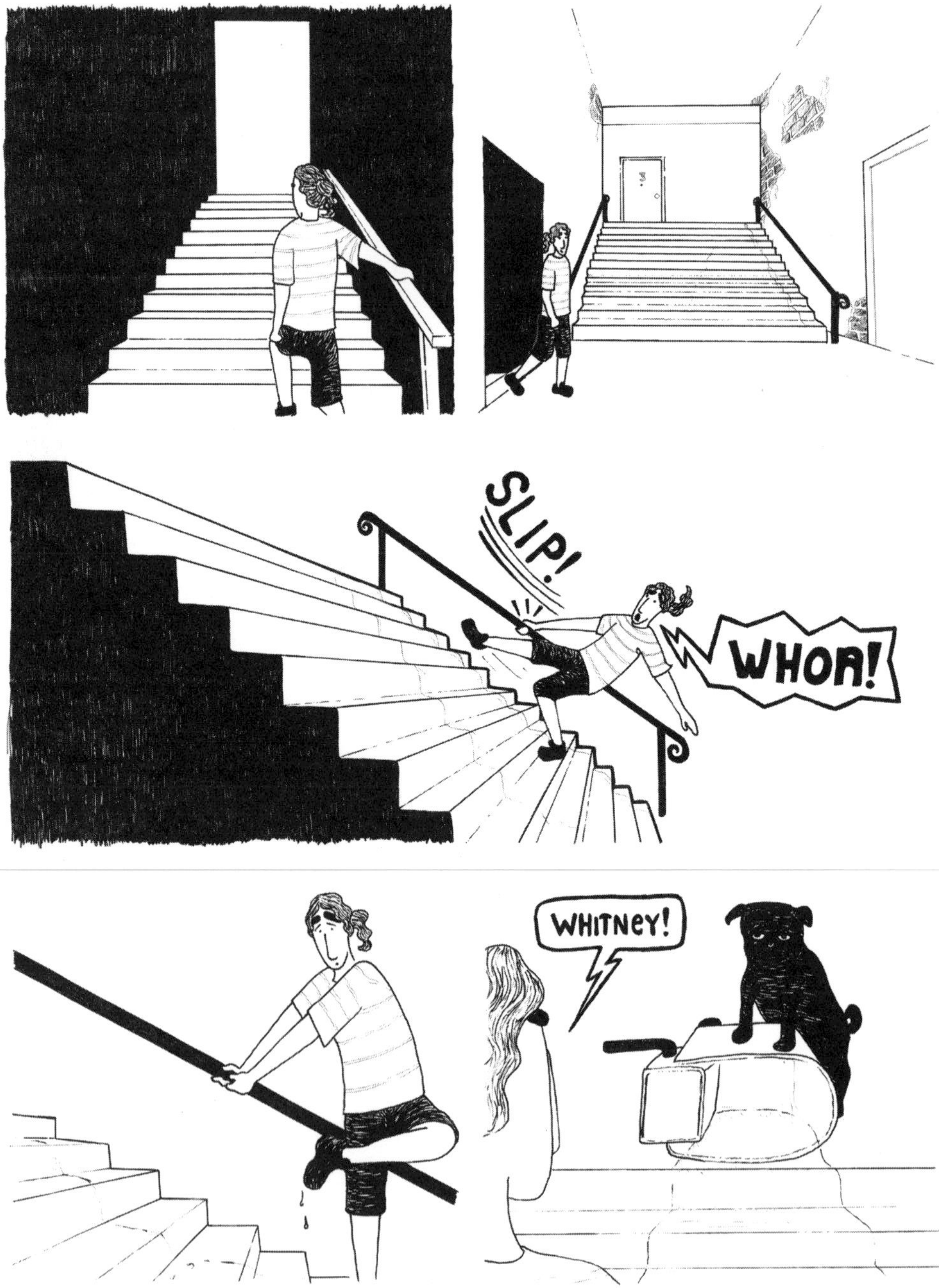
SLIP!
WHOA!
WHITNEY!

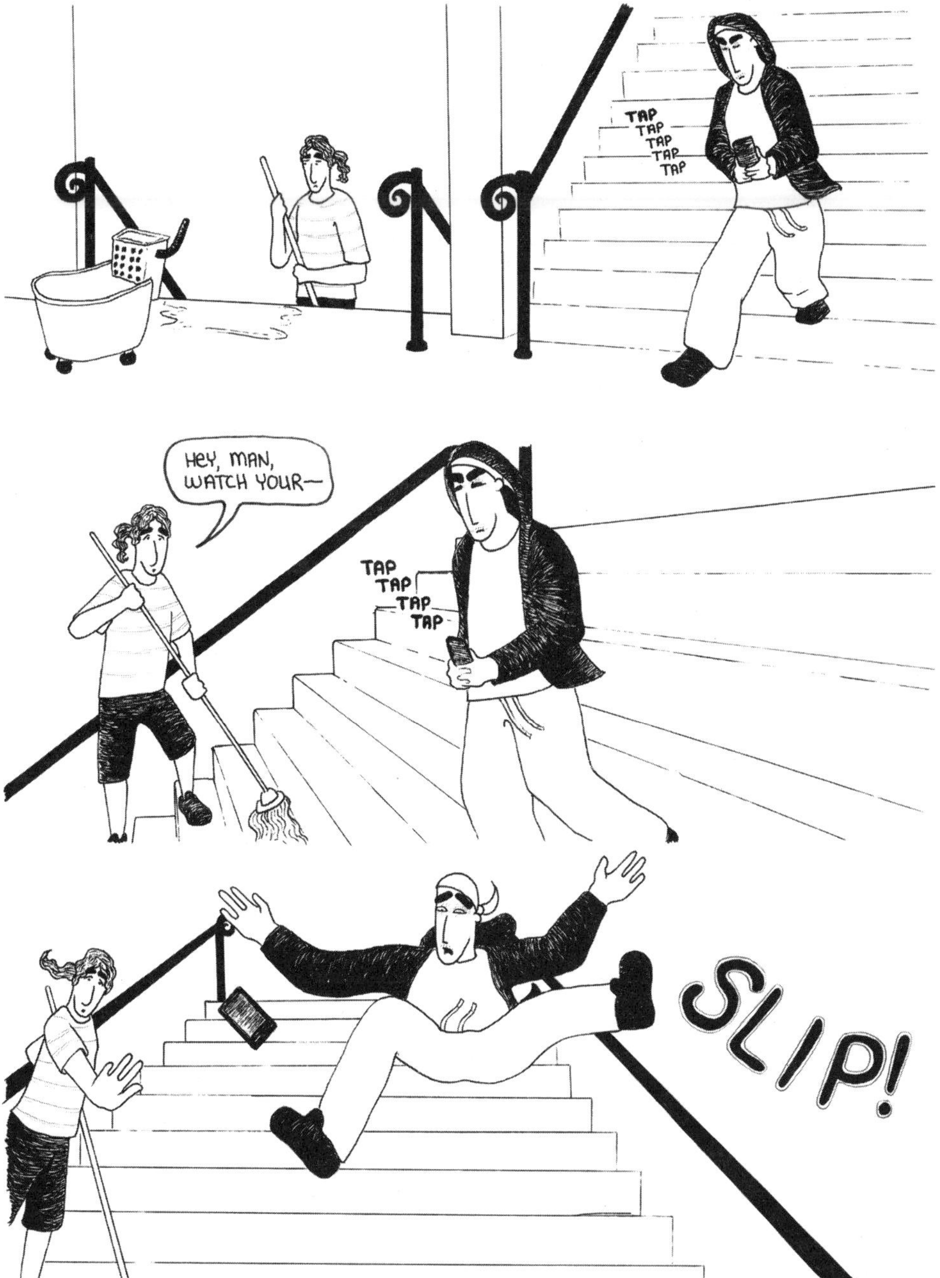
TAP
TAP
TAP
TAP
TAP
HEY, MAN, WATCH YOUR—
TAP
TAP
TAP
TAP
SLIP!

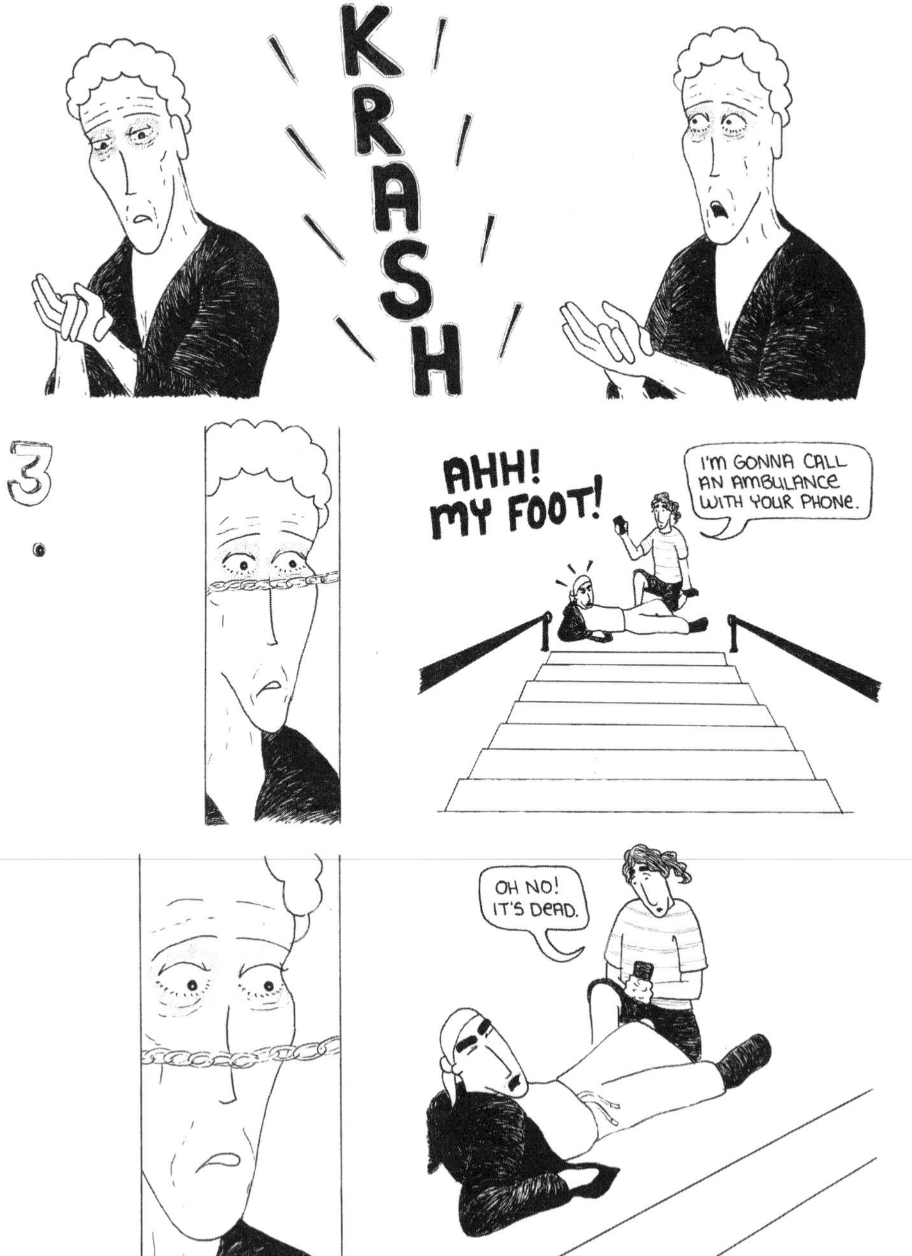
KRASH
3.
AHH! MY FOOT!
I'M GONNA CALL AN AMBULANCE WITH YOUR PHONE.
OH NO! IT'S DEAD.

CHAPTER 6

fluid -
Tom
Tyler
9:17

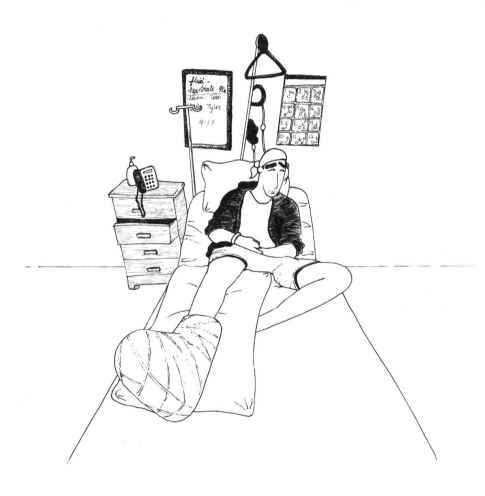

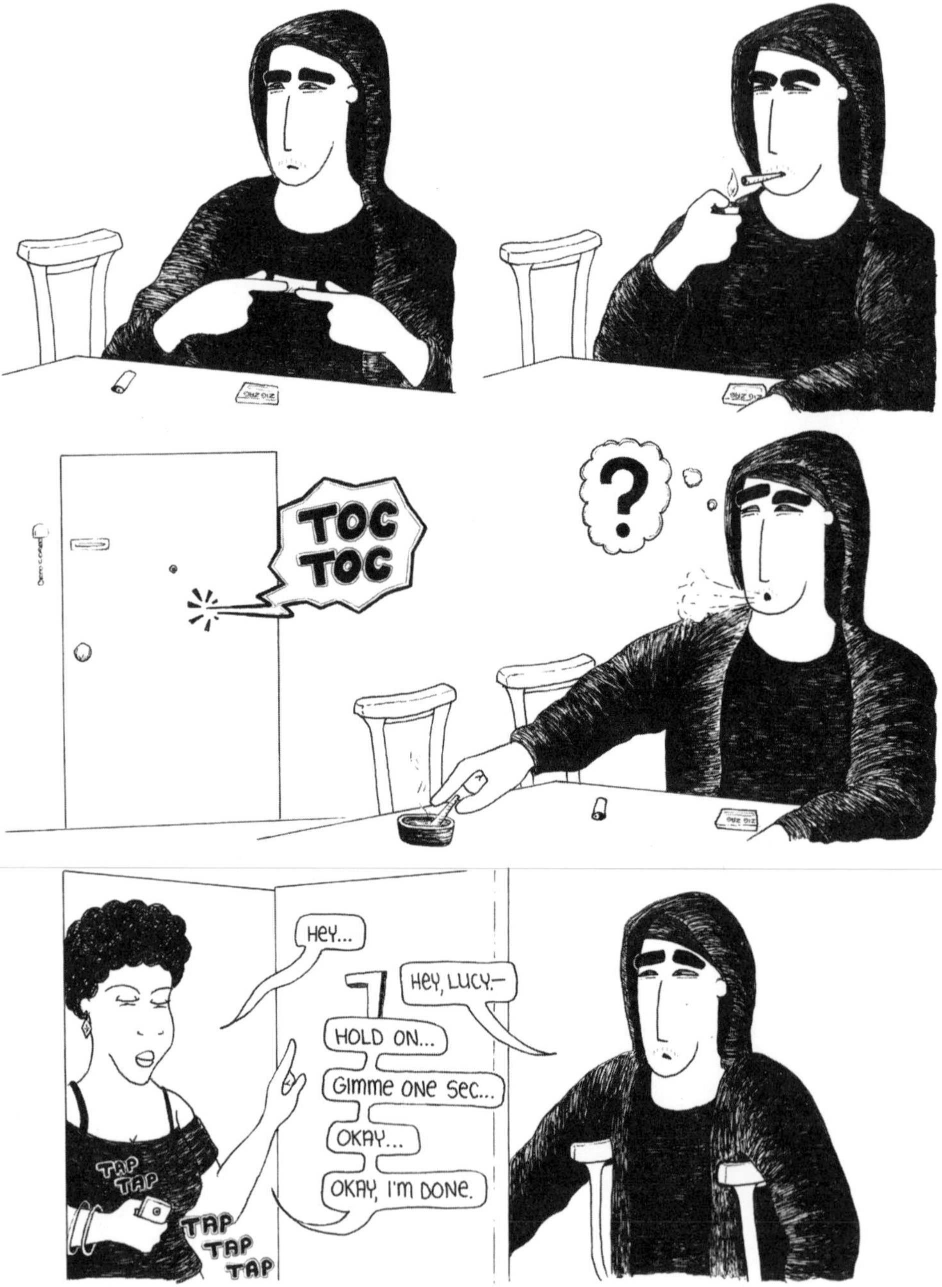
TOC
TOC
?
HEY...
HEY, LUCY.–
HOLD ON...
GIMME ONE SEC...
OKAY...
OKAY, I'M DONE.
TAP
TAP
TAP
TAP
TAP

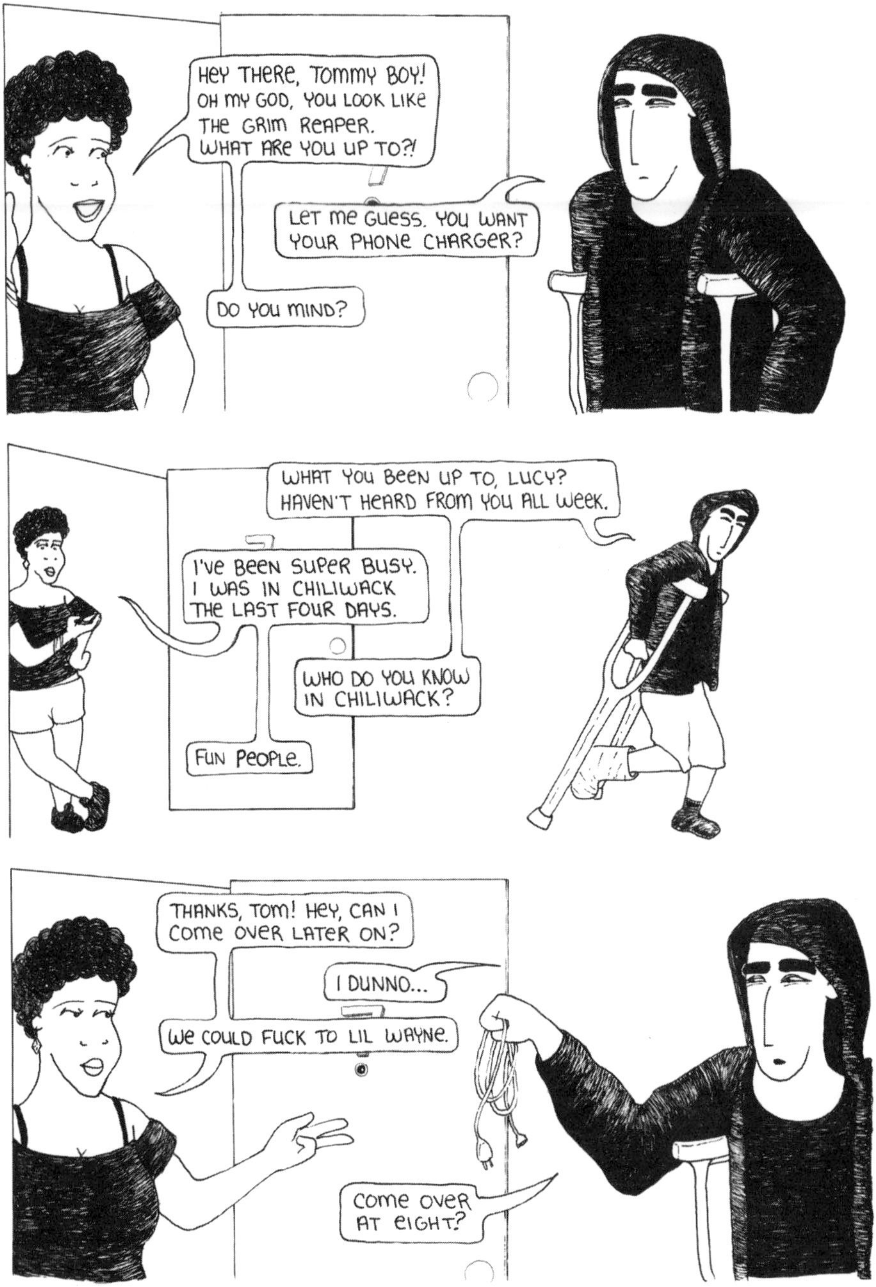
HEY THERE, TOMMY BOY! OH MY GOD, YOU LOOK LIKE THE GRIM REAPER. WHAT ARE YOU UP TO?!
LET ME GUESS. YOU WANT YOUR PHONE CHARGER?
DO YOU MIND?
WHAT YOU BEEN UP TO, LUCY? HAVEN'T HEARD FROM YOU ALL WEEK.
I'VE BEEN SUPER BUSY. I WAS IN CHILIWACK THE LAST FOUR DAYS.
WHO DO YOU KNOW IN CHILIWACK?
FUN PEOPLE.
THANKS, TOM! HEY, CAN I COME OVER LATER ON?
I DUNNO...
WE COULD FUCK TO LIL WAYNE.
COME OVER AT EIGHT?

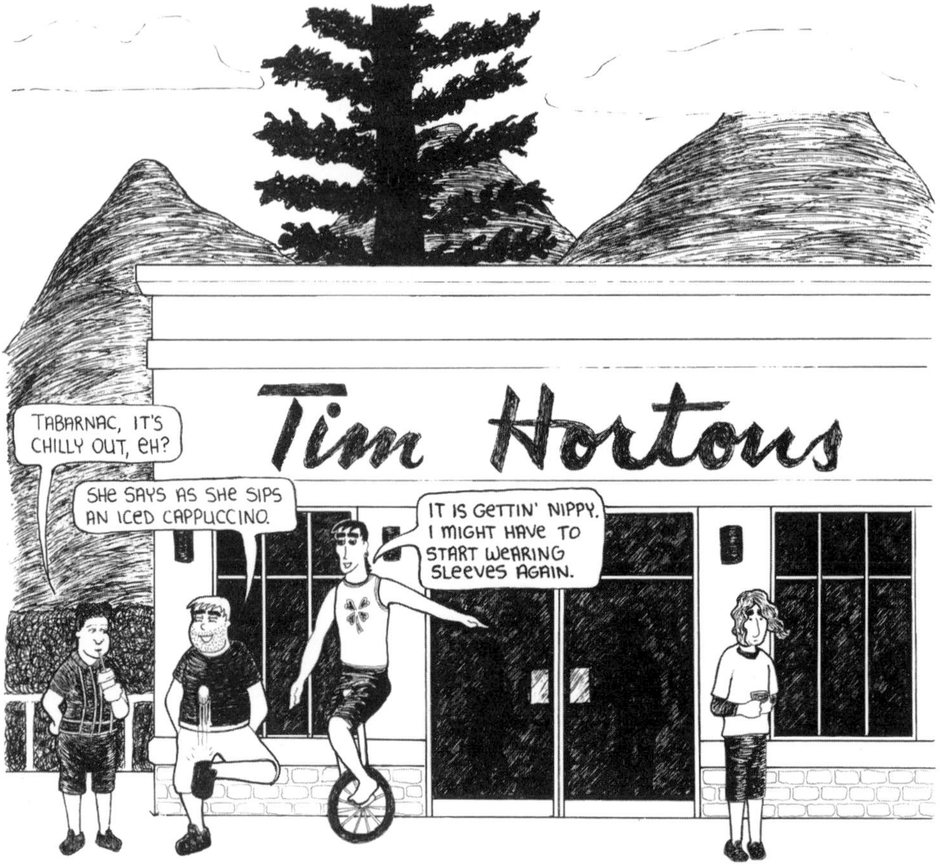
TABARNAC, IT'S CHILLY OUT, EH?
SHE SAYS AS SHE SIPS AN ICED CAPPUCCINO.
IT IS GETTIN' NIPPY. I MIGHT HAVE TO START WEARING SLEEVES AGAIN.
Tim Hortons

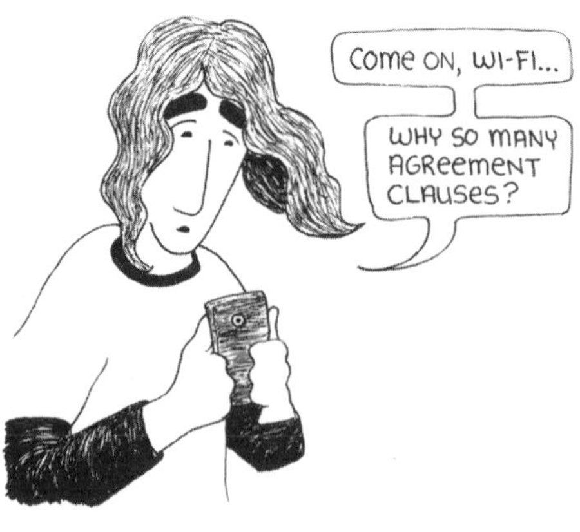
COME ON, WI-FI...
WHY SO MANY AGREEMENT CLAUSES?

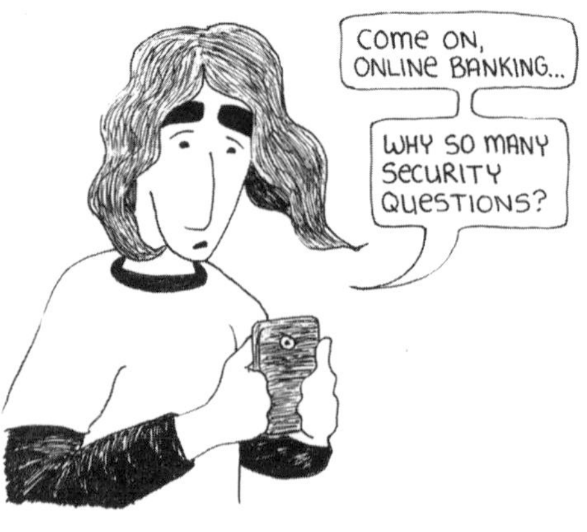
COME ON, ONLINE BANKING...
WHY SO MANY SECURITY QUESTIONS?

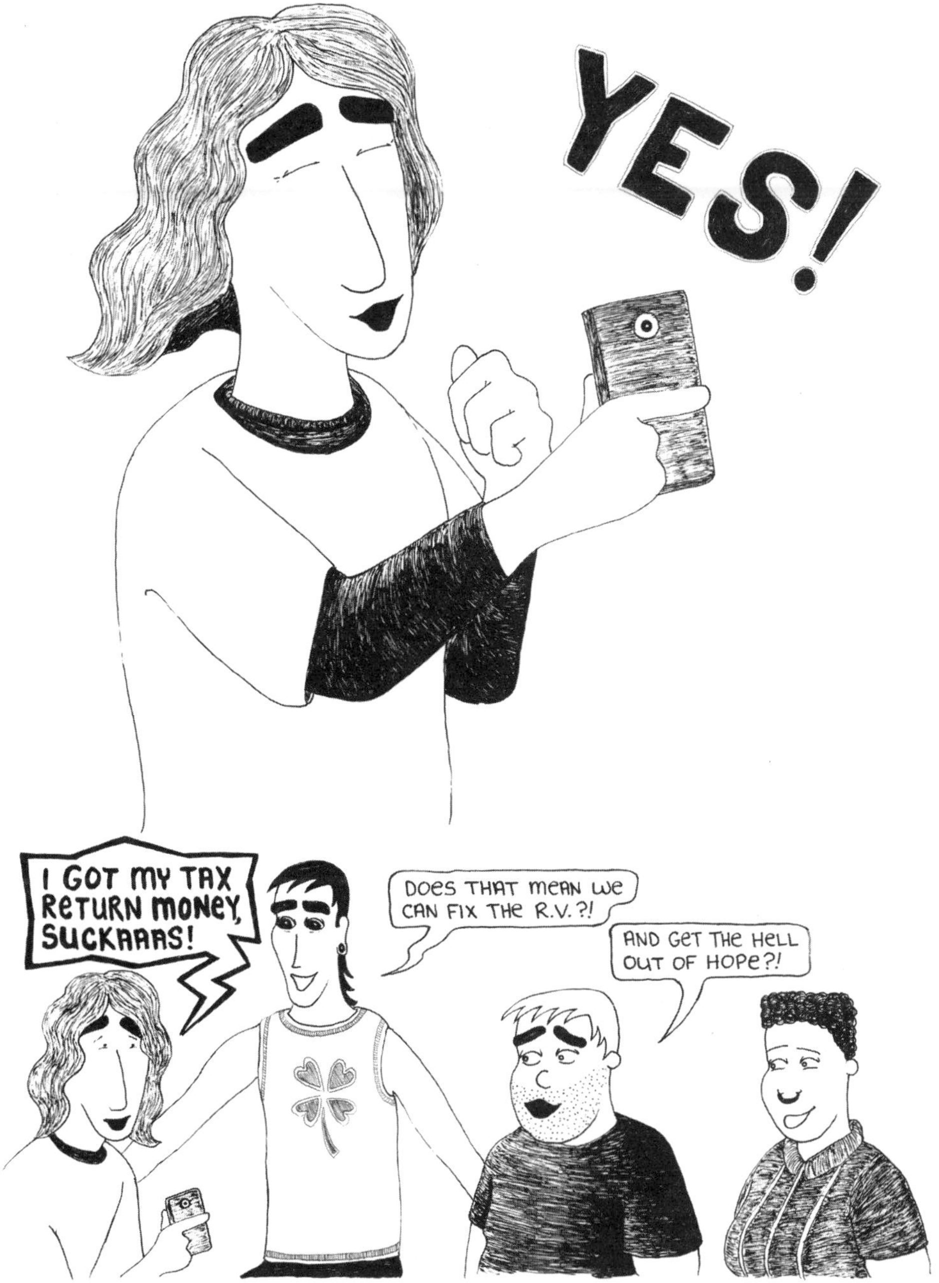
YES!
I GOT MY TAX RETURN MONEY, SUCKAAAS!
DOES THAT MEAN WE CAN FIX THE R.V.?!
AND GET THE HELL OUT OF HOPE?!

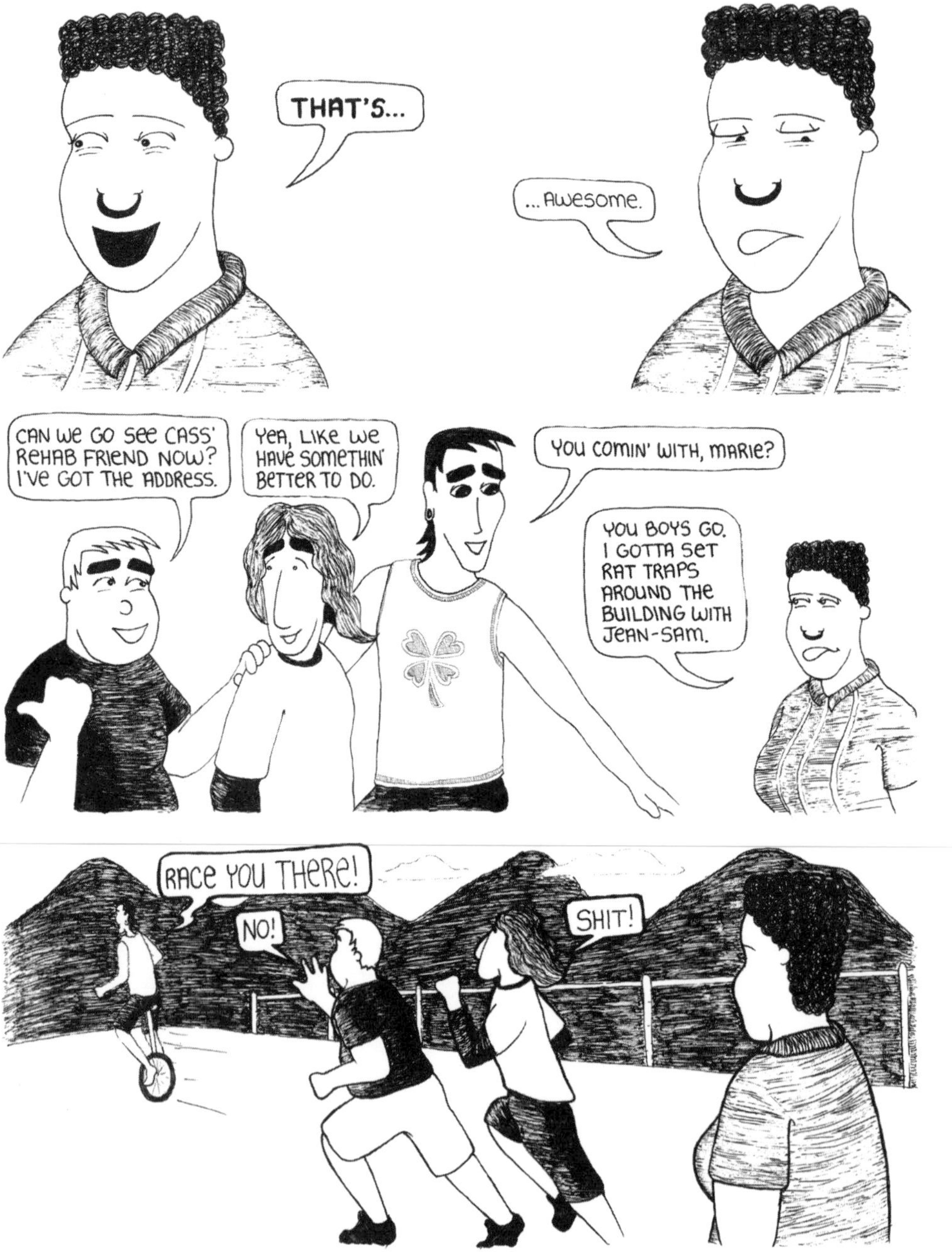
THAT'S...
...AWESOME.
CAN WE GO SEE CASS' REHAB FRIEND NOW? I'VE GOT THE ADDRESS.
YEA, LIKE WE HAVE SOMETHIN' BETTER TO DO.
YOU COMIN' WITH, MARIE?
YOU BOYS GO. I GOTTA SET RAT TRAPS AROUND THE BUILDING WITH JEAN-SAM.
RACE YOU THERE!
NO!
SHIT!

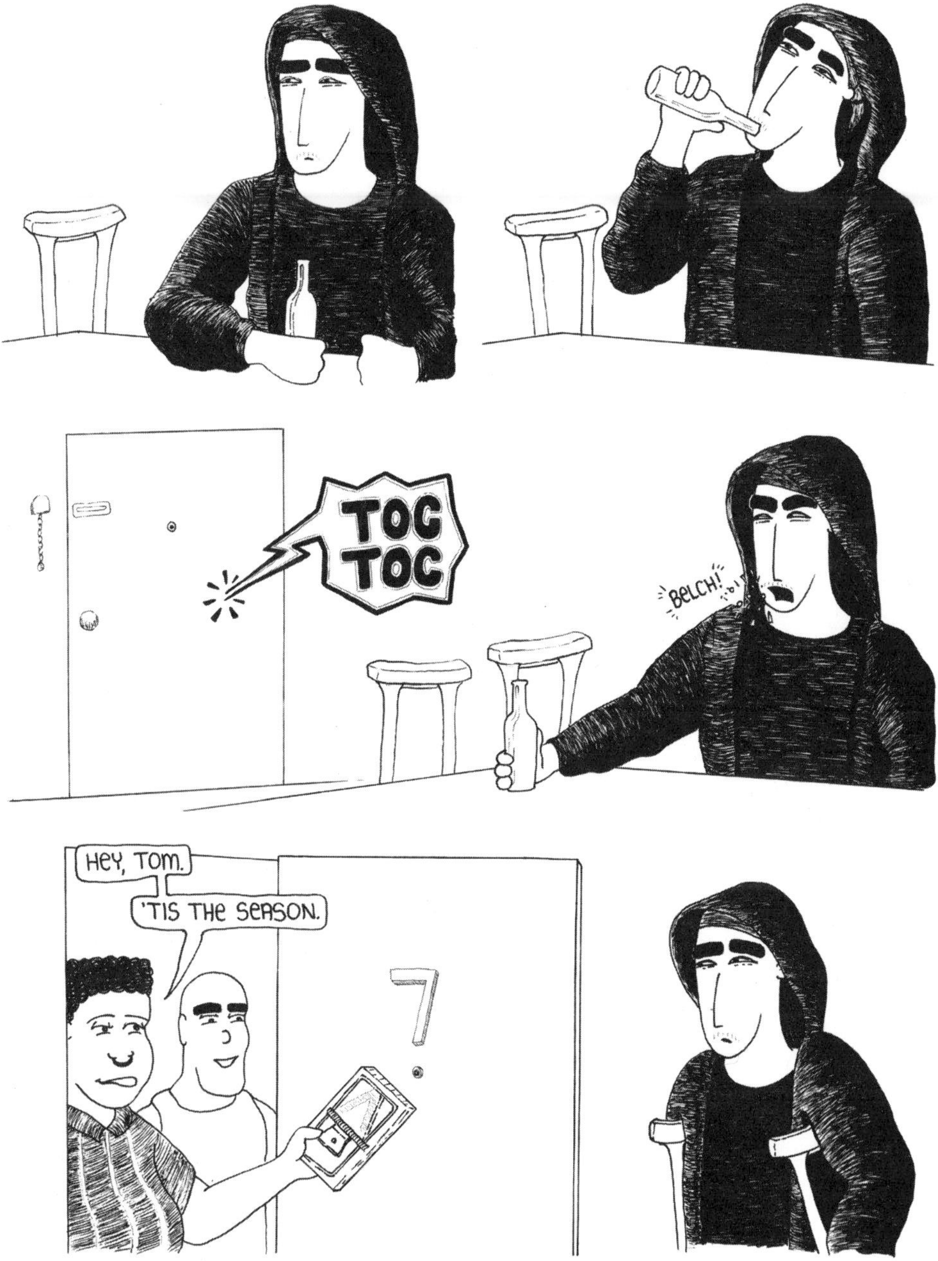
TOC
TOC
BELCH!
HEY, TOM.
'TIS THE SEASON.
7

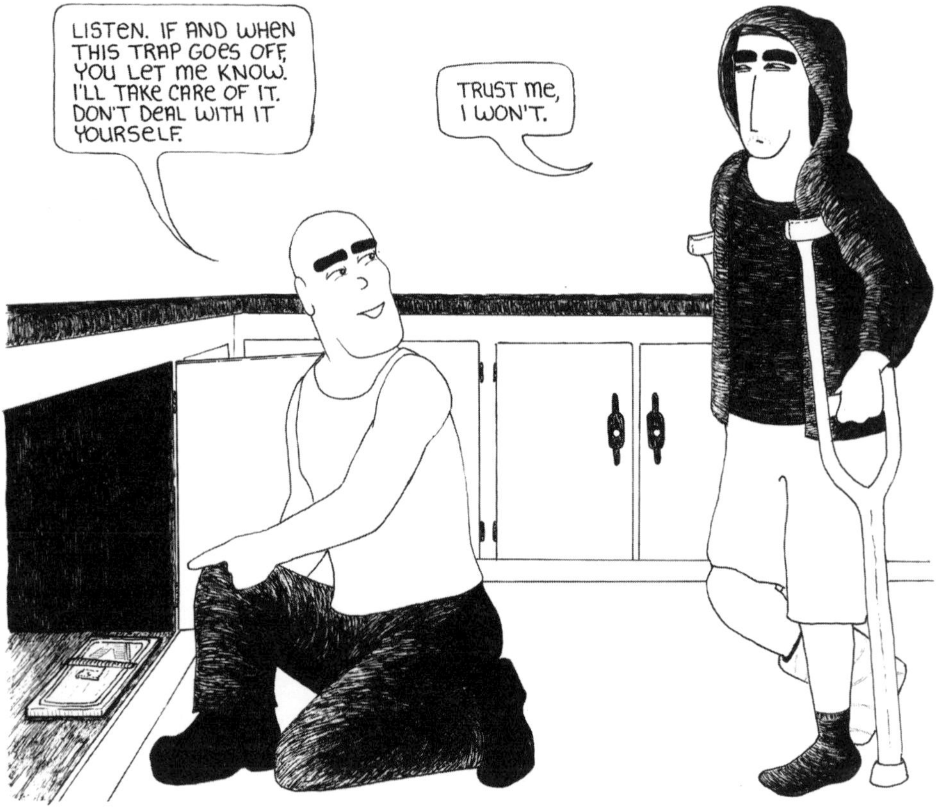
LISTEN. IF AND WHEN THIS TRAP GOES OFF, YOU LET ME KNOW. I'LL TAKE CARE OF IT. DON'T DEAL WITH IT YOURSELF.
TRUST ME, I WON'T.

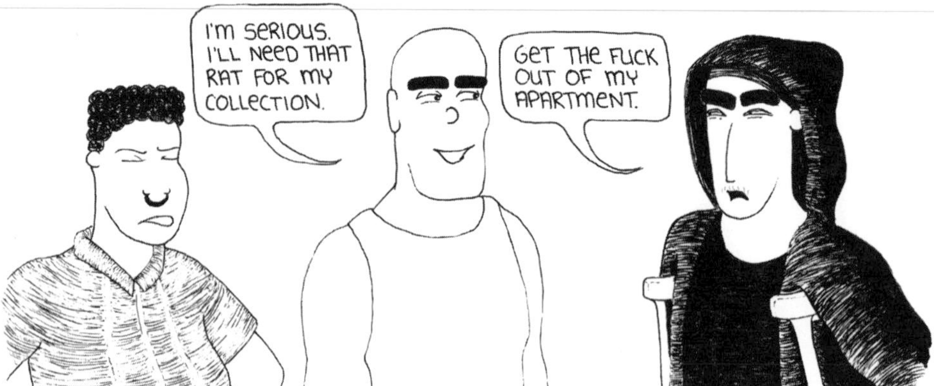
I'M SERIOUS. I'LL NEED THAT RAT FOR MY COLLECTION.
GET THE FUCK OUT OF MY APARTMENT.

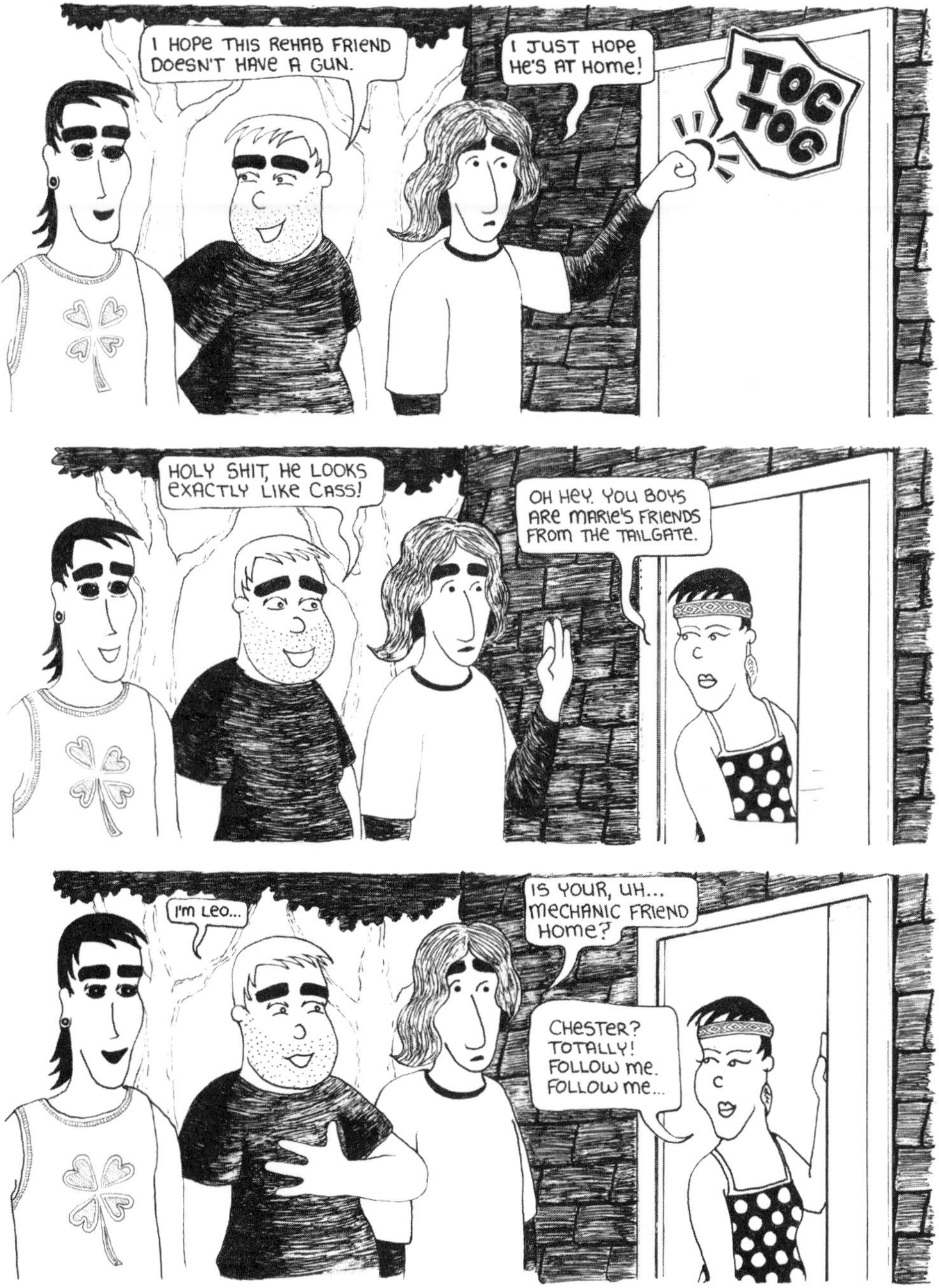
I HOPE THIS REHAB FRIEND DOESN'T HAVE A GUN.
I JUST HOPE HE'S AT HOME!
TOC TOC
HOLY SHIT, HE LOOKS EXACTLY LIKE CASS!
OH HEY. YOU BOYS ARE MARIE'S FRIENDS FROM THE TAILGATE.
I'M LEO...
IS YOUR, UH... MECHANIC FRIEND HOME?
CHESTER? TOTALLY! FOLLOW ME. FOLLOW ME...

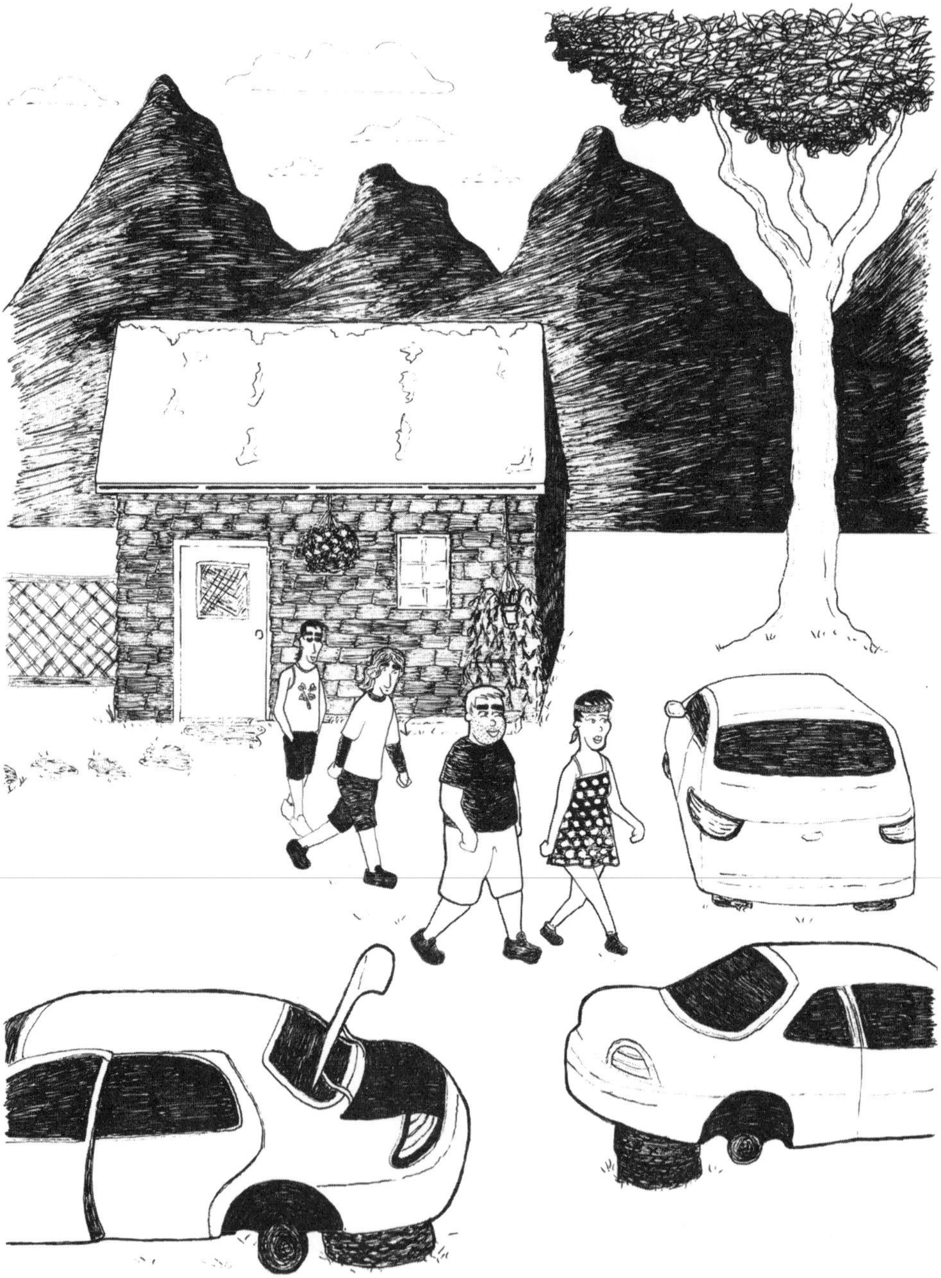

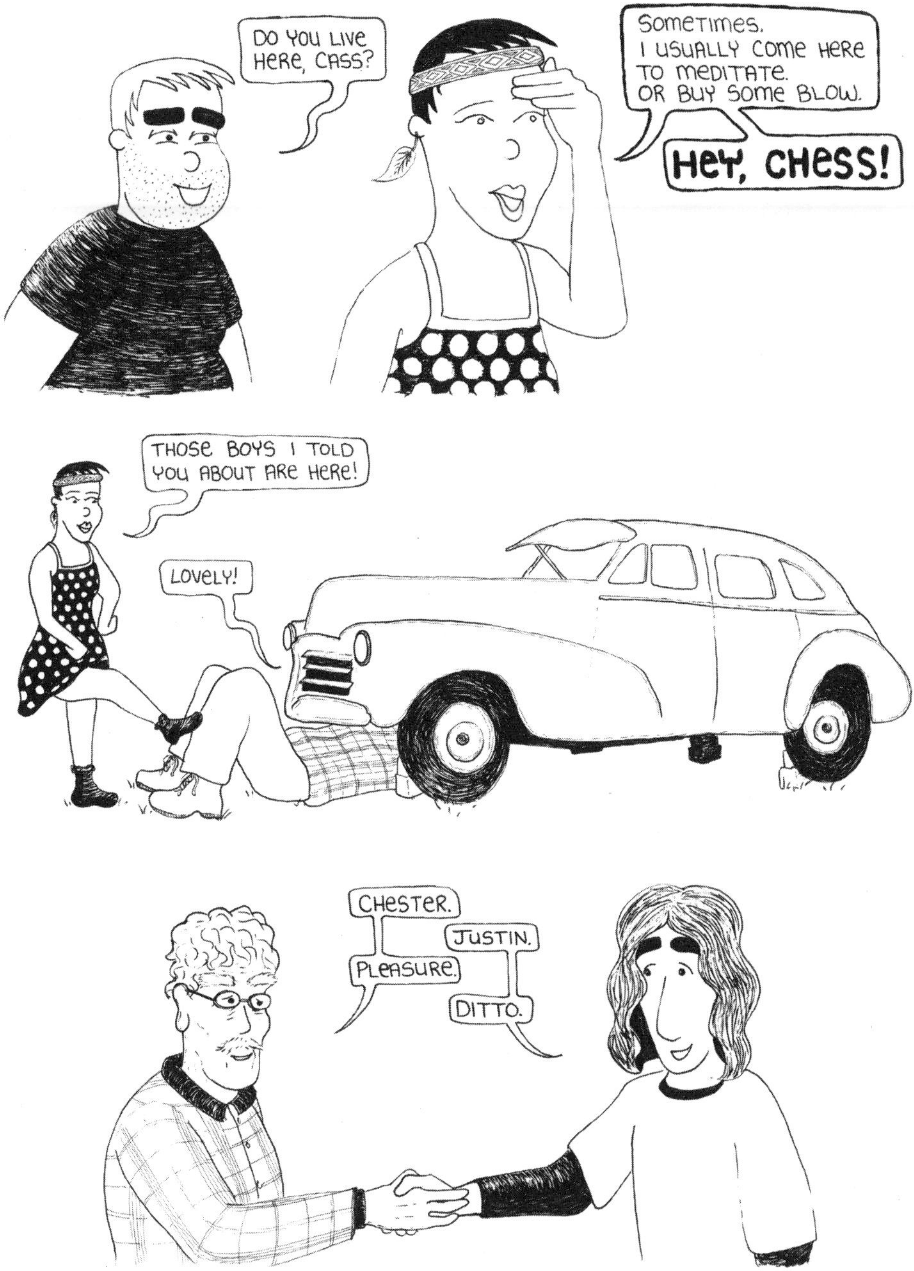
DO YOU LIVE HERE, CASS?
SOMETIMES. I USUALLY COME HERE TO MEDITATE. OR BUY SOME BLOW.
HEY, CHESS!
THOSE BOYS I TOLD YOU ABOUT ARE HERE!
LOVELY!
CHESTER.
JUSTIN.
PLEASURE.
DITTO.

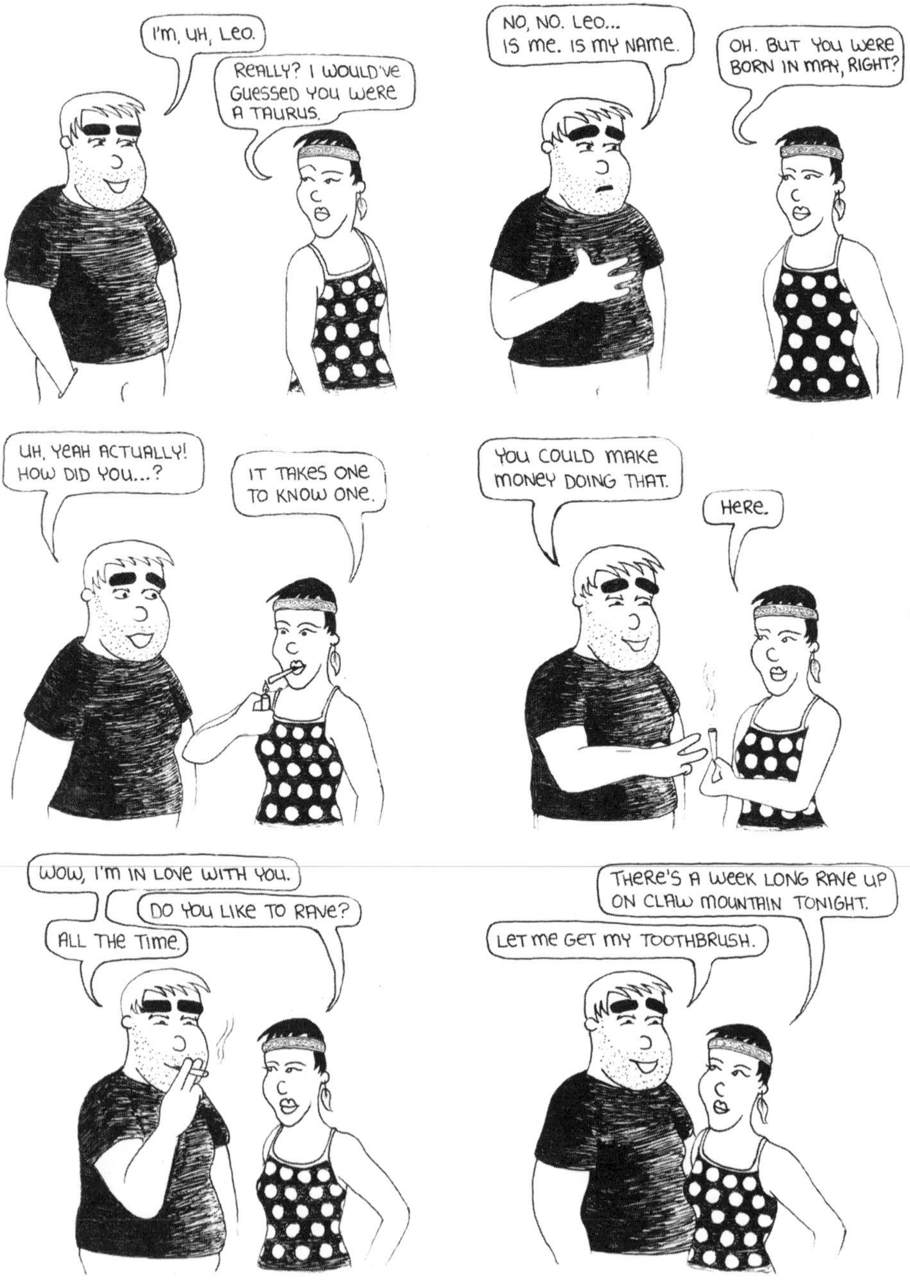
I'M, UH, LEO.
REALLY? I WOULD'VE GUESSED YOU WERE A TAURUS.
NO, NO. LEO... IS ME. IS MY NAME.
OH. BUT YOU WERE BORN IN MAY, RIGHT?
UH, YEAH ACTUALLY! HOW DID YOU...?
IT TAKES ONE TO KNOW ONE.
YOU COULD MAKE MONEY DOING THAT.
HERE.
WOW, I'M IN LOVE WITH YOU.
DO YOU LIKE TO RAVE?
ALL THE TIME.
THERE'S A WEEK LONG RAVE UP ON CLAW MOUNTAIN TONIGHT.
LET ME GET MY TOOTHBRUSH.

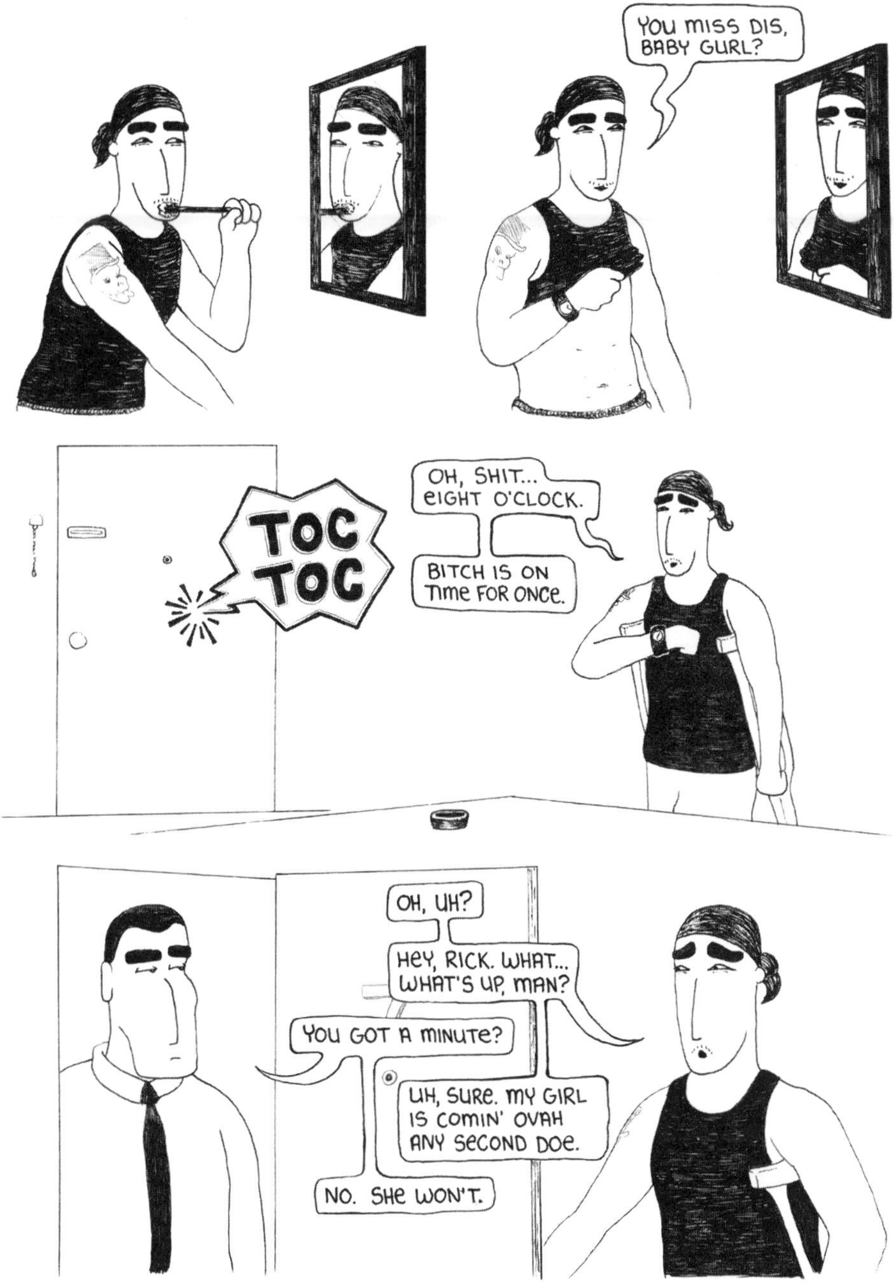

YOU MISS DIS, BABY GURL?
TOC TOC
OH, SHIT... EIGHT O'CLOCK.
BITCH IS ON TIME FOR ONCE.
OH, UH?
HEY, RICK. WHAT... WHAT'S UP, MAN?
YOU GOT A MINUTE?
UH, SURE. MY GIRL IS COMIN' OVAH ANY SECOND DOE.
NO. SHE WON'T.

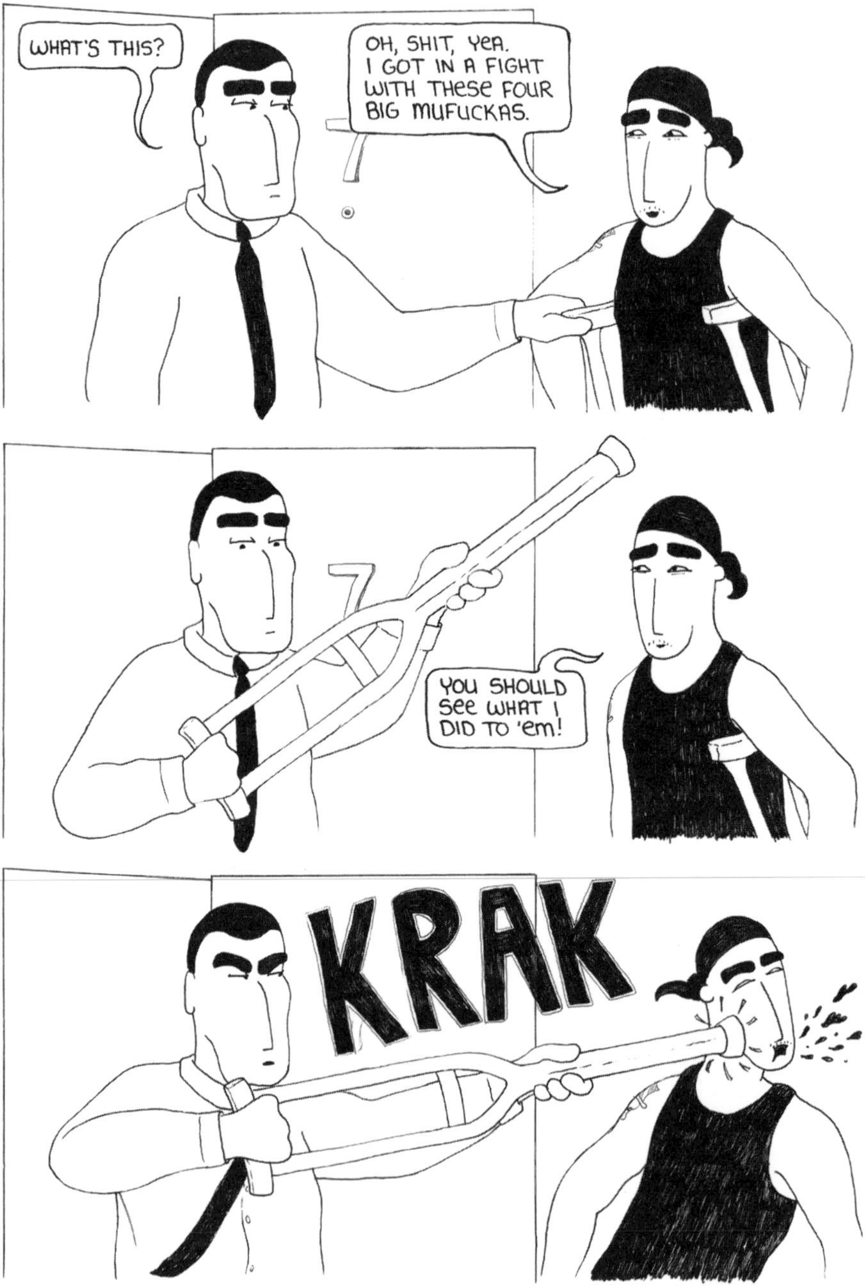
WHAT'S THIS?
OH, SHIT, YEA. I GOT IN A FIGHT WITH THESE FOUR BIG MUFUCKAS.
YOU SHOULD SEE WHAT I DID TO 'EM!
KRAK

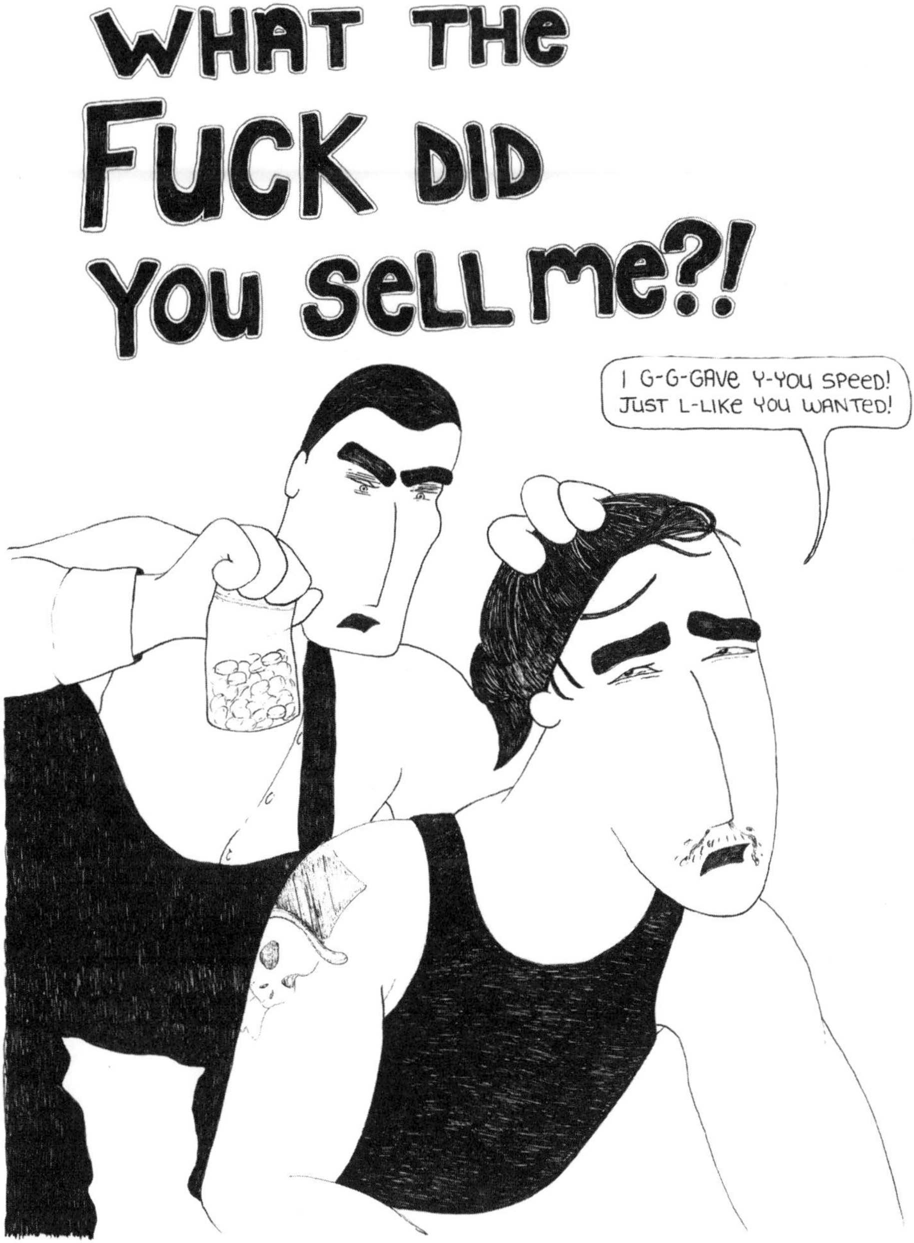
WHAT THE FUCK DID YOU SELL ME?!
I G-G-GAVE Y-YOU SPEED! JUST L-LIKE YOU WANTED!

BULL! YOU SOLD me SHIT PILLS! YOU THINK I'M A CHUMP?!

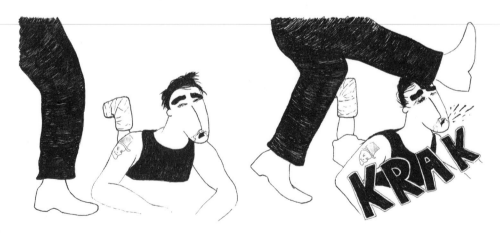

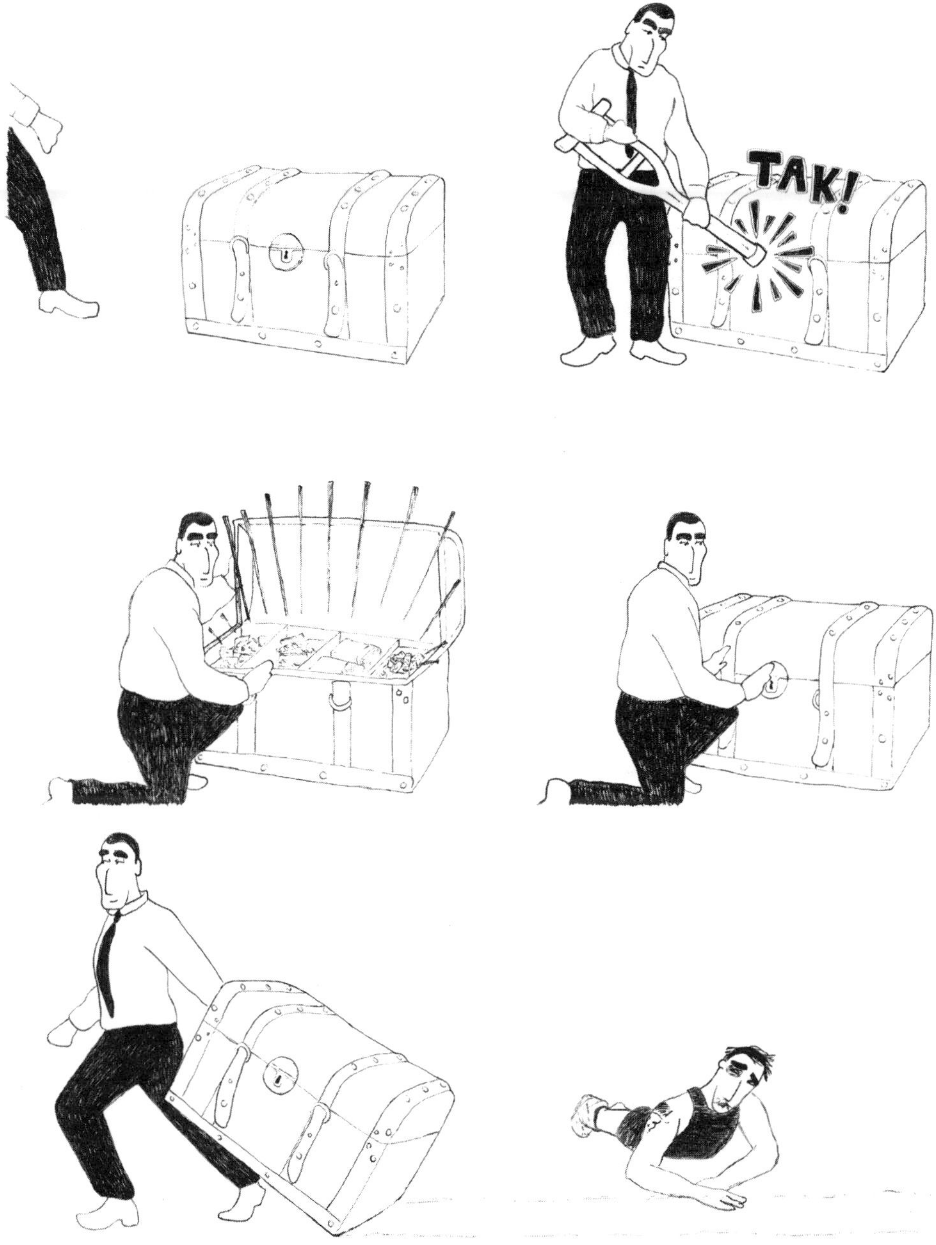
TAK!

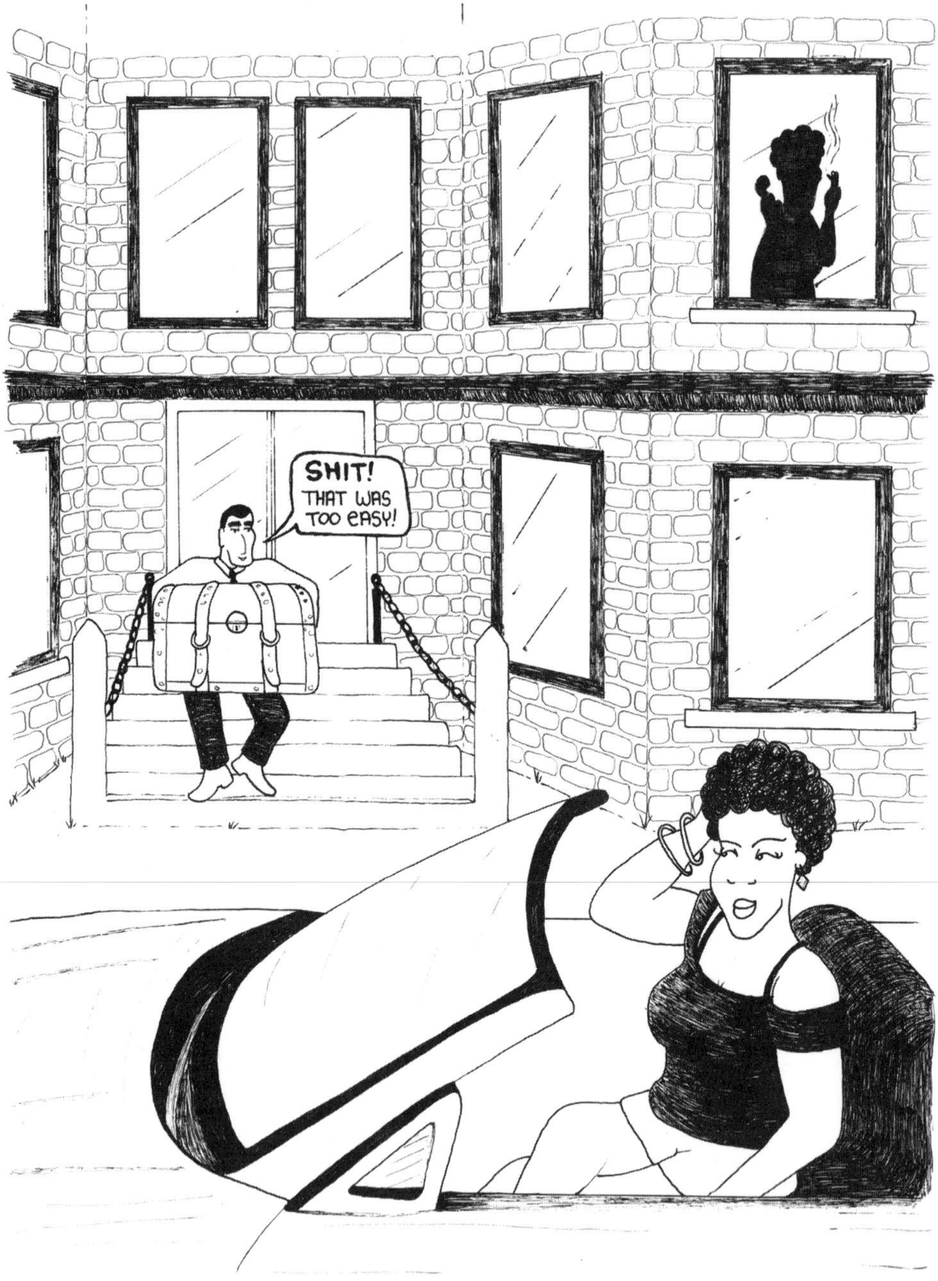
SHIT! THAT WAS TOO EASY!

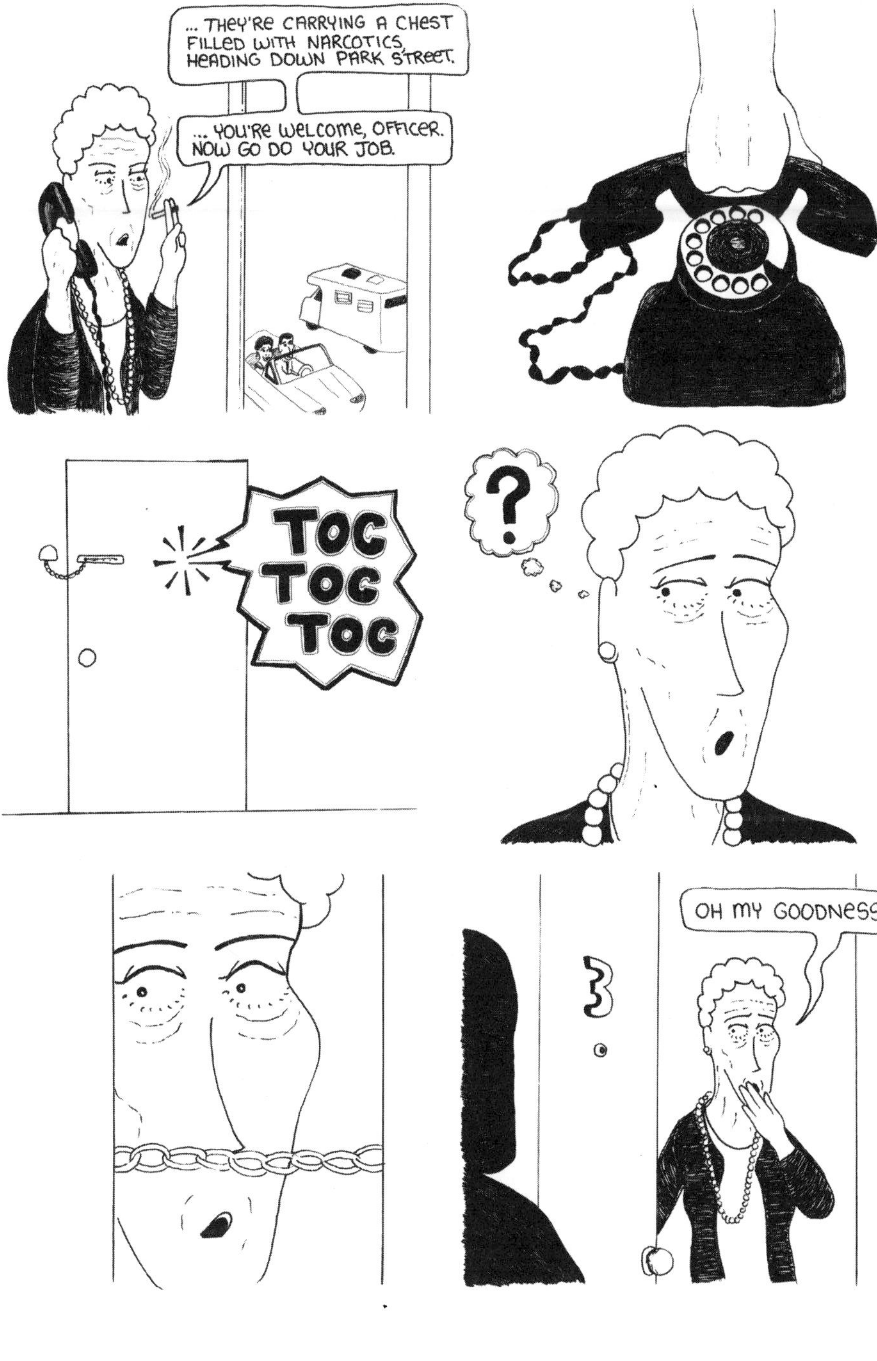

... THEY'RE CARRYING A CHEST FILLED WITH NARCOTICS, HEADING DOWN PARK STREET.
... YOU'RE WELCOME, OFFICER. NOW GO DO YOUR JOB.
TOC TOC TOC
?
OH MY GOODNESS...

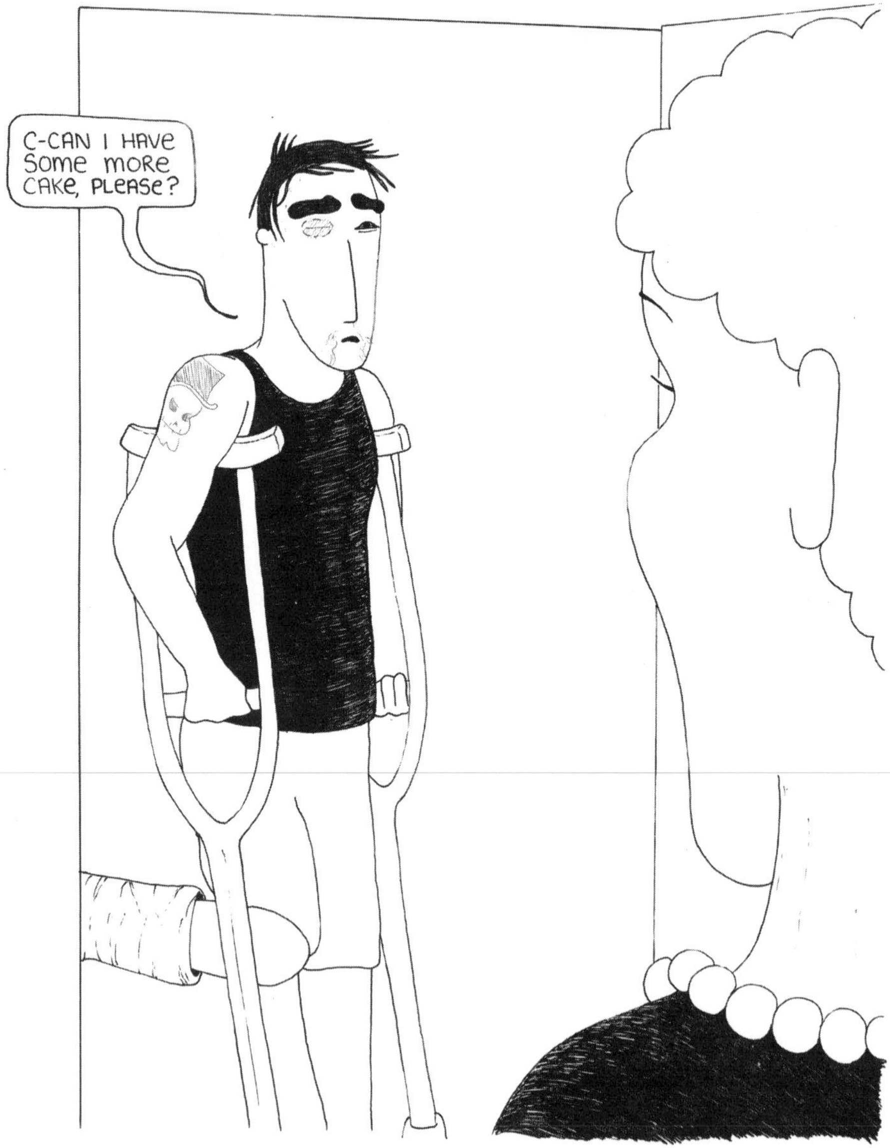
C-CAN I HAVE SOME MORE CAKE, PLEASE?

CHAPTER 7

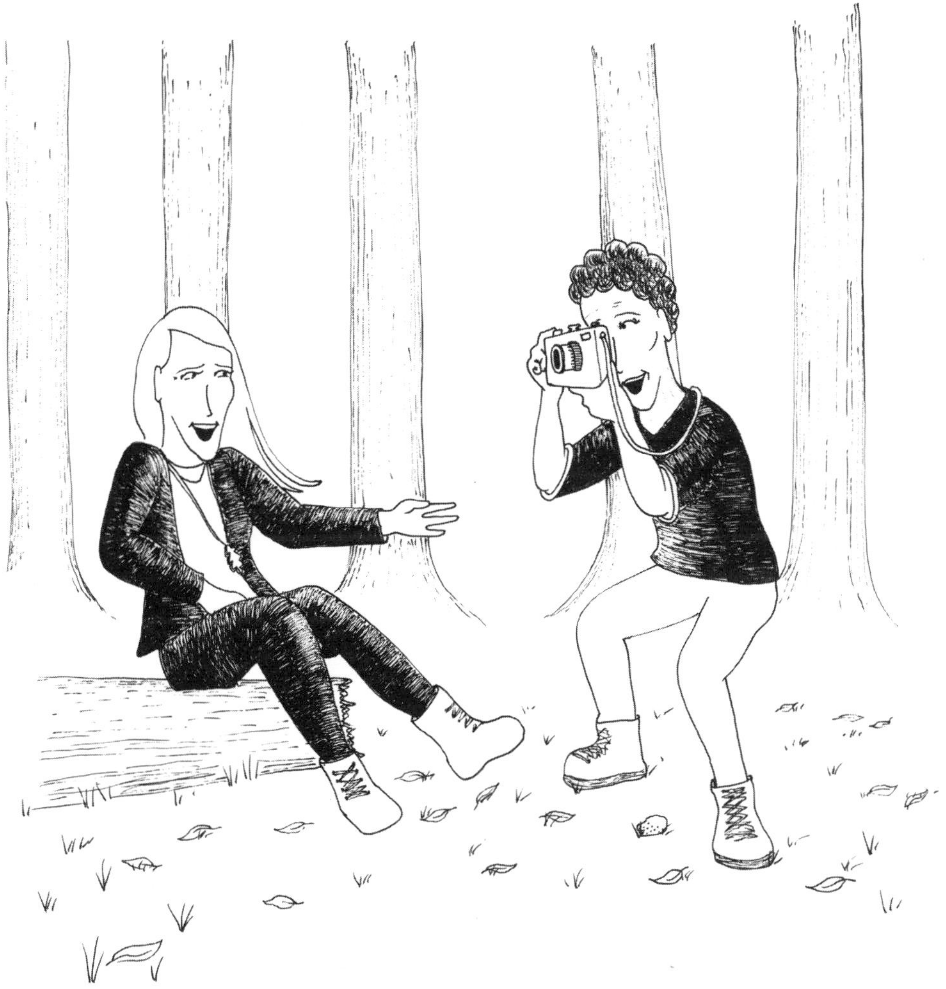

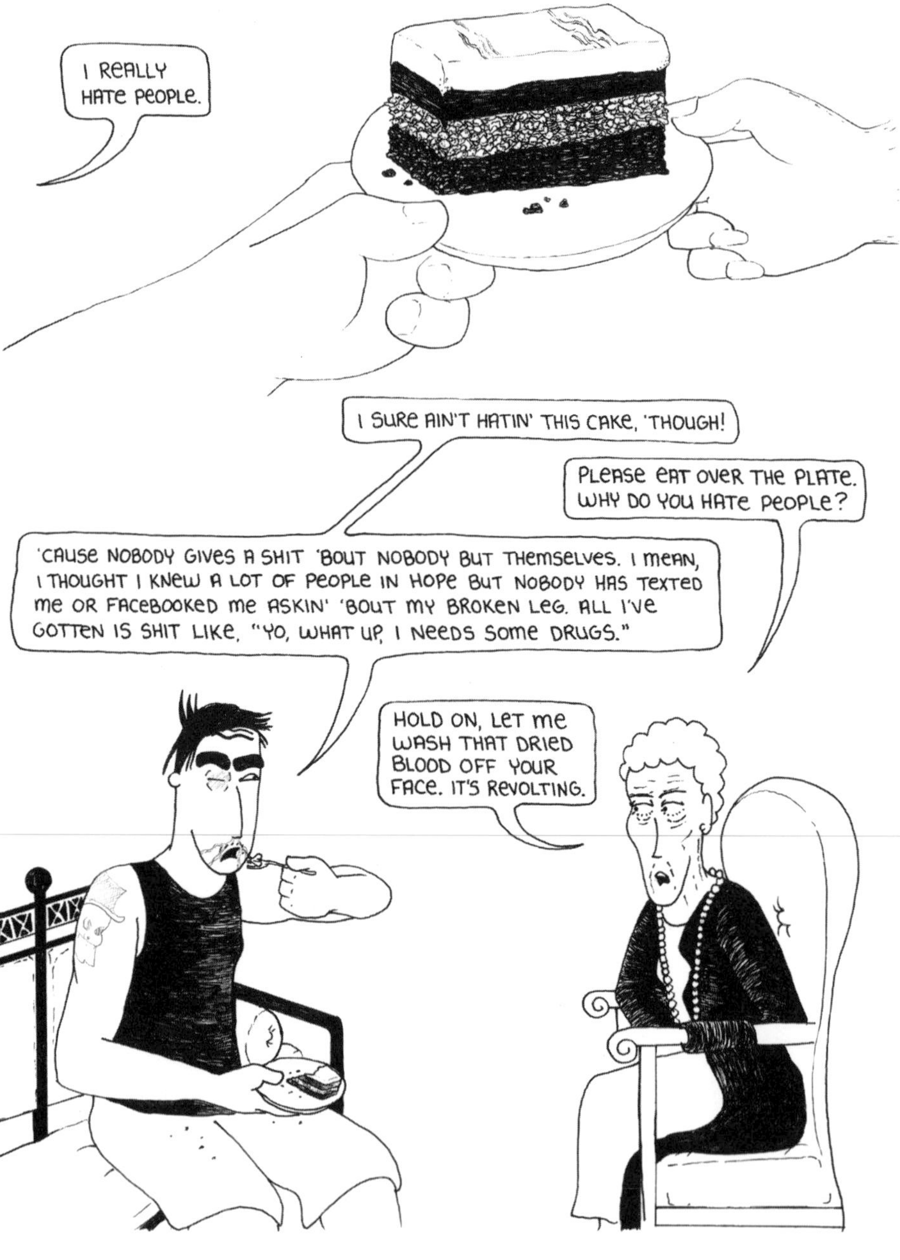
I REALLY HATE PEOPLE.
I SURE AIN'T HATIN' THIS CAKE, 'THOUGH!
PLEASE EAT OVER THE PLATE. WHY DO YOU HATE PEOPLE?
'CAUSE NOBODY GIVES A SHIT 'BOUT NOBODY BUT THEMSELVES. I MEAN, I THOUGHT I KNEW A LOT OF PEOPLE IN HOPE BUT NOBODY HAS TEXTED ME OR FACEBOOKED ME ASKIN' 'BOUT MY BROKEN LEG. ALL I'VE GOTTEN IS SHIT LIKE, "YO, WHAT UP, I NEEDS SOME DRUGS."
HOLD ON, LET ME WASH THAT DRIED BLOOD OFF YOUR FACE. IT'S REVOLTING.

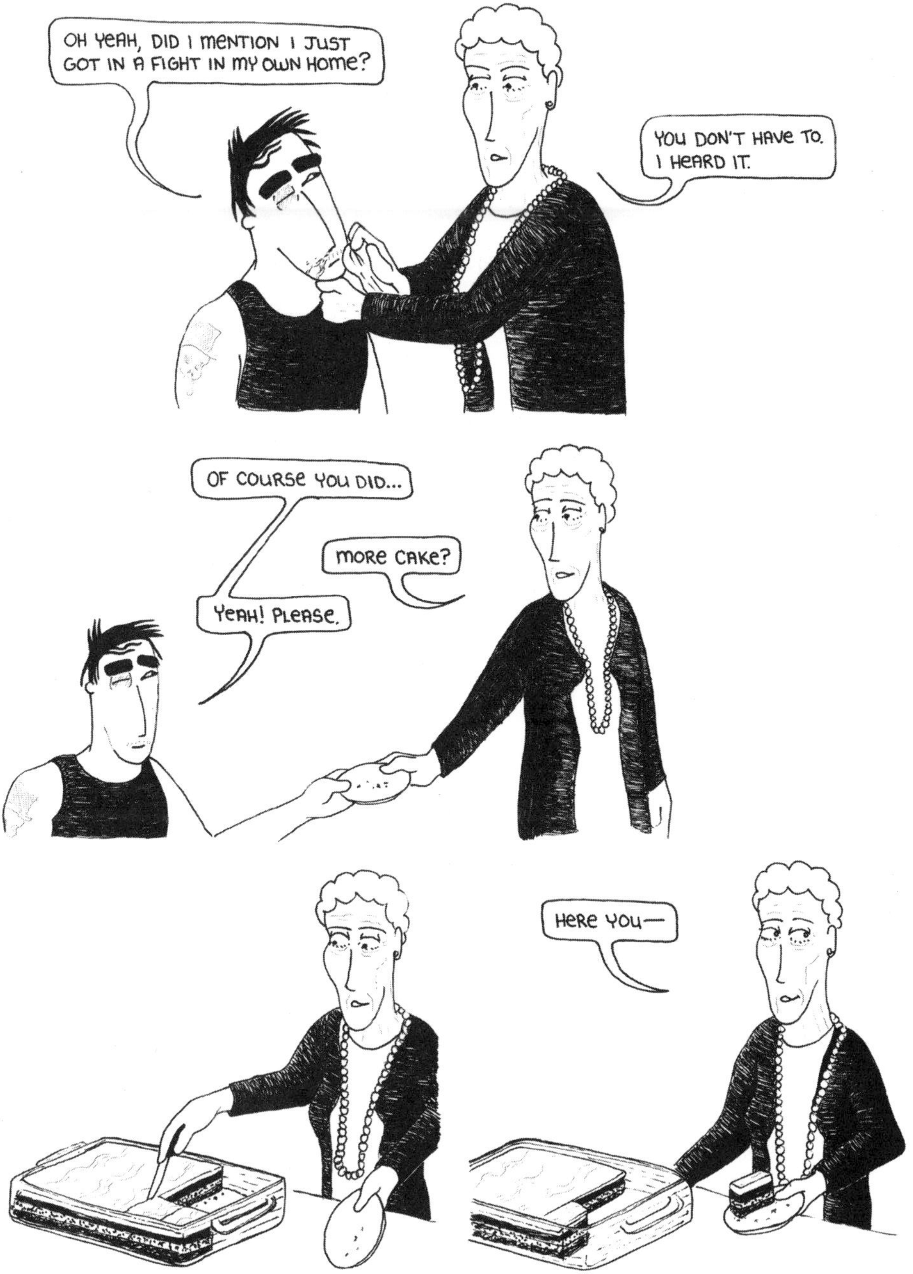
OH YEAH, DID I MENTION I JUST GOT IN A FIGHT IN MY OWN HOME?
YOU DON'T HAVE TO. I HEARD IT.
OF COURSE YOU DID...
MORE CAKE?
YEAH! PLEASE.
HERE YOU—

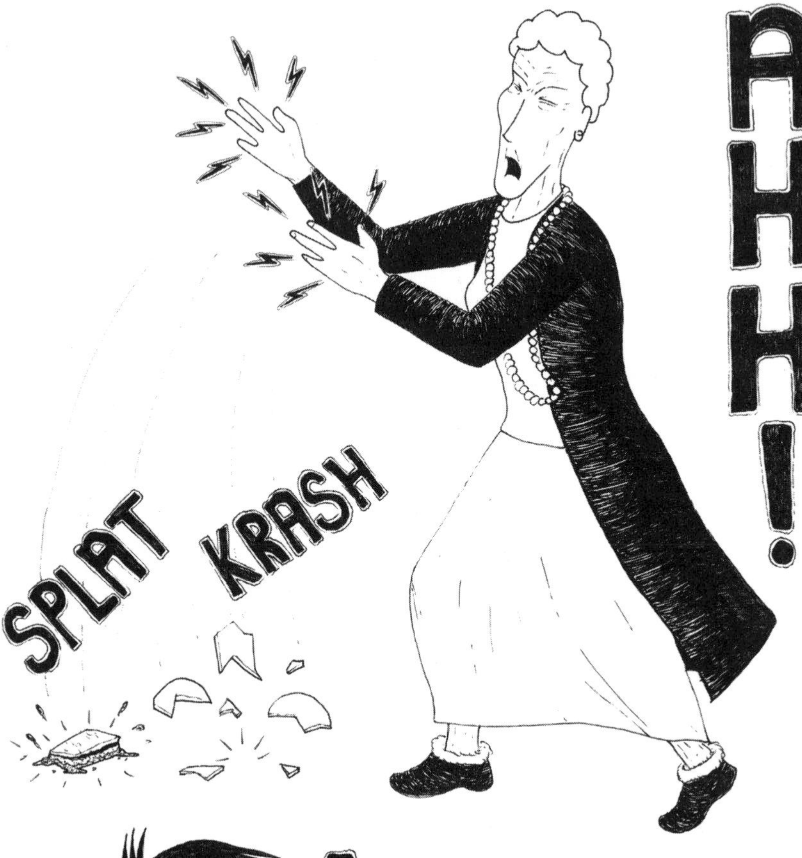
AHHH!
SPLAT
KRASH

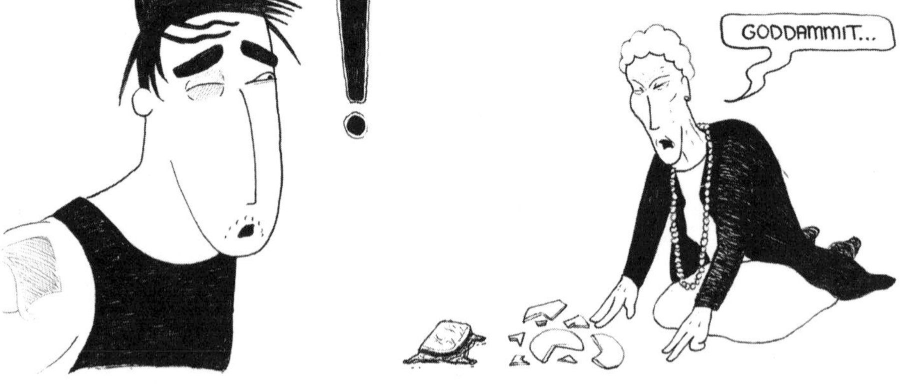
!
GODDAMMIT...

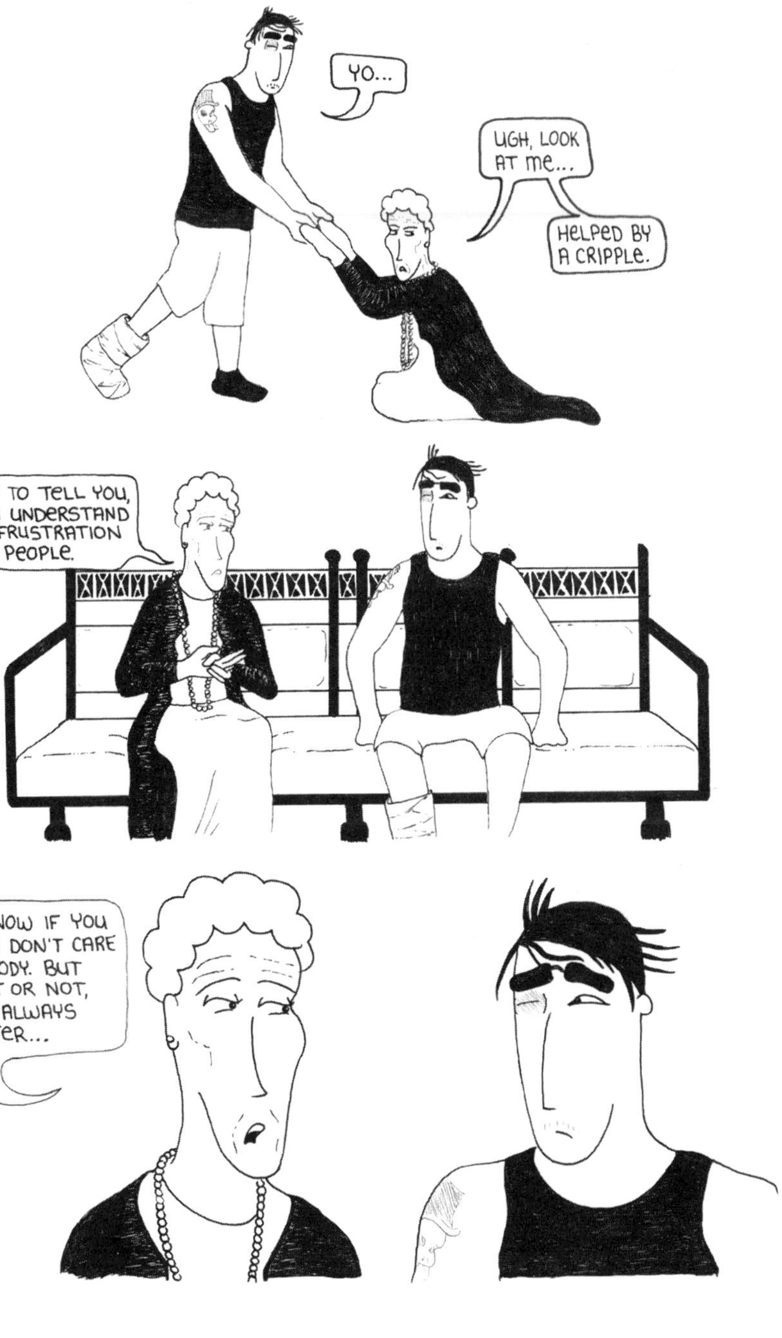
YO...
UGH, LOOK AT ME...
HELPED BY A CRIPPLE.
I HAVE TO TELL YOU, TOM. I UNDERSTAND YOUR FRUSTRATION WITH PEOPLE.
I DON'T KNOW IF YOU NOTICED; I DON'T CARE FOR ANYBODY. BUT BELIEVE IT OR NOT, I WASN'T ALWAYS THIS BITTER...

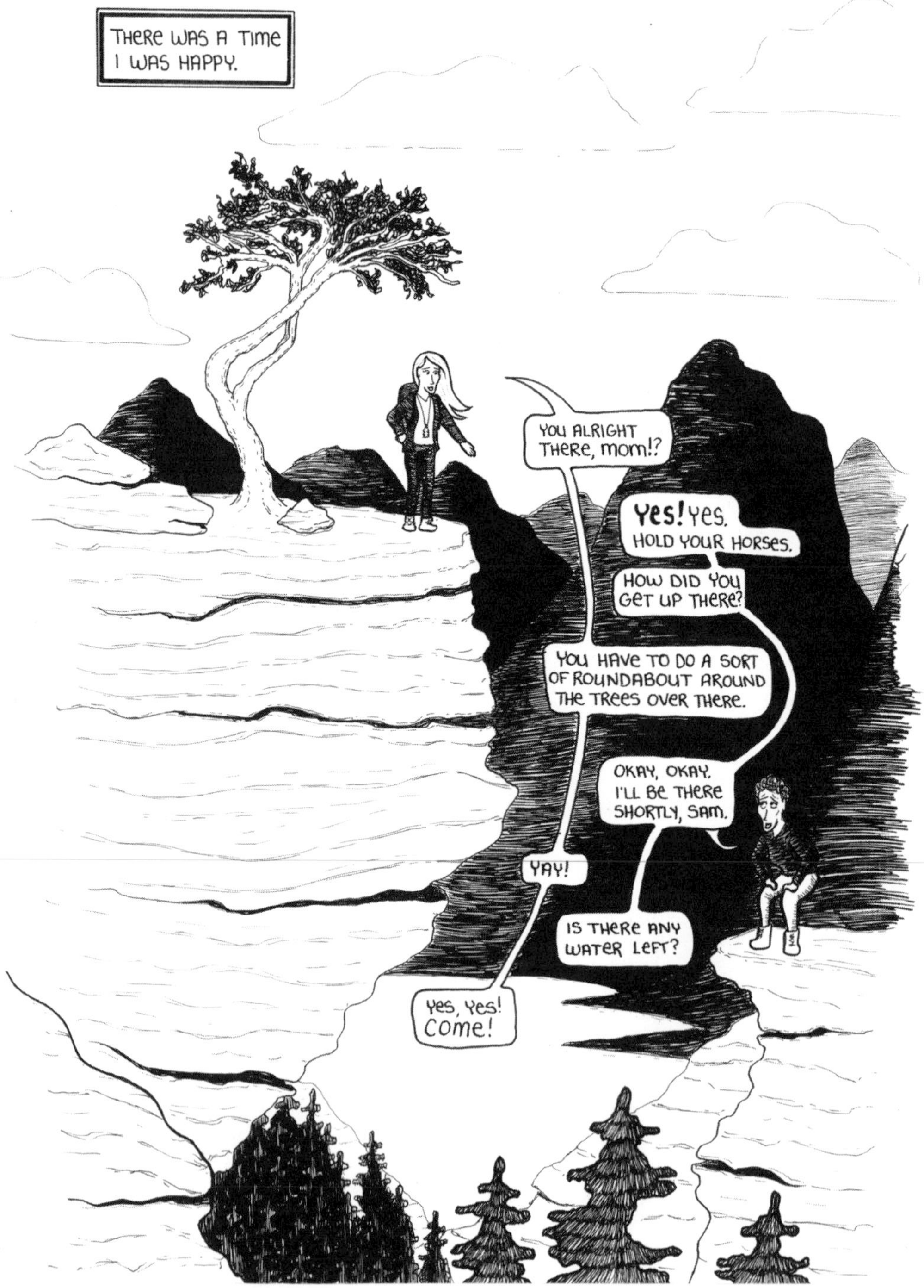
THERE WAS A TIME I WAS HAPPY.
YOU ALRIGHT THERE, MOM!?
YES! YES. HOLD YOUR HORSES.
HOW DID YOU GET UP THERE?
YOU HAVE TO DO A SORT OF ROUNDABOUT AROUND THE TREES OVER THERE.
OKAY, OKAY. I'LL BE THERE SHORTLY, SAM.
YAY!
IS THERE ANY WATER LEFT?
YES, YES! COME!

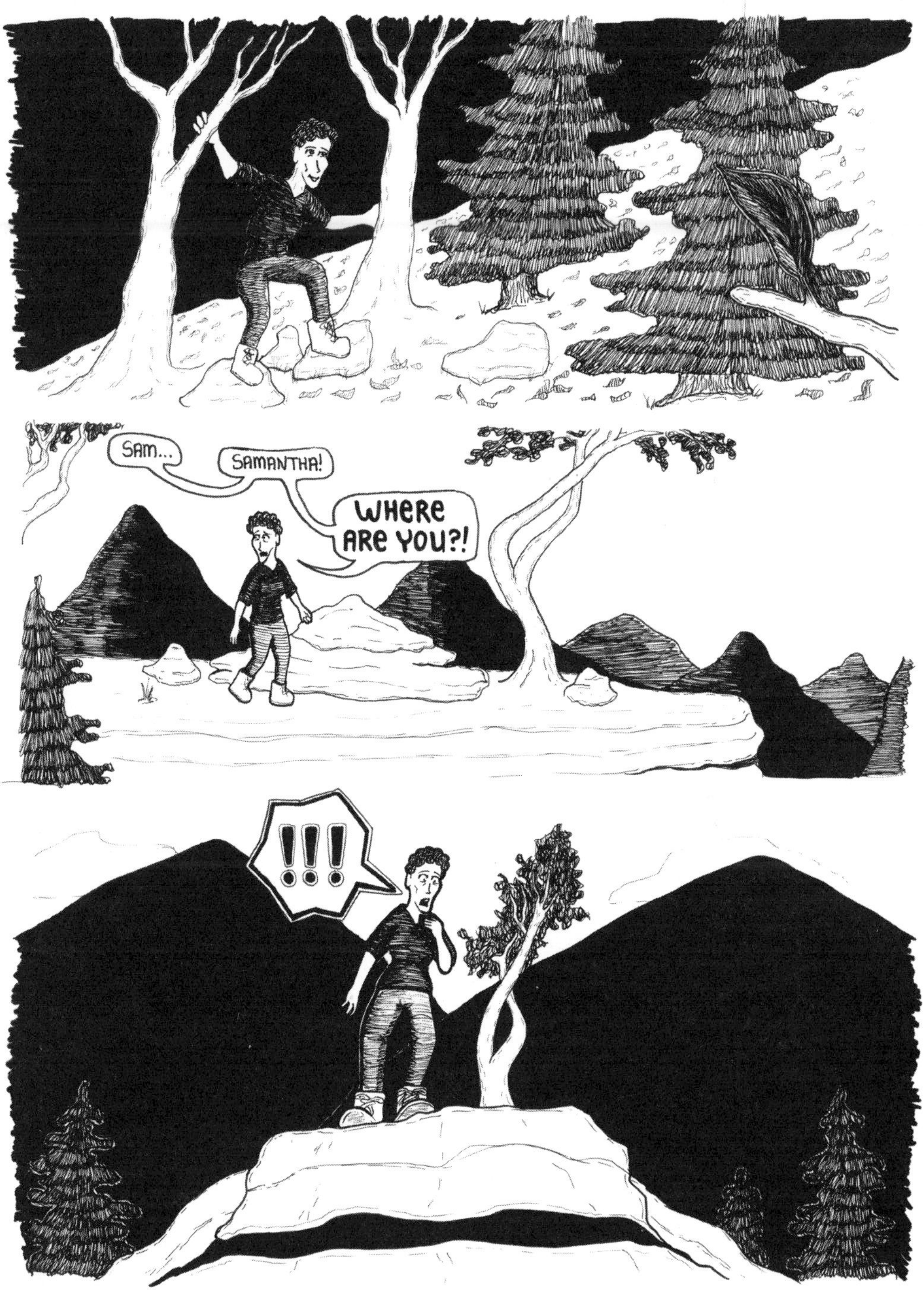
SAM...
SAMANTHA!
WHERE ARE YOU?!
!!!

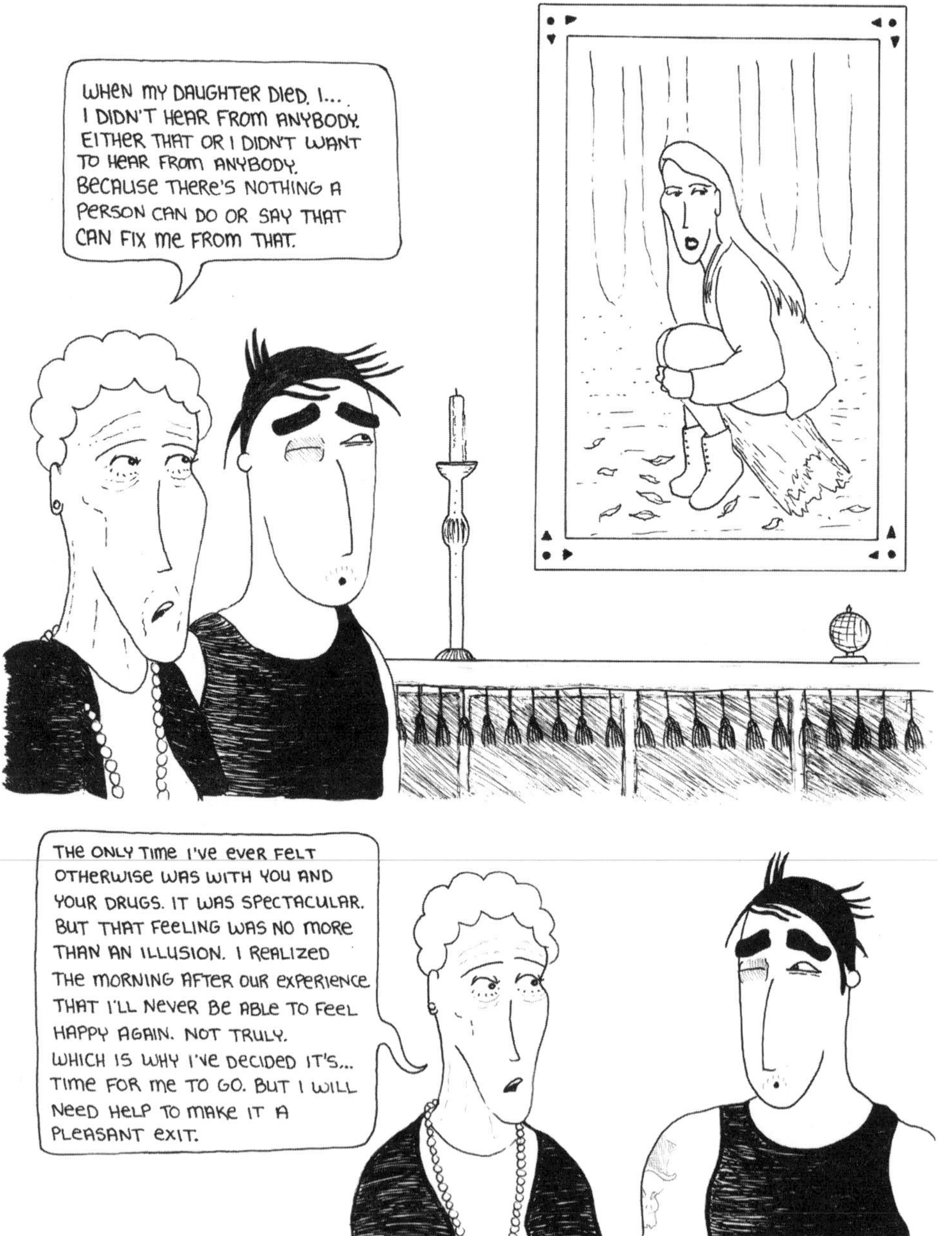
WHEN MY DAUGHTER DIED, I... I DIDN'T HEAR FROM ANYBODY. EITHER THAT OR I DIDN'T WANT TO HEAR FROM ANYBODY. BECAUSE THERE'S NOTHING A PERSON CAN DO OR SAY THAT CAN FIX ME FROM THAT.
THE ONLY TIME I'VE EVER FELT OTHERWISE WAS WITH YOU AND YOUR DRUGS. IT WAS SPECTACULAR. BUT THAT FEELING WAS NO MORE THAN AN ILLUSION. I REALIZED THE MORNING AFTER OUR EXPERIENCE THAT I'LL NEVER BE ABLE TO FEEL HAPPY AGAIN. NOT TRULY. WHICH IS WHY I'VE DECIDED IT'S... TIME FOR ME TO GO. BUT I WILL NEED HELP TO MAKE IT A PLEASANT EXIT.

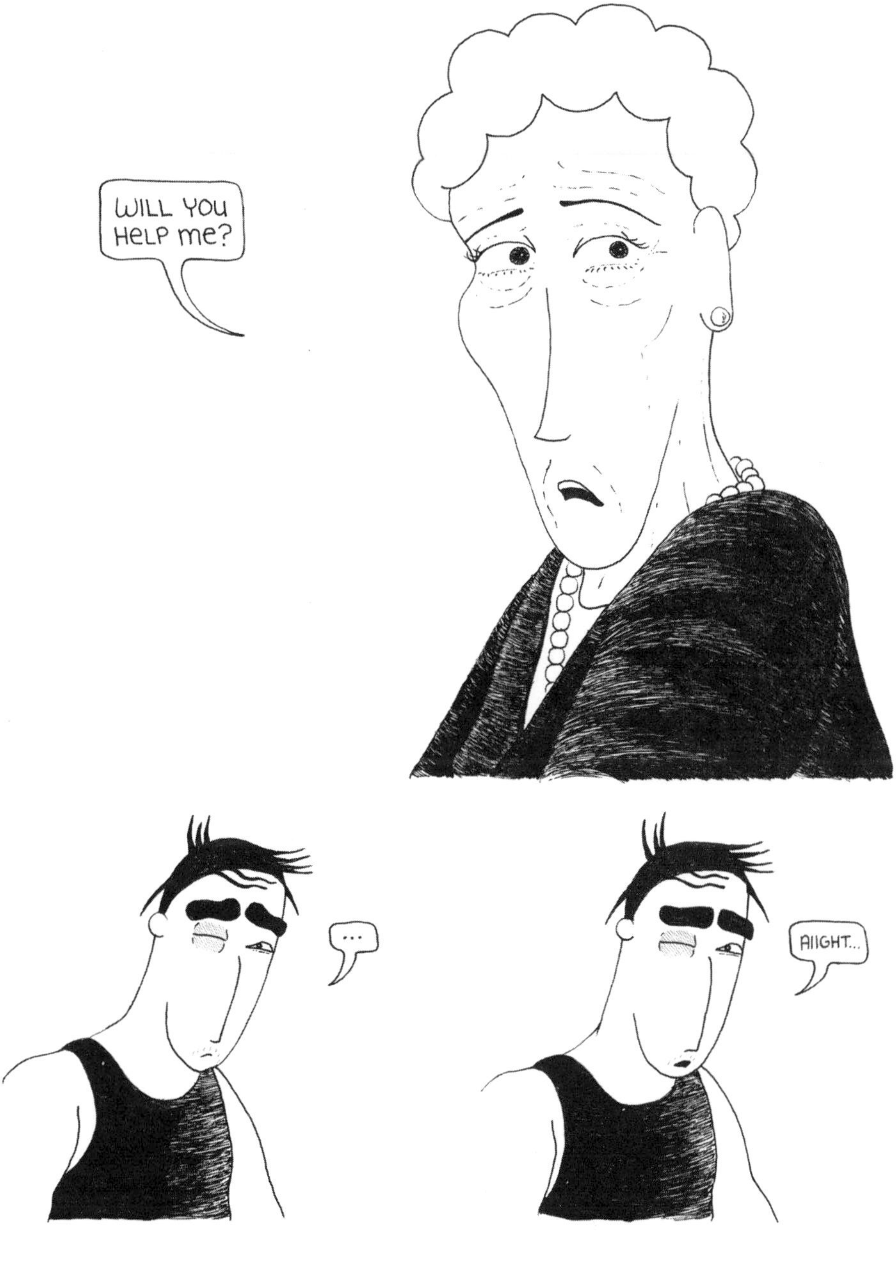
WILL YOU HELP me?
...
AIIGHT...

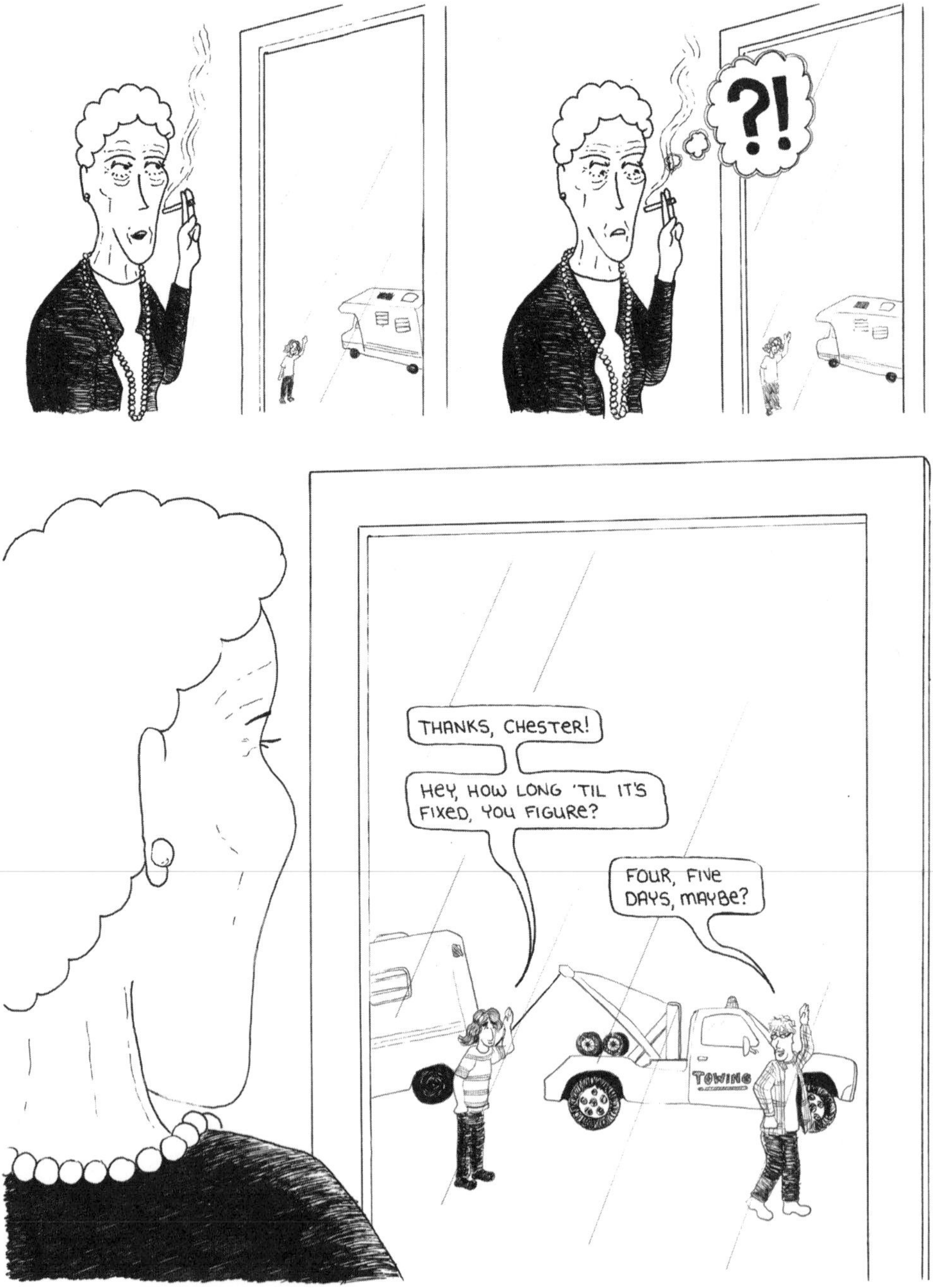
?!
THANKS, CHESTER!
HEY, HOW LONG 'TIL IT'S FIXED, YOU FIGURE?
FOUR, FIVE DAYS, MAYBE?
TOWING

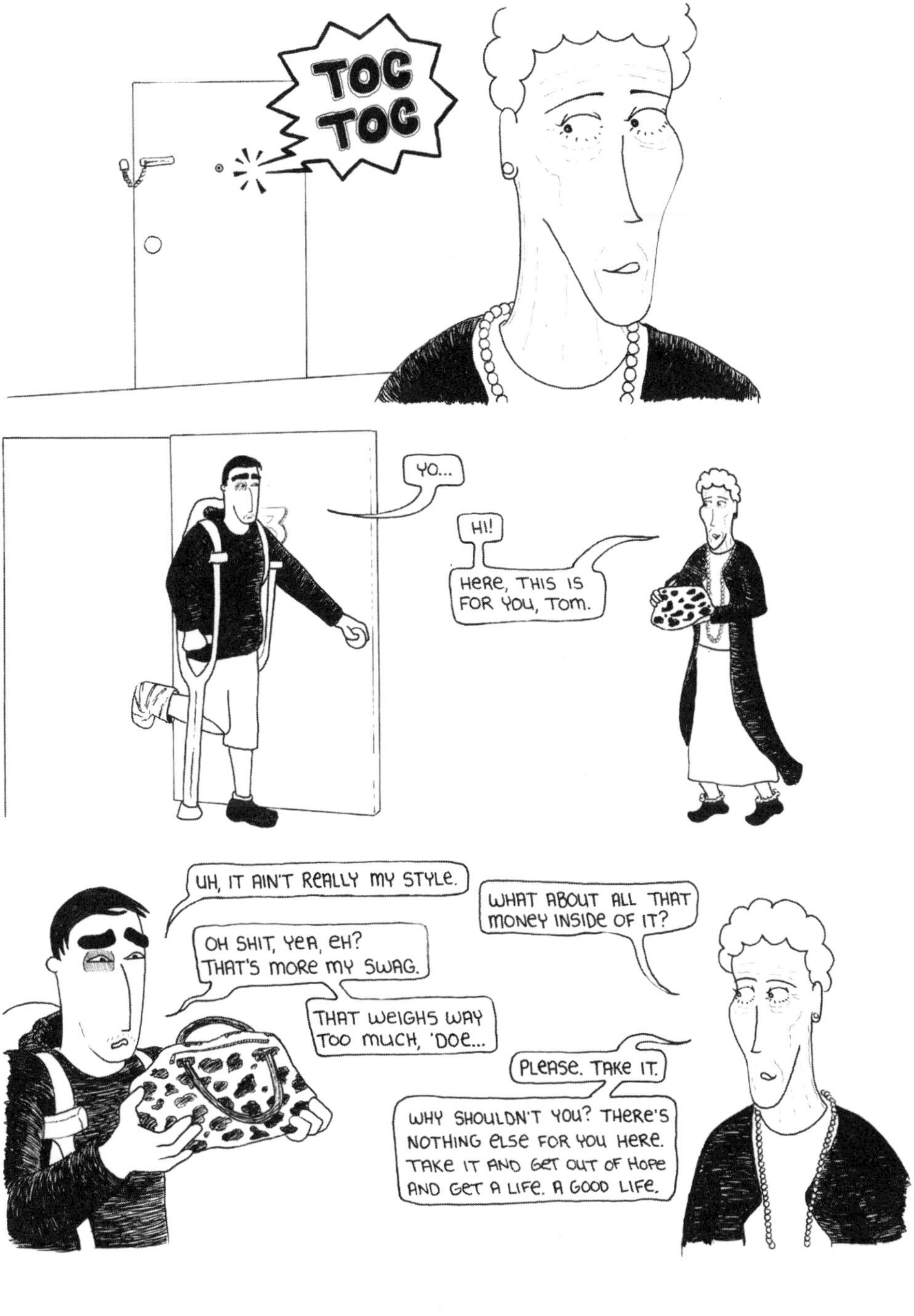
TOC TOC
YO...
HI!
HERE, THIS IS FOR YOU, TOM.
UH, IT AIN'T REALLY MY STYLE.
WHAT ABOUT ALL THAT MONEY INSIDE OF IT?
OH SHIT, YEA, EH? THAT'S MORE MY SWAG.
THAT WEIGHS WAY TOO MUCH, 'DOE...
PLEASE. TAKE IT.
WHY SHOULDN'T YOU? THERE'S NOTHING ELSE FOR YOU HERE. TAKE IT AND GET OUT OF HOPE AND GET A LIFE. A GOOD LIFE.

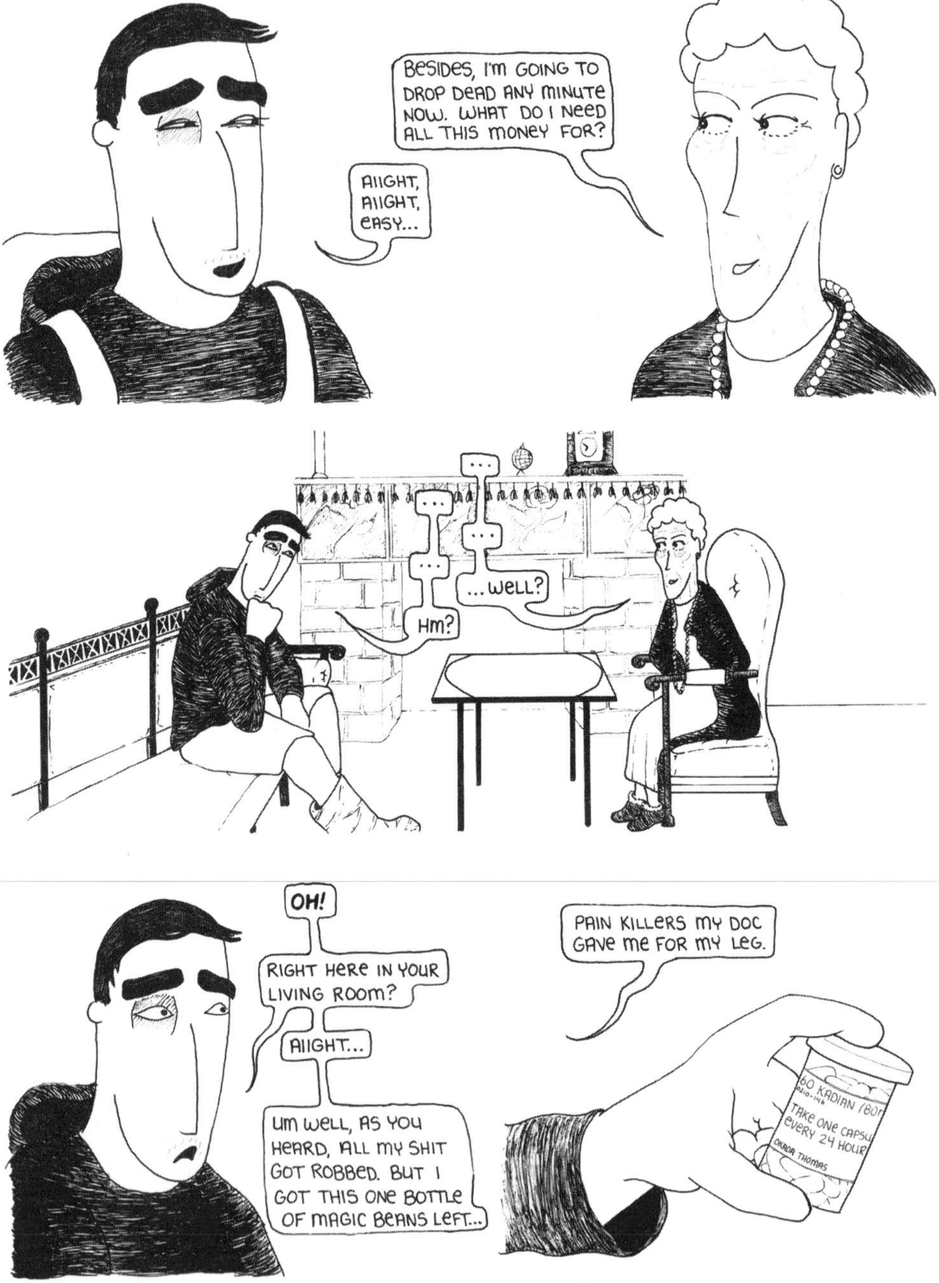
BESIDES, I'M GOING TO DROP DEAD ANY MINUTE NOW. WHAT DO I NEED ALL THIS MONEY FOR?
AIIGHT, AIIGHT, EASY...
...
...
...
...
Hm?
...WELL?
OH!
RIGHT HERE IN YOUR LIVING ROOM?
AIIGHT...
UM WELL, AS YOU HEARD, ALL MY SHIT GOT ROBBED. BUT I GOT THIS ONE BOTTLE OF MAGIC BEANS LEFT...
PAIN KILLERS MY DOC GAVE ME FOR MY LEG.

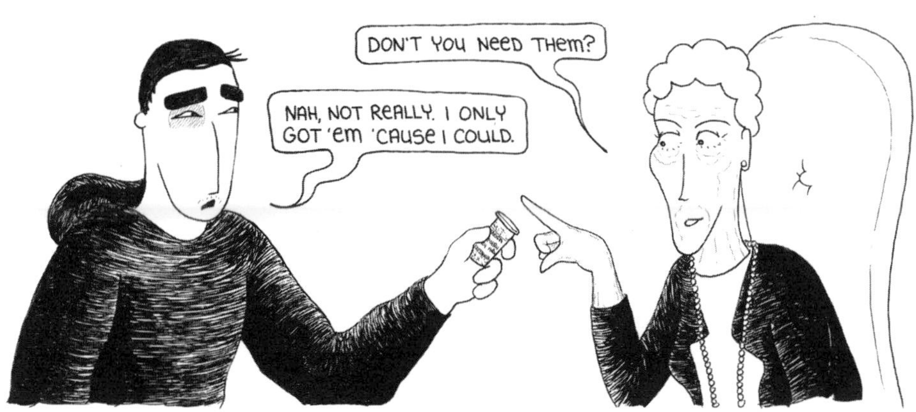
DON'T YOU NEED THEM?
NAH, NOT REALLY. I ONLY GOT 'EM 'CAUSE I COULD.

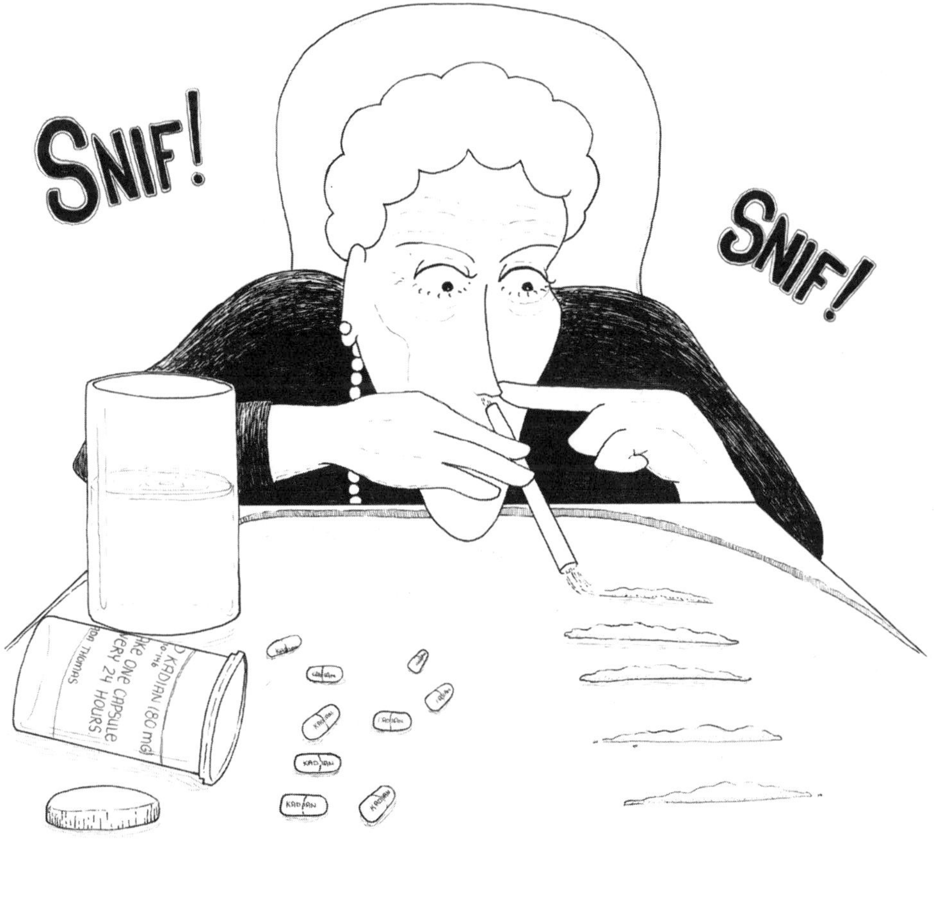
SNIF!
SNIF!
KADIAN 180 mg

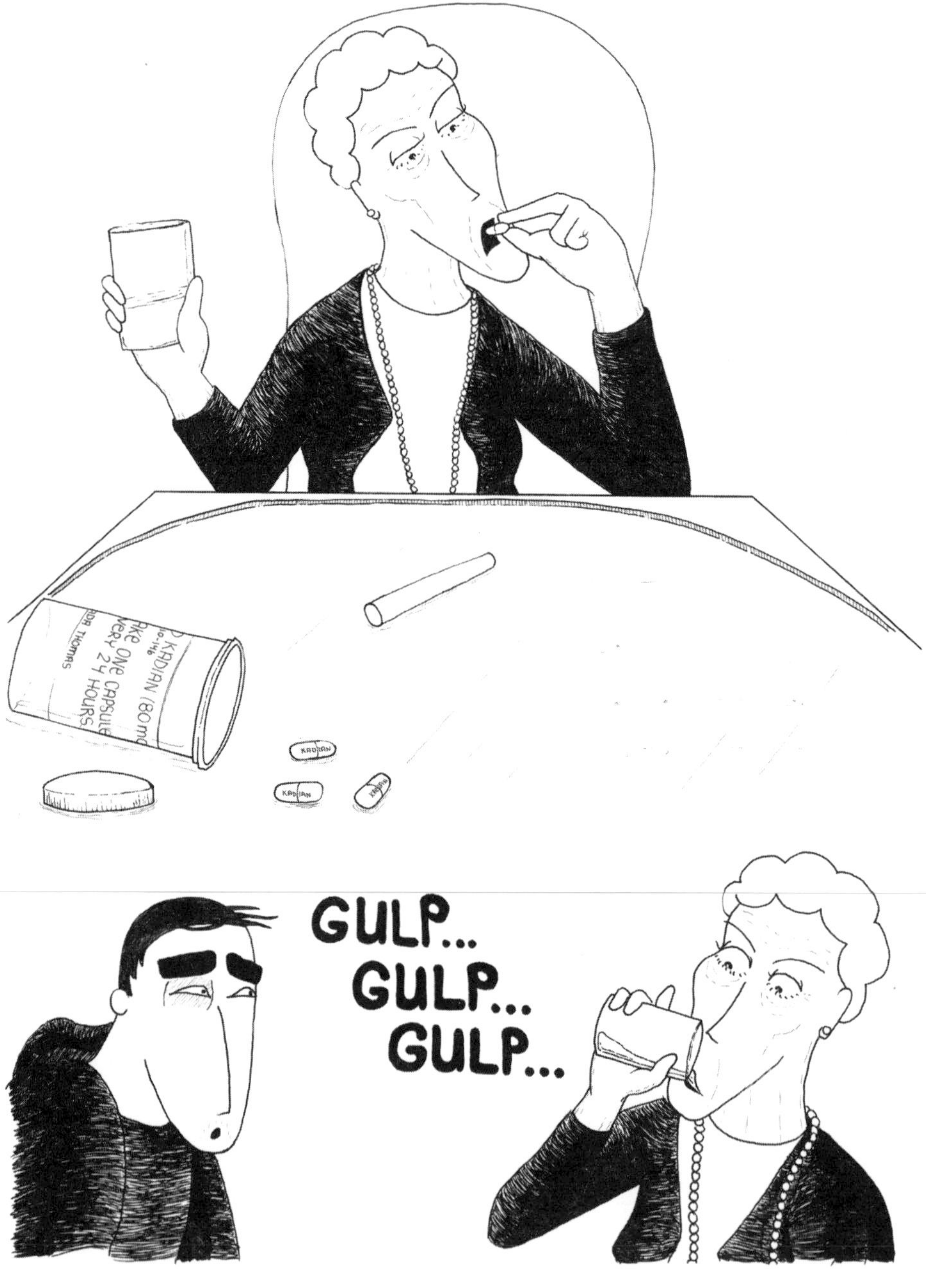
KADIAN
KADIAN
GULP...
GULP...
GULP...

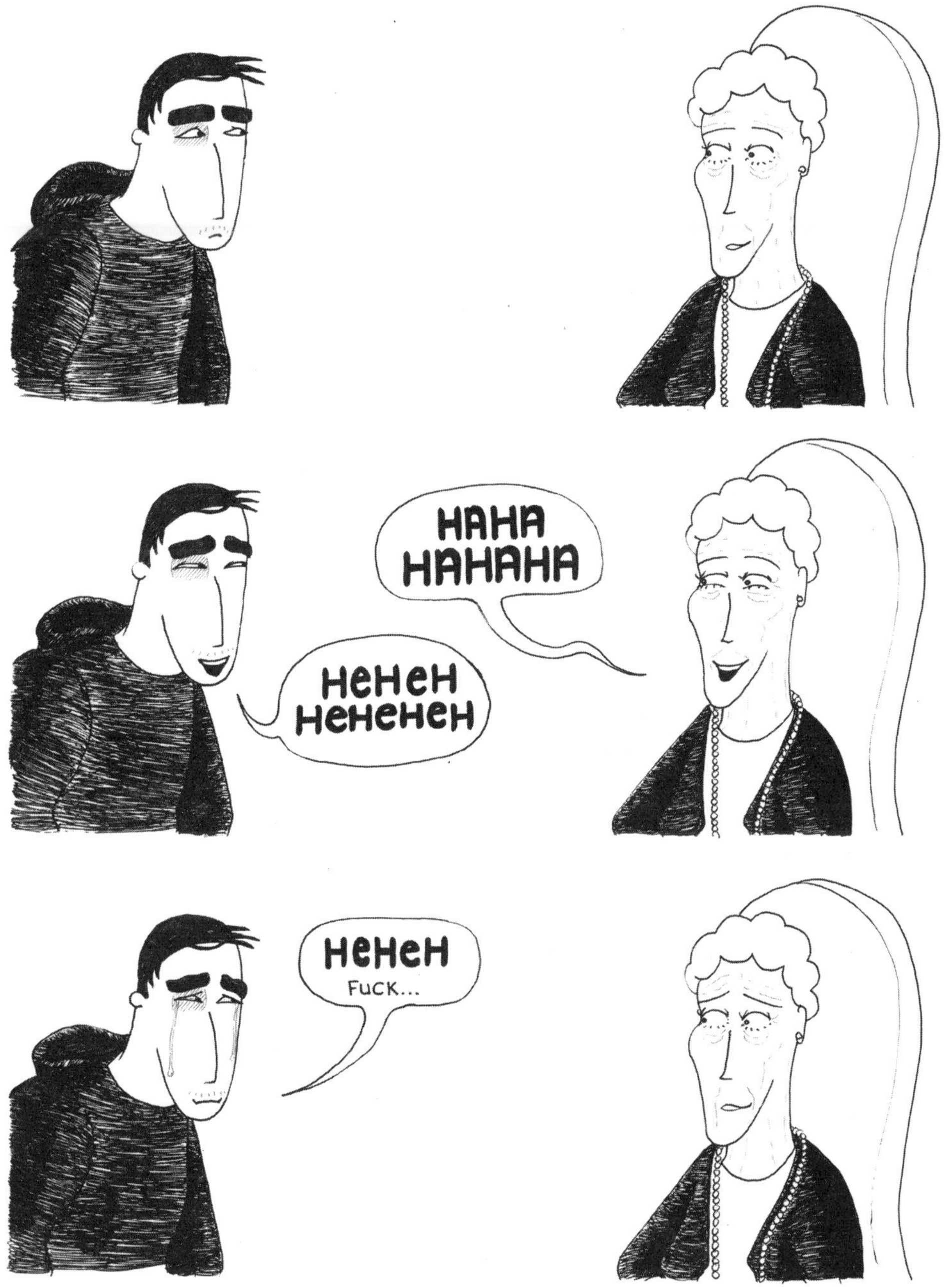
HAHA HAHAHA
HEHEH HEHEHEH
HEHEH
FUCK...

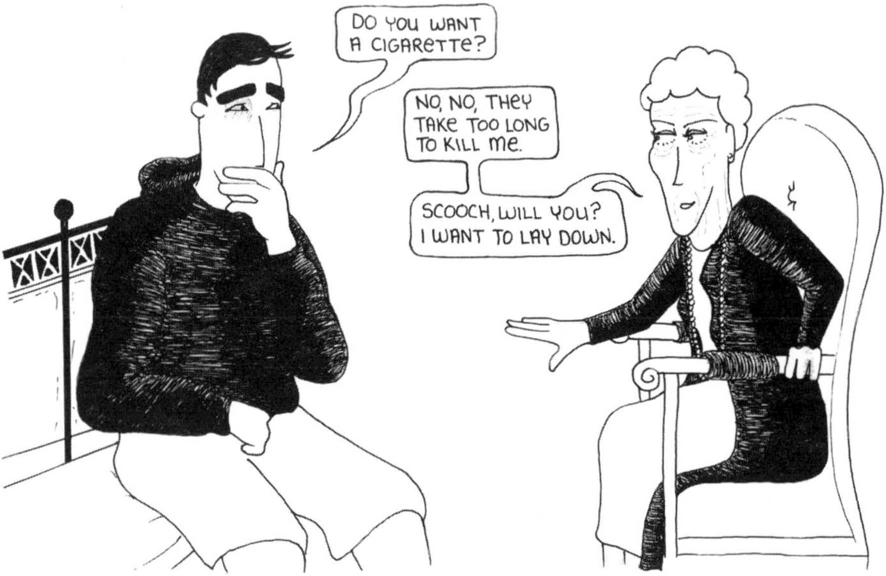
DO YOU WANT A CIGARETTE?
NO, NO, THEY TAKE TOO LONG TO KILL ME.
SCOOCH, WILL YOU? I WANT TO LAY DOWN.

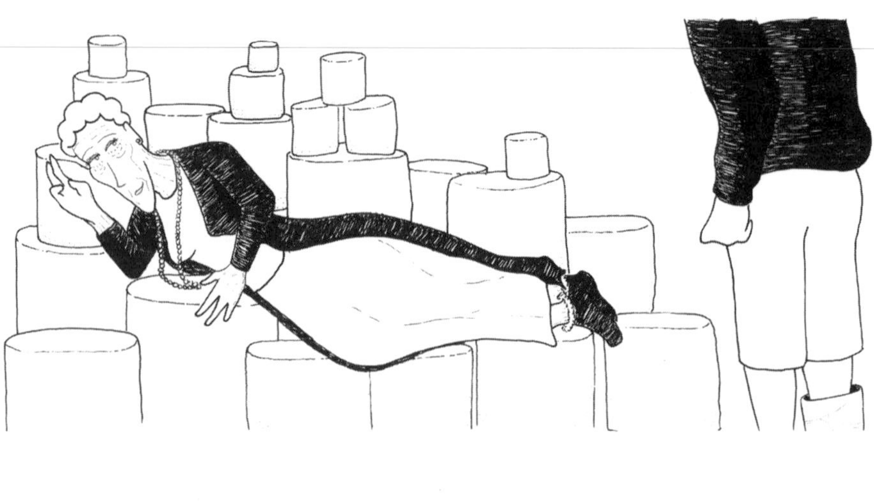

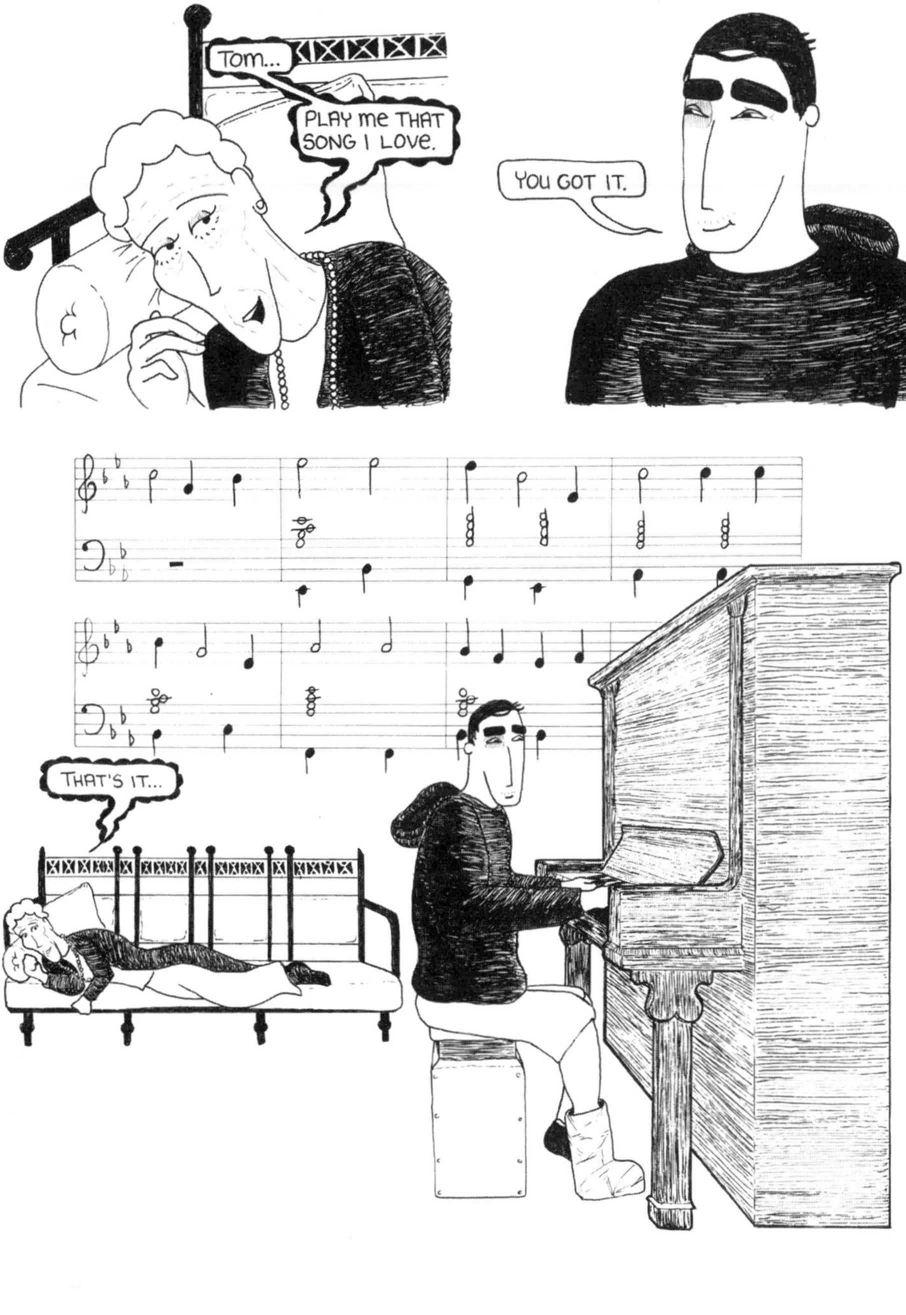

Tom...
PLAY ME THAT SONG I LOVE.
YOU GOT IT.
THAT'S IT...

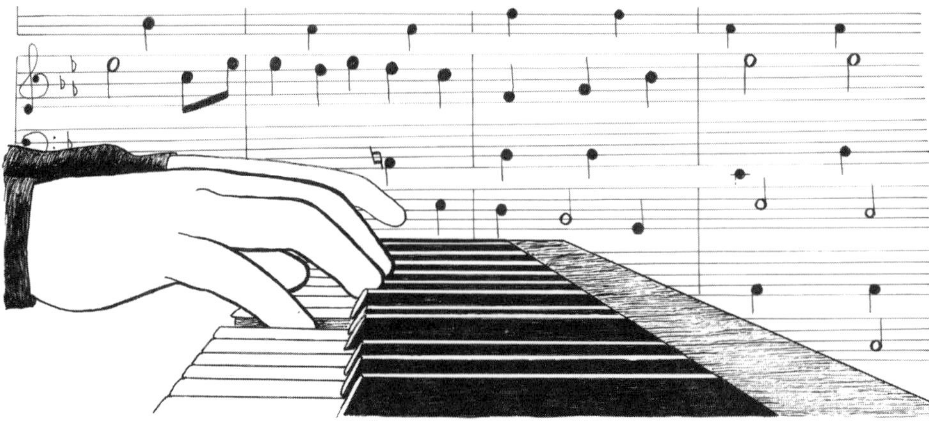

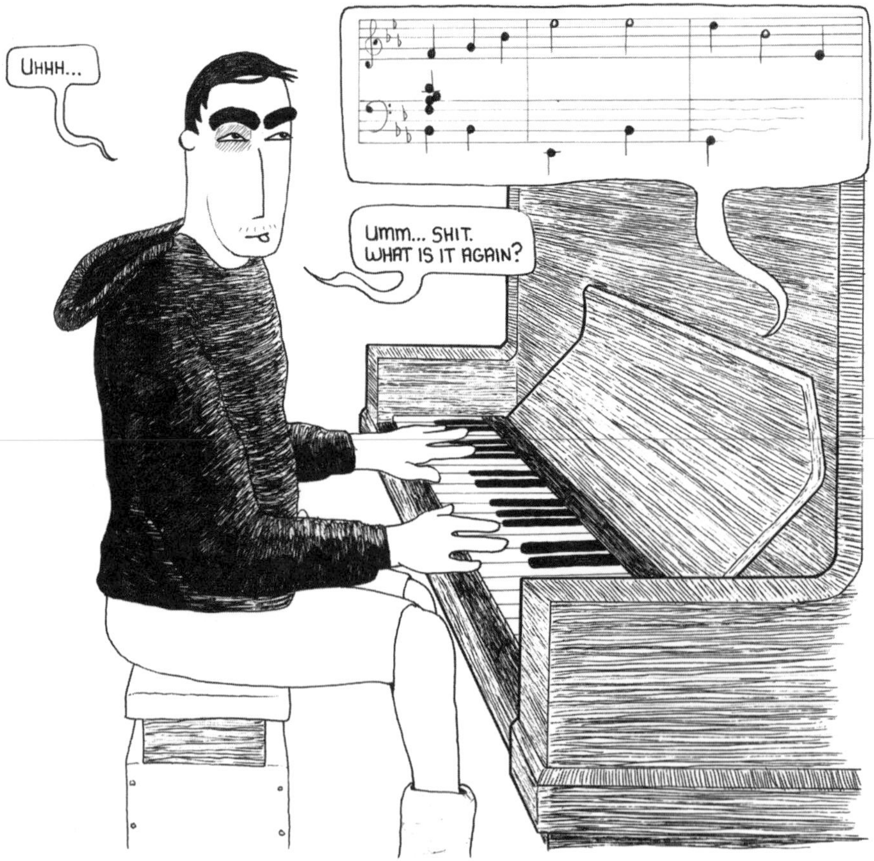
UHHH...
UMM... SHIT. WHAT IS IT AGAIN?

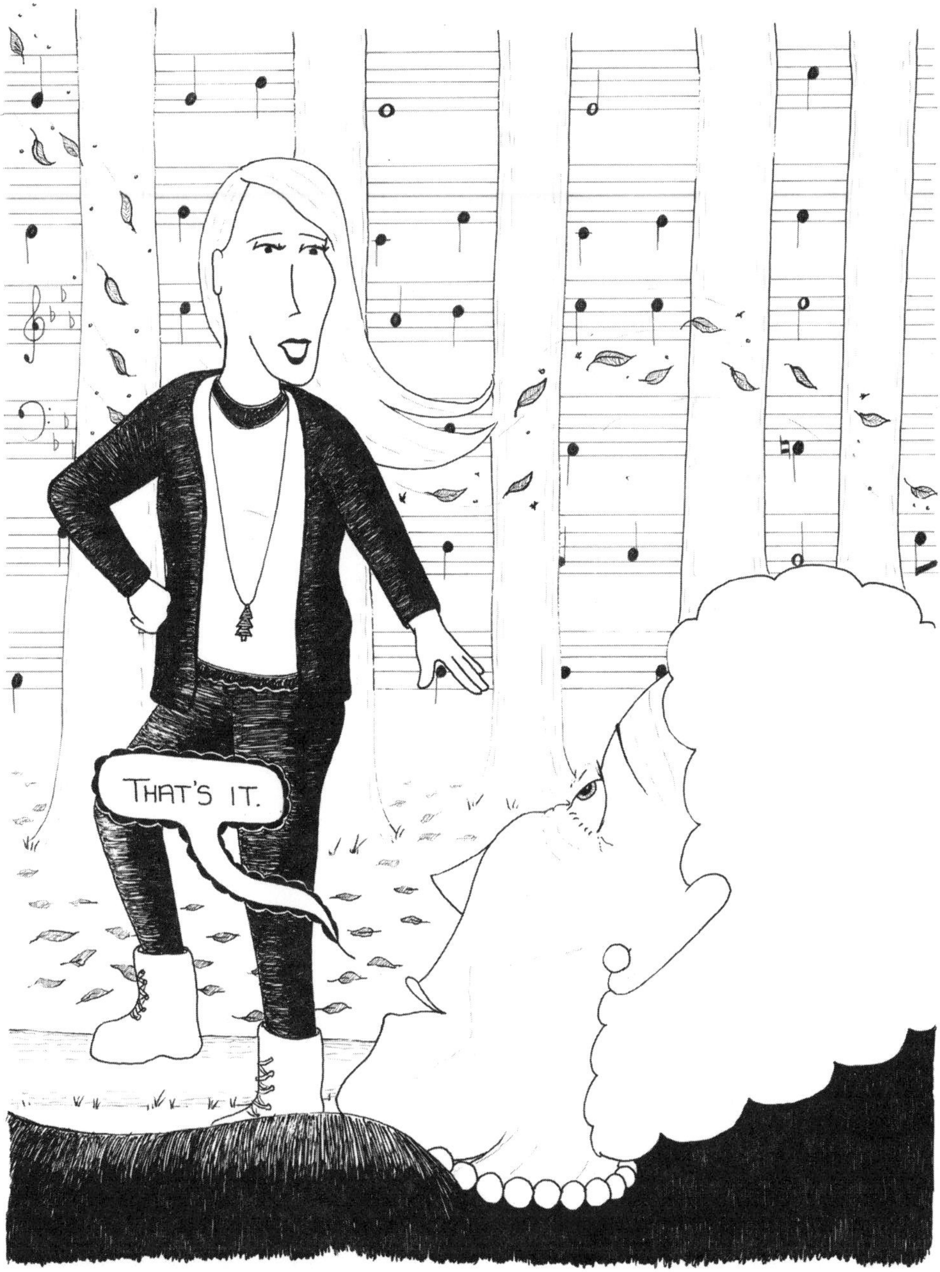
THAT'S IT.

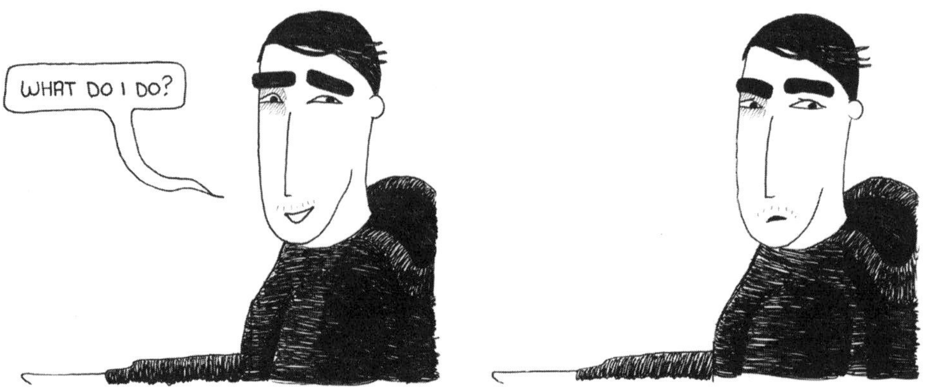
WHAT DO I DO?

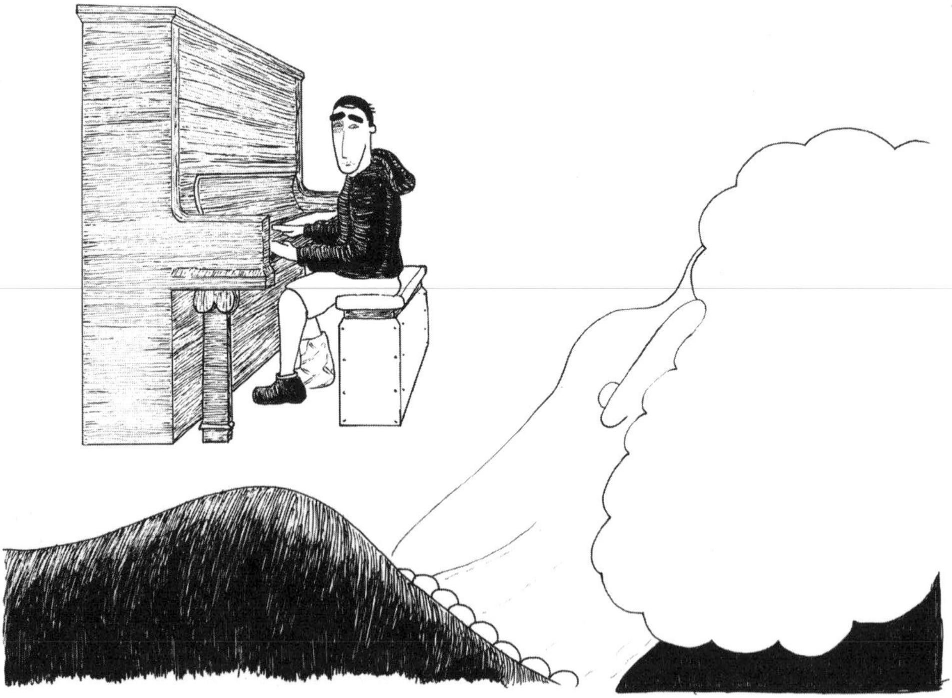

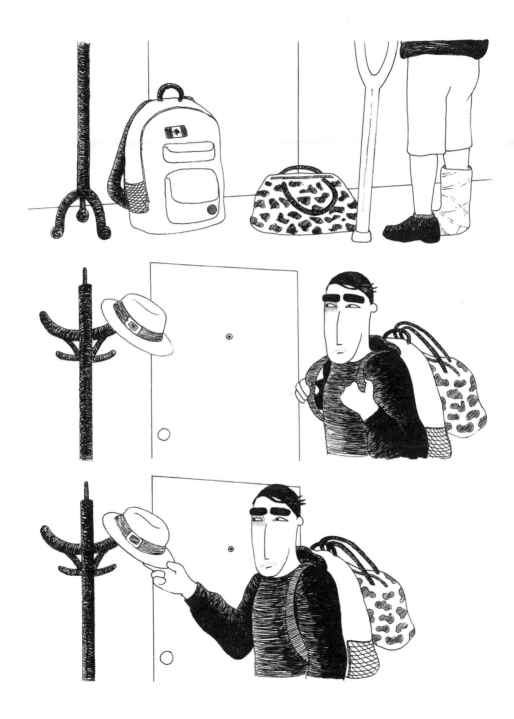

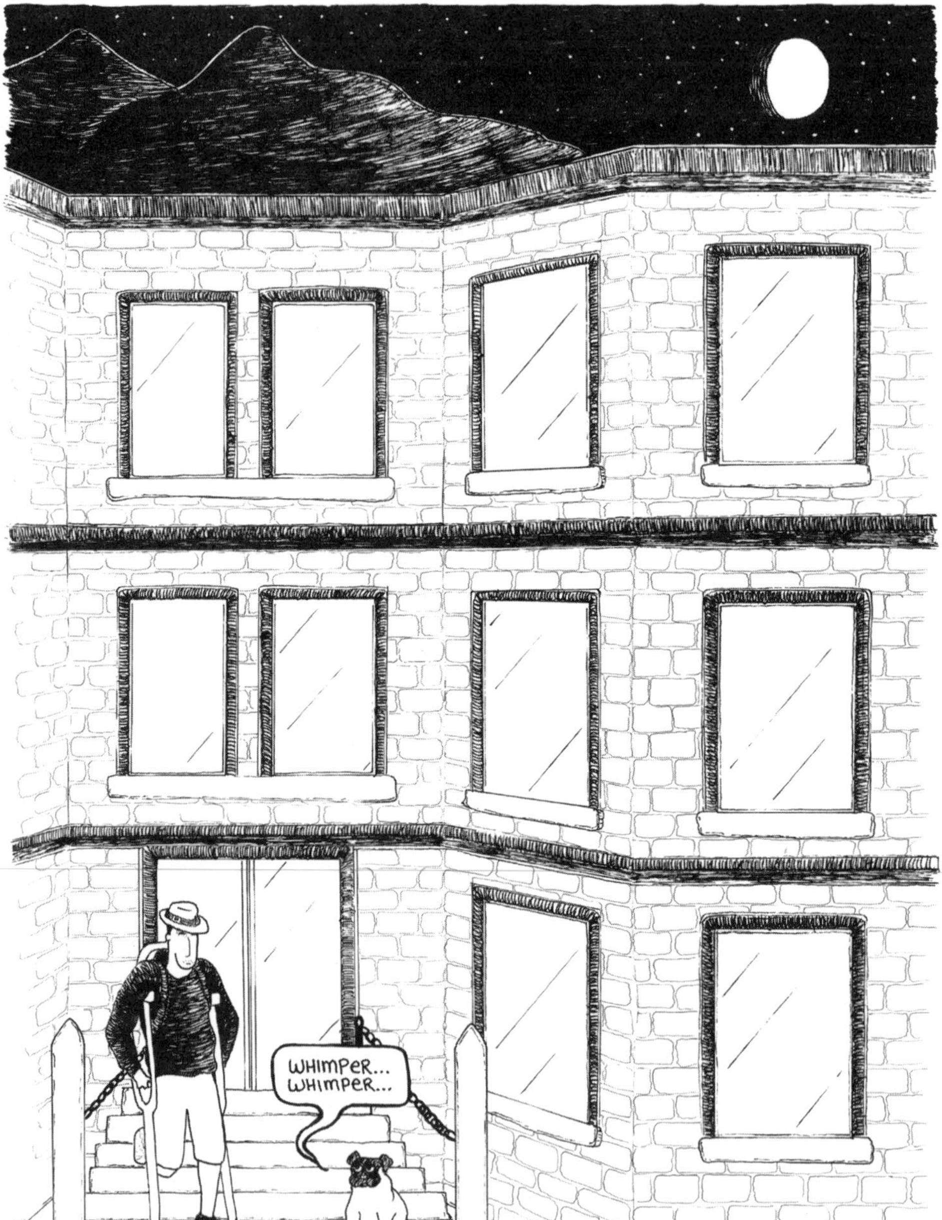
WHIMPER...
WHIMPER...

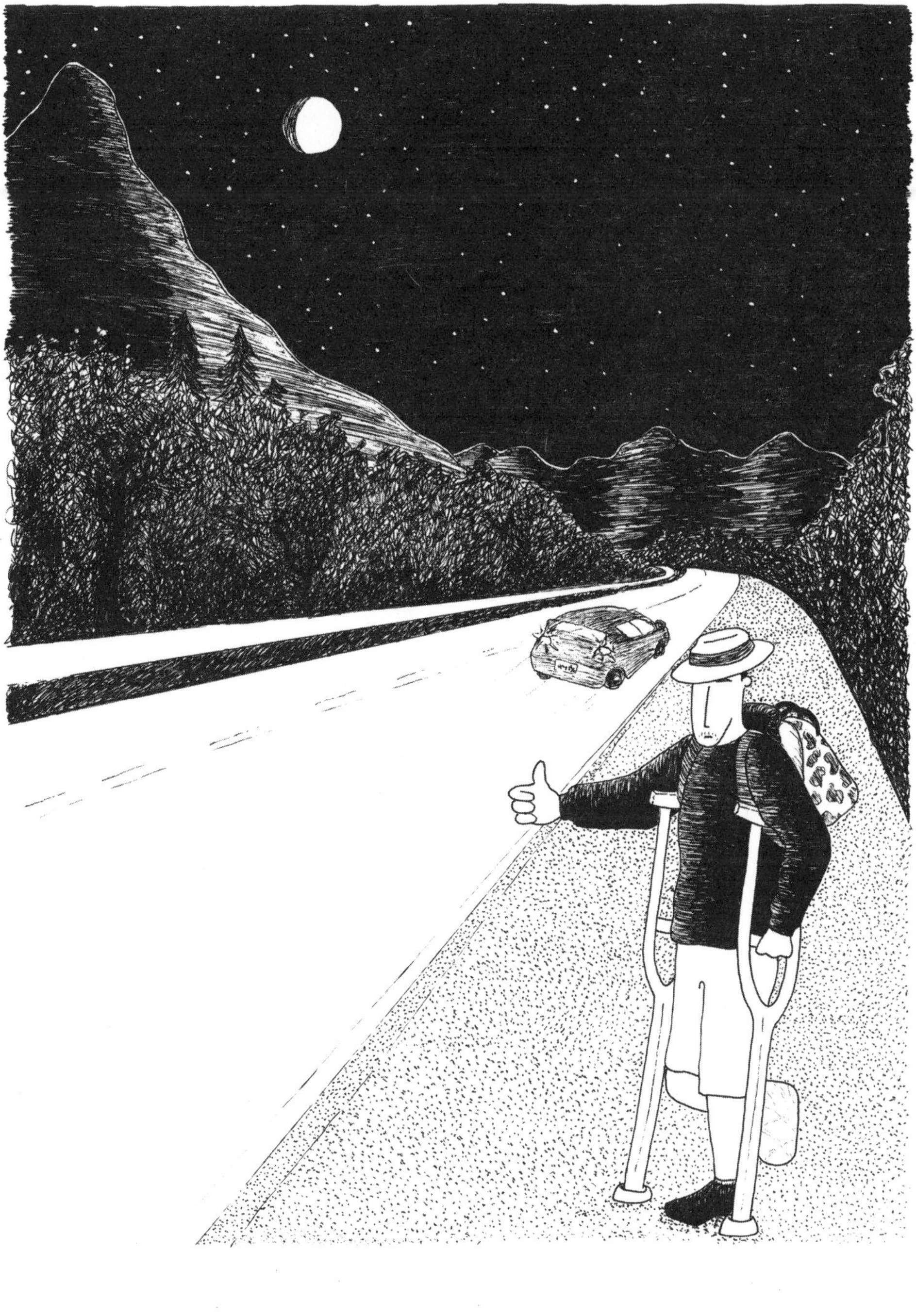

CHAPTER 8

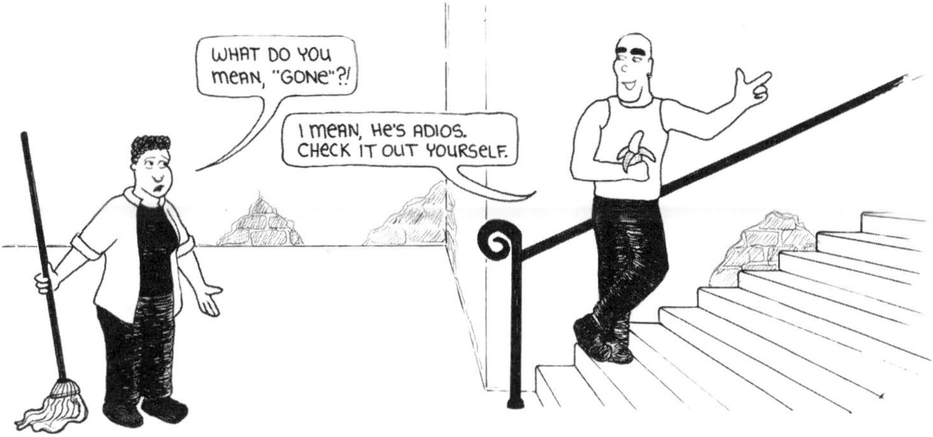
WHAT DO YOU MEAN, "GONE"?!
I MEAN, HE'S ADIOS. CHECK IT OUT YOURSELF.

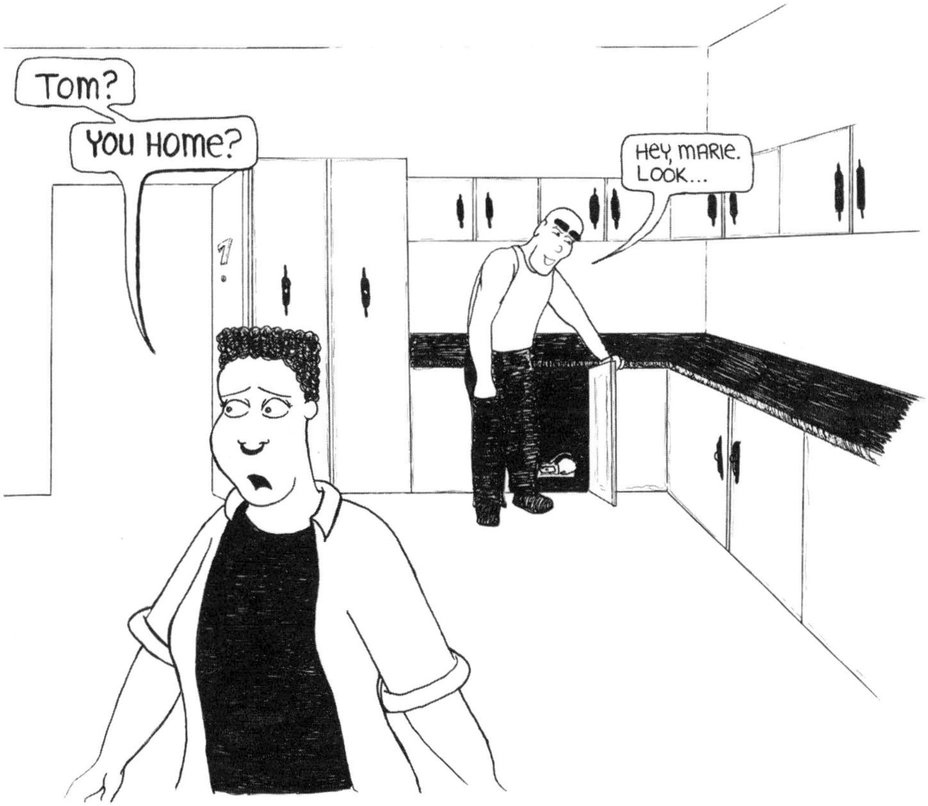
Tom?
You Home?
HEY, MARIE. LOOK...

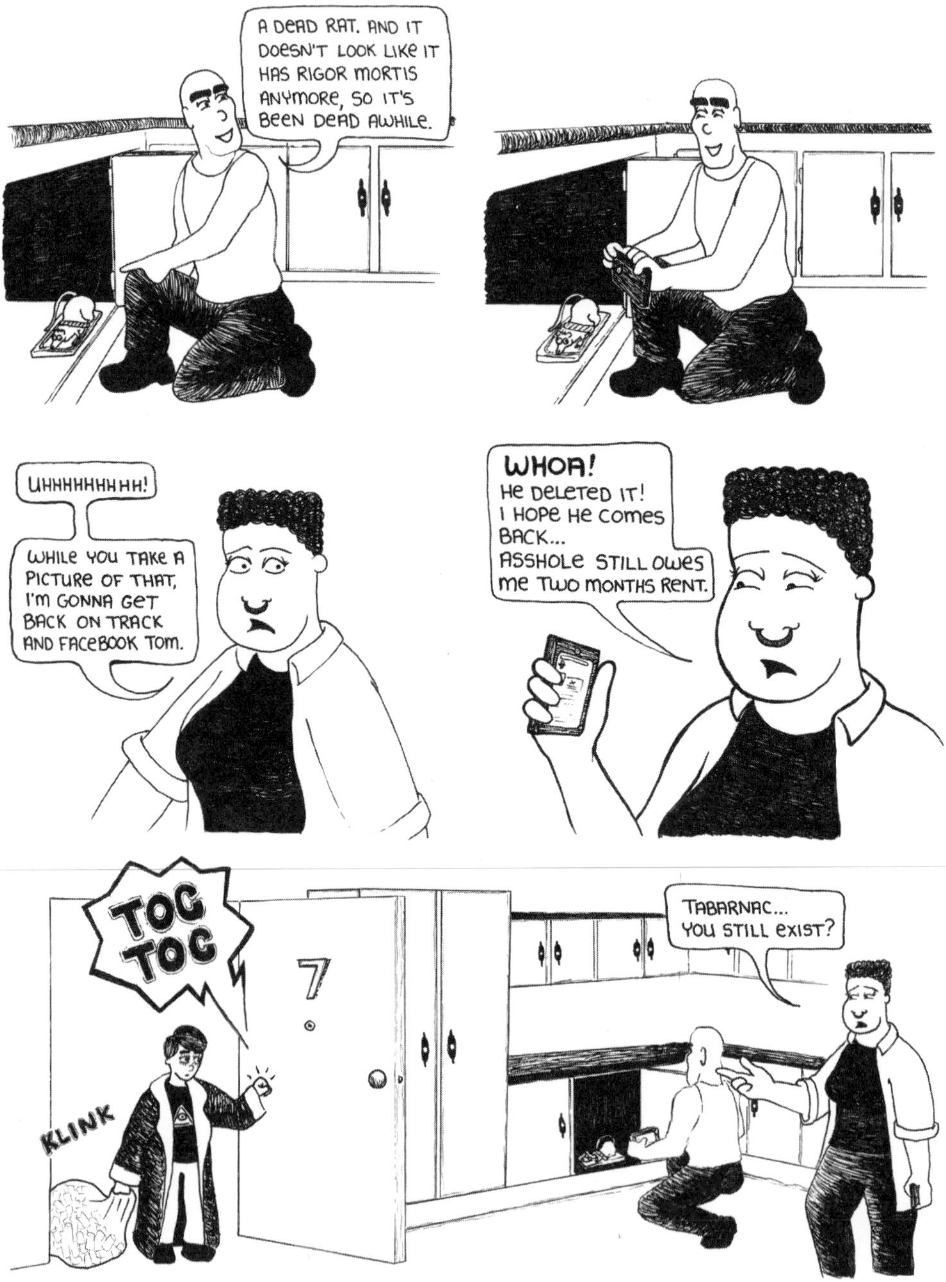
A DEAD RAT. AND IT DOESN'T LOOK LIKE IT HAS RIGOR MORTIS ANYMORE, SO IT'S BEEN DEAD AWHILE.
UHHHHHHHHH!
WHILE YOU TAKE A PICTURE OF THAT, I'M GONNA GET BACK ON TRACK AND FACEBOOK TOM.
WHOA!
HE DELETED IT! I HOPE HE COMES BACK... ASSHOLE STILL OWES ME TWO MONTHS RENT.
TOC TOC
7
KLINK
TABARNAC... YOU STILL EXIST?

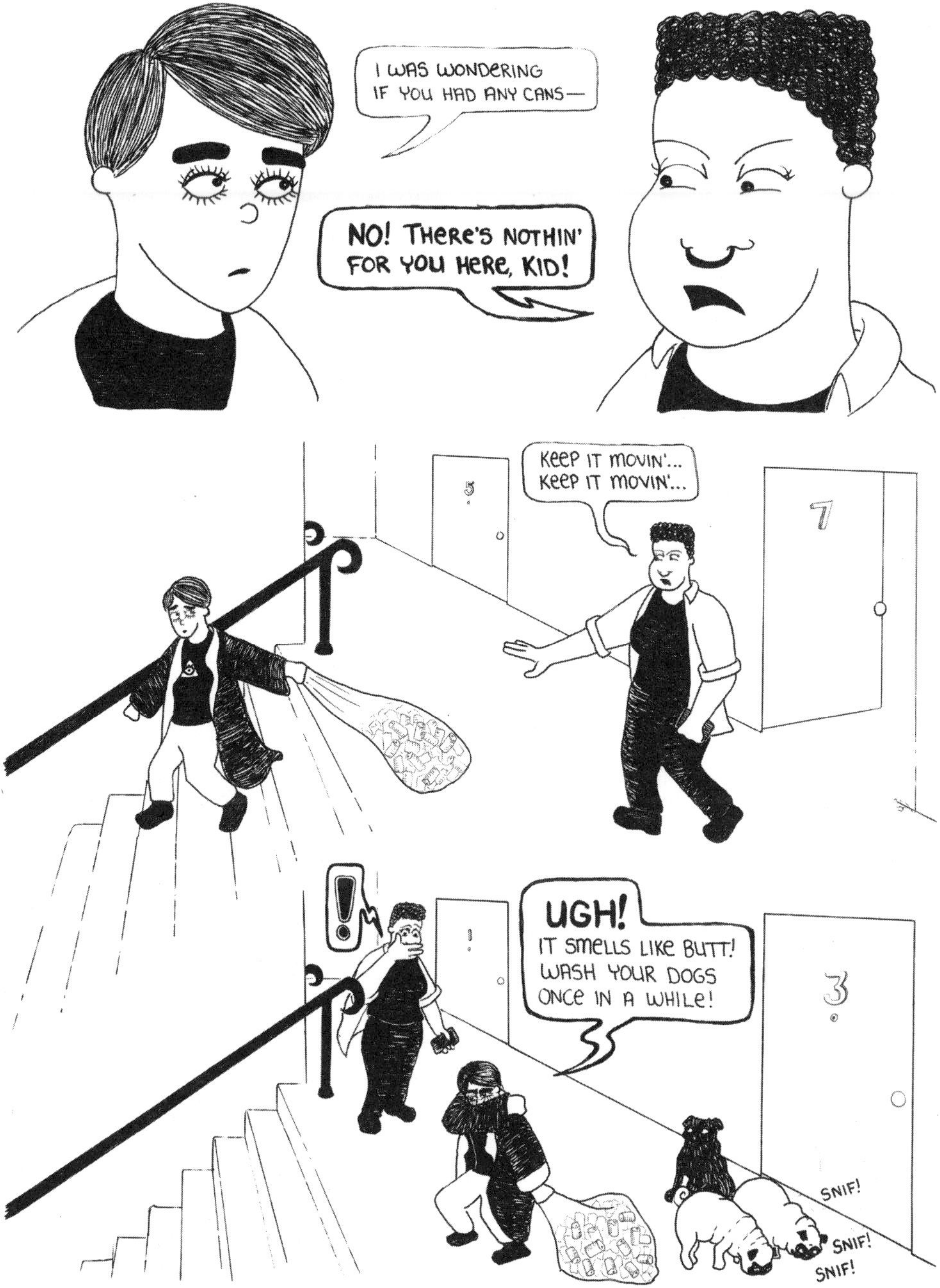
I WAS WONDERING IF YOU HAD ANY CANS—
NO! THERE'S NOTHIN' FOR YOU HERE, KID!
KEEP IT MOVIN'... KEEP IT MOVIN'...
!
UGH!
IT SMELLS LIKE BUTT! WASH YOUR DOGS ONCE IN A WHILE!
SNIF!
SNIF!
SNIF!

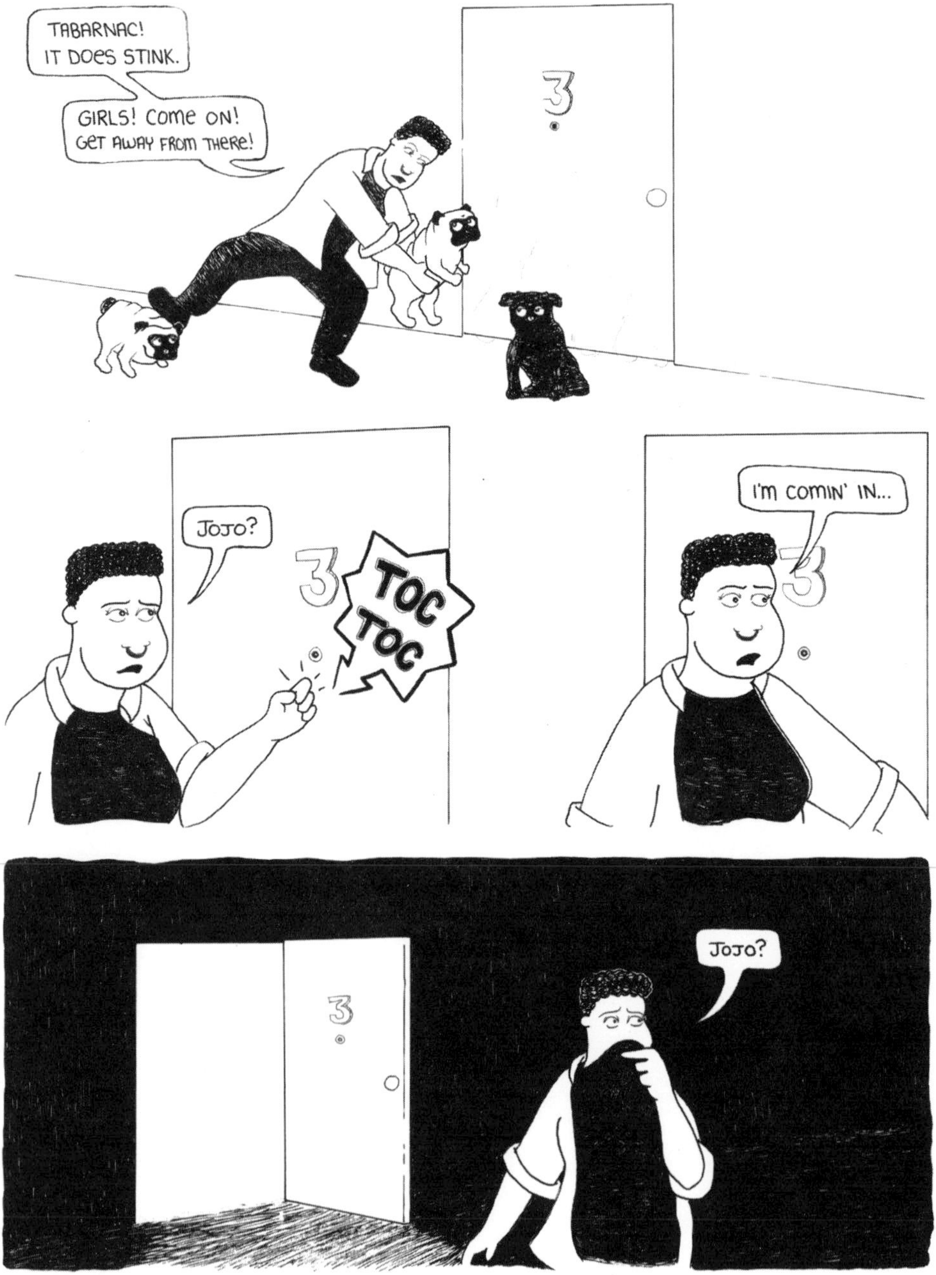
TABARNAC! IT DOES STINK.
GIRLS! COME ON! GET AWAY FROM THERE!
3
JOJO?
3
TOC TOC
I'M COMIN' IN...
3
3
JOJO?

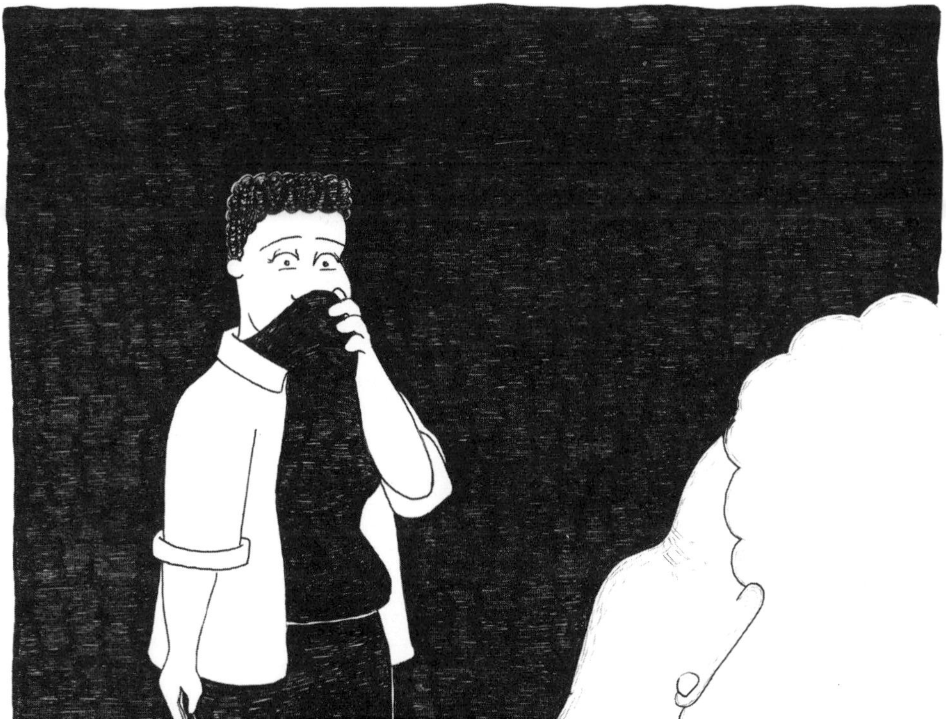

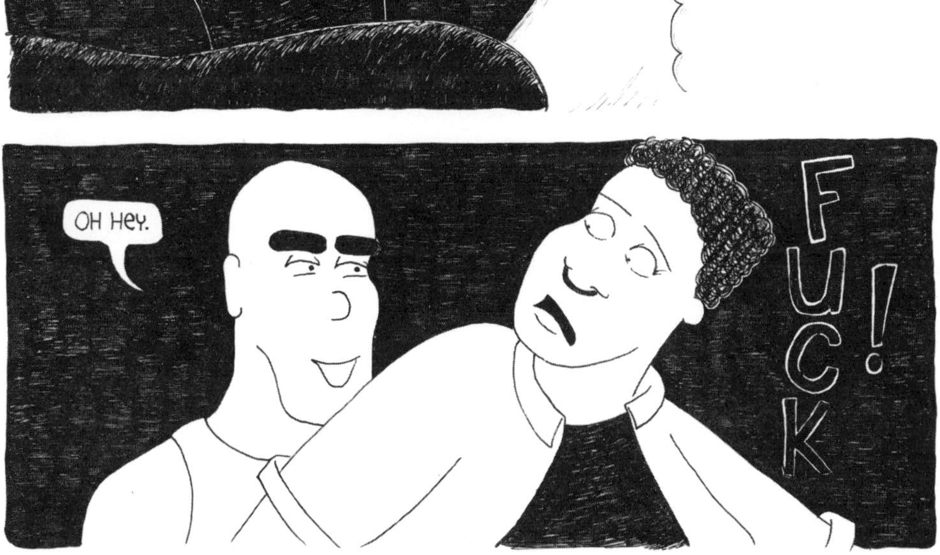

OH HEY.
FUCK!

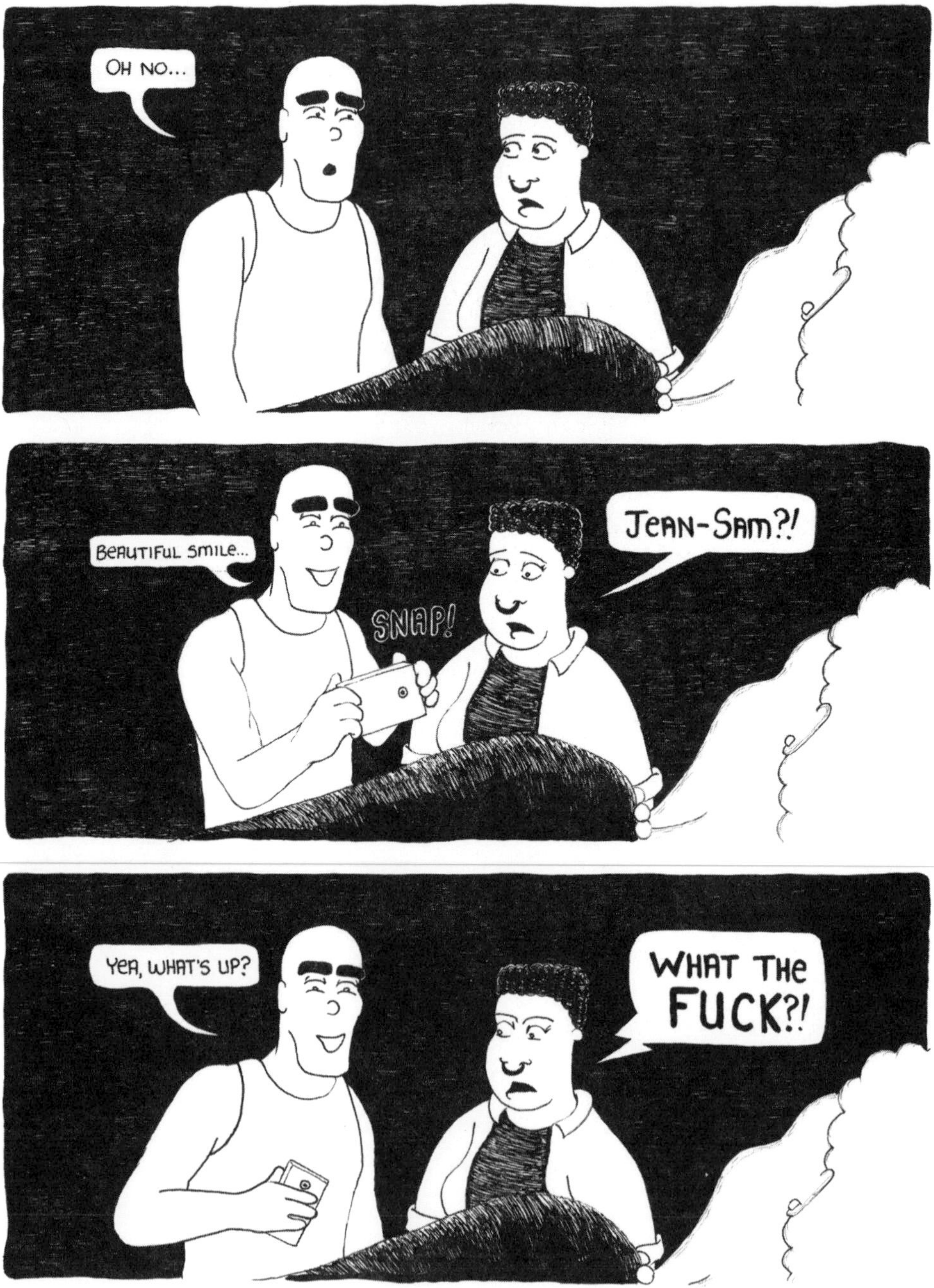
OH NO...
BEAUTIFUL SMILE...
SNAP!
JEAN-SAM?!
YEA, WHAT'S UP?
WHAT THE FUCK?!

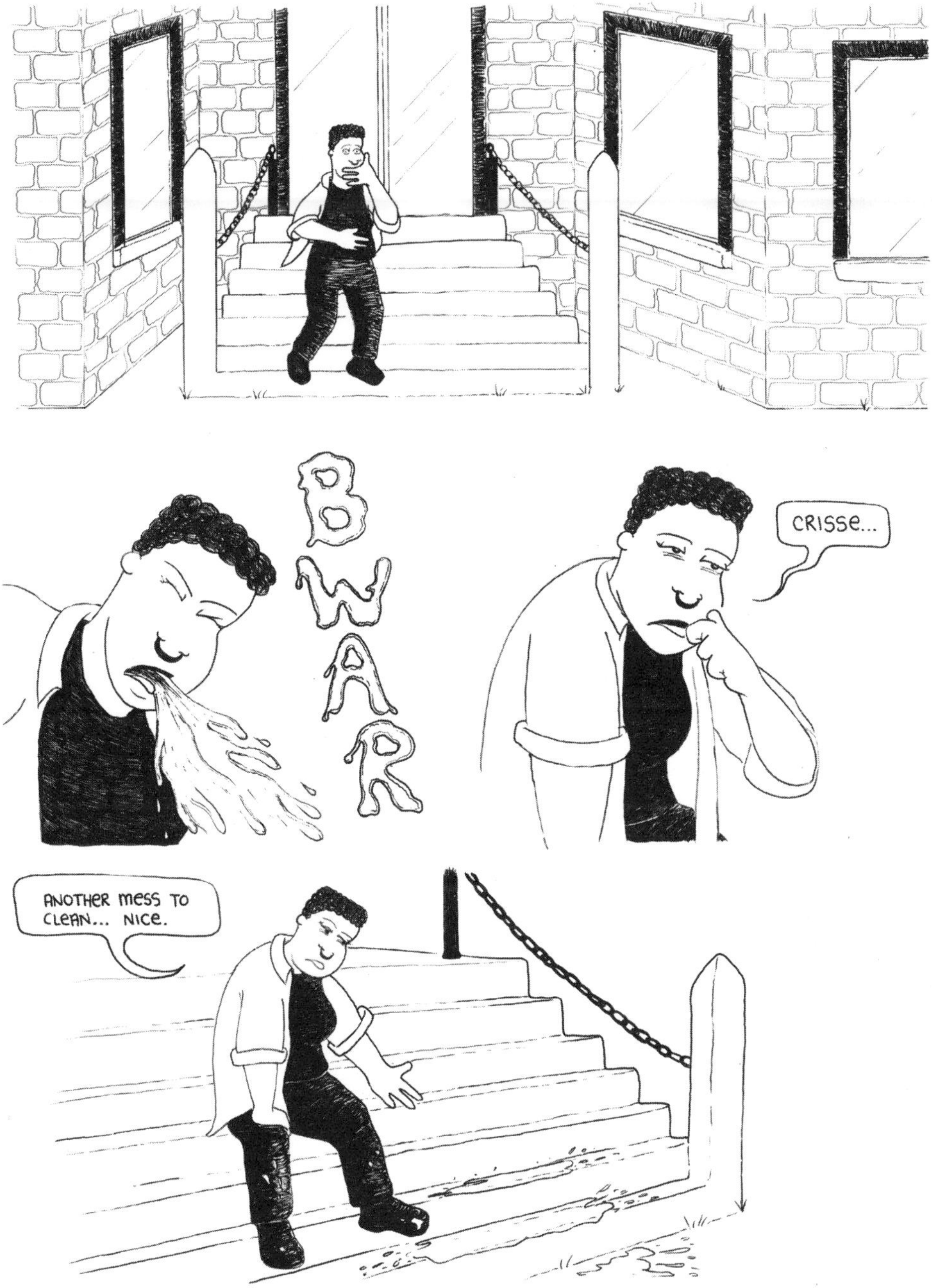
BWAR
CRISSE...
ANOTHER MESS TO CLEAN... NICE.

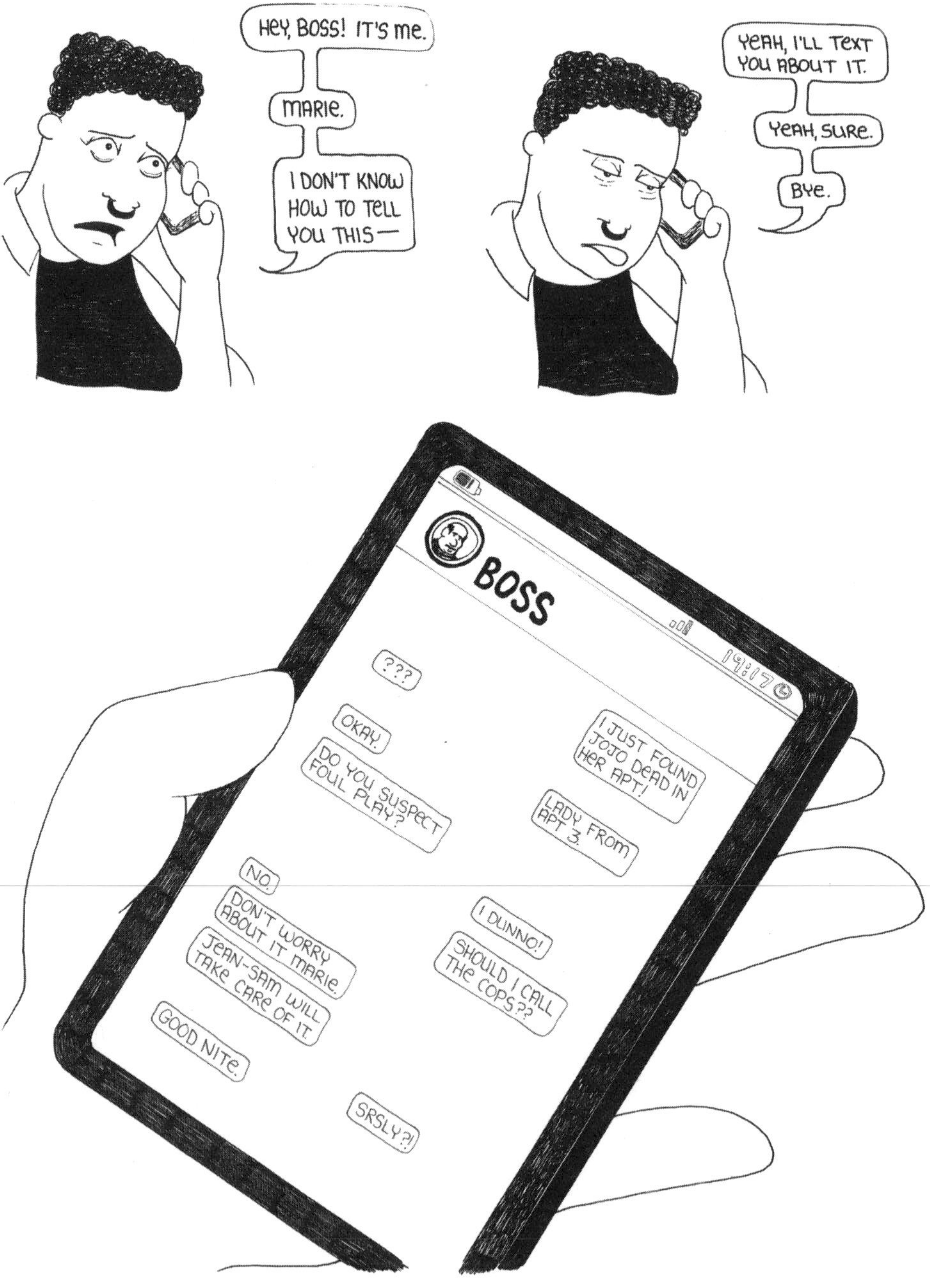
HEY, BOSS! IT'S ME.
MARIE.
I DON'T KNOW HOW TO TELL YOU THIS—
YEAH, I'LL TEXT YOU ABOUT IT.
YEAH, SURE.
BYE.
BOSS
19:17
???
I JUST FOUND JOJO DEAD IN HER APT!
OKAY.
DO YOU SUSPECT FOUL PLAY?
LADY FROM APT 3.
NO.
I DUNNO!
DON'T WORRY ABOUT IT MARIE.
SHOULD I CALL THE COPS??
JEAN-SAM WILL TAKE CARE OF IT.
GOOD NITE.
SRSLY?!

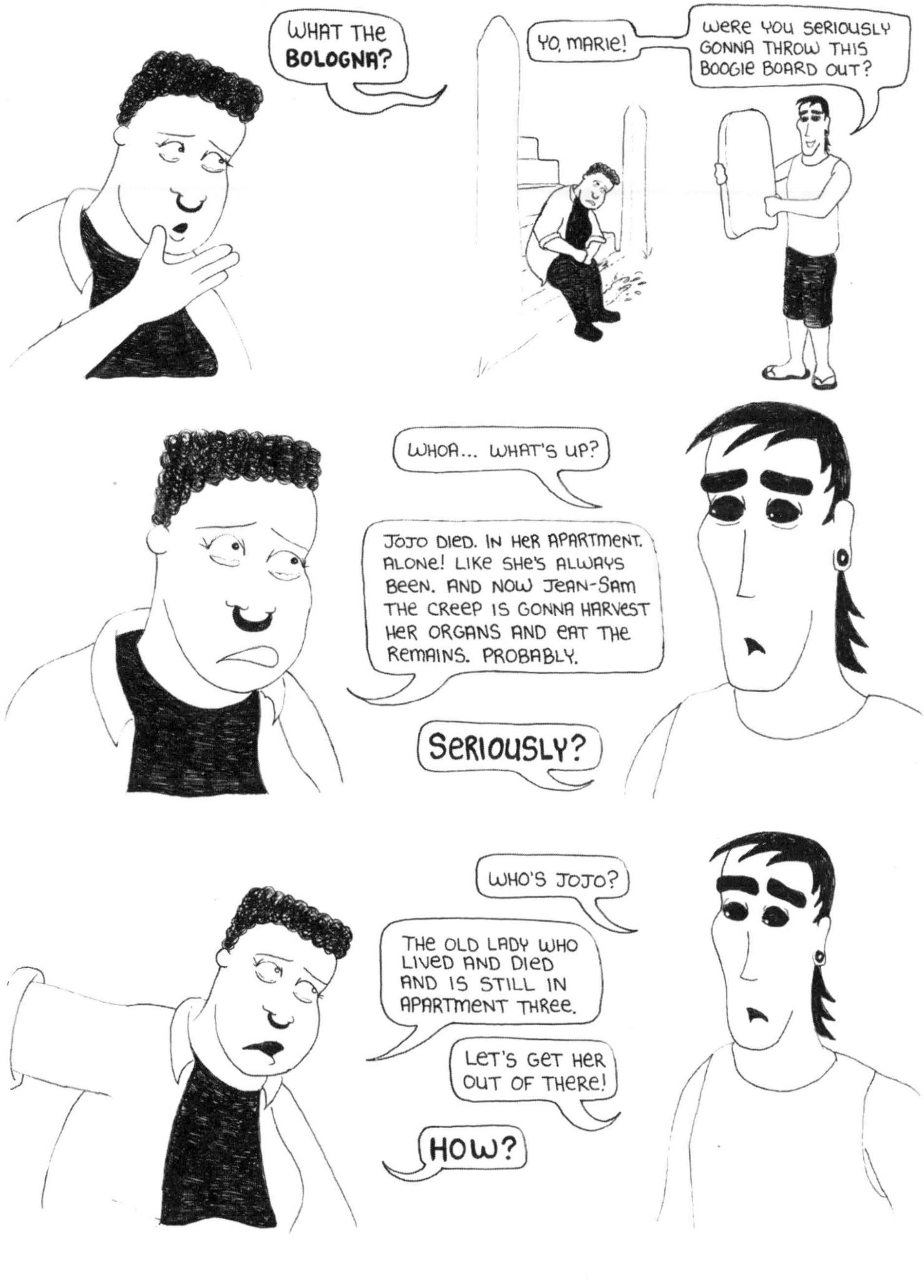
WHAT THE BOLOGNA?
YO, MARIE!
WERE YOU SERIOUSLY GONNA THROW THIS BOOGIE BOARD OUT?
WHOA... WHAT'S UP?
JOJO DIED. IN HER APARTMENT. ALONE! LIKE SHE'S ALWAYS BEEN. AND NOW JEAN-SAM THE CREEP IS GONNA HARVEST HER ORGANS AND EAT THE REMAINS. PROBABLY.
SERIOUSLY?
WHO'S JOJO?
THE OLD LADY WHO LIVED AND DIED AND IS STILL IN APARTMENT THREE.
LET'S GET HER OUT OF THERE!
HOW?

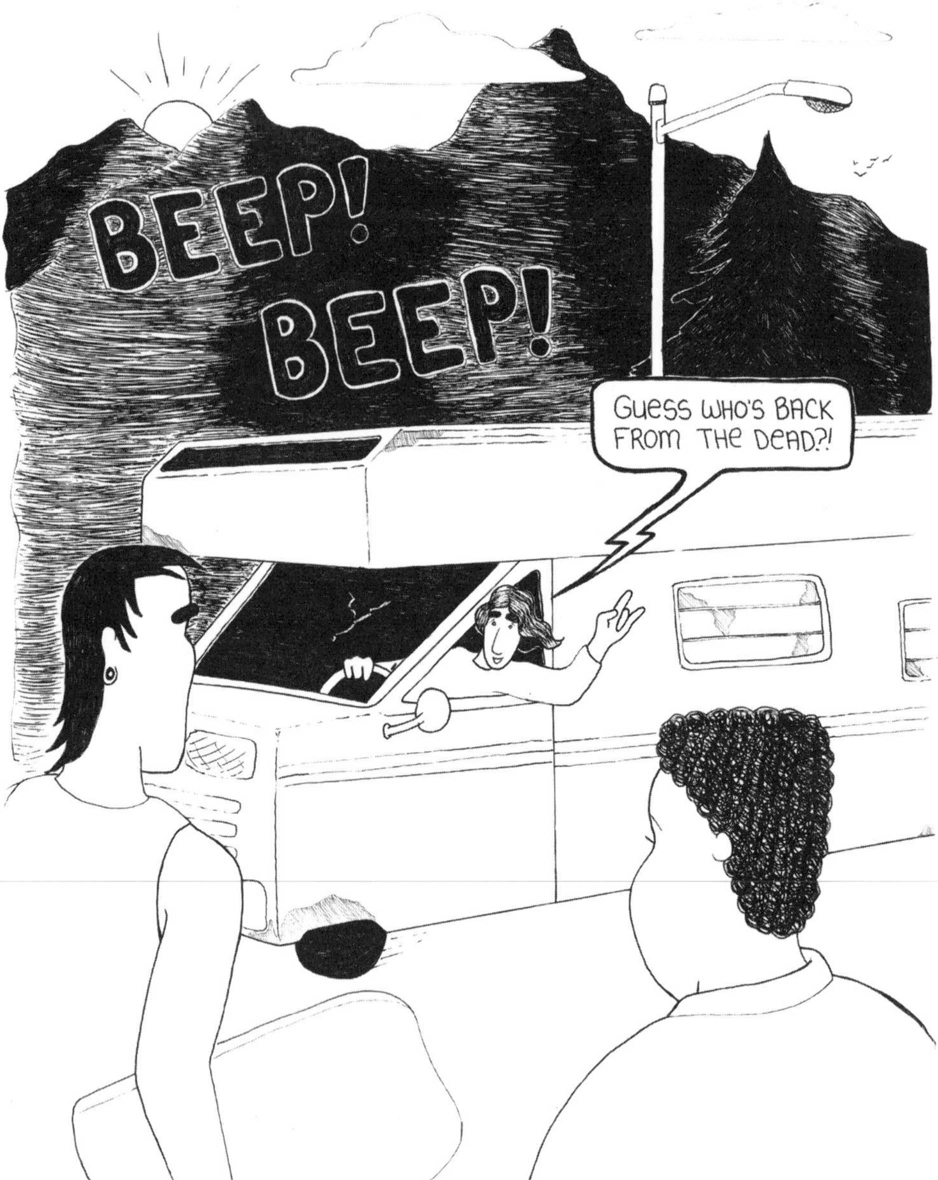
BEEP!
BEEP!
GUESS WHO'S BACK FROM THE DEAD?!

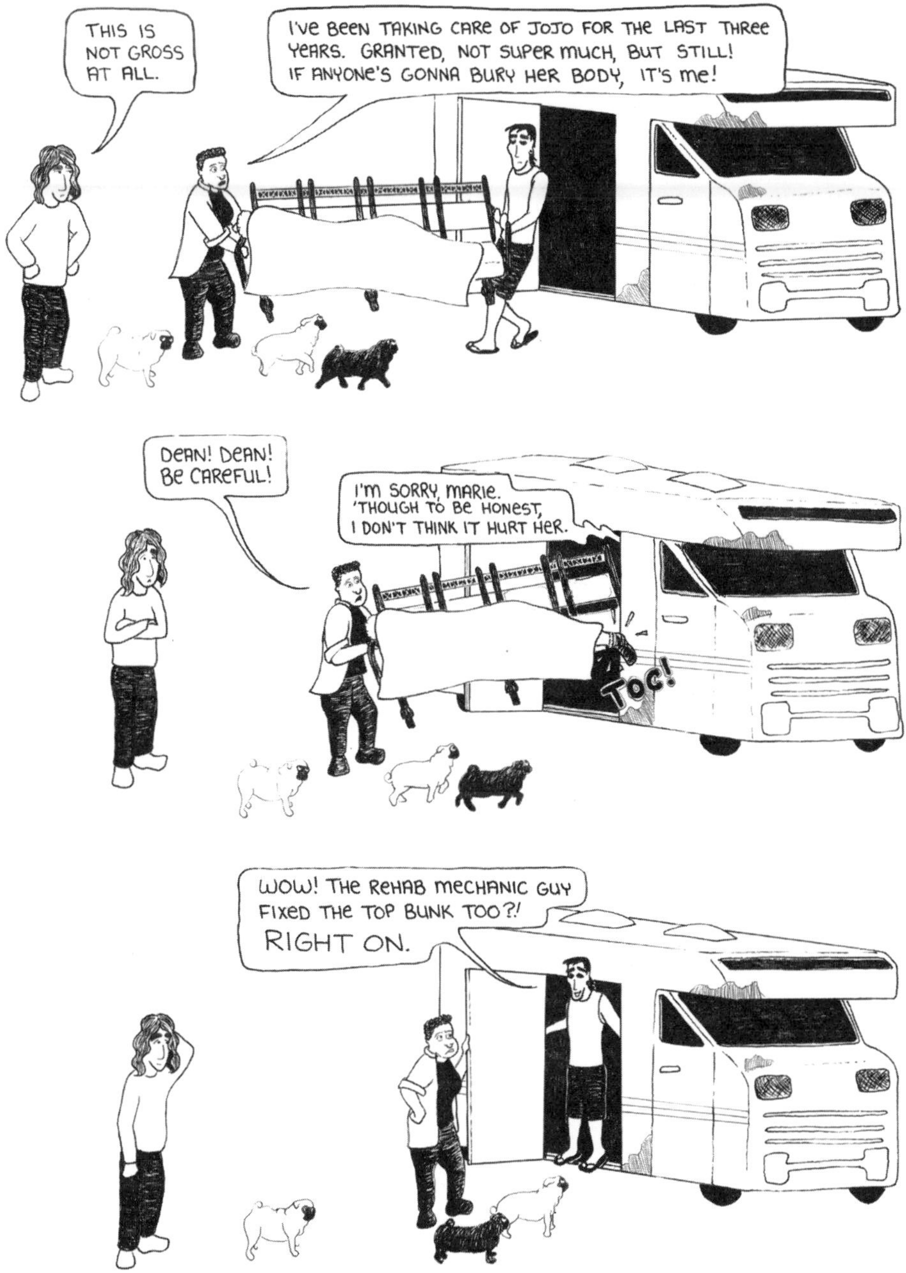
THIS IS NOT GROSS AT ALL.
I've BEEN TAKING CARE OF JOJO FOR THE LAST THREE YEARS. GRANTED, NOT SUPER MUCH, BUT STILL! IF ANYONE'S GONNA BURY HER BODY, IT'S me!
DEAN! DEAN! Be CAREFUL!
I'm SORRY, mARIe. 'THOUGH TO BE HONEST, I DON'T THINK IT HURT HER.
TOC!
WOW! THE REHAB MECHANIC GUY FIXED THE TOP BUNK TOO?!
RIGHT ON.

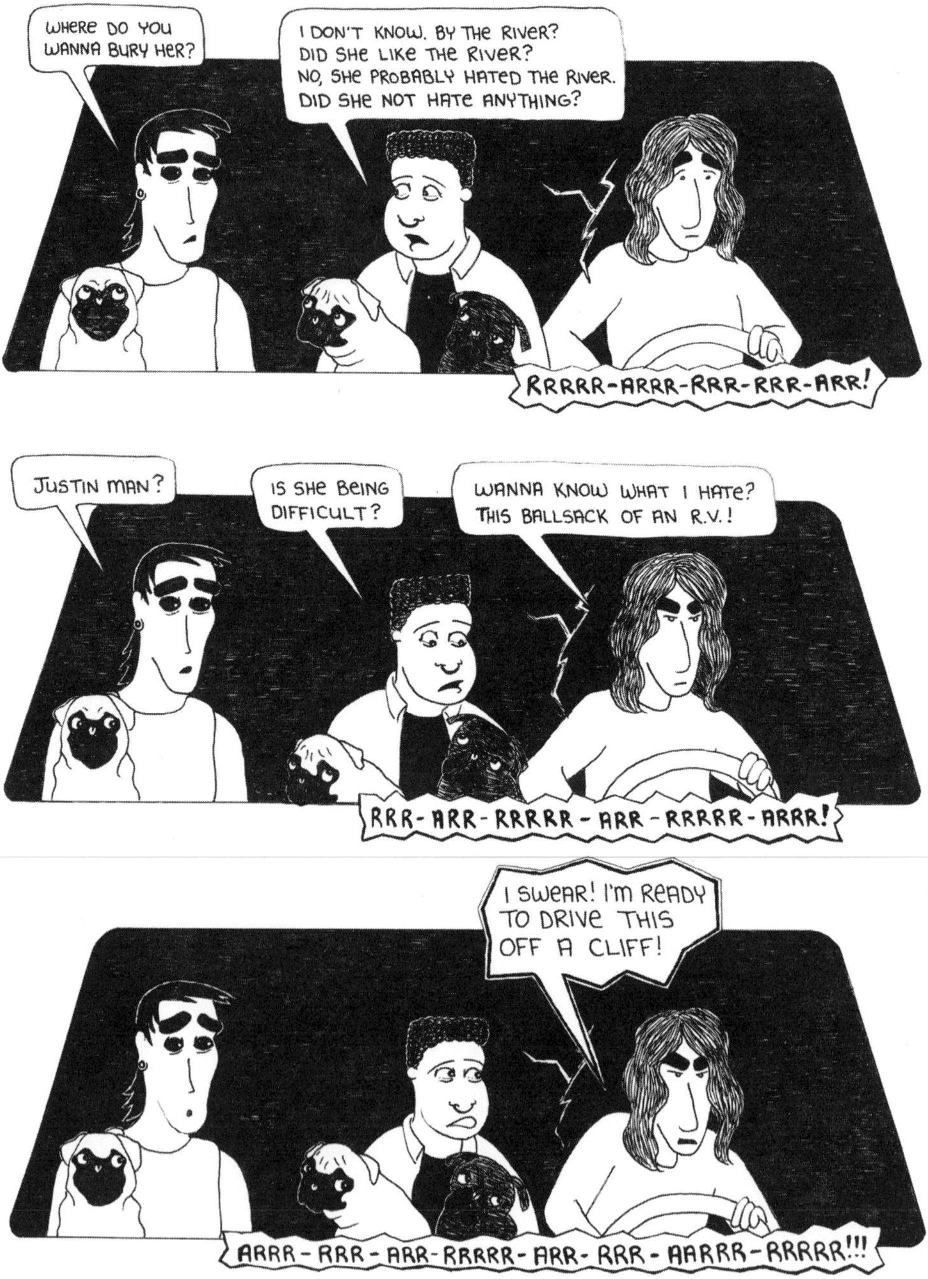
WHERE DO YOU WANNA BURY HER?
I DON'T KNOW. BY THE RIVER? DID SHE LIKE THE RIVER? NO, SHE PROBABLY HATED THE RIVER. DID SHE NOT HATE ANYTHING?
RRRRR-ARRR-RRR-RRR-ARR!
JUSTIN MAN?
IS SHE BEING DIFFICULT?
WANNA KNOW WHAT I HATE? THIS BALLSACK OF AN R.V.!
RRR-ARR-RRRRR-ARR-RRRRR-ARRR!
I SWEAR! I'M READY TO DRIVE THIS OFF A CLIFF!
ARRR-RRR-ARR-RRRRR-ARR-RRR-AARRR-RRRRR!!!

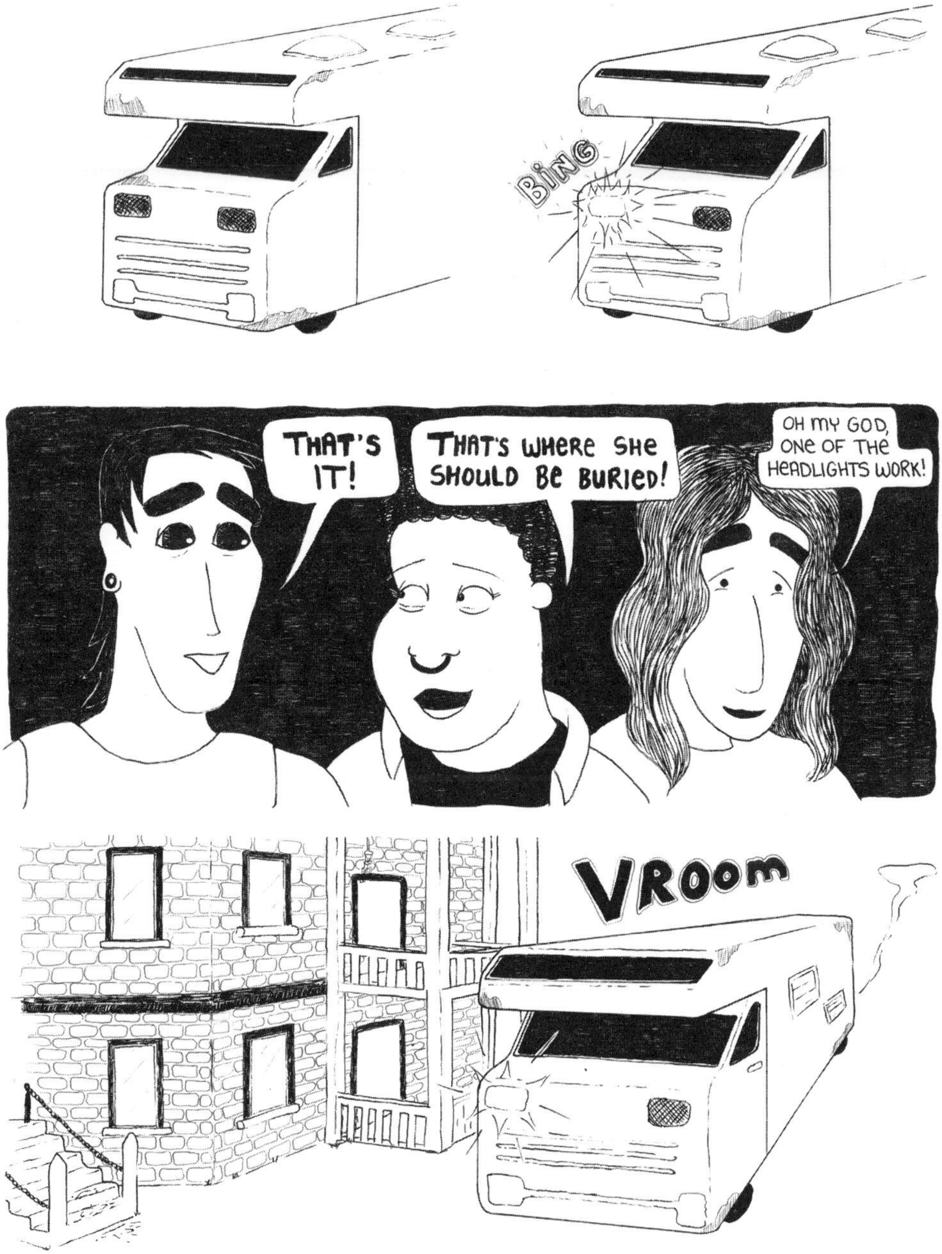
BING
THAT'S IT!
THAT'S WHERE SHE SHOULD BE BURIED!
OH MY GOD, ONE OF THE HEADLIGHTS WORK!
VROOM

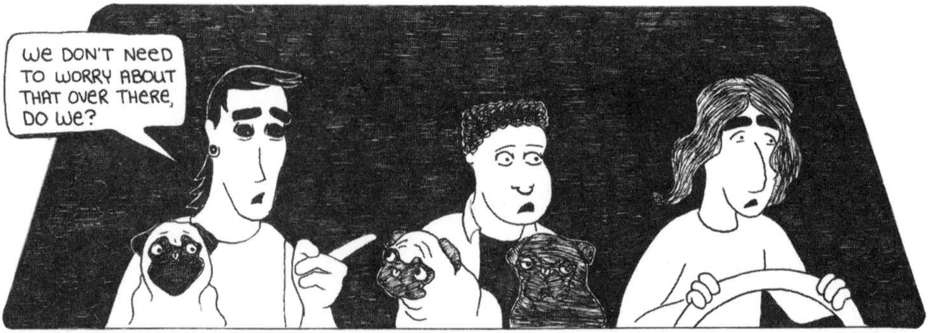
WE DON'T NEED TO WORRY ABOUT THAT OVER THERE, DO WE?

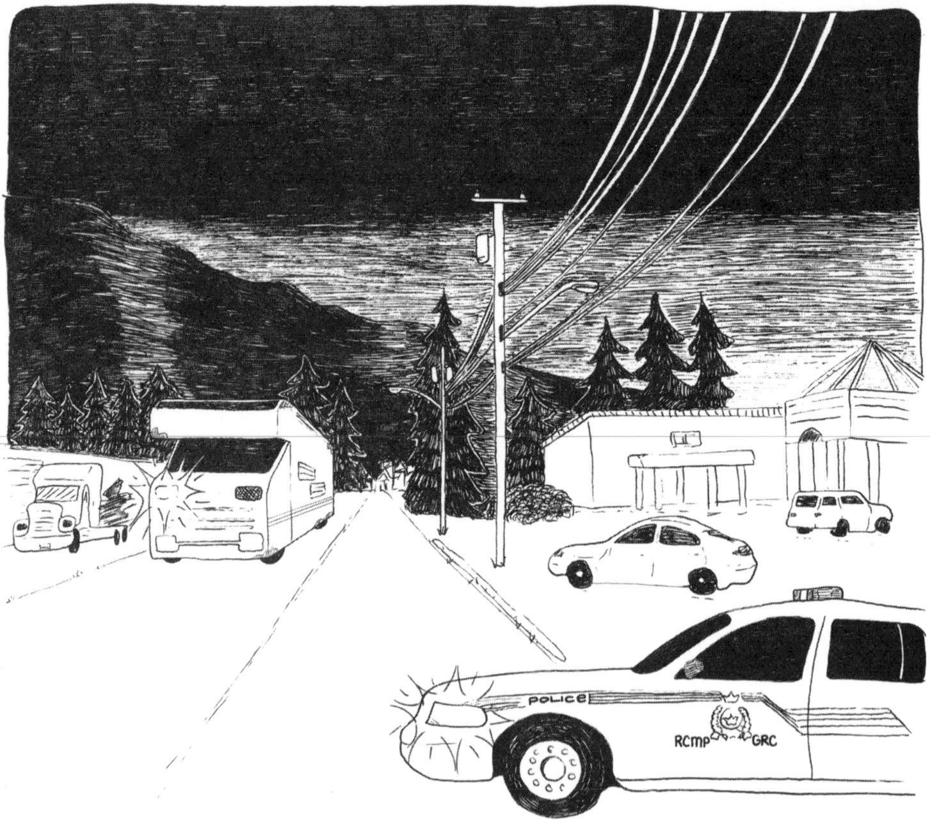
POLICE
RCMP
GRC

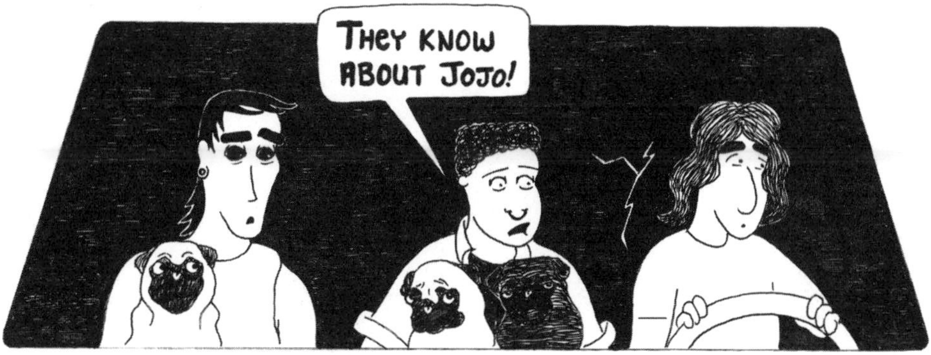
THEY KNOW ABOUT JOJO!

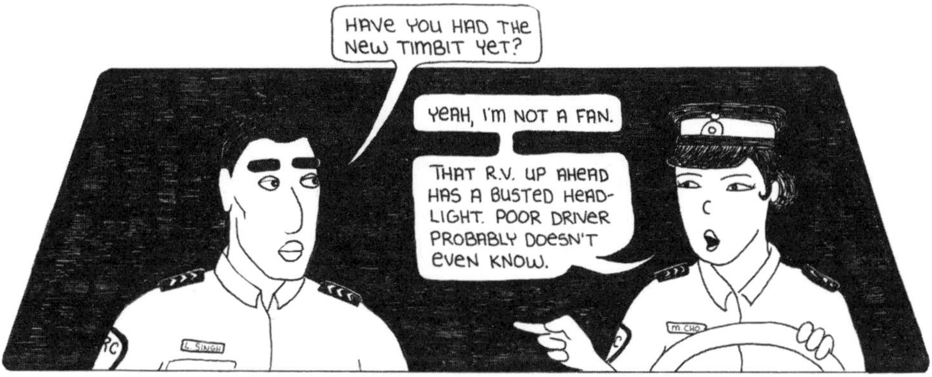
HAVE YOU HAD THE NEW TIMBIT YET?
YEAH, I'M NOT A FAN.
THAT R.V. UP AHEAD HAS A BUSTED HEAD-LIGHT. POOR DRIVER PROBABLY DOESN'T EVEN KNOW.
L. SINGH
M. CHO

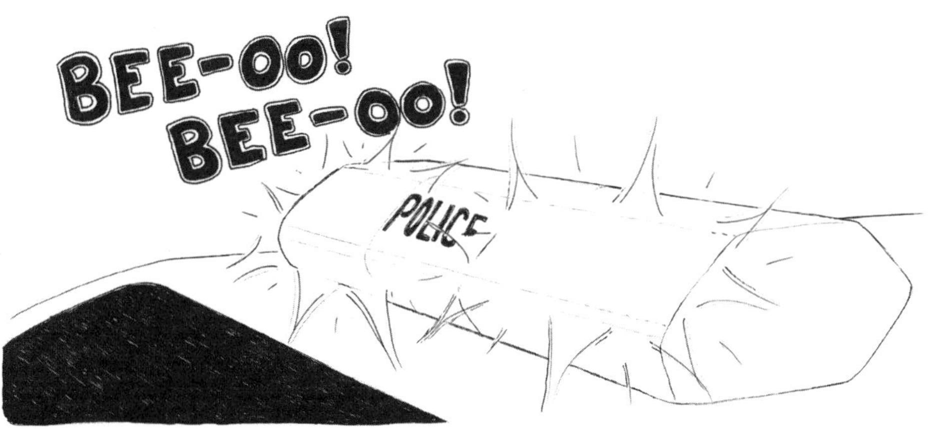
BEE-OO! BEE-OO!
POLICE

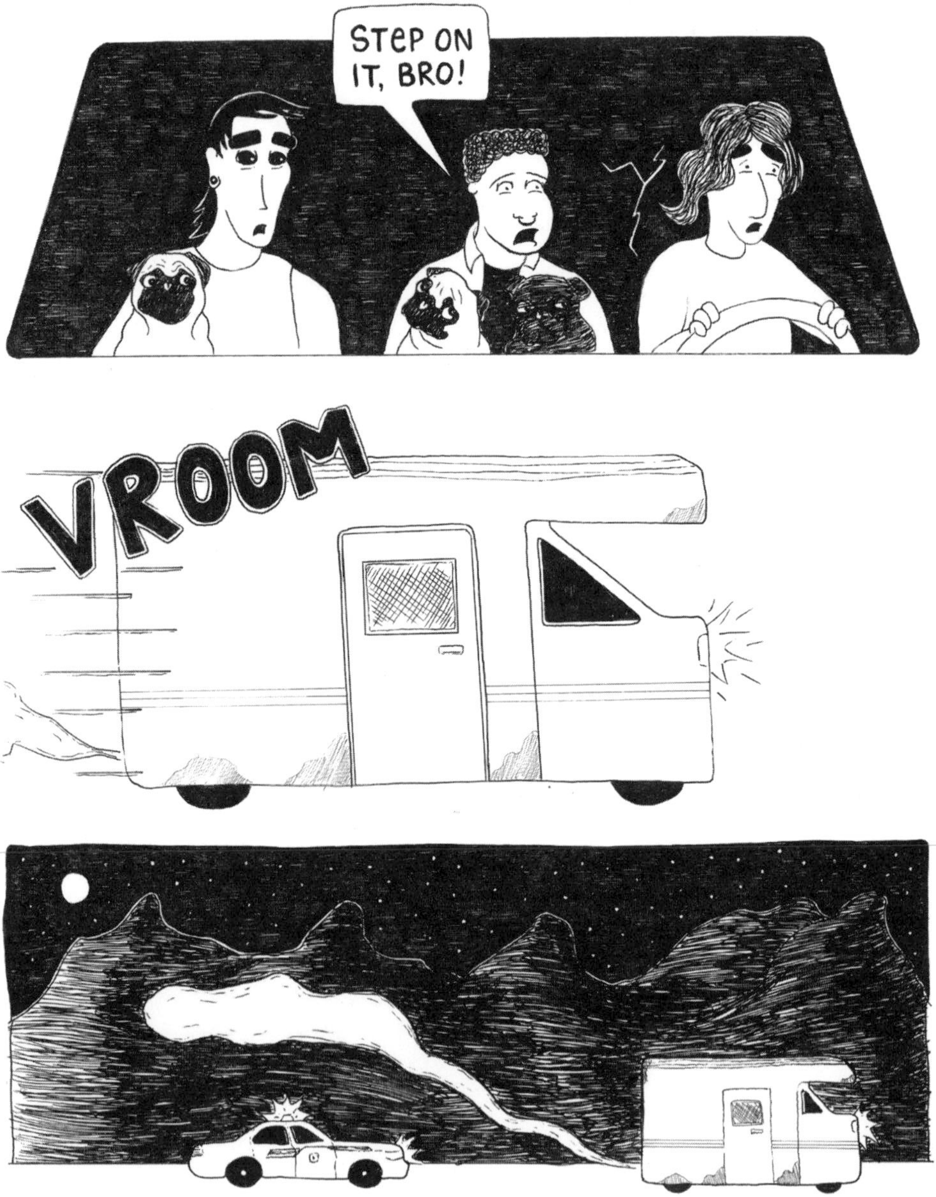
STEP ON IT, BRO!
VROOM

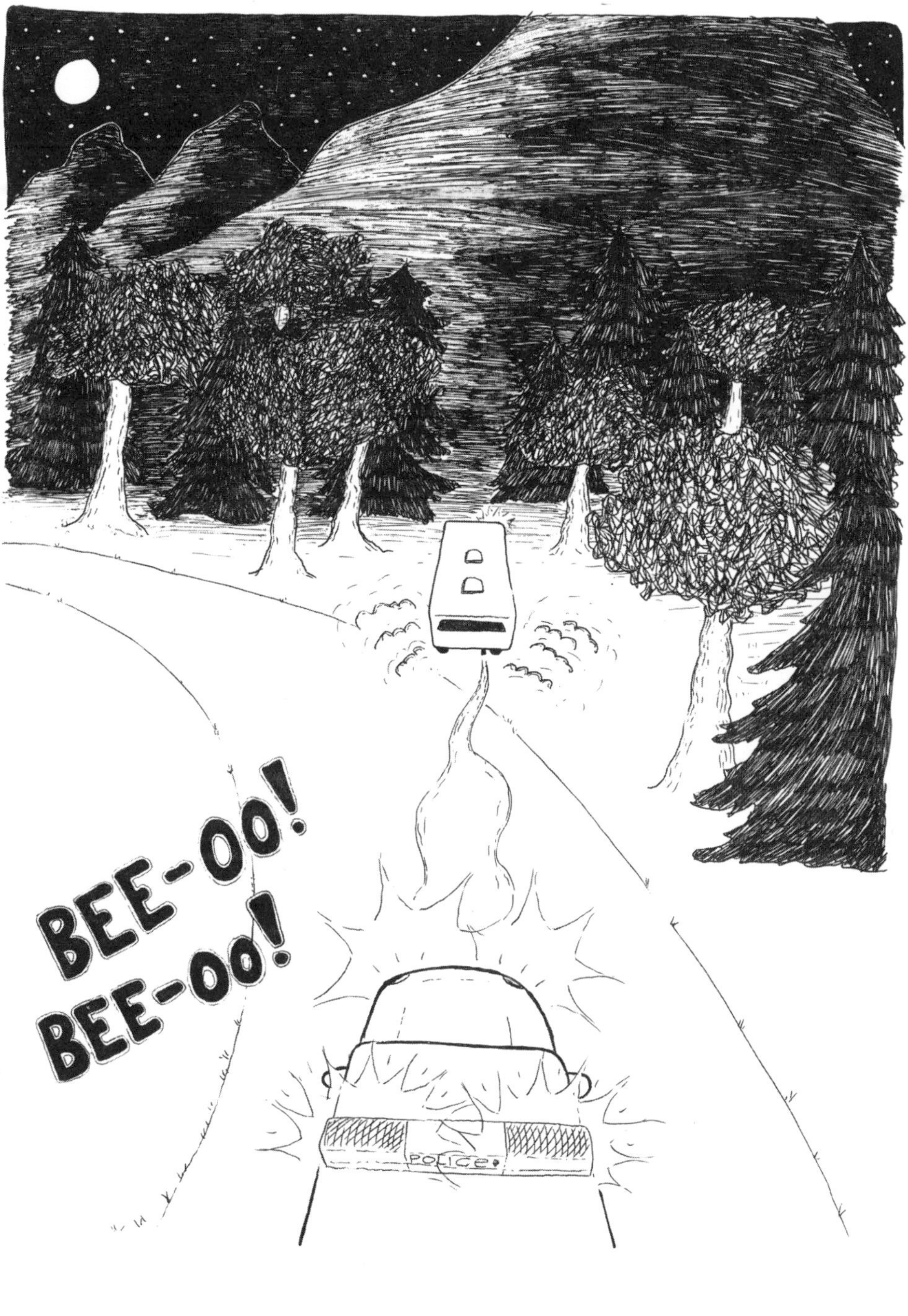
BEE-OO!
BEE-OO!
POLICE

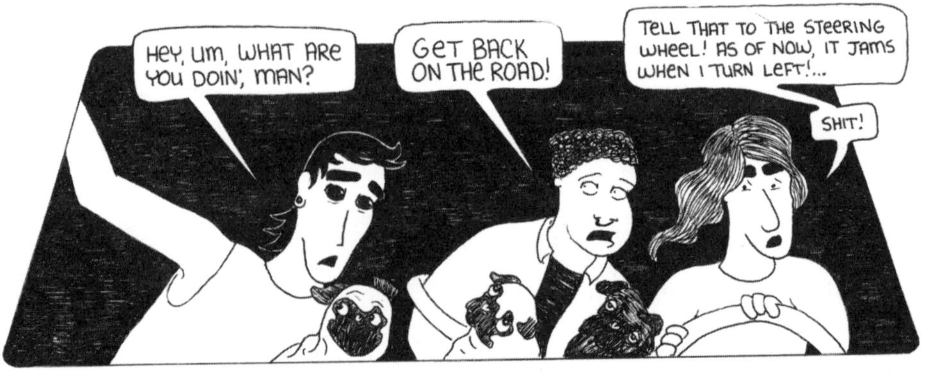
HEY, UM, WHAT ARE YOU DOIN', MAN?
GET BACK ON THE ROAD!
TELL THAT TO THE STEERING WHEEL! AS OF NOW, IT JAMS WHEN I TURN LEFT!...
SHIT!

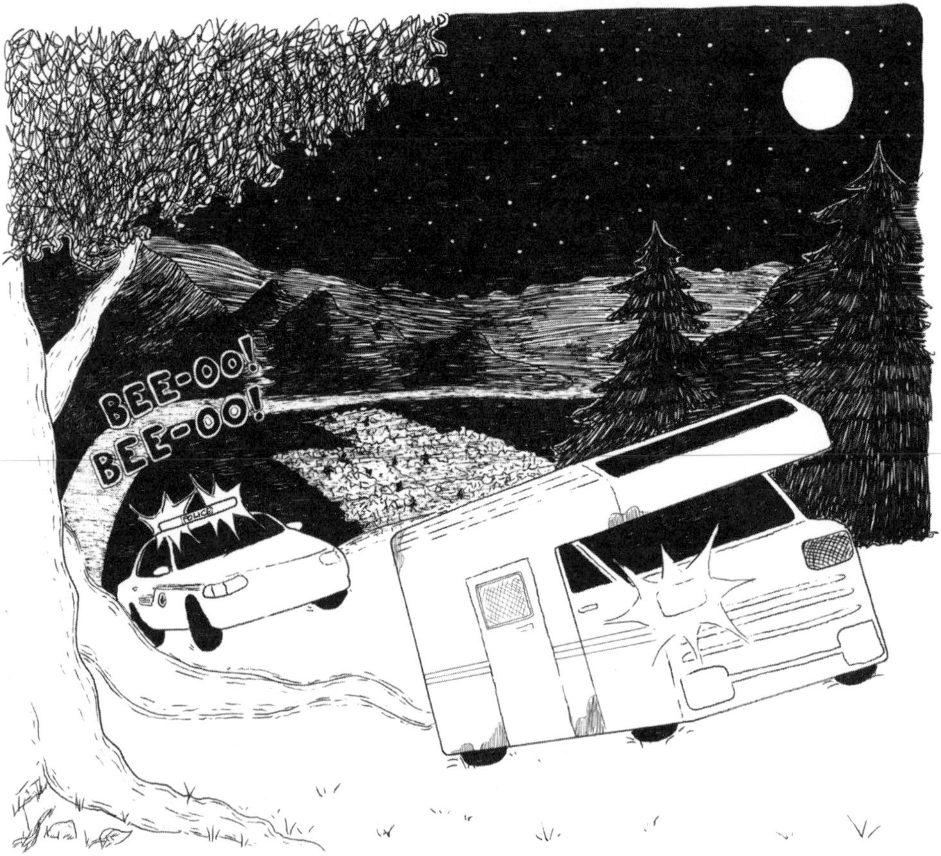
BEE-OO! BEE-OO!
POLICE

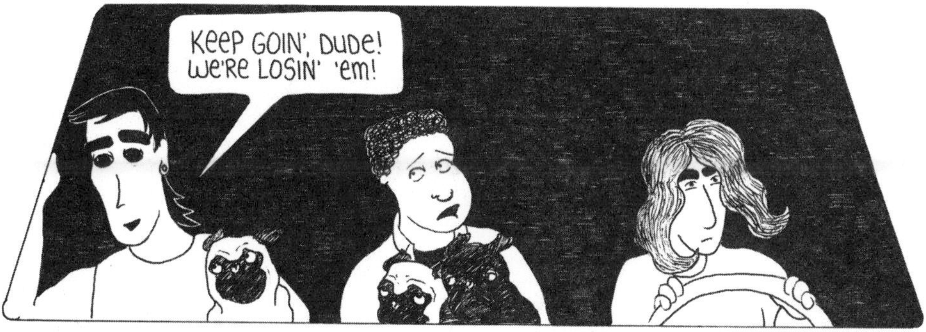
KEEP GOIN', DUDE! WE'RE LOSIN' 'EM!

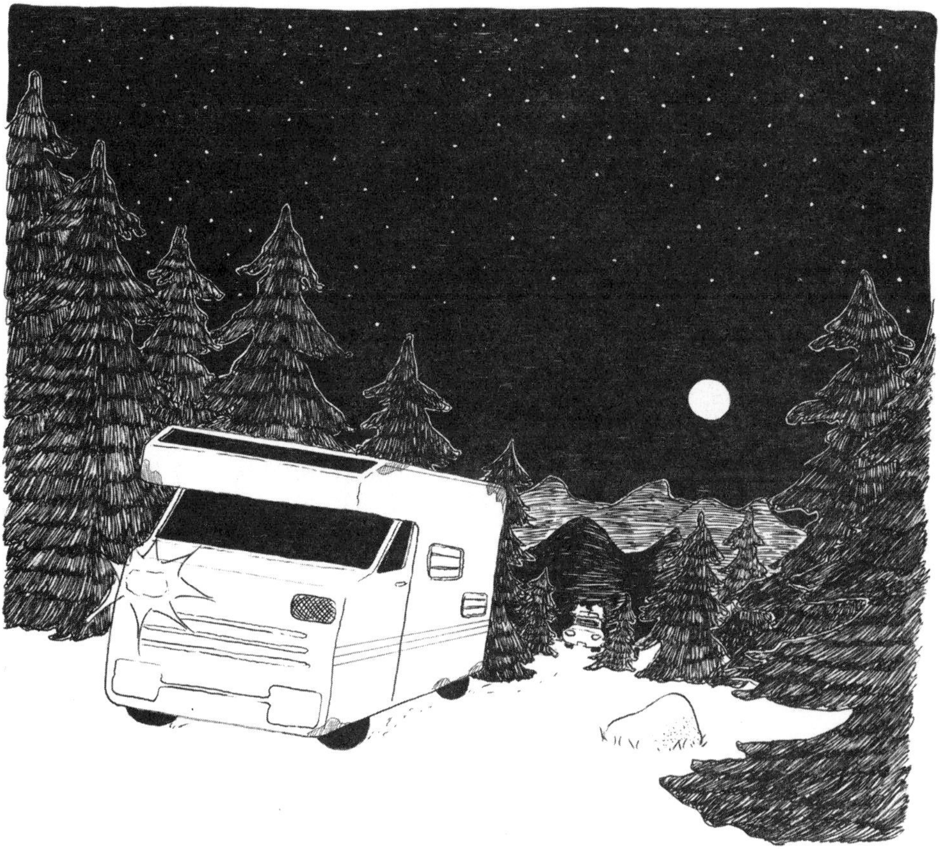

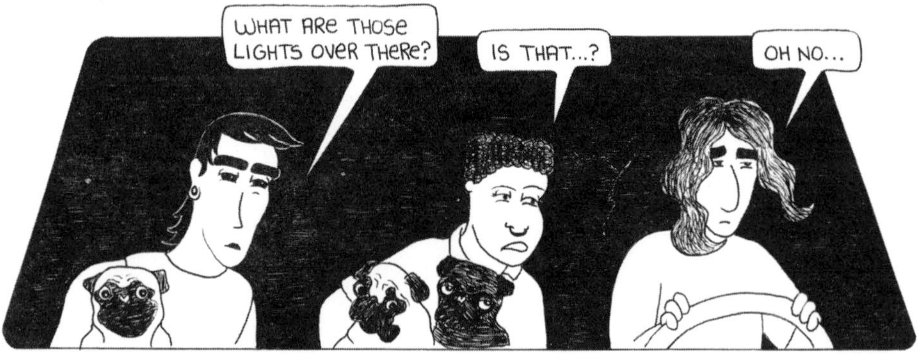
WHAT ARE THOSE LIGHTS OVER THERE?
IS THAT...?
OH NO...

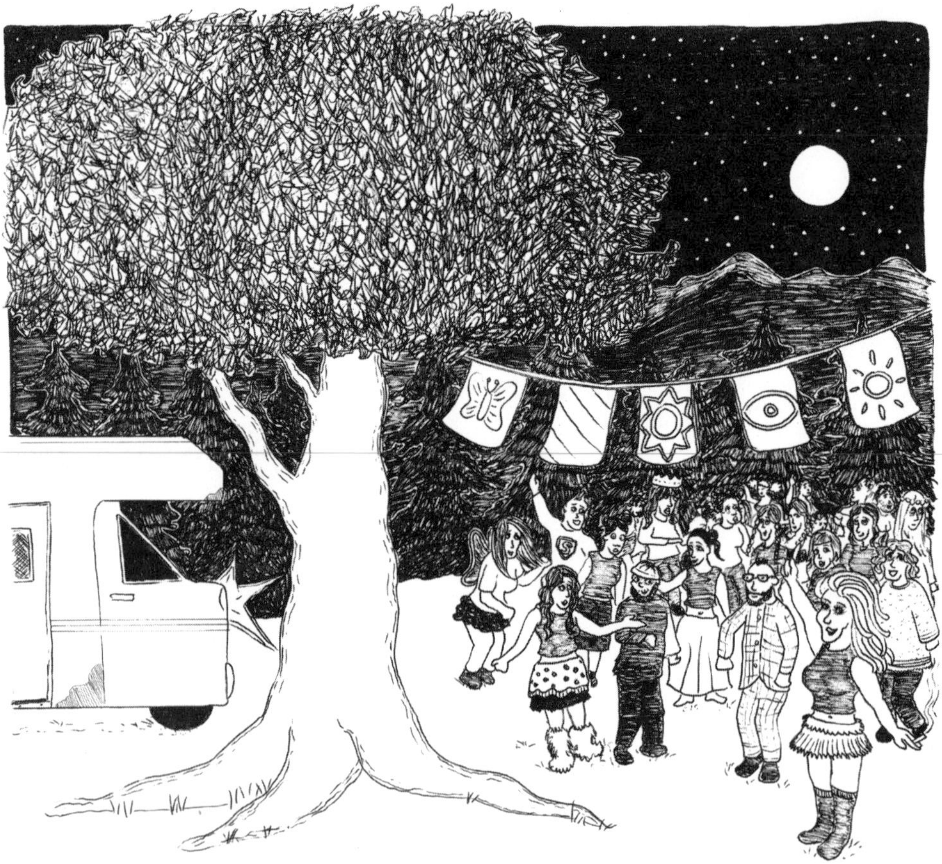

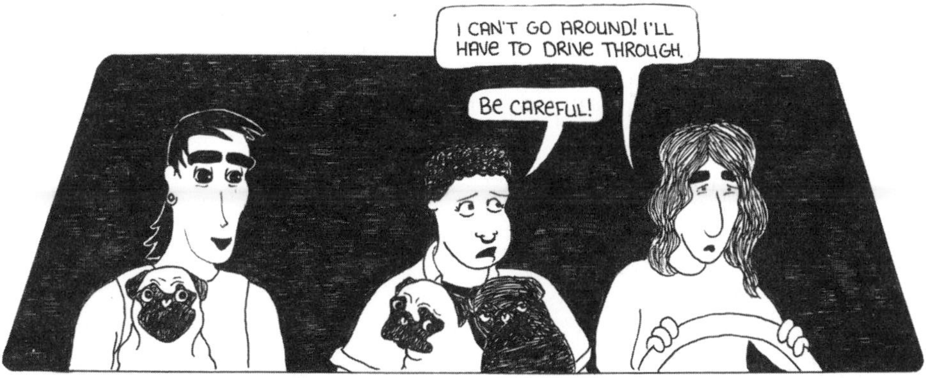
I CAN'T GO AROUND! I'LL HAVE TO DRIVE THROUGH.
Be CAREFUL!

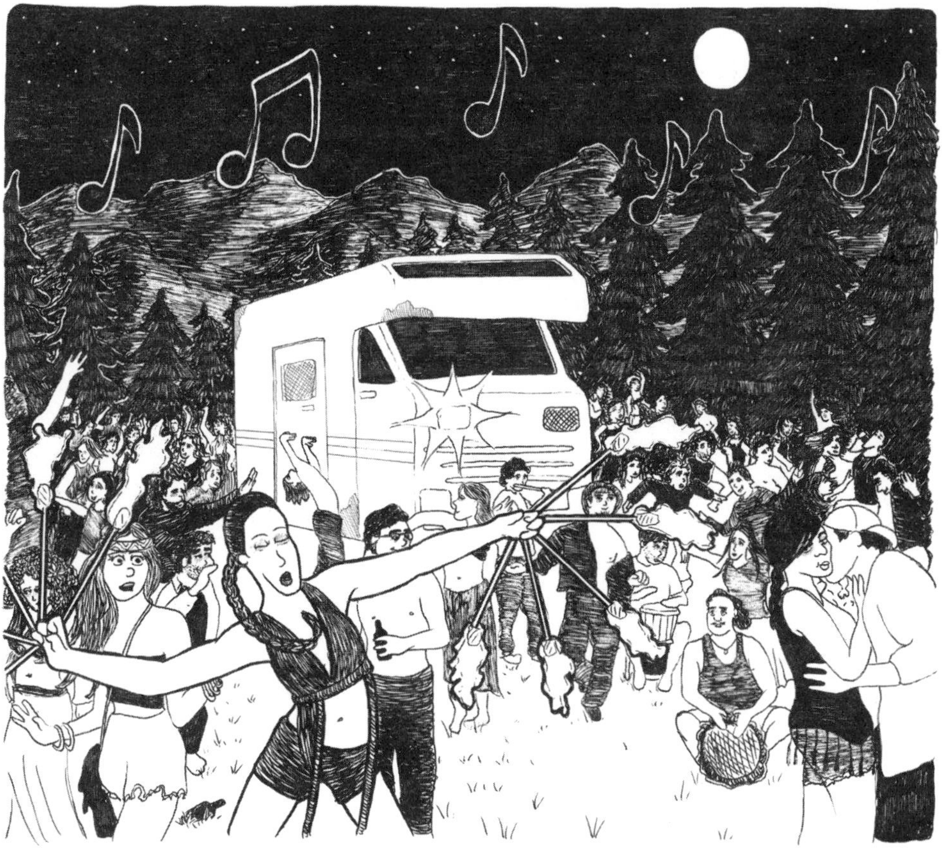

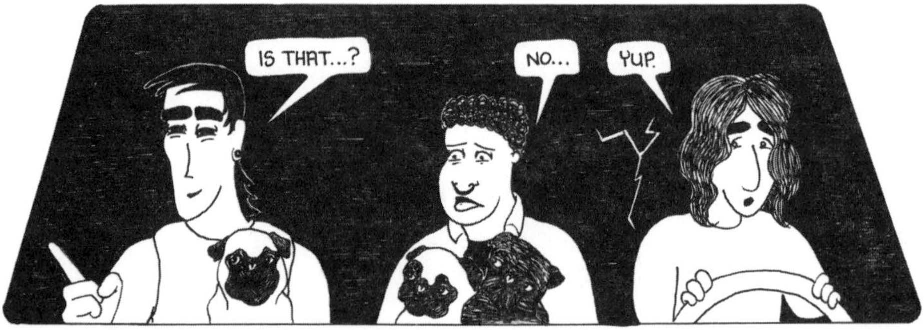
IS THAT...?
NO...
YUP.

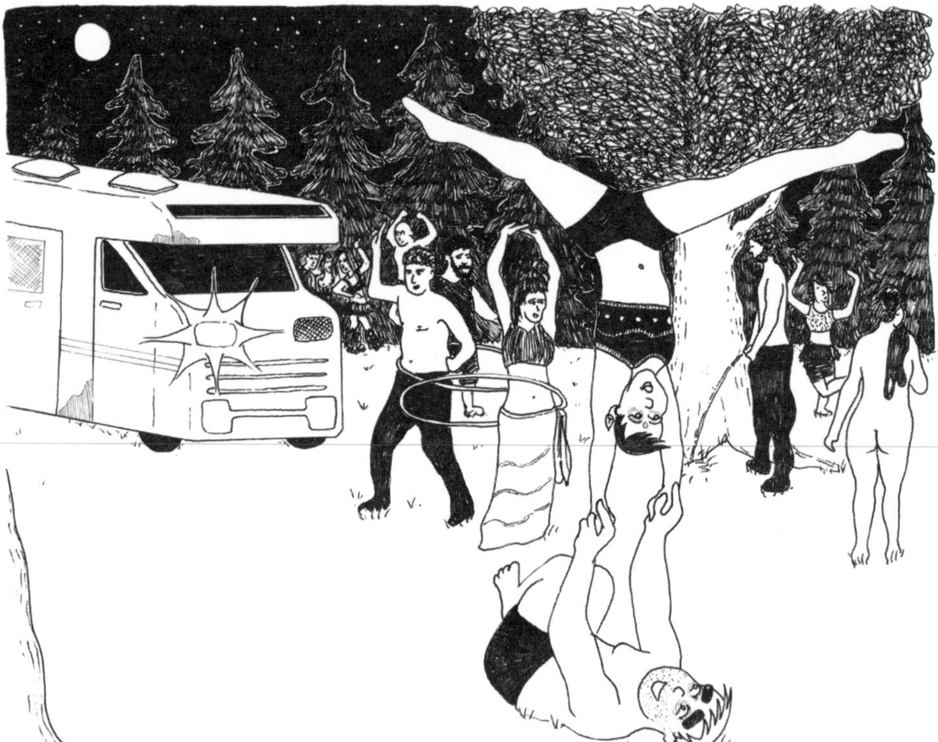

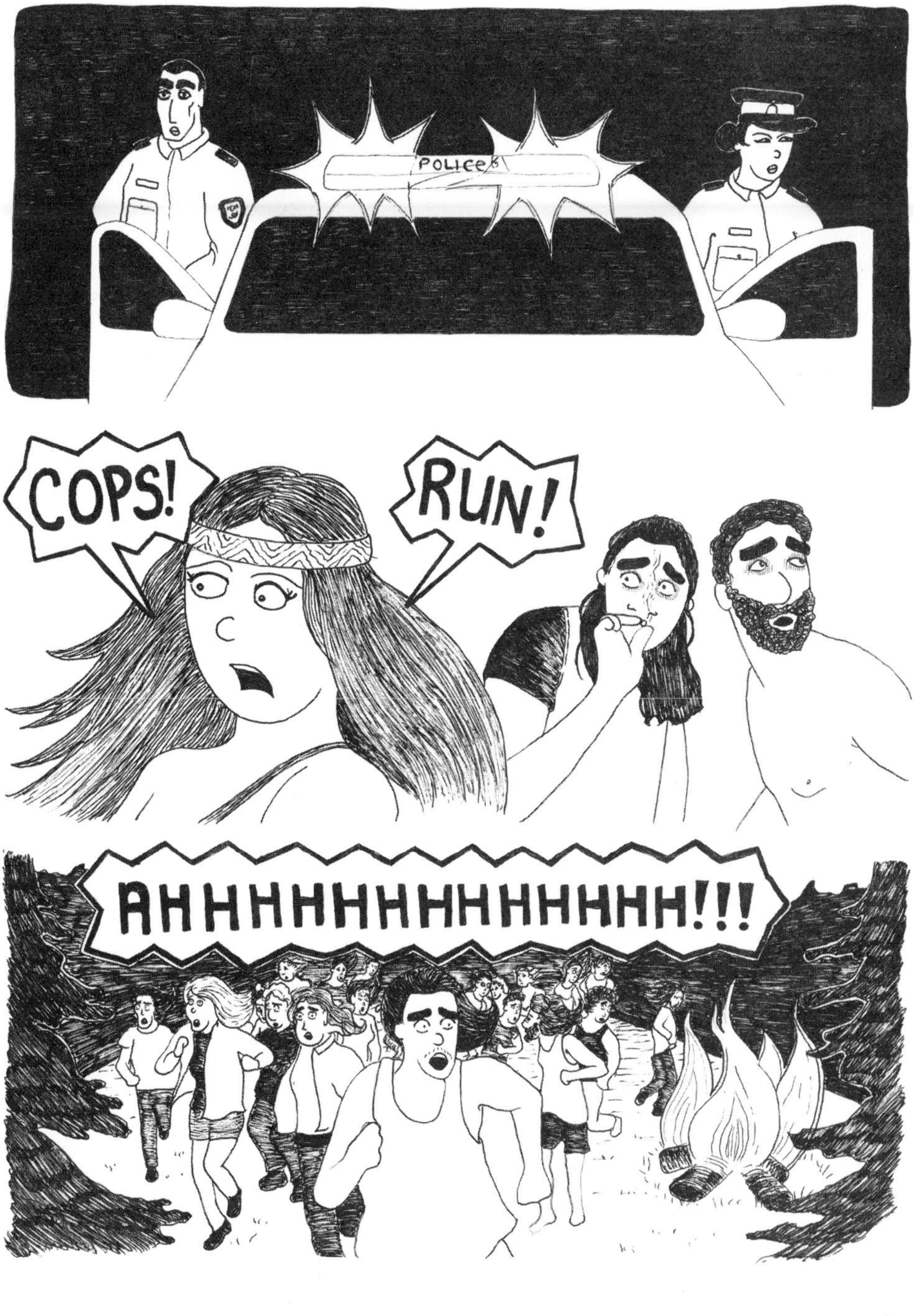
POLICE
COPS!
RUN!
AHHHHHHHHHHHH!!!

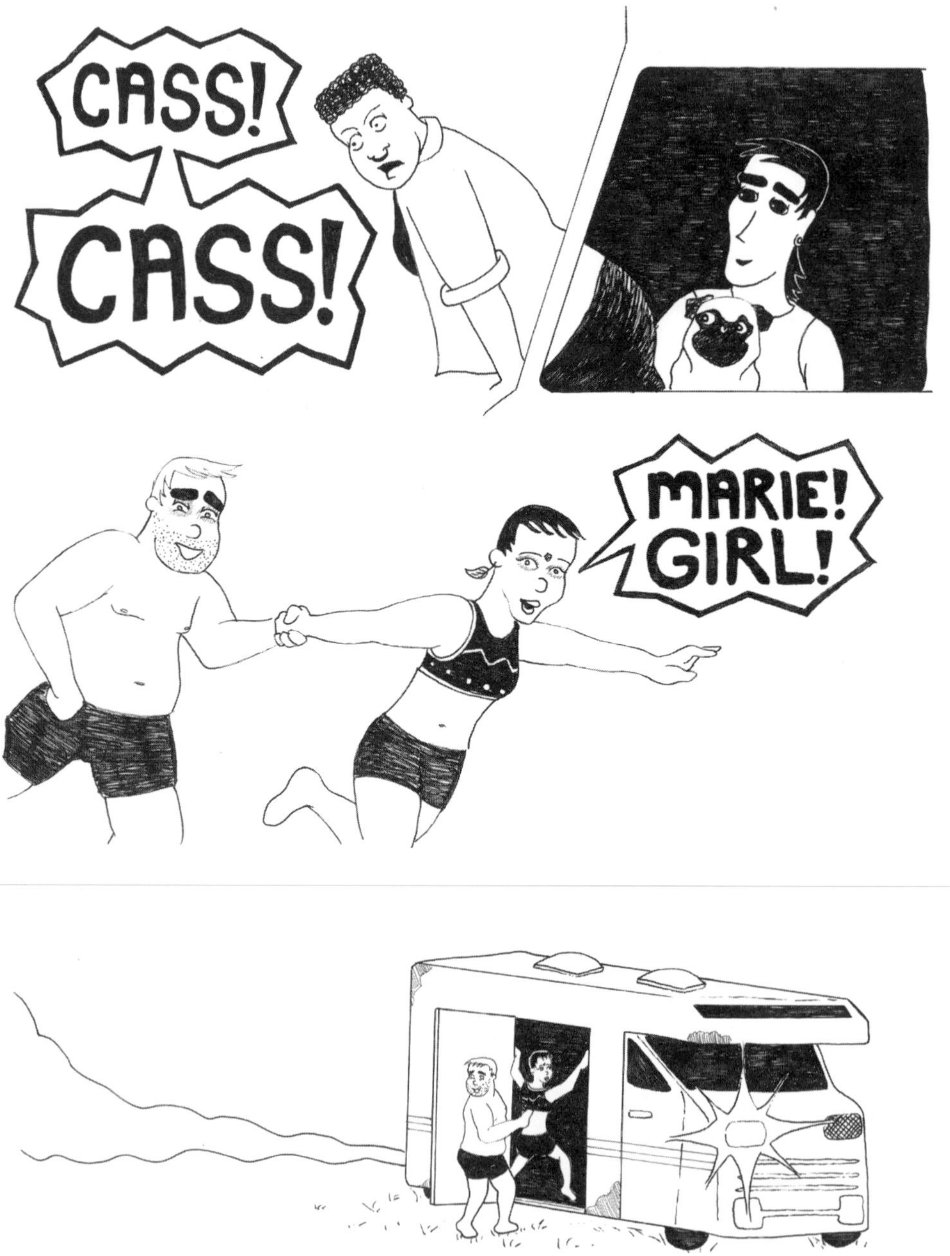
CASS!
CASS!
MARIE! GIRL!

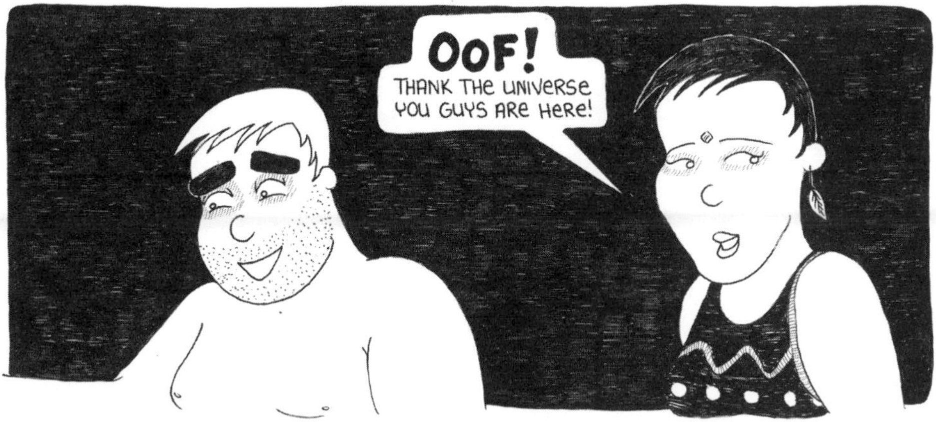
OOF!
THANK THE UNIVERSE YOU GUYS ARE HERE!

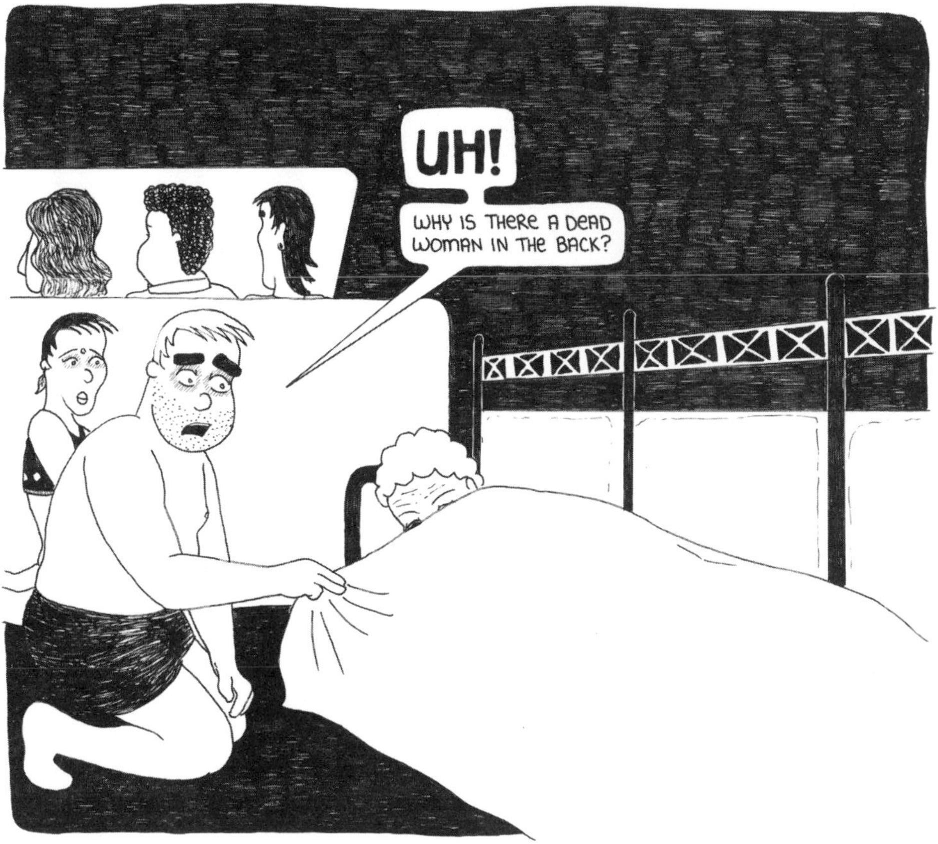
UH!
WHY IS THERE A DEAD WOMAN IN THE BACK?

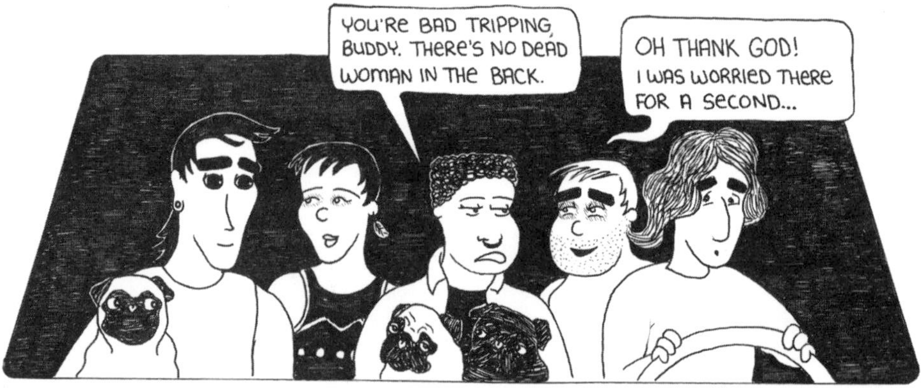
YOU'RE BAD TRIPPING, BUDDY. THERE'S NO DEAD WOMAN IN THE BACK.
OH THANK GOD! I WAS WORRIED THERE FOR A SECOND...

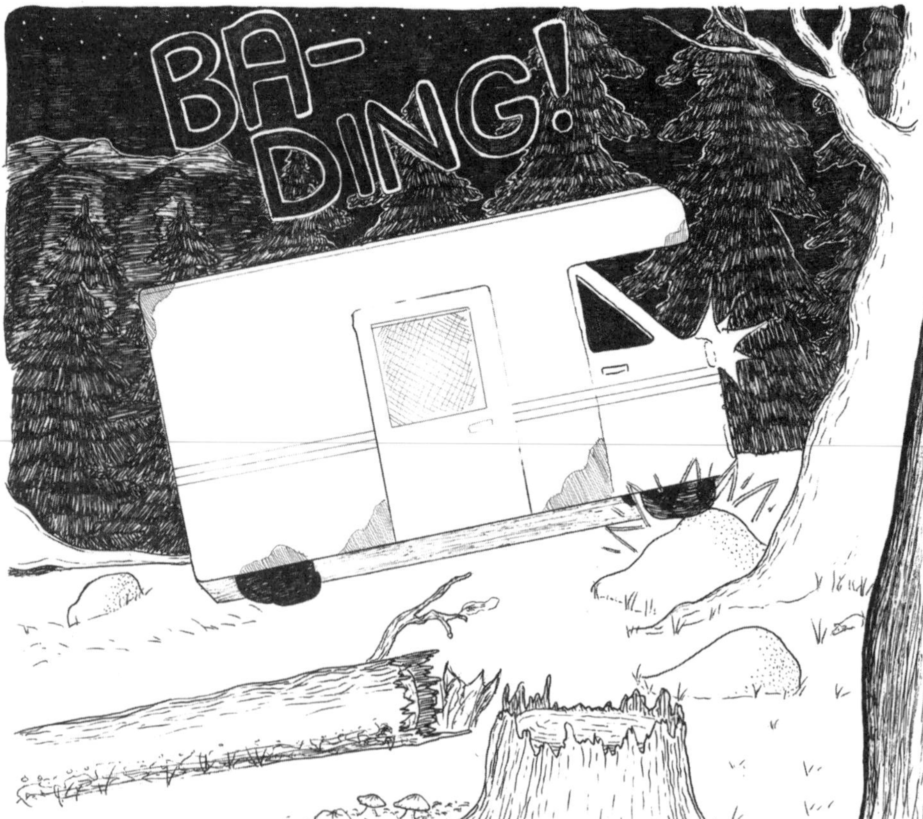
BA-DING!

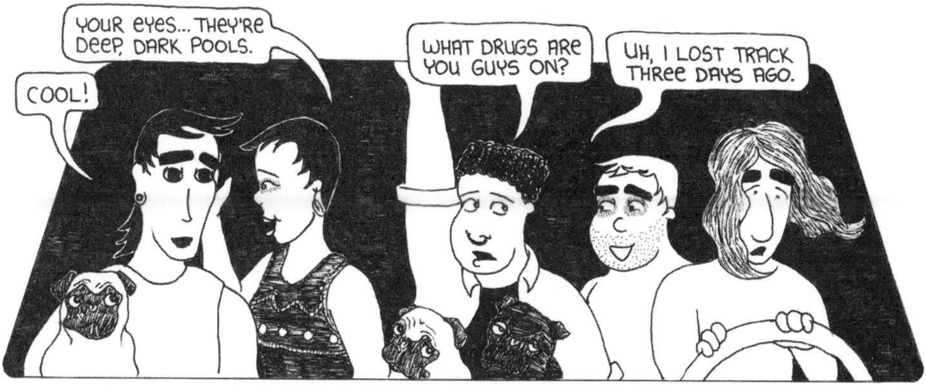
YOUR EYES... THEY'RE DEEP, DARK POOLS.
COOL!
WHAT DRUGS ARE YOU GUYS ON?
UH, I LOST TRACK THREE DAYS AGO.

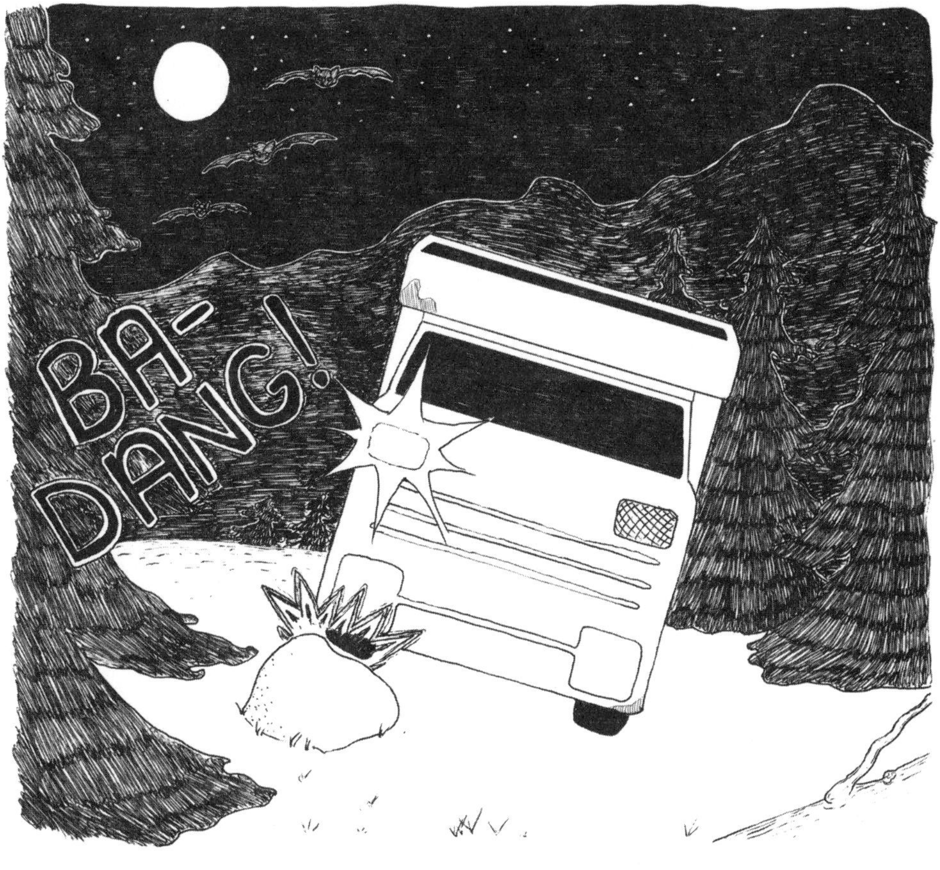
BA-DANG!

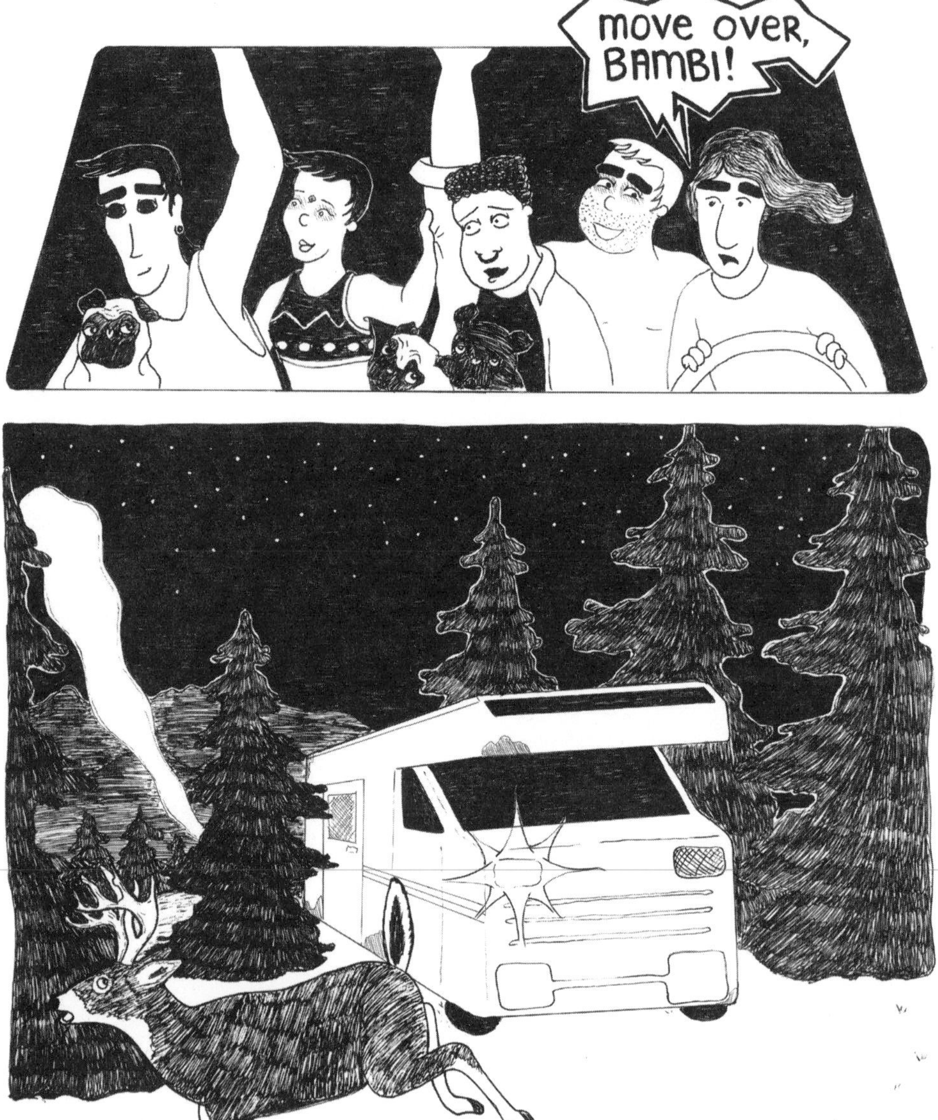
move over, BAMBI!

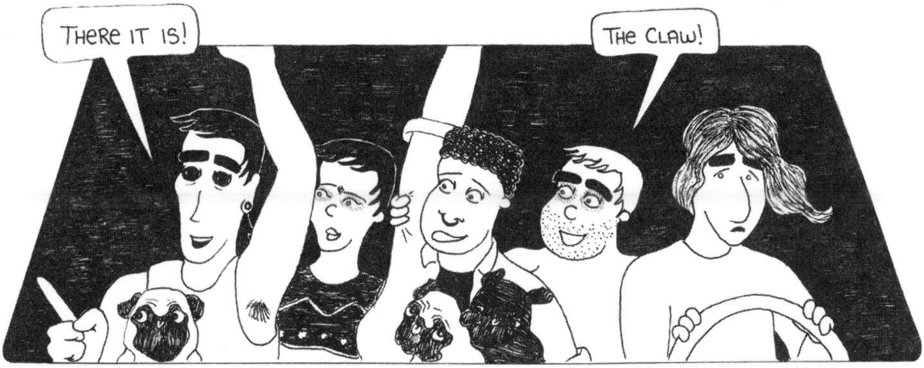
THERE IT IS!
THE CLAW!

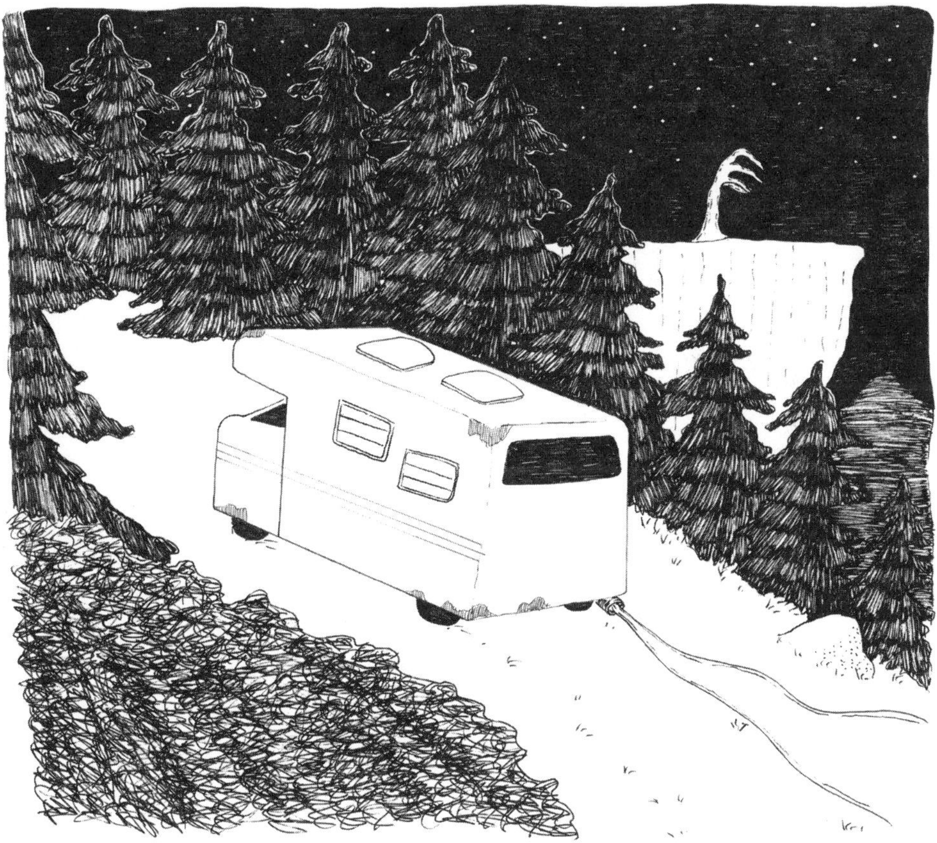

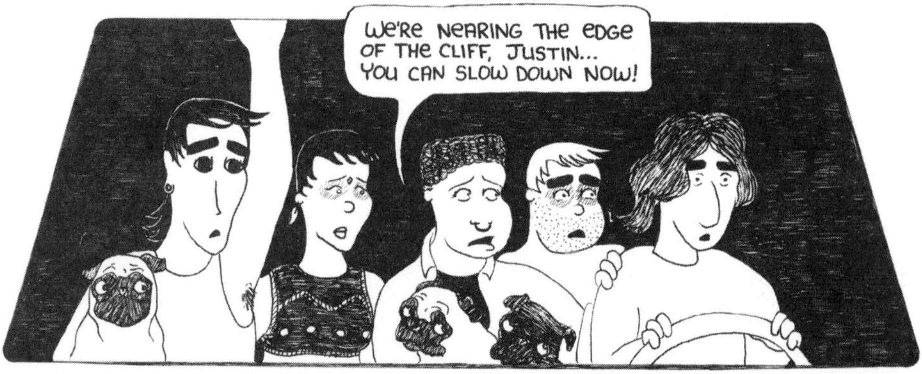
WE'RE NEARING THE EDGE OF THE CLIFF, JUSTIN... YOU CAN SLOW DOWN NOW!

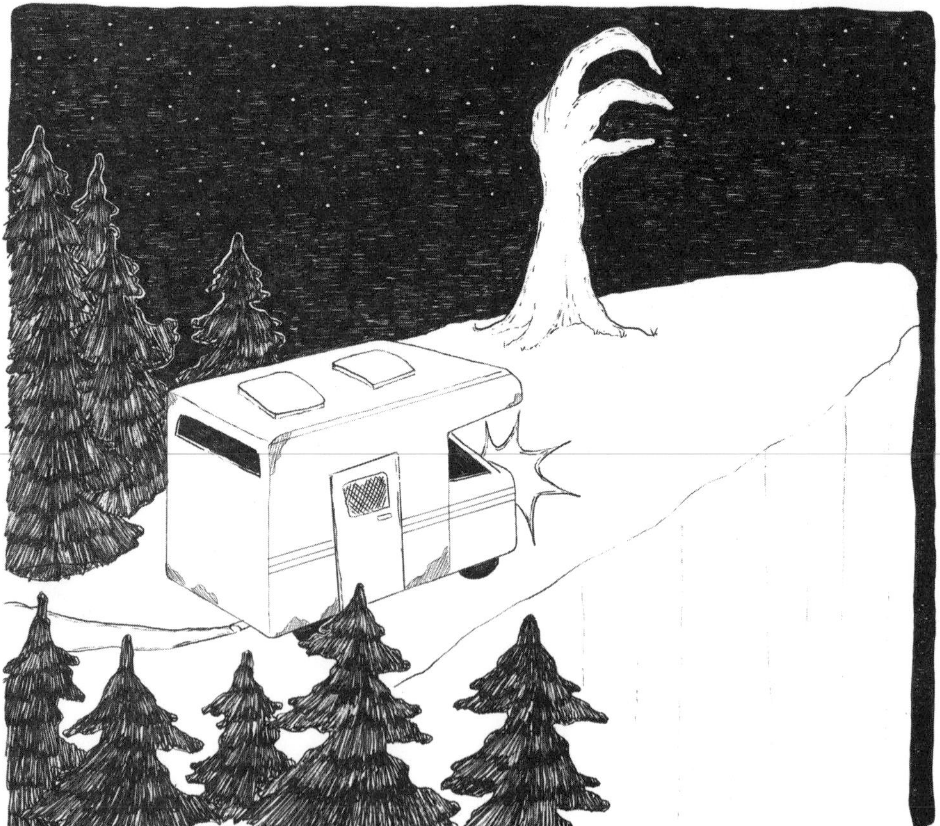

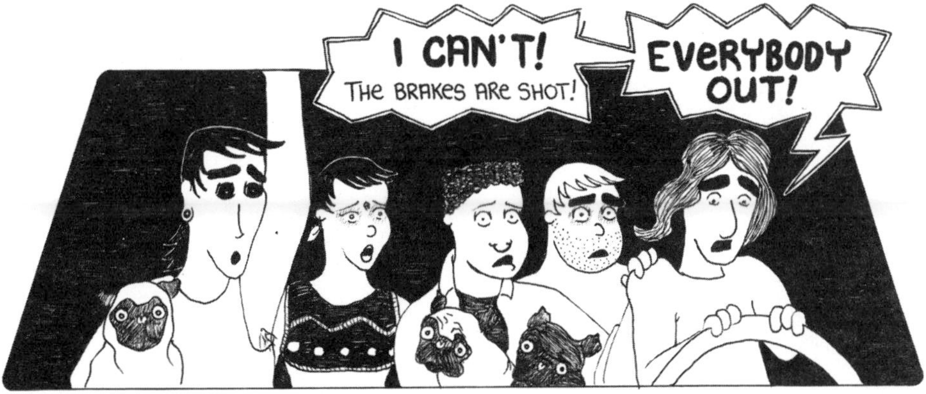
I CAN'T!
The BRAKES ARE SHOT!
EVERYBODY OUT!

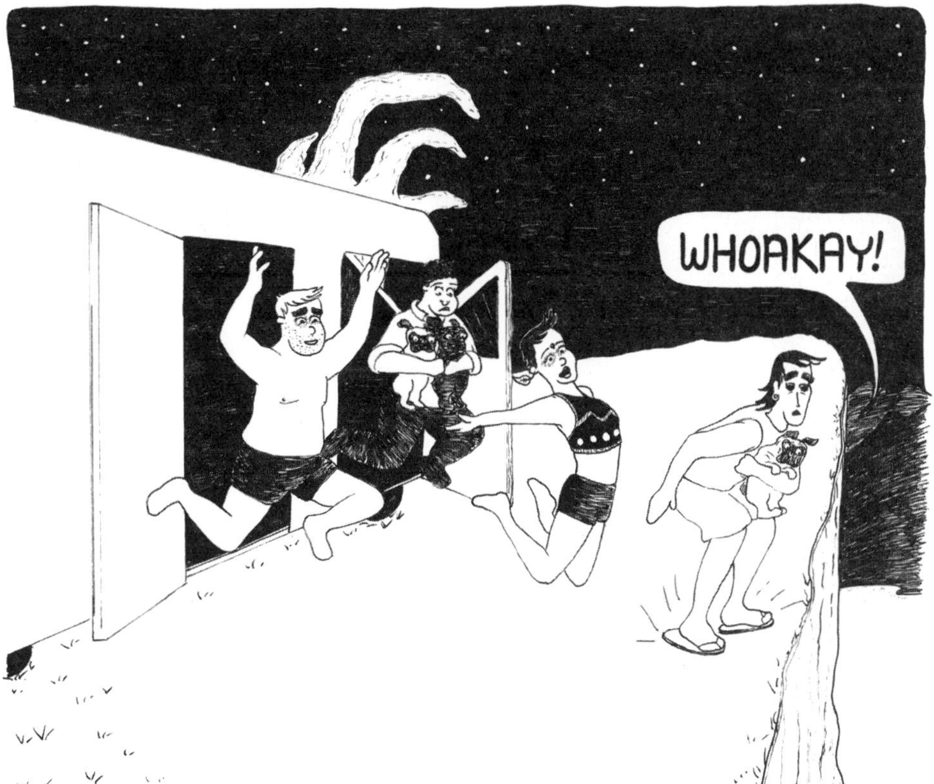
WHOAKAY!

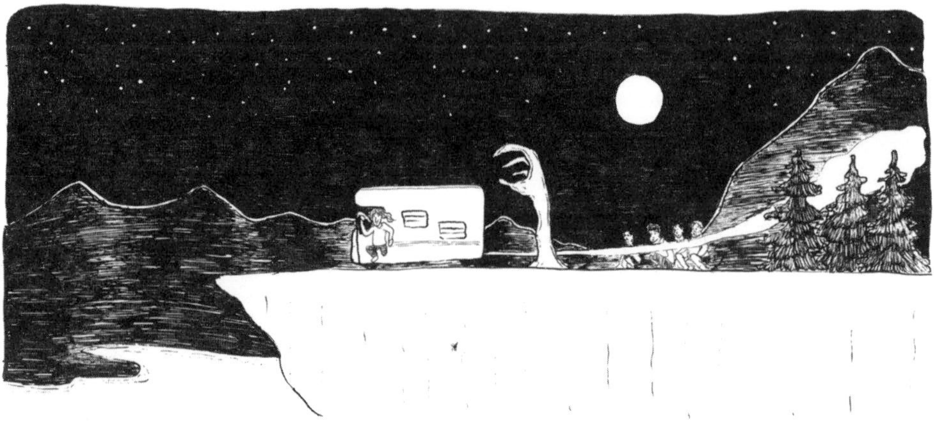

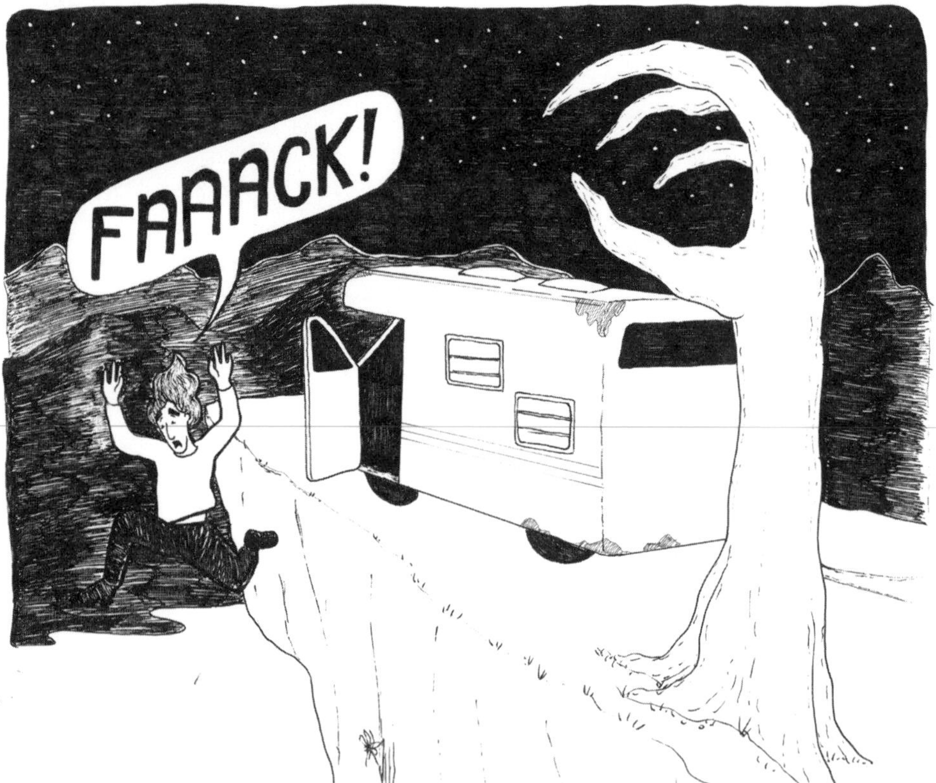
FAAACK!

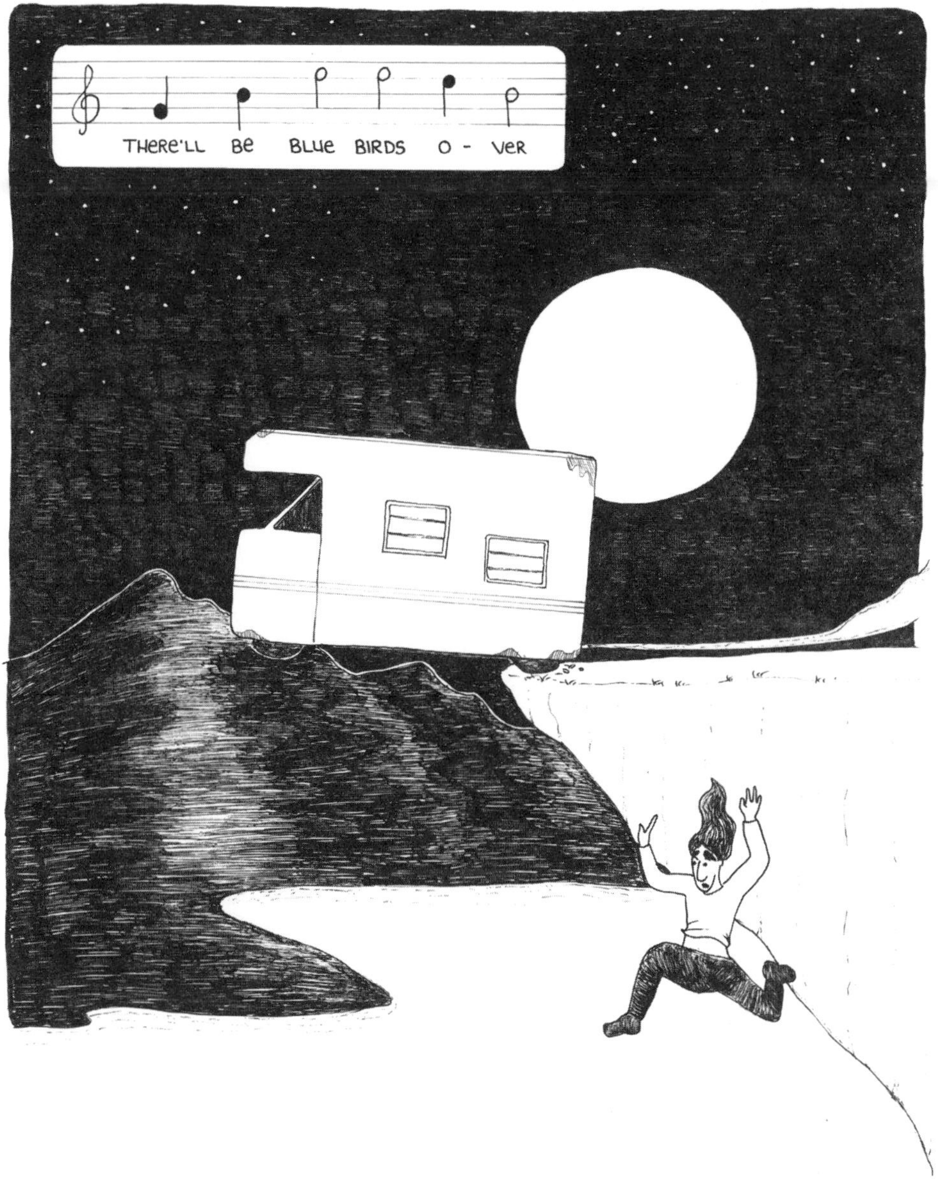
THERE'LL BE BLUE BIRDS O - VER

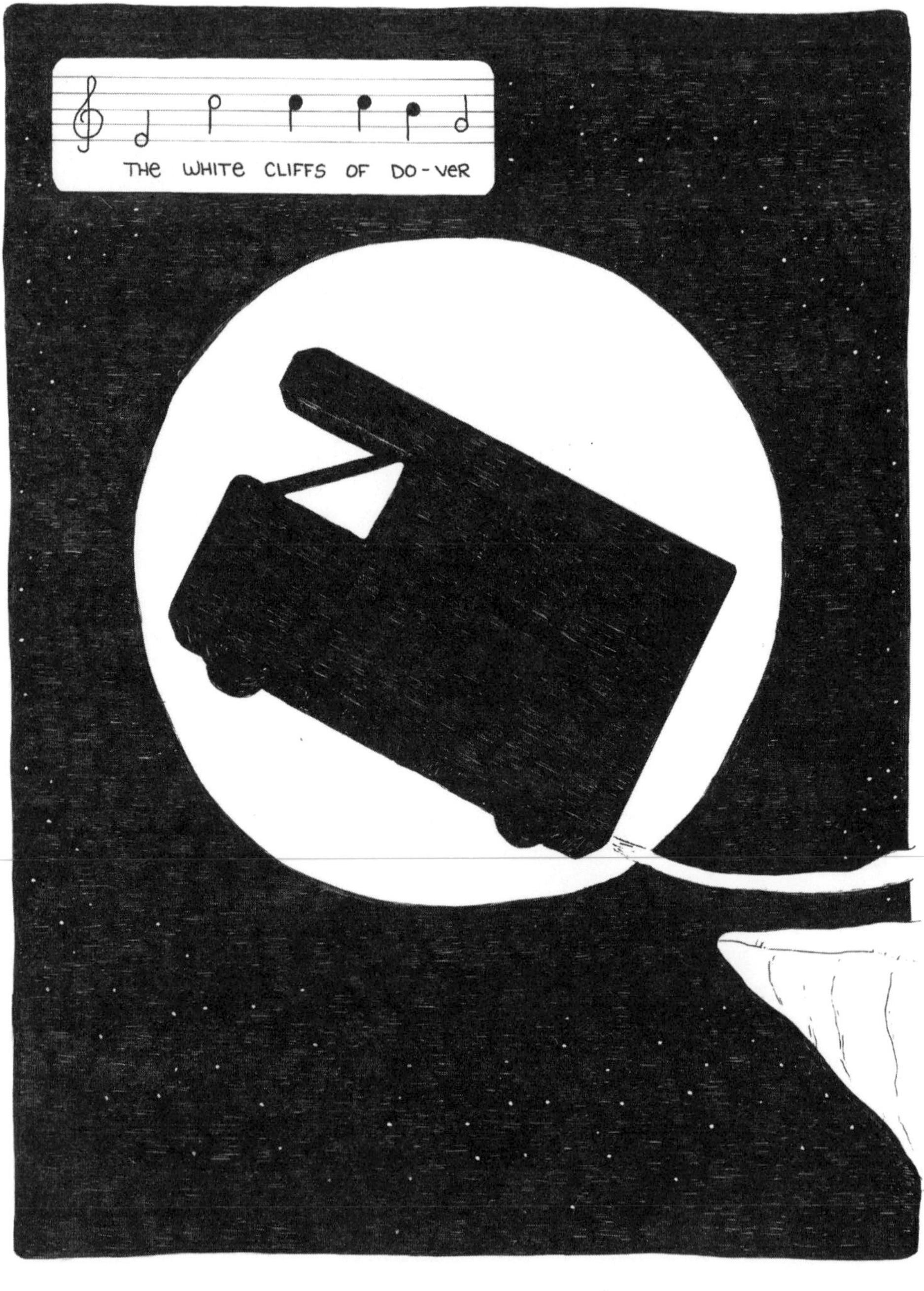
THE WHITE CLIFFS OF DO-VER

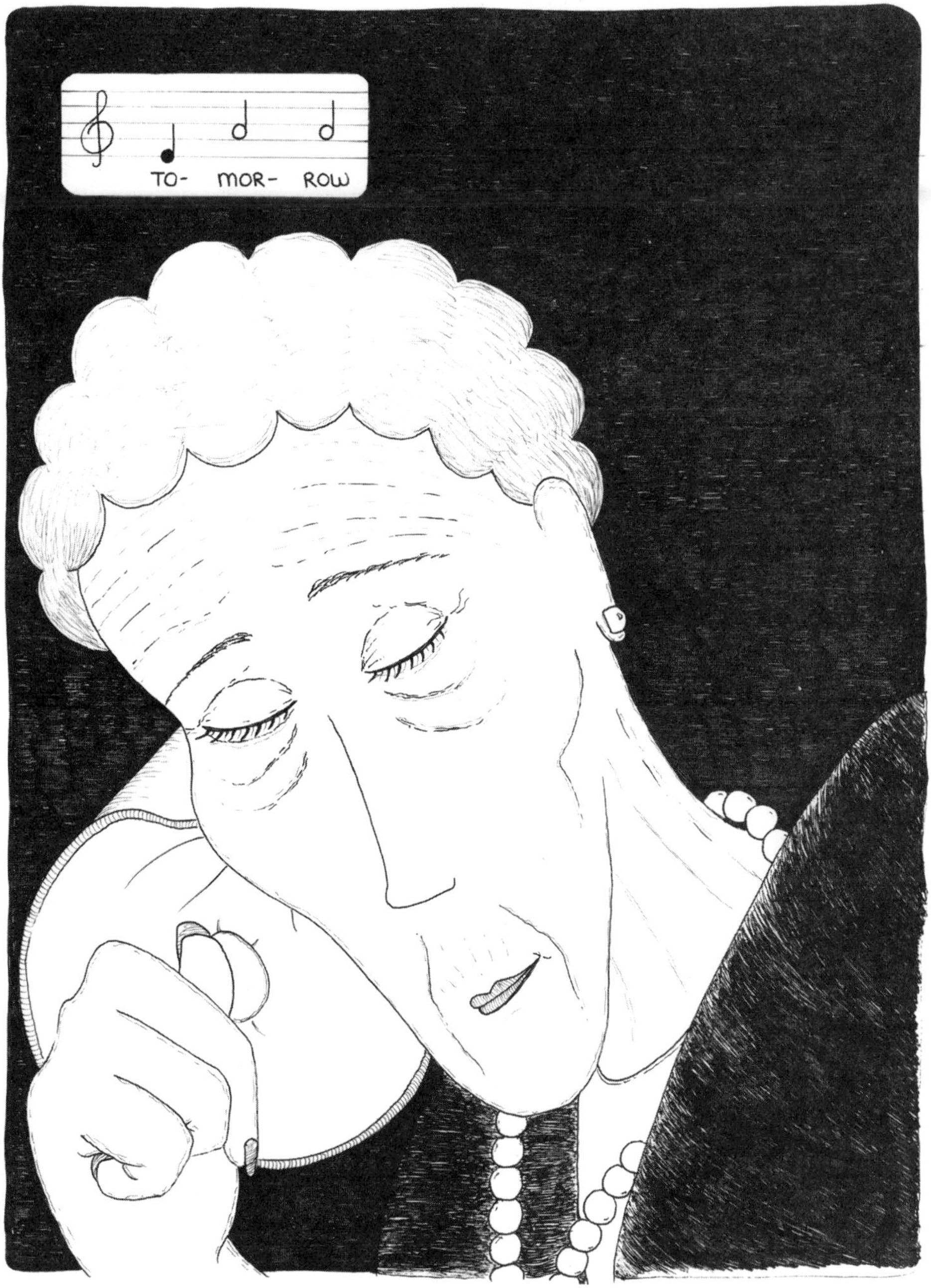
TO- MOR- ROW

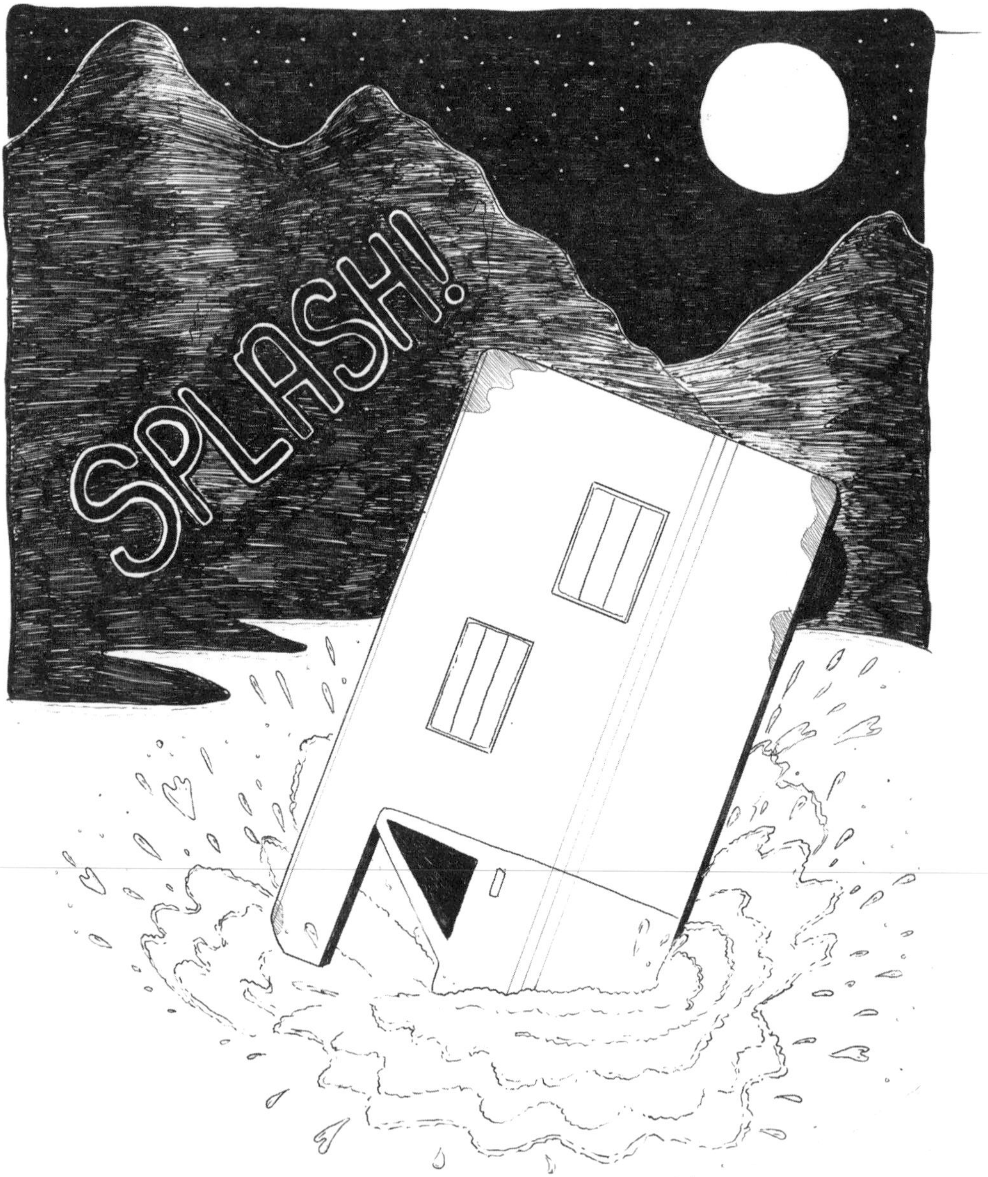
SPLASH!

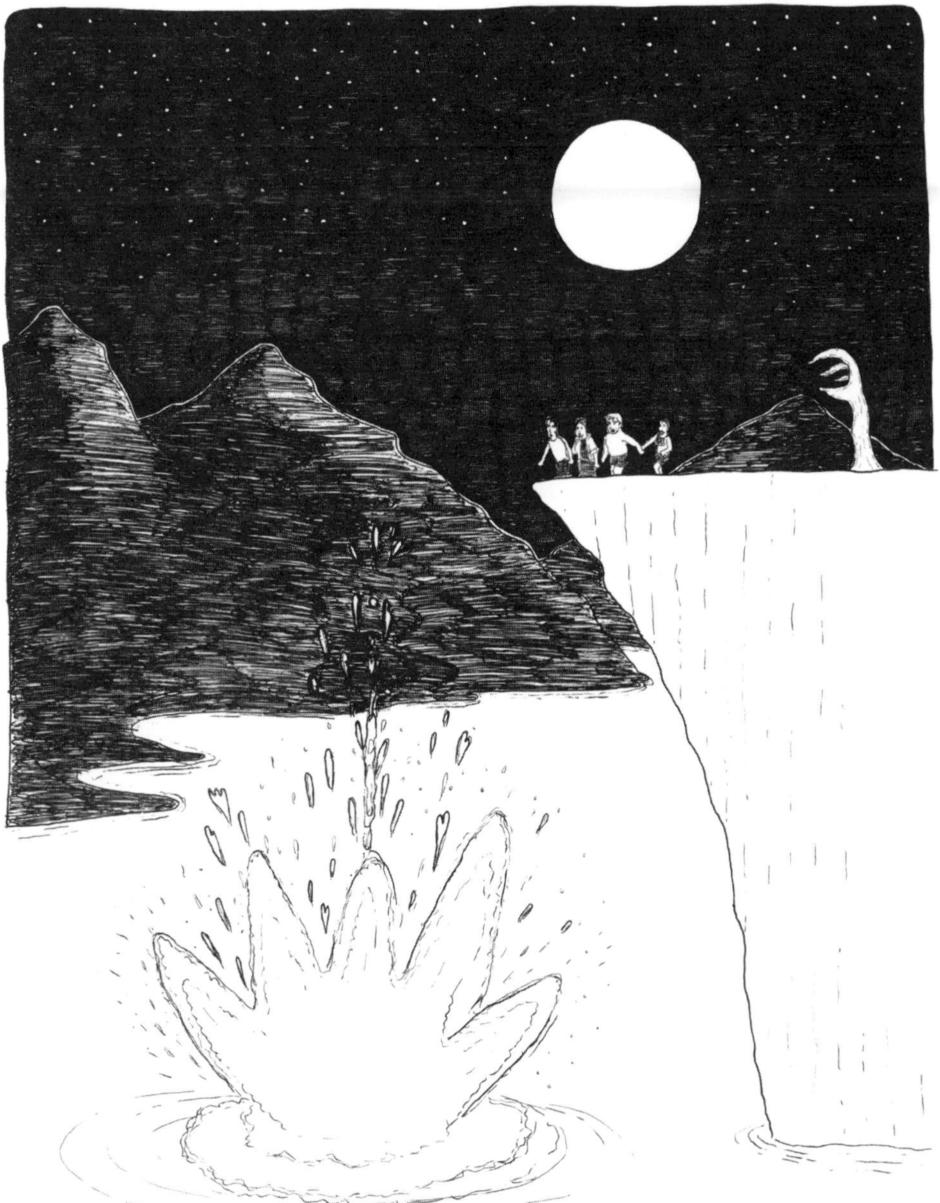

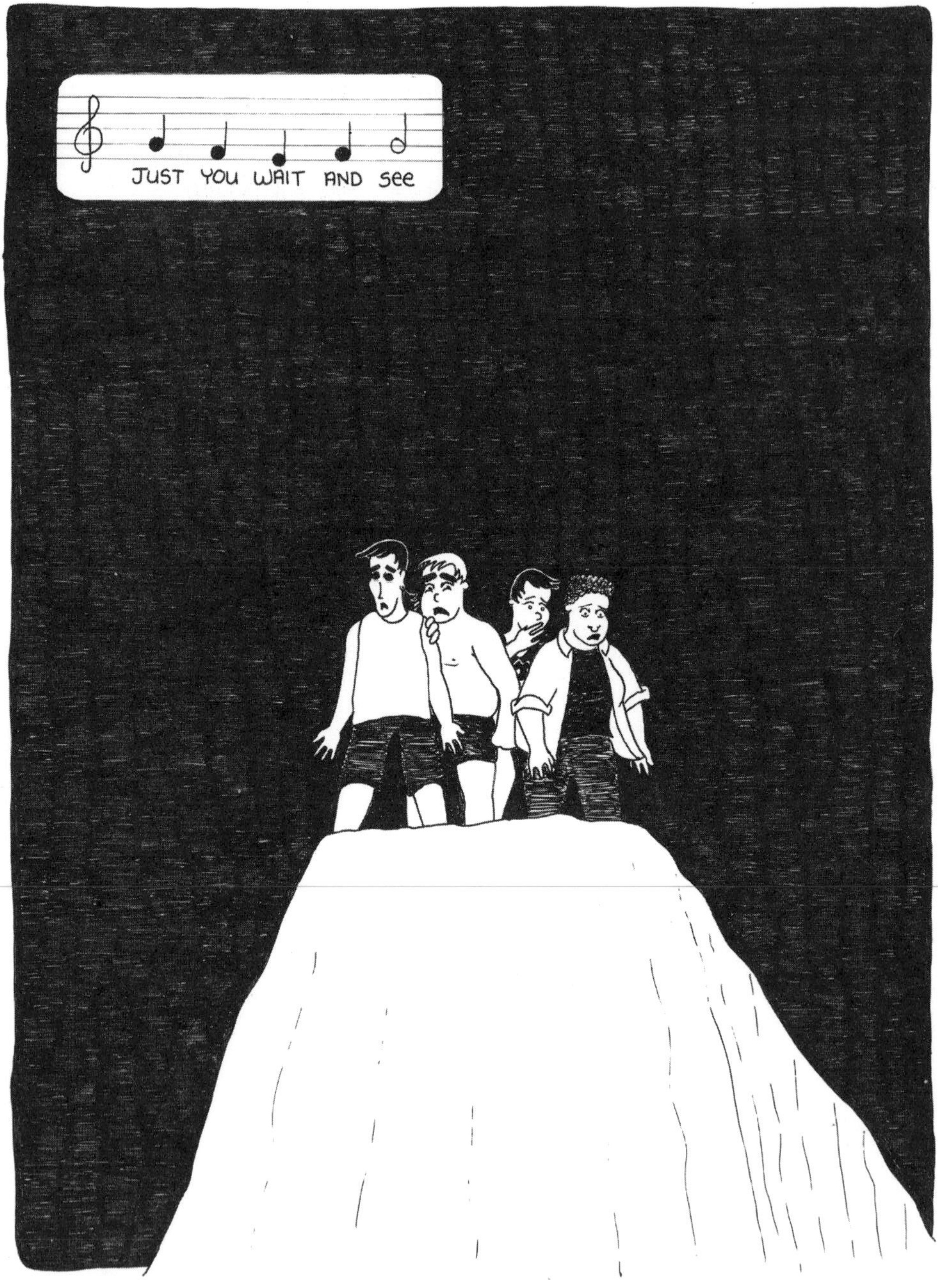
JUST YOU WAIT AND SEE

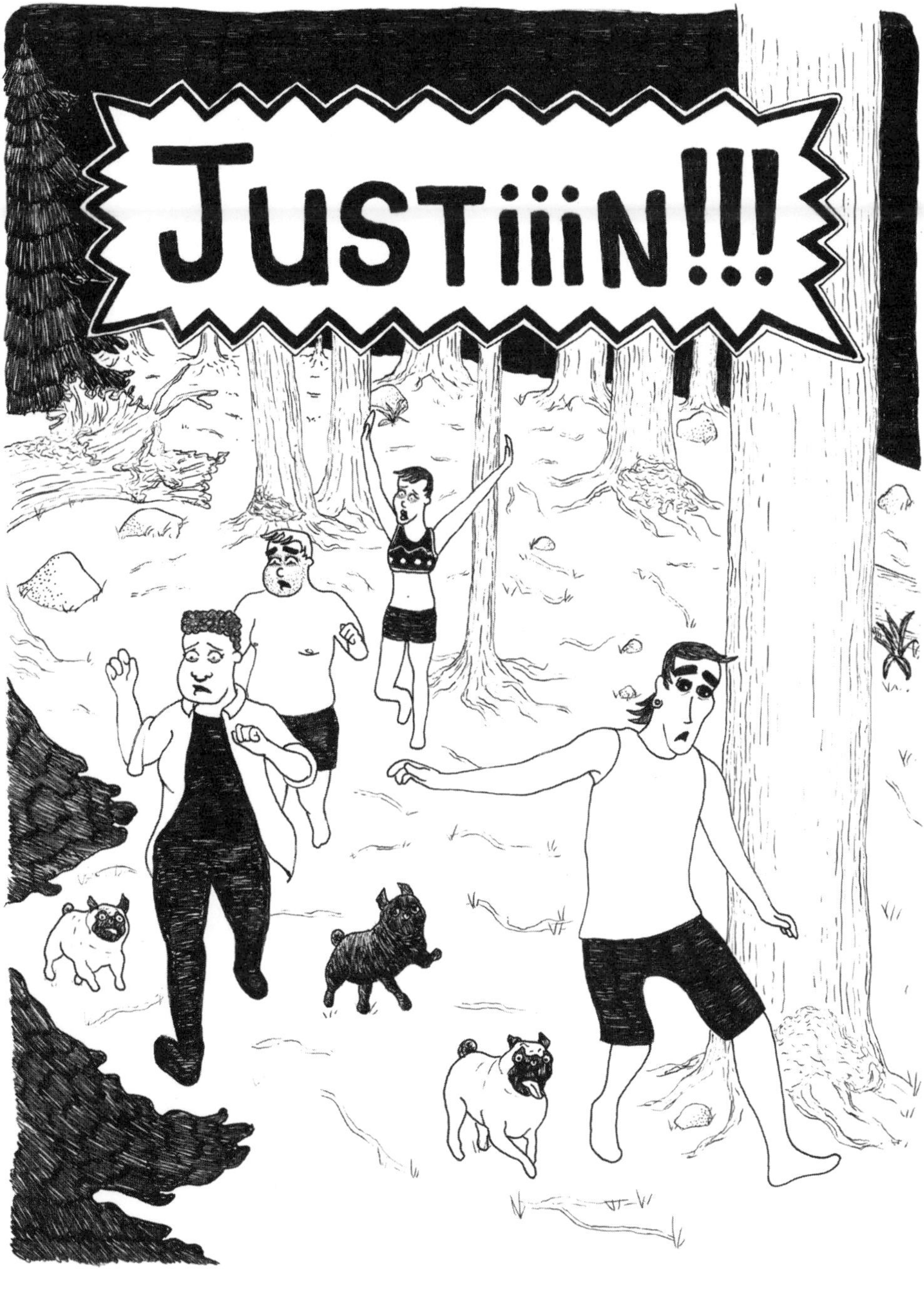
JUSTiiiN!!!

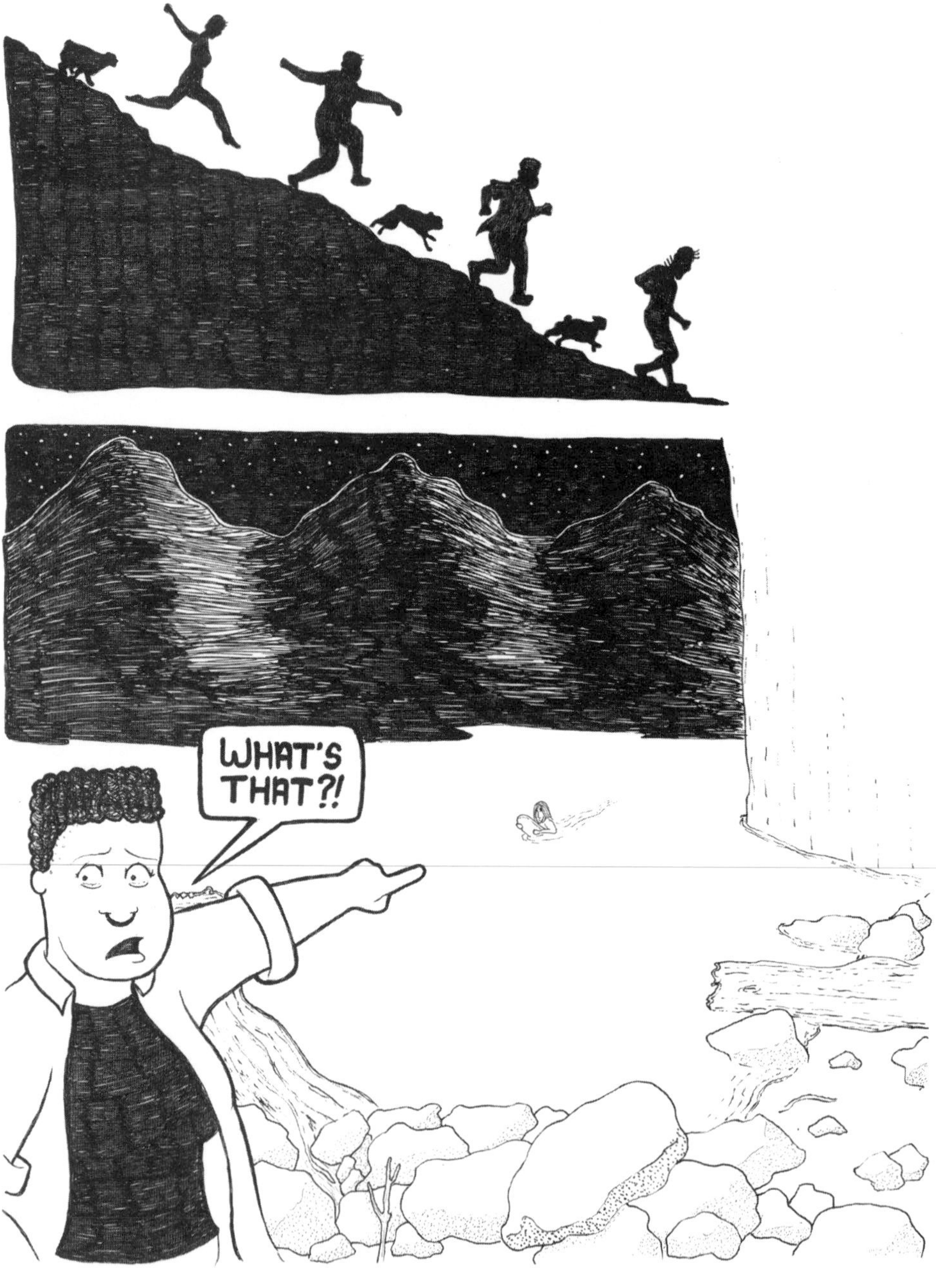
WHAT'S THAT?!

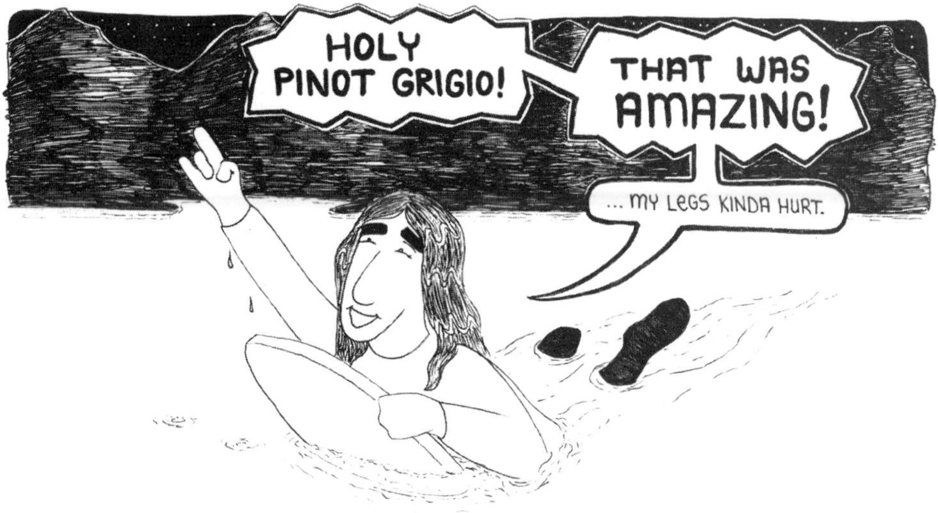
HOLY PINOT GRIGIO!
THAT WAS AMAZING!
... MY LEGS KINDA HURT.

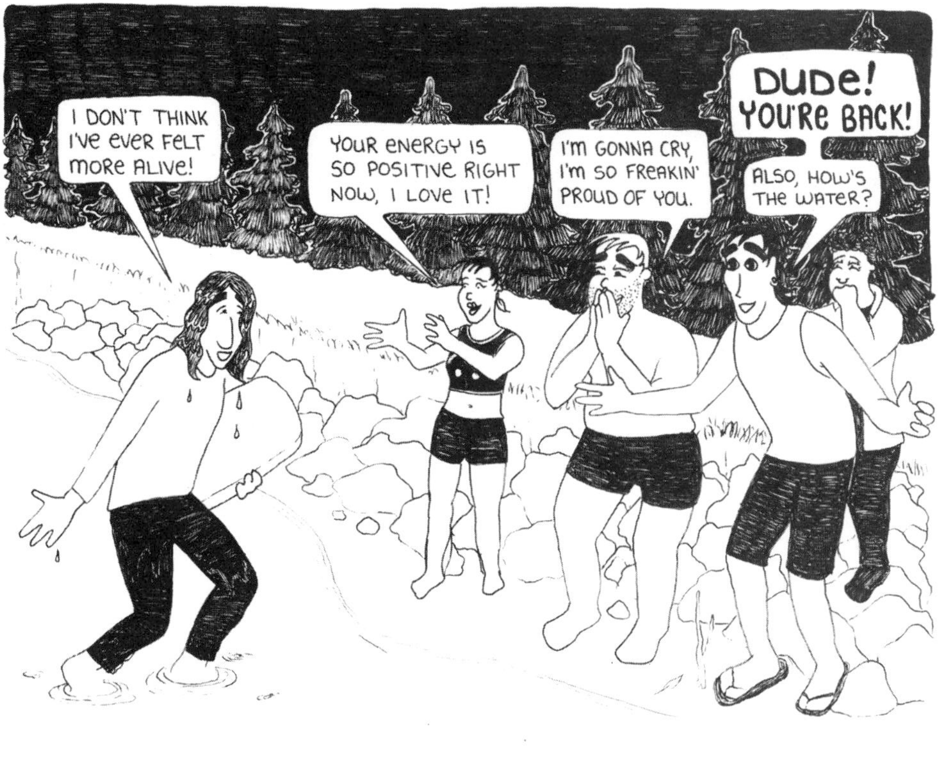
I DON'T THINK I'VE EVER FELT MORE ALIVE!
YOUR ENERGY IS SO POSITIVE RIGHT NOW, I LOVE IT!
I'M GONNA CRY, I'M SO FREAKIN' PROUD OF YOU.
DUDE! YOU'RE BACK!
ALSO, HOW'S THE WATER?

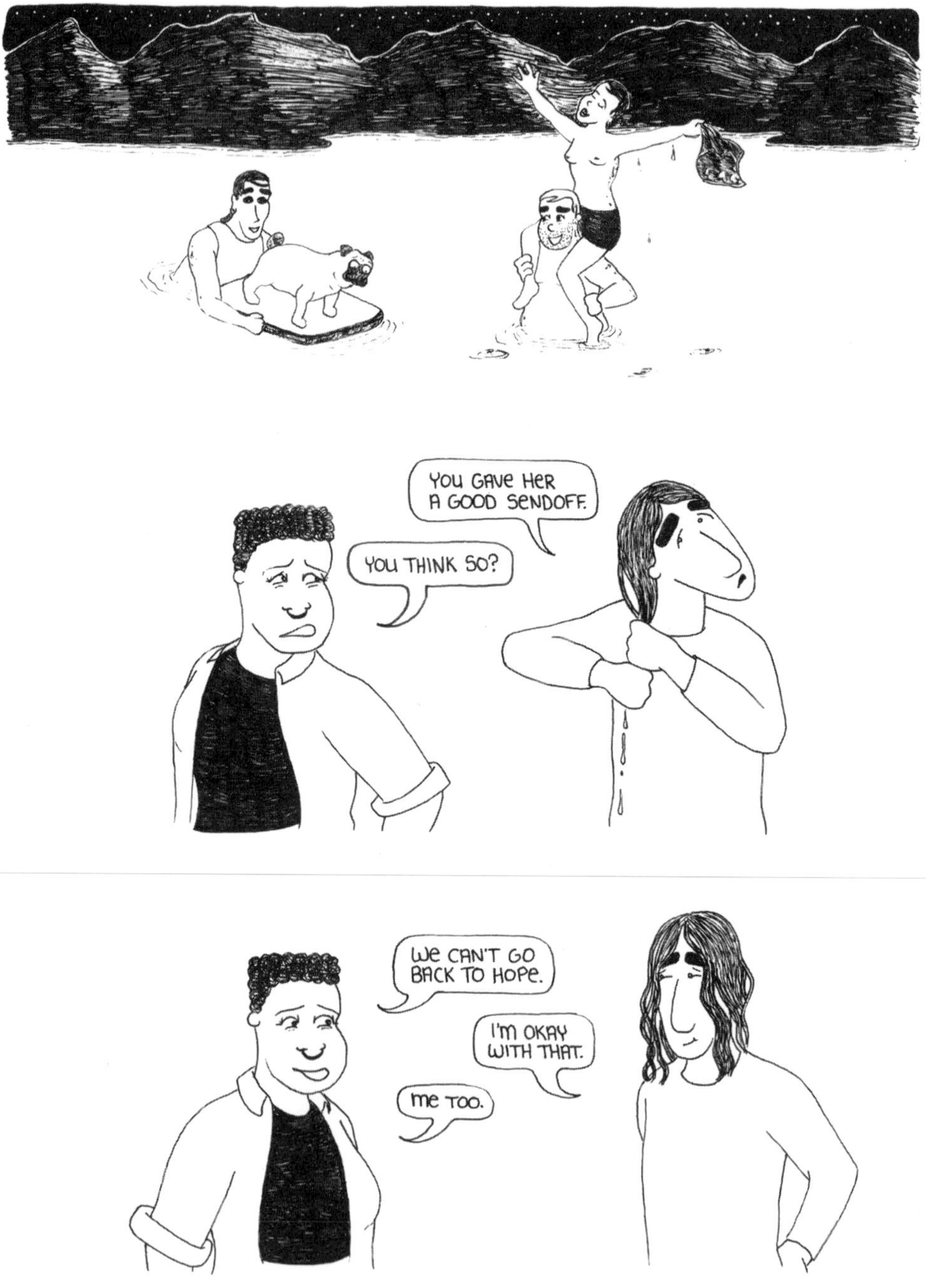
YOU GAVE HER A GOOD SENDOFF.
YOU THINK SO?
WE CAN'T GO BACK TO HOPE.
I'M OKAY WITH THAT.
ME TOO.

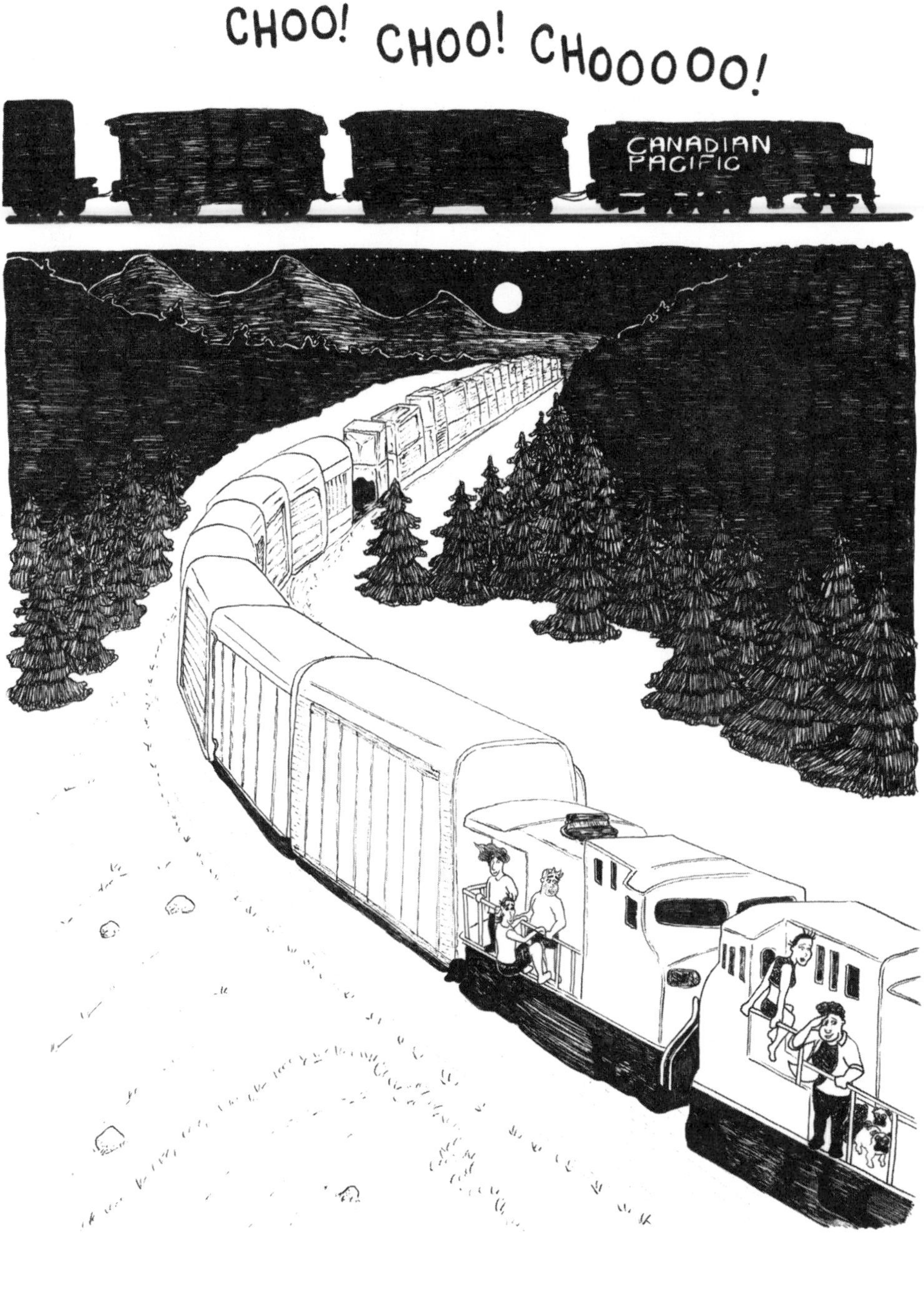
CHOO! CHOO! CHOOOOOO!
CANADIAN PACIFIC

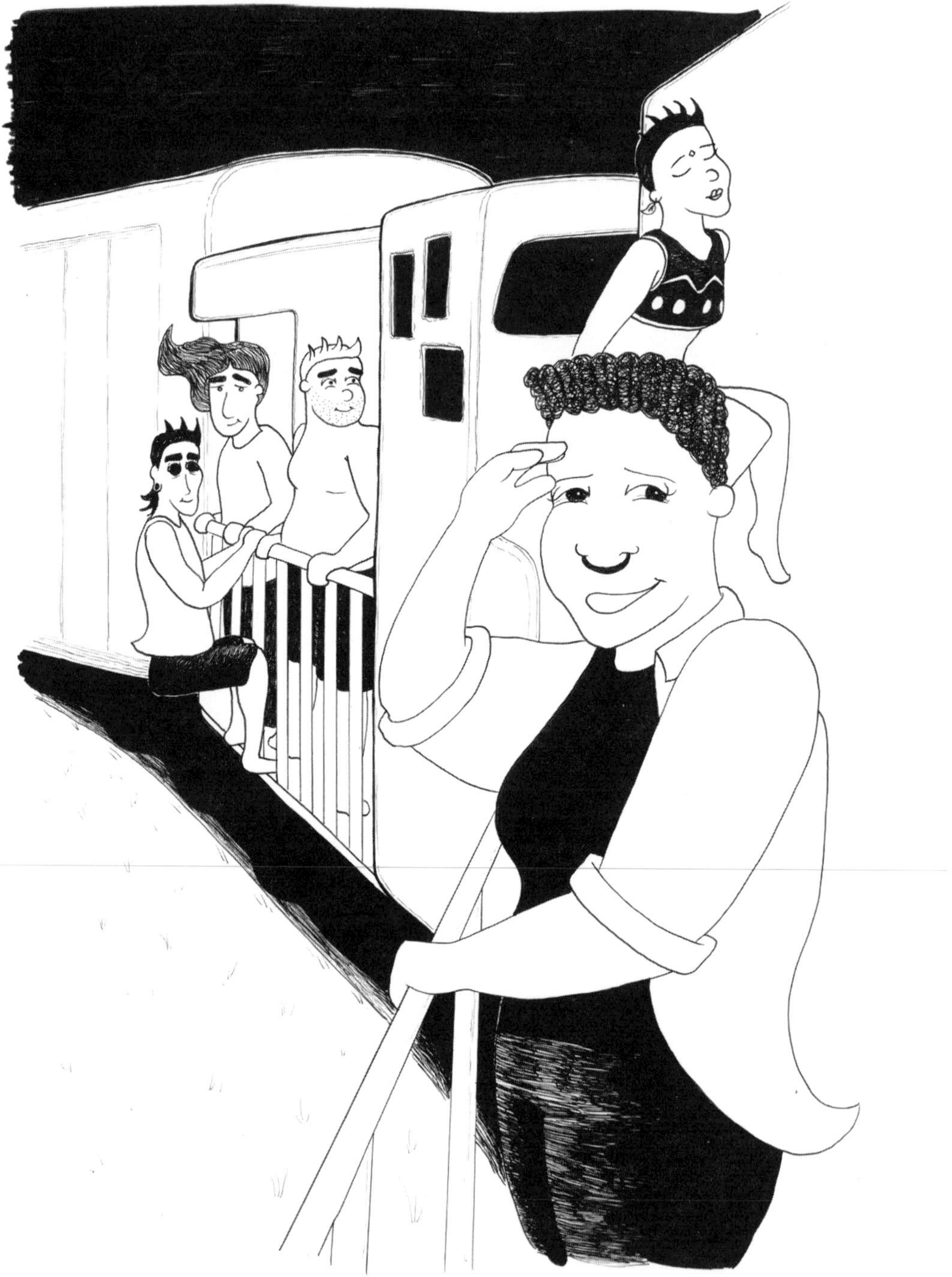

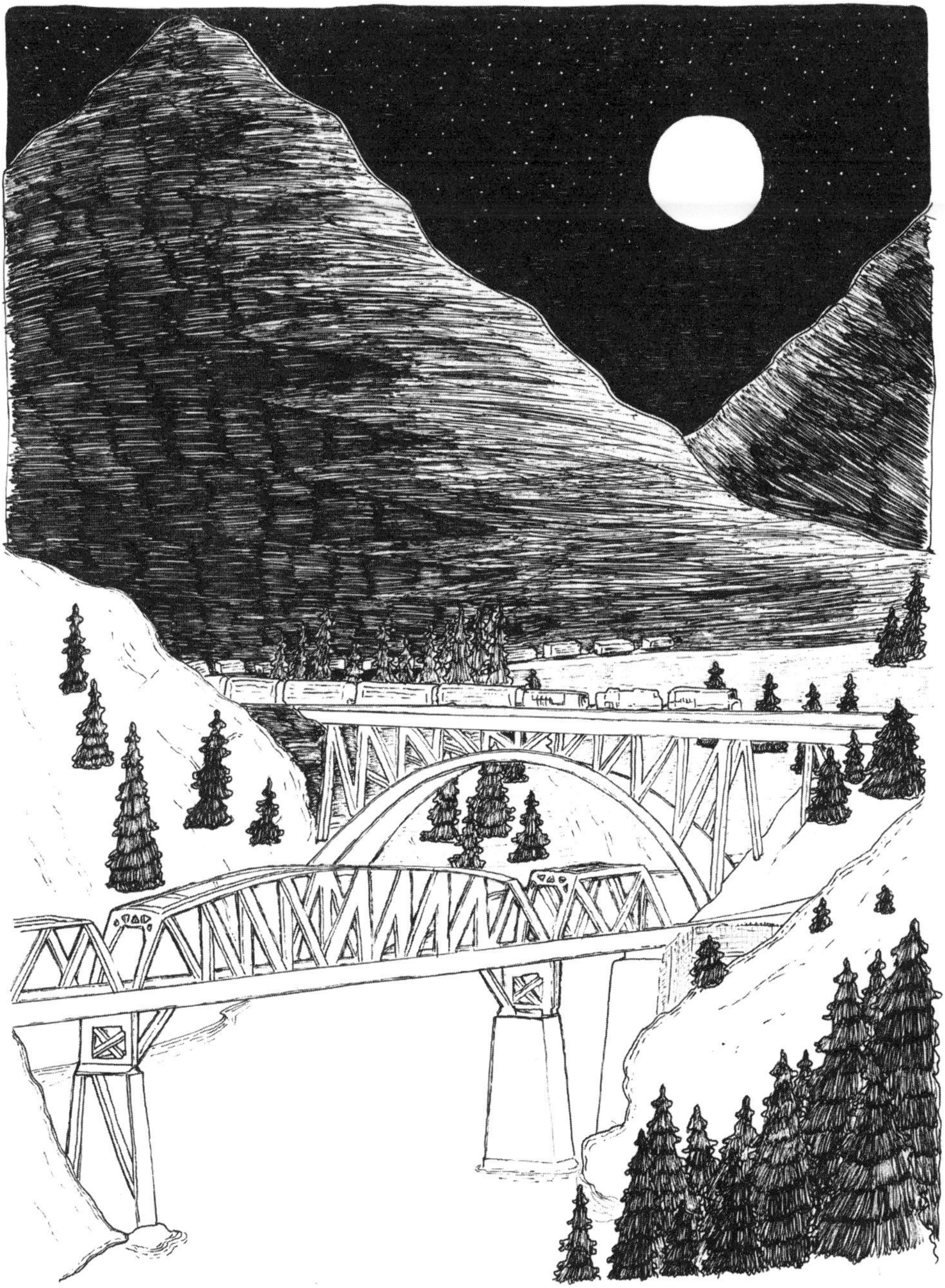

EPiLOGUE

PHOTO EXHIBIT
"LiFe WUZ HERE"
NOV 12-19

RECREATION CEN..

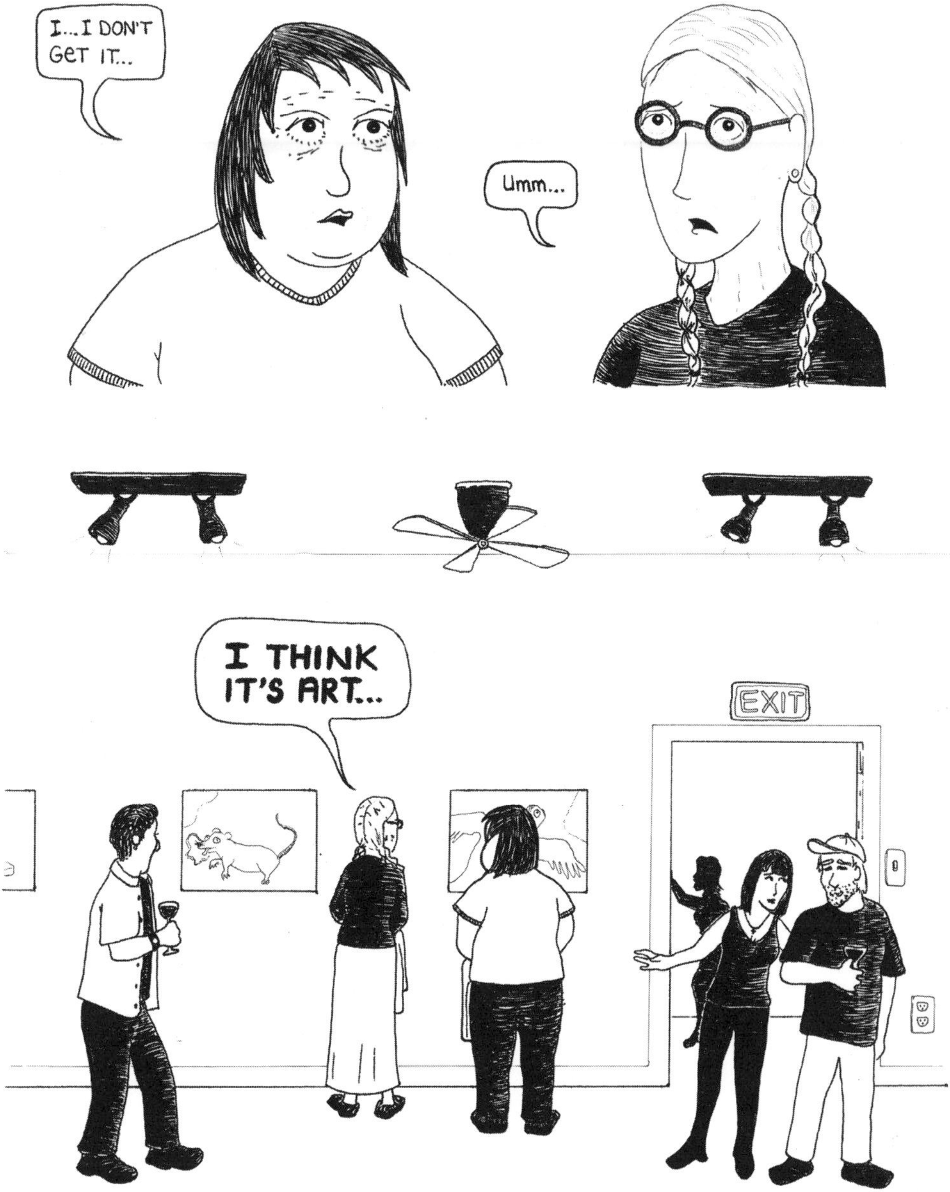
I... I DON'T GET IT...
Umm...
I THINK IT'S ART...
EXIT

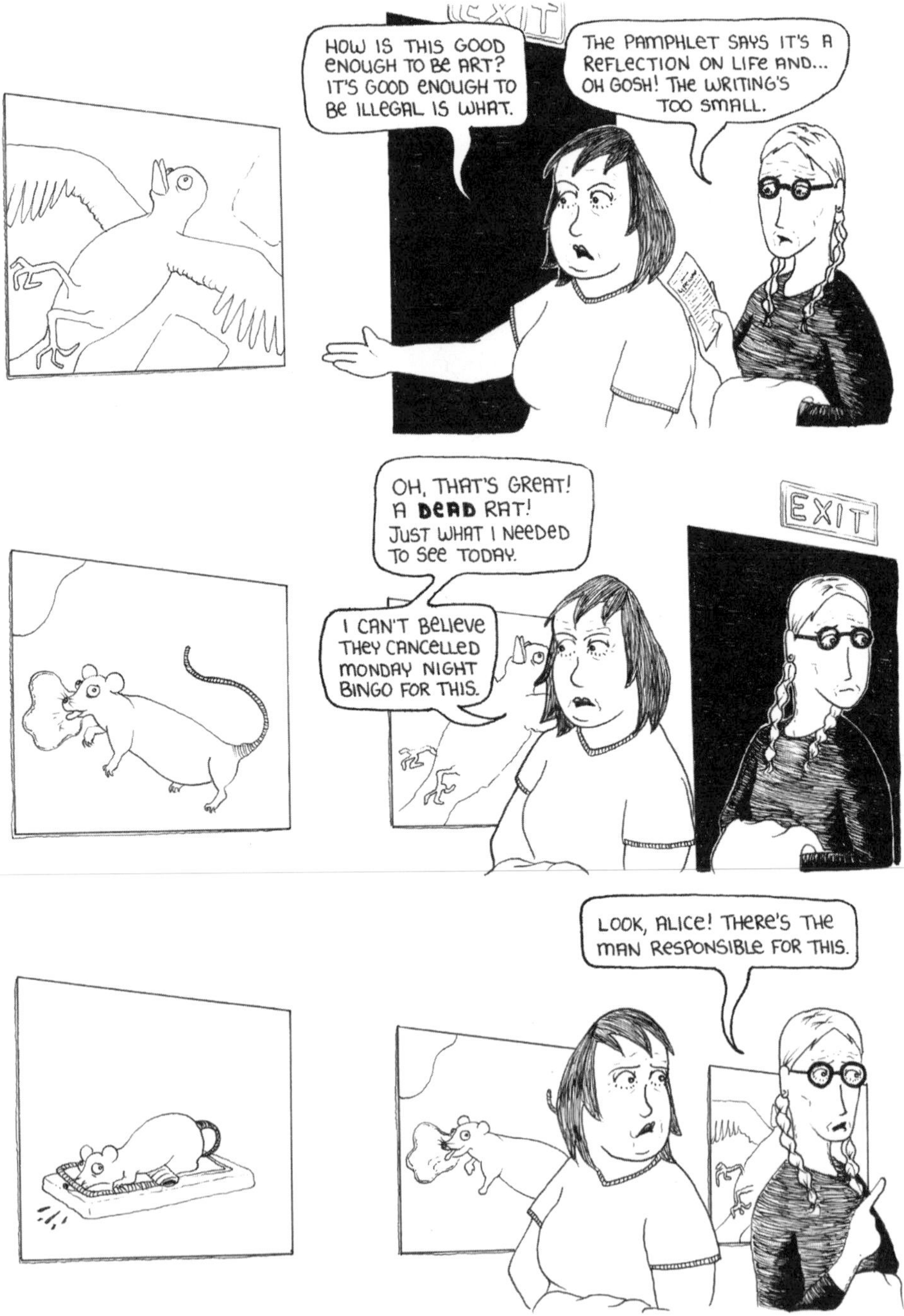
EXIT
HOW IS THIS GOOD ENOUGH TO BE ART? IT'S GOOD ENOUGH TO BE ILLEGAL IS WHAT.
THE PAMPHLET SAYS IT'S A REFLECTION ON LIFE AND... OH GOSH! THE WRITING'S TOO SMALL.
EXIT
OH, THAT'S GREAT! A **DEAD** RAT! JUST WHAT I NEEDED TO SEE TODAY.
I CAN'T BELIEVE THEY CANCELLED MONDAY NIGHT BINGO FOR THIS.
LOOK, ALICE! THERE'S THE MAN RESPONSIBLE FOR THIS.

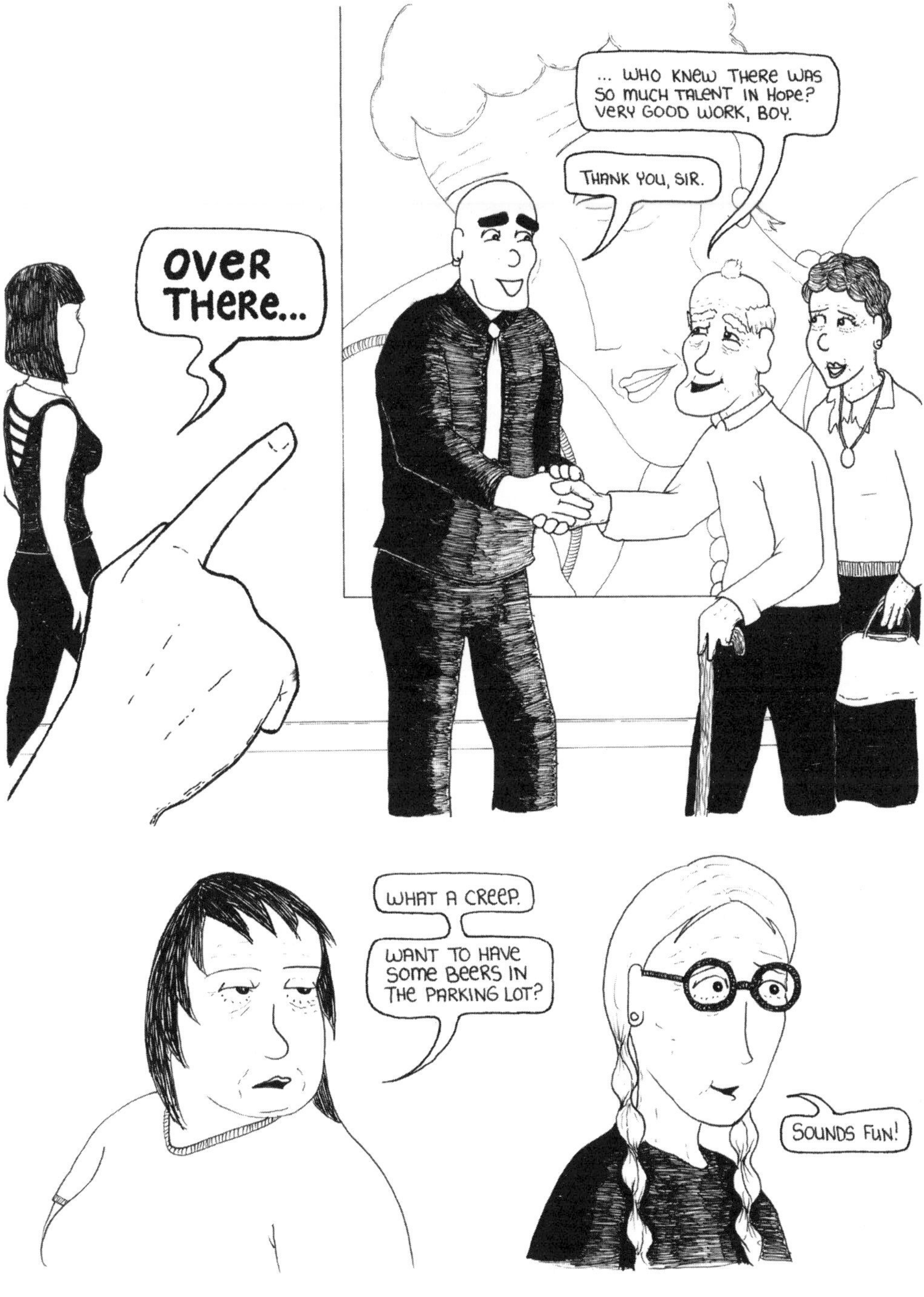
OVER THERE...
... WHO KNEW THERE WAS SO MUCH TALENT IN HOPE? VERY GOOD WORK, BOY.
THANK YOU, SIR.
WHAT A CREEP.
WANT TO HAVE SOME BEERS IN THE PARKING LOT?
SOUNDS FUN!